T0223122

Lecture Notes in Artificial Intelligence 1229

Subseries of Lecture Notes in Computer Science
Edited by J. G. Carbonell and J. Siekmann

Lecture Notes in Computer Science

Edited by G. Goos, J. Hartmanis and J. van Leeuwen

Springer
Berlin
Heidelberg
New York
Barcelona
Budapest
Hong Kong
London
Milan
Paris
Santa Clara
Singapore
Tokyo

Gerhard K. Kraetzschmar

Distributed
Reason Maintenance
for Multiagent Systems

Springer

Series Editors
Jaime G. Carbonell, Carnegie Mellon University, Pittsburgh, PA, USA
Jörg Siekmann, University of Saarland, Saarbrücken, Germany

Author

Gerhard K. Kraetzschmar
University of Ulm, Department of Neural Information Processing
Oberer Eselsberg, D-89069 Ulm, Germany
E-mail: gkk@neuro.informatik.uni-ulm.de
www: http://www.informatik.uni-ulm.de/ni/staff/gkk.html

Cataloging-in-Publication Data applied for

Die Deutsche Bibliothek - CIP-Einheitsaufnahme

Kraetzschmar, Gerhard:
Distributed reason maintenance for multiagent systems / Gerhard
Kreetzschmar. - Berlin ; Heidelberg ; New York ; Barcelona ;
Budapest ; Hong Kong ; London ; Milan ; Paris ; Santa Clara ;
Singapore ; Tokyo : Springer, 1997
  (Lecture notes in computer science ; Vol. 1229 : Lecture notes in
  artificial intelligence)
  ISBN 3-540-63606-4

This book constitutes the dissertation thesis of the author
accepted by the School of Engineering at the University of Erlangen-Nürnberg.

CR Subject Classification (1991): I.2.11, I.2, C.2.4, F.4.1

ISBN 3-540-63606-4 Springer-Verlag Berlin Heidelberg New York

© Springer-Verlag Berlin Heidelberg 1997
Printed in Germany

Typesetting: Camera ready by author
SPIN 10548725   06/3142 – 5 4 3 2 1 0   Printed on acid-free paper

To my parents.

Abstract

Reason maintenance technology has been successfully applied in many AI systems. Reason maintenance systems help to maintain logical dependencies between data and support assumption-based reasoning, which has useful applications in a wide spectrum of domains ranging from diagnosis to planning.

Most reason maintenance systems, however, have been developed with a single agent in mind, i.e. there is only one problem solver using the services of the reason maintenance system. Only few reason maintenance systems are known that claim to be suited for application in multiagent systems. None of these systems adequately supports multiple-context reasoning in a distributed environment, although this functionality is highly desirable in many domains, e.g. for distributed planning, scheduling, and control. Thus, as multiagent systems become increasingly attractive for solving larger and more complex problems, the need for adequate reason maintenance technology for multiagent systems arises.

This book provides an in-depth investigation of a restricted class of multiple-context assumption-based multiagent reasoning problems. Logics for formalizing the underlying kind of reasoning are provided and a description of the functionality desirable to adequately support the reasoning processes of such systems is derived. A revised reason maintenance system architecture is presented that lays a solid foundation for building distributed reason maintenance systems for use in multiagent systems. The architecture is applied in the construction of the two systems XFRMS and MXFRMS, which provide a solid foundation for building more complex utilities, such as plan or schedule maintenance systems.

The results of the problem analysis and task-specific requirements suggest several fundamental changes and extensions of existing reason maintenance technology in order to make it applicable in planning, scheduling, and control. The single agent reason maintenance system XFRMS is therefore developed first, which incorporates and illustrates the key ideas of those improvements and enhancements. XFRMS provides functionality that partially matches those of de.Kleer's ATMS, but focuses on consequence finding, consistency checking, and context determination, while the generation of explanations or the construction of interpretations are neglected. The main improvement in comparison with the ATMS, however, is that XFRMS tackles the key problem of using ATMS-based systems in planning domains: computational complexity, especially the predictability of resource use for particular instances of a problem class. By making context management an explicit task of XFRMS and giving the problem solver explicit control over the number of contexts under consideration, the resource demands of XFRMS can be controlled by the problem solver. The potentially exponential growth of resource demands by the ATMS can be avoided especially in those cases, where the structure of the dependency net would force the ATMS to construct exponentially many contexts, although the problem solver is interested in comparatively few contexts (maybe several dozen or a few hundred). Furthermore, the XFRMS allows the problem solver to explicitly delete contexts it no longer considers relevant.

The technology developed for the single agent case is then further enhanced to the multiagent or distributed case. The problem analysis shows that standard approaches to formalize the underlying kind of assumption-based reasoning for the multiagent case is not well-suited for the intended domain. Facetted Horn Propositional Logic (FHPL) is then developed to present a more adequate tool for the formalization of such problems.

Next, we show that the value of full ATMS functionality is rather doubtful in a multiagent setting: it easily incurs large computational cost and may have side effects that endanger agent autonomy and other desirable properties of agents. Resolving design conflicts when implementing a full ATMS-type distributed reason maintenance system requires several decisions to be made with serious consequences for functionality, efficiency, and applicability of the system. Instead of taking too many such choices and thereby restricting its possible uses, the multiagent reason maintenance system MXFRMS provides a solid base layer functionality which can build the foundation of more specialized reason maintenance services. Also, MXFRMS extends the techniques developed for XFRMS to avoid or at least control the problem of computational complexity. In particular, the XFRMS labelling scheme proves to be much better suited for distribution while giving the programmer better control on how tightly agent autonomy is to be enforced.

The two systems XFRMS and MXFRMS now provide a solid foundation for building more complex utilities, such as plan or schedule maintenance systems. The final chapter gives a perspective on potential uses and future extensions.

Preface

This book investigates the problem of maintaining and managing data dependencies in multiagent systems, a particular type of distributed system. The work described in this text is part of my thesis work and was developed in the context of the PEDE research project [Stoyan et al., 1992], which dealt with planning and execution in distributed environments. The PEDE project served as a unifying framework for research done both at the Knowledge Acquisition Research Group (FG WE) at FORWISS Erlangen and at the Artificial Intelligence Department of the University of Erlangen (IMMD-8), both of which are led by Prof. Dr. Herbert Stoyan. The PEDE project was loosely associated with the Special Research Area 182 on Multiprocessor and Network Configurations (SFB 182, see e.g. [Wedekind, 1992] and [Wedekind, 1994]), a large nationally-funded research effort that was coordinated and headed by Prof. Dr. Hartmut Wedekind.

Acknowledgements

My thesis project benefitted from the support provided to me by a number of people, whose efforts I hereby would like to gratefully acknowledge. Sorry to all those I have forgotten to mention.

Unquestionably, my thesis advisor Prof. Dr. Herbert Stoyan played a key role during my thesis work. He created the lively and inspiring work environment in which my thesis work was done and was also a constant source of questions and new ideas. Prof. Dr. Hartmut Wedekind made it possible for me to come to FORWISS. He provided support and advice throughout my time in Erlangen. I also thank Prof. Dr. Peter Mertens for giving advice and supporting me first during my time as student and later on as a researcher at FORWISS. The early work for this thesis, in particular the system DARMS described later on, was done jointly with Prof. Dr. Clemens Beckstein . This fruitful cooperation is documented by several papers accepted at international workshops. He continued to support my thesis work by carefully reviewing drafts.

I now work in the group of Prof. Dr. Günther Palm at University of Ulm and I am very grateful to Prof. Palm for making it possible for me to finish this work. With Prof. Dr. Bernhard Nebel I had several valuable discussions regarding the parts of my thesis related to logics. I am very grateful to

Prof. Dr. Jörg Siekmann for accepting my thesis for publication in the Lecture Notes in Artificial Intelligence series, published by Springer-Verlag. Many thanks also to Alfred Hofmann and Anna Kramer of Springer-Verlag for their help and their patience.

My colleague and friend Dr. Josef Schneeberger did an outstanding job in motivating and supporting my effort to finish this thesis. When he came to FORWISS in late 1992, he took over a good deal of the administrative duties and management tasks that until then had accumulated on me. As a consequence, I was able to free my mind for doing this research. His interest in my work and his advice were always very inspiring and helpful. Both Josef and myself would never have managed to do all the work we did in the last few years without the help and support of Margarethe Griffaton, the secretary of both the Knowledge Acquisition Research Group and the Knowledge Processing Group at FORWISS. She is a real jewel and I hope she will always get the recognition she deserves for her work and commitment.

My colleagues Christiane Förtsch, Rainer Gastner, Ernst Lutz, Michael Müller, and Gerhard Tobermann at FORWISS, and Markus Kesseler, Hans Weber, and Thomas Stürmer at IMMD-8, created a stimulating and fruitful atmosphere. I thank them all for the good time I had in Erlangen. I also owe a lot to the students that I advised during my time at FORWISS: Rainer Basler, Christoph Dotzel, Robert Fuhge, Tim Geisler, Jürgen Gövert, Sabine Iserhardt, Joachim Klausner, Jörn Kriegel, Rolf Reinema, Joachim Rick, and Martin Riederer.

I had many great discussions on various topics related to my thesis with my long-time friend Michael Beetz from Yale University and many other people from the German and the international DAI community: Jürgen Müller, Donald Steiner, Kurt Sundermeyer, Klaus Fischer, Ed Durfee, Yoav Shoham, Mike Wooldridge, Mike Huhns, Gilad Zlotkin, Jeff Rosenschein, Mike Wellman, and Les Gasser, to mention just a few.

My brother Alfred and his wife Sabine, my sister Renate with her friend Horst, and my friends Elisabeth and Winfried Barth with their daughter Luisa, Annette and Michael Beetz with Nicola, Monique Neumann and Roger Knab with sons Julian and Marius, Lisa and Ernst Lutz, and Gabi and Thomas Ruf with their kids Maximilian and Stefanie, all helped to make life enjoyable for my family, despite my never having enough time to contribute much myself. My parents showed extremely good farsight in the early stages of my education, thereby laying the foundation for my career, and provided moral and financial support later on. They continue to give me the security of a good and intact family. For this and a thousand other reasons, my thesis is devoted to my parents.

More than everybody else, my wife Iris and my son Thomas had to take the heaviest load of long nights and weekends spent in the office. Iris and Thomas, I thank you with all my love.

Contents

1 Introduction   **1**
   1.1   Motivation 1
   1.2   The PEDE Project 3
   1.3   Sketch of the Problem 9
   1.4   Solution Approach 12
   1.5   Contributions and Results 19
   1.6   Outline of the Book 21

2 Single Agent Reason Maintenance   **25**
   2.1   Analysis of Assumption-Based Reasoning 25
      2.1.1   The Lonely Secretary's Nightmare 26
      2.1.2   Tasks in Assumption-Based Reasoning 30
   2.2   Formalization of Assumption-Based Reasoning 32
      2.2.1   Logics for Formalizing Reasoning 32
      2.2.2   Horn Propositional Logic 34
      2.2.3   A HPL Formalization of The Lonely Secretary's Nightmare   38
   2.3   Generic Single Agent Reason Maintenance 43
      2.3.1   Components of Single Agent RMS Specifications 44
      2.3.2   Generic RMS Logical State 45
      2.3.3   Generic RMS Logical Query Interface 45
      2.3.4   Generic RMS State Change Interface 47
      2.3.5   Generic RMS State Query Interface 47
      2.3.6   Relaxation of Protocol Assumptions 47
   2.4   Standard Single Agent Reason Maintenance Technology . . . 48
      2.4.1   Design Tradeoffs 48
      2.4.2   RMS Architecture 50
      2.4.3   RMS Families 50
      2.4.4   The ATMS 52
      2.4.5   Some ATMS Derivates 54
   2.5   Review of Single Agent Reason Maintenance 55

**3 XFRMS: A Single Agent Focus-Based Reason Maintenance
System   57**
  3.1 Overview on XFRMS 57
  3.2 XFRMS Specification 58
       3.2.1 XFRMS Logical State 58
       3.2.2 XFRMS Logical Query Interface 60
       3.2.3 XFRMS State Change Interface 61
       3.2.4 XFRMS State Query Interface 63
  3.3 XFRMS Architecture 64
  3.4 XFRMS Implementation 66
       3.4.1 Representation: Mapping Logical State to XFRMS State 66
       3.4.2 Labels 68
       3.4.3 Integrity Constraints 68
       3.4.4 Exploiting Labels in Query Processing 69
       3.4.5 Label Propagation 71
       3.4.6 Updating XFRMS States and Correctness of Label
              Propagation 74
  3.5 XFRMS Complexity Considerations 78
       3.5.1 Space Complexity 79
       3.5.2 Runtime Complexity 79
  3.6 Summary of XFRMS 81

4 Multiagent Reason Maintenance   83
  4.1 Analysis of Multiagent Assumption-Based Reasoning 83
       4.1.1 The Secretaries' Nightmare 83
       4.1.2 Desirability of Multiagent Assumption-Based Reasoning
              Support 91
       4.1.3 Subtle Issues in Multiagent Assumption-Based Reasoning 92
       4.1.4 Tasks in Multiagent Assumption-Based Reasoning . . . 96
  4.2 Formalization of Multiagent Assumption-Based Reasoning . . . 99
       4.2.1 Logics for Formalizing Multiagent Reasoning 99
       4.2.2 Facetted Horn Propositional Logic 105
              4.2.2.1 Basic Idea: A Road Map for FHPL 105
              4.2.2.2 FHPL: Language Syntax 106
              4.2.2.3 FHPL: Language Semantics 111
              4.2.2.4 FHPL: Calculus 118
              4.2.2.5 Discussion: Some Properties of FHPL 122
       4.2.3 A FHPL Formalization of The Secretaries' Nightmare . 123
  4.3 Generic Multiagent Reason Maintenance 131
       4.3.1 Components of Multiagent RMS Specifications 134
       4.3.2 Generic Multiagent RMS Logical State 135
       4.3.3 Generic Multiagent RMS Logical Query Interface . . . 136
       4.3.4 Generic Multiagent RMS State Change Interface 138

4.3.5   Generic Multiagent RMS State Query Interface 139
4.3.6   Relaxation of Protocol Assumptions 139
4.4   Standard Multiagent Reason Maintenance Technology 141
4.4.1   Design Tradeoffs 142
4.4.2   Multiagent RMS Architectures 143
4.4.3   Multiagent RMS Families 147
4.4.4   The DTMS and the BRTMS 150
4.4.5   The DATMS 151
4.4.6   The DARMS 152
4.4.6.1   Multiagent RMS Requirements 153
4.4.6.2   Key Ideas 154
4.4.6.3   Architecture of DARMS Modules 155
4.4.6.4   Functional Interface and DARMS Behavior . . 158
4.4.6.5   Formal Specification of DARMS 160
4.4.6.6   Applying DARMS 164
4.4.6.7   Discussion and Conclusions 169
4.5   Review of Multiagent Reason Maintenance 170

5 MXFRMS: A Multiagent Focus-Based Reason Maintenance
   System   171
5.1   Overview on MXFRMS 171
5.2   MXFRMS System Architecture 175
5.2.1   Multiagent System Architecture 176
5.2.2   MXFRMS System Architecture Perspectives 178
5.2.3   Agent-Oriented MXFRMS System Architecture View . 178
5.2.4   Logical MXFRMS System Architecture View 180
5.2.5   Implementational MXFRMS System Architecture View 182
5.2.6   An Open MXFRMS Architecture 186
5.3   MXFRMS Specification 188
5.3.1   MXFRMS Global Logical State 188
5.3.2   MXFRMS Facet Logical State 191
5.3.3   MXFRMS Logical Query Interface 197
5.3.4   MXFRMS State Change Interface 199
5.3.5   MXFRMS State Query Interface 206
5.3.6   MXFRMS System Level Functionality 209
5.4   MXFRMS Facet Module Architecture 211
5.5   MXFRMS Implementation 212
5.5.1   Representation: Mapping Logical State to MXFRMS
         State 213
5.5.2   Labels 215
5.5.3   Integrity Constraints 216
5.5.4   Process Structure of Facet Modules 217
5.5.5   Exploitation of Labels in Query Processing 218

5.5.6   Label Propagation 220
5.5.7   Updating MXFRMS States 226
5.5.8   MXFRMS Facet Communication Interface 235
5.5.9   Correctness of Label Propagation 238
5.6   MXFRMS Complexity Considerations 247
5.6.1   Space Complexity 248
5.6.2   Runtime Complexity 248

6   Conclusions   251
6.1   History and Review of Work Done 251
6.2   Major Results and Contributions 253
6.3   The Work in Perspective 254
6.4   Future Work 258
6.5   Summary 260

Bibliography   261

List of Figures   275

List of Tables   277

List of Acronyms   277

Chapter 1

Introduction

1.1 Motivation

Multiagent systems (MAS) have received much attention recently, especially within the Distributed Artificial Intelligence[1] (DAI) community, a very active subfield of Artificial Intelligence[2] (AI). Both the number of papers related to multiagent systems in conferences and workshops and the number of attendees interested in them have significantly increased over the past years. This development has led to the organization of a biannual conference, the International Conference on Multiagent Systems, which was held for the first time [Lesser, 1995] in San Francisco in 1995. Once a subfield of Artificial Intelligence holds its own conference, it is commonly believed to have matured to the extent that applications incorporating the concepts of the field can be developed, and both interest in the field as well as the amount of work being done justify a separate conference. Machine Learning [ML, 1993], Knowledge Representation [KR, 1992], [KR, 1994], and AI Planning and Scheduling [Hendler and McDermott, 1992], [Hammond, 1994] are examples for such developments.

So far, however, hardly any practical applications of multiagent systems are known to be used in everyday business processes or by a large number of users. Most systems described in research papers are laboratory or small demonstration systems. Widely known big success stories for multiagent systems, which could play a role similar to that of the rule-based configuration system XCON

---

[1]For an introduction to DAI, see e.g. [Bond and Gasser, 1988b] and [Müller, 1993].

[2]See the DAI-related sessions in the proceedings of major AI conferences, e.g. [IJCAI, 1991], [IJCAI, 1993], [IJCAI, 1995], [AAAI, 1991], [AAAI, 1992], [AAAI, 1993], [AAAI, 1994], [ECAI, 1992], and [ECAI, 1994]. Furthermore, the number of workshops on DAI and MAS seems to constantly increase, see e.g. the MAAMAW workshops in Europe, the DAI workshops in the U.S., and a number of workshops held in conjunction with the major AI conferences like IJCAI, AAAI, or ECAI. In Germany, the DAI special interest group (FG 1.1.6 Verteilte Künstliche Intelligenz) within the "Gesellschaft für Informatik" is very active and organizes about two workshops per year.

(also known as R1, see [McDermott, 1982], [McDermott, 1984]) in the expert systems area, are still not known. This situation is in contrast to the large and increasing need for multiagent systems technology that can utilize recent and future developments in networking[3] and interoperability[4] technology to provide a new and improved platform for distributed, but cooperating software systems like multiagent systems. The multiagent systems approach is viewed as one of the most promising paradigms for the integration of business processes within a single enterprise, for coupling business processes of several cooperating enterprises, and for new and innovative software applications for the consumer market.

We believe the unsatisfactory situation in multiagent systems is largely due to the fact that adequate support technology for building multiagent systems in an efficient and effective way is still missing in many areas. Like any distributed system, multiagent systems are very difficult to design and implement. Generic, application-independent concepts and implementational frameworks are needed to facilitate application system development. Two examples for the enabling role of such concepts, taken from from classical software technology, are the *Remote Procedure Call* and the *Client-Server Architecture*. Many concepts and ideas developed for standalone systems, however, do not carry over to multiagent or distributed systems without major redesign.[5] An example for this phenomenon, again from standard software technology, are databases. If several application programs, each of which connects to one or more different databases, communicate and exchange data, additional measures must be taken in order to ensure data consistency and integrity on a global level. This has led to the development of distributed database technology (see e.g. [Schneider, 1982], [Wedekind, 1988], [Oezsu and Valduriez, 1991], [Bell and Grimson, 1992], [Wedekind, 1994]).

An AI example for a single agent concept that does not easily carry over to multiagent systems is reason maintenance. Reason maintenance systems (RMSs)[6] are often used to solve the *context determination problem* and the *belief revision problem* (these terms will be explained later on) in practical applications. We will illucidate later on, that standard reason maintenance technology is more or less useless in multiagent systems, and that the whole idea of reason maintenance must be reinvented for multiagent settings. New

---

[3]For example, the INTERNET or high-speed digital data highways.

[4]See e.g. work done in the ARPA Knowledge Sharing Effort (KSE) project [Neches et al., 1991a], in particular the Interlingua Knowledge Interchange Format (KIF) [Genesereth et al., 1993a] and the agent communication protocol Knowledge and Query Manipulation Language (KQML) [Finin et al., 1993a].

[5]See e.g. [Bond and Gasser, 1988a] for an overview on problems related to the development of multiagent and other DAI systems.

[6]See e.g. [Doyle, 1979] or [de Kleer, 1986a] for early systems, [Martins, 1991] for a guide to the relevant literature, and [Beckstein, 1994] for a coherent and formal treatment of many single agent RMS systems and techniques.

and improved technology must be provided to solve the *distributed context determination problem* and the *distributed belief revision problem* occurring in many multiagent systems. Once this kind of improved technology is readily available, multiagent systems that need to solve these problems can be built better and faster. Thus, the work described here is a step towards improving multiagent systems technology by providing computational support that eases multiagent systems development.

1.2   The PEDE Project

The PEDE project [Stoyan et al., 1992] investigates planning, scheduling and control in distributed environments. One of the main hypotheses of the PEDE project is that such problems can best be solved by multiagent systems that consist of knowledge-based agents performing planning, scheduling and execution tasks and whose organizational structure matches the organizational structure of the enterprise the multiagent system is embedded in. Thus, we deal with multiagent systems consisting mainly of communicating, knowledge-based planners, schedulers, and agents that control the execution of tasks or operations. The goal of the PEDE project is to enhance existing and to develop new technology that allows the use of typical AI concepts and ideas, expecially from planning and scheduling, in multiagent systems that solve PEDE problems.

The PEDE Research Approach   In the PEDE project, we take the following basic research approach:

- A large class of problems, which we call PEDE[7] problems (defined below) and which encompasses problems involving planning, scheduling and control of execution in dynamic multiagent environments, is identified and chosen as the primary domain of interest.

- A common (sub)problem occurring in many, if not all, PEDE problems, is selected as research topic. This subproblem is the typical occurrence of lots of dependencies between problem solving data that represent relevant pieces of information. Another feature of this problem is that such data are typically held, maintained and communicated among several problem solving agents.

- A central hypothesis is set forth. In the PEDE project, this hypothesis is that explicitly representing and maintaining the data dependencies mentioned above is advantageous, if not crucial, for effective and efficient solutions of PEDE problems.

---

[7]PEDE = Planning and Execution in Distributed Environments

- The goal of the research is to provide effective and efficient computational support for solving the problem selected as research topic; in our case, distributed reason maintenance systems are developed that allow the maintenance and management of such data dependencies in distributed and multiagent systems.

- Applying the newly developed or enhanced technology should significantly ease the design and construction of application systems that solve instances of the chosen problem class. Within PEDE, we use the distributed reason maintenance technology developed and described in this text to simplify the design and implementation of distributed planning and scheduling systems.

PEDE Problems Consider a company that manufactures, assembles and sells transmission parts for various types of customers throughout the world. Many agents throughout the company are involved to continuously acquire orders, design the ordered parts, generate process plans for them, plan and schedule production, manufacture the parts, assemble the transmissions, and finally deliver the orders to the customer. In order to achieve a desired overall system behavior (at the top level: making profit), most of these activities must first be planned and scheduled and then their execution must be controlled. The planning and execution of activities takes place in different spatial locations at different times and is performed by different human or artificial (machines, robots, etc.) agents. Even for a single order, this is a very complex task.

Many other scenarios — ranging from logistics to office automation — could be presented that show many of the same characteristics, although they are from completely different domains. Therefore, we can identify a large class of problems sharing some crucial common characteristics:

DEFINITION 1.2.1 (PEDE PROBLEM)
*A **PEDE problem** is a complex task the solution of which requires the functionally, spatially and temporally distributed planning and execution of tasks by several agents in a dynamically changing environment.*

Functional distribution of subtasks is often necessary, because no single agent is able to solve the problem on its own while meeting the given task specifications. Thus, several agents must cooperate to solve the overall problem (*cooperation* problem). *Spatial* distribution of subtasks may be necessary, because some agents reside at fixed, spatially distributed locations, and therefore, information and material must be transported to them in order to enable them to contribute to the solution. Thus, spatial distribution introduces the problems of *logistics* and *communication*. *Temporal* distribution of subtasks is often necessary, because not all subtasks can be performed at the same time for technical reasons (unaccessability) or because objects needed to perform several subtasks must be used exclusively (tools) or at different locations (parts). Therefore, subtasks may have to be performed in a synchronized or mutually exclusive manner (*coordination* problem).

Planning and execution of tasks means that agents are rational and deliberative, i.e. they try to figure out effective and efficient ways to achieve their goals and the possible effects of them prior to actually performing actions. The joint consideration of both planning and execution makes a problem much more complex than simple planning: one must supervise the correct execution of plans generated, adequately react to failures, e.g. by revising plans, and ensure the achievement of the initial, top-level goal.

The aspect of having to act in a dynamically changing world means that the likelihood of world states at execution time being different from those assumed at planning time increases significantly with the length of the interval between these two points of time.

Finally, there are several reasons for a task to be classified as *complex*:

- The task must be decomposed into many (often highly interdependent) subtasks.

- The solution space is very large.

- Many levels of abstraction are needed.

- Many agents are necessary to perform the task.

The identification of problem classes and their formal characterizations are essential requirements for developing computational models that are principally suitable as solutions for many practical problems. PEDE problems are such a problem class.

Multiagent Planning and Scheduling Systems We propose the use of multiagent systems for solving PEDE problems. These multiagent systems may consist of quite different kinds of agents, ranging from very primitive, simple agents to very complex, rational agents. In the following, we consider rational agents with the following characteristics:

- Agents do one or more of *i)* generating, *ii)* modifying, or *iii)* executing plans and schedules.[8]

- It is not only possible, but the standard case, that plans generated by one agent are executed by one or several other agents.

---

[8]Schedules are considered special cases of plans. Therefore, we often simply refer to plans when we also implicitly refer to schedules.

- Planning and scheduling decisions made by the agents often depend on assumptions, i.e. propositions about future world states which cannot definitely be guaranteed to become true.[9]

- Agents communicate with each other and thereby exchange information about plans. In particular, they may exchange partial or even complete plans containing information depending on assumptions.

Another problem characteristic to be taken into account is that the environment of the agents is changing dynamically. The coincidence of assumptions and dependencies in plans, communication of plans between agents, and dynamically changing agent environments makes multiagent planning and scheduling difficult.

Assumptions and Dependencies in Planning and Scheduling   There is a variety of techniques available for solving planning and scheduling tasks.[10] As Figure 1.1 illustrates, planners and schedulers (implicitly) introduce assumptions (about future states of the world) as well as dependencies (among parts of the plan and other relevant pieces of information). This is not a real problem if a static world is assumed. Giving up the static world assumption, however, forces agents to adapt to new situations. In practice, this problem

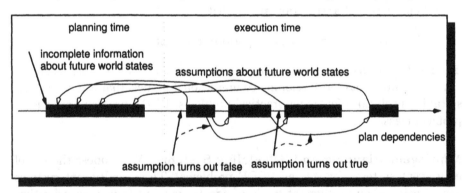

Figure 1.1: Assumptions and dependencies in dynamic planning and scheduling domains.

At planning time t_{plan}, the planner makes decisions based on an incomplete model of the world (thick arrow top left) and assumptions about certain future world states (thin arrows above timeline). Thereby, dependencies between planned operations are created (thin arrows below timeline). The assumptions underlying such dependencies can often be verified or falsified during execution (thick arrows below timeline), which allows to remove dependencies (usually if an assumption turns out true) or to take apropriate measures for repairing the plan or at least avoiding damage and waste (if the assumption turns out false).

---

[9]Later, we represent these assumptions explicitly in plans.
[10]See e.g. [Allen et al., 1990] or [Sycara, 1990].

is often solved by throwing away the old plan and generating a completely new one. If this is not possible, e.g. for reasons like cost of computing new plans[11], then human intervention is necessary to cope with such a situation and human job shop schedulers/controllers locally adapt the plan reflecting minor changes. We argue that it is useful to explicitly maintain and manage assumptions and the dependencies they introduce among parts of plans, because it allows for simpler adaptation of complex plans to new situations.[12]

Attempts to explicitly deal with the assumptions made during planning have successfully been made for single agent scenarios, e.g. by [Beetz et al., 1992] or [Petrie, 1991]. Such approaches usually employ reason maintenance systems such as de Kleers ATMS, which are application-independent tools for solving the problem of maintaining data and dependencies between them. The general idea of reason maintenance systems is to build problem solving systems according to a two-level architecture, which consists of a problem solver (PS) module and a reason maintenance (RMS) module that interact with each other as follows:

- The problem solver informs the RMS module about relevant propositions and assumptions. It also provides the logical dependencies between them, called justifications.

- The RMS module maintains the appropiate data structures for the information provided by the problem solver and keeps these data structures consistent. It also answers queries posed by the problem solver, like whether a proposition holds given certain assumptions.

The task to be solved if an RMS is to be used in a planing application is to find an adequate mapping of data and dependencies relevant in the domain onto the functionality provided by an RMS.

Factoring out the functionality for reason maintenance results in much simpler architectures for the problem solving modules, as they do not have to care about reason maintenance at all. Also, the problem solving system is divided into a domain-independent part (the RMS module) and a domain-dependent part (the PS module), which eases reuse and maintenance of the overall system.

---

[11]Production planning systems often take several hours to produce a plan on a large mainframe.

[12]There is a tradeoff between the cost of maintaining dependencies and the cost of adapting a plan to a new situation. It has been shown, that the computational cost for replanning is, in the worst case, even worse than for generating a new plan [Nebel and Köhler, 1995]. However, practice seems to suggest that repairing existing plans is preferable to computing new ones in most scenarios, especially if the cost for executing the plan are taken into account.

Distributed Planning and Scheduling   As already mentioned previously, in a multiagent planning and scheduling scenario several agents create plans or schedules (e.g. a job shop scheduling agent receiving an order from the stock control agent), which are usually executed by several other agents (various agents controlling e.g. machines, robots, and transportation devices). In such a scenario agents commonly communicate partial or complete plans, or other information based on them, such as orders to execute a particular operation at a particular time. As Figure 1.2 illustrates, this severely complicates the administration of data and dependencies between them. As will be shown

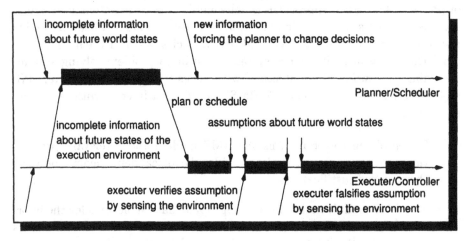

Figure 1.2:   Assumptions and dependencies in distributed planning and scheduling.

Activities of a planning agent and a plan execution agent are displayed along two timelines. As before, the planning agent must make decisions based on an incomplete model of the world state and on assumptions about future world states in both its own (e.g. the operation being the most suited one) as well as the executer environment (such as the availability of a workpiece or tool). The dependencies and their underlying assumptions get communicated to the executer. From then on, both planner and executer may receive new information that verifies or falsifies assumptions, thereby necessitating updates to the plans in both agents.

in later chapters, currently available reason maintenance technology does not suffice to cope with the problems posed by distributed planning and scheduling scenarios and other PEDE problems. The main deficiencies are inadequate handling of multiple contexts, lack of support for representing temporal dependencies and missing communicative capabilities for application in distributed environments.

The approach we follow in the PEDE project is to extend and enhance reason maintenance technology for use in multiagent systems. In particular, the systems developed here, XFRMS and MXFRMS, are considered as a solid basis for further research and developments towards multiagent planning and scheduling technology. Some viable paths for future research are the integration of support for temporal dependencies, which has been investigated already for the single agent case by others in our group [Geisler, 1994], and the addition of functionality for maintaining (multiagent) plans and schedules, e.g. similar to the functionality of the PNMS system [Lindner, 1992].

Summary of the PEDE Approach Summarizing, the idea is to make plan representations rich enough to enable plan generating agents, information providing agents, and plan executing agents to explicitly reason about the assumptions underlying planning decisions and keep other interested agents automatically informed on changes to these assumptions. In order to keep planning and scheduling architectures reasonably simple, there is a need for a general utility incorporating a mechanism to maintain and manage such dependencies. The text shows that no adequate technology was available to maintain and manage dependencies like those occurring in planning and scheduling problems in distributed systems. The goal of our work is to provide this technology.

1.3 Sketch of the Problem

As motivated in the previous section, we use multiagent planning and scheduling systems for solving PEDE problems. In such multiagent systems, each of these agents typically has to represent one or more plans or schedules and — more or less explicitly — a significant number of past, current, and future states of the world. Some typical examples for tasks such an agent must perform are to decide whether an operation will lead to a desired effect, to check whether an operation can be performed at a certain time, to ensure that all requirements of an operation are met, and so on.[13] In order to perform such operations, the causal and temporal dependencies between various aspects of the domain, formalized in a domain theory[14], and the previous planning and scheduling decisions, e.g. operations performed prior to the one on hand, must be taken into account. In particular, inconsistent situations, like a workpiece required to be at two different places at the same time or two operations to be performed by a single executor at the same time, must be detected. Because of such dependencies, the modification of plans and schedules due to changed environment conditions is an especially hard problem in planning and scheduling applications. Thus, the question is

1. how planning and scheduling agents can represent several alternative plans or schedules and multiple world states, including the dependencies between relevant data items,

---

[13]See e.g. [Beetz and Lefkowitz, 1989a],[Beetz et al., 1992], or [Lindner, 1992] for discussion of tasks a planner must perform.

[14]In planning, this includes a theory of action.

2. how they can maintain consistency of plans and schedules, and

3. how they can effectively update these representations when additional planning and scheduling decisions are made or new information about world states becomes known.

Previous work in planning[15] has shown, that these problems can be solved for single agent planners by applying *multiple context, assumption-based reasoning*. The planning and scheduling agents investigated here are assumed to apply a restricted form of this kind of reasoning. The agents express relevant knowledge about the planning and scheduling domain in a propositional Horn clause logic, i.e. as a

- set of (elementary) propositions $p, q, r, \ldots$, and a

- set of (propositional) definite Horn clauses of the form "*if p and q then r*".

Propositions are used to represent problem solver decisions, like executing an operation on a certain machine at a certain time, and to describe aspects of world states, like a part being available or a machine being busy. Horn clauses are used to express causal and other dependencies between propositions as logical constraints. Horn clauses of the form "*if p and q then $\perp$*" are used to declare contradictions and to formulate conditions for material inconsistency, while Horn clauses of the form "*if $\top$ then p*" are used to declare as premises propositions that must hold in all situations.

Let us assume that a planning or scheduling agent maintains a database which consists *only of clauses* and wants to determine whether a particular proposition is a consequence of a particular set of planning decisions in a particular world state. Then, the agent must first *assume* the propositions representing these planning decisions and the world state (i.e. it simulates adding the propositions to the database of clauses)[16] and then determine whether the proposition of interest is a logical consequence of the clauses and the assumptions. Each such logical consequence is called a belief, and all beliefs induced by a particular set of assumptions (which is also referred to as an *environment*) are called a *context*. Thus, the above problem is called the **context determination problem**. Determining whether a particular proposition should be believed in a certain environment (consequence finding) is a simpler variant of the context determination problem that we sometimes refer to as the **consequence determination problem**. If $\perp$ is in the context, then the context is considered inconsistent, which means that some of the propositions representing planning and scheduling decisions and aspects of world states result in a

---

[15]See e.g. [Morris and Nado, 1986], [Fikes et al., 1987], [Beetz and Lefkowitz, 1989b], and [Lindner, 1992].

[16]Thus, the assumptions are assumed to hold, while by default all other propositions are assumed not to hold.

contradiction. Alternative plans and schedules as well as different world states can be represented by different contexts which are characterized by different environments, i.e. by different sets of underlying assumptions.[17]

Whenever the agents make new planning and scheduling decisions or learn new information about the world, they have to update their clause databases. Any change to an agent's clause database, however, may result in changes to the contexts the agent is interested in. The problem of updating contexts because of changes to the clause database is called the **belief revision problem**. In particular, planning and scheduling agents will be interested in detecting new inconsistencies, which represent conflicts in planning decisions.

We now consider several such planning and scheduling agents which have to cooperate and communicate with each other in order to exchange information (beliefs) about their local planning and scheduling decisions and their local knowledge about the world states. In particular, we assume that agents have to base their local decision making on information received from other agents via communication and to formulate dependencies between their local problem solving data and communicated data. This has consequences for the consistency of plans and schedules: agents may have to find out whether their local planning and scheduling decisions do not conflict with those of one or more other agents. Otherwise, agents may have locally consistent, but mutually inconsistent plans (like a part planned to be at two different places at the same time by different agents). Finally, whenever an agent modifies its local plan or schedule, other agents may be affected and must be notified of such changes.

Earlier in this section, we have outlined that single agent planners and schedulers can perform certain planning subtasks (represent and reason with several alternative plans and world states, maintain consistency, and update plans and world states), if they apply multiple-context assumption-based reasoning and if they can solve the context determination problem and the belief revision problem. The question arising is how multiple-context assumption-based reasoning can be applied to multiagent systems. That is, we have to look at *multiagent, multiple-context, assumption-based reasoning*.

An immediate question is what communication of beliefs exactly means in the context of multiple-context assumption-based reasoning. It must be discussed how an agent can represent and reason with such communicated beliefs. An adequate formalization of multiple context assumption-based reasoning in multiagent systems is needed. This includes a discussion of issues like consistency of beliefs from different perspectives (from an agent's local viewpoint, for an arbitrary group of agents, and from the global (i.e. all agents) view-

---

[17]Note, that each environment uniquely determines an associated context. This means that — unless additional restrictions are set forth — different contexts are always characterized by different environments, but different environments may result in the same context.

point). Assuming that planning and scheduling agents in a multiagent system apply assumption-based reasoning in a similar manner as outlined above, then

- the **distributed consequence determination problem**,

- the **distributed context determination problem**, and

- the **distributed belief revision problem**

must be investigated and solved. The main difference between the non-distributed and the distributed variants of the context determination problem is that in order to solve the latter an agent will have to take into account dependencies (clauses) that involve communicated beliefs. In particular, an agent must be able to find out whether a communicated belief is a logical consequence of a certain set of assumptions or not. Communicated beliefs also make the distributed belief revision problem more difficult. In single agent systems, belief revision can only be caused by the agent updating its local database. In multiagent systems, however, an update of an agent's clause database may as well force several other agents to revise their beliefs. In particular, an agent that updates it's local database of dependencies may have to inform other agents about these changes.

Once an adequate formalization of multiagent multiple-context assumption-based reasoning is available, the question arises how multiagent systems can make effective and efficient use of this kind of reasoning. Computational support for applying multiagent assumption-based reasoning in application systems is required. Modules that provide functionality for solving the context determination and belief revision problems with reasonable performance must be specified, designed and implemented.

1.4   Solution Approach

Reason Maintenance Systems (RMSs)[18] are commonly used in single agent systems to solve the context determination and belief revision problems. We suggest the extension and enhancement of reason maintenance technology to the multiagent (distributed) case and the development of Distributed Reason Maintenance Systems (DRMSs). DRMSs are re-usable, application-independent software components that can be used in application software systems to solve the *distributed* context determination problem and the *distributed* belief revision problem.

A standard method of software technology is to provide support systems, i.e. off-the-shelf software components (as libraries, modules, or subsystems)

---

[18] Also commonly known as Truth Maintenance Systems (TMSs). See [Beckstein, 1994] for a brief history and discussion of these terms.

that ease and accelerate the development of large applications. Such support systems typically provide functionality for solving common subproblems and performing tasks that are reasonably self-contained and can be described in an application-independent manner. Examples are database systems, libraries for constructing graphical user interfaces, graphics modules, and statistics packages. Because such support systems are specialized for solving a particular problem, they provide their functionality with great efficiency.[19]

The representation and maintenance of a database of beliefs and of the dependencies between them is a coherent and important subproblem by itself. This suggests that specialized support systems should be used to solve this subproblem. Reason Maintenance Systems (RMSs) are such support systems commonly used for solving the context determination and the belief revision problems. If such a reason maintenance system is used, the architecture of a problem solving agent is structured into two levels (see Figure 1.3): the application-independent RMS and the application-specific core problem solver (PS). The problem solver tells the RMS about relevant propositions, assumptions, and dependencies. The RMS stores this information, updates it automatically, and utilizes it to provide fast responses to problem solver queries, which require the context determination and belief revison problems to be solved.

The basic idea of a reason maintenance system is that it compiles propositions and dependencies into a dependency net and assigns *labels* to propositions (and possibly the dependencies). These labels are compact representation of context information and thus the basis for providing answers to problem solver queries efficiently, i.e. for solving the context determination problem. Labels must be updated by label propagation procedures whenever the database of propositions and dependencies is modified; updating the labels means solving instances of the belief revision problem.

An overview and thorough description of single agent reason maintenance technology, including a classification of systems, can be found in [Beckstein, 1994]. Due to the requirements of the intented application domain (PEDE), we are only interested in *multiple-context assumption-based reason maintenance systems*. The prototypical example for such an RMS is de Kleer's *basic* ATMS (see [de Kleer, 1986a], a widely known and very popular system. However, the ATMS exhibits some deficiencies when used in (single agent) planning or scheduling applications:

- *Inadequate support for context management.* The ATMS has no knowledge about the specific contexts the problem solver is interested in. In

---

[19]Of course, this does not mean that a certain functionality, like maintaining a particular set of data or performing a special graphics function, could not be implemented more efficiently, but this would typically take a large programming effort that one must usually pay for with loss of generality and compatability.

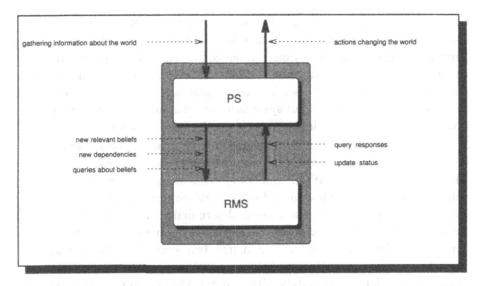

Figure 1.3: The two-level software architecture.

The problem solving agent is structured into a core problem solver (PS) and a reason maintenance system (RMS). Due to the availability of new information about the world or its own
inference, the problem solver declares new propositions as relevant, formulates additional
data dependencies, and queries the RMS about the belief status of relevant propositions.
The RMS responds with information about the update status of the belief database or responses to the queries.

principle, the ATMS implicitly considers all contexts as relevant, i.e. it
must be able to construct the context for all possible subsets of assumptions. As the number of assumptions increases, this feature may force the
ATMS to construct and maintain very complex labels, even if the problem
solver is interested only in a very small number of contexts. Also, queries
to the ATMS must always explicitly provide an environment as argument;
there is no support for a *current environment* or *focus*. Determining the
complete context of an environment is also not directly supported by the
ATMS, but often useful in planning and scheduling applications. Finally,
environments are automatically constructed and deleted by the ATMS;
there is no way for the problem solver to force the ATMS to delete environments not of interest any more. Altogether, we believe that the ATMS
does not always provide adequate support for managing problem solver
contexts, in particular not for planning and scheduling applications.

- *Exponentially growing resource demands.* As a consequence of its complex labels, the resource demands of the ATMS for space and time are
  almost impossible to predict. The actual use of resources mainly depends
  on the specific set of clauses maintained by the ATMS and can grow ex-

ponentially with the number of assumptions.[20] That the problem solver
has no effective control on the resource demands of its associated ATMS
is especially in those cases a nuisance, where the problem solver wants
to maintain large numbers of data, dependencies and assumptions, but
is interested only in comparatively few of the contexts that the ATMS
would construct.

Furthermore, the ATMS compromises on information hiding by giving pointers
to its internal data structures to the problem solver. Although this can lead
to limited efficiency gains, it must be considered bad programming practice.
As communicating pointers to local data structures to another agent, which
is supposed to relate the information represented by this pointer to its own
information, is not meaningful, this feature seems especially inappropriate for
multiagent scenarios. It seems to be a good idea to provide remedies for these
deficiencies first before actually tackling the multiagent case.

As is shown in later chapters, fixing the ATMS deficiencies requires significant modifications that suggest an alternative architecture for an RMS. This
architecture features an RMS design based on three modules: a dependency
net unit, a context management unit, and a communication and control unit.
The XFRMS system presented later on is a reason maintenance system that
implements this new architecture. Furthermore, XFRMS improves information
hiding by providing a representation language-oriented problem solver interface.

Getting around the problem of exponentially growing resource demands
and improving the functionality for managing environments and contexts requires further extensive changes. Both problems are caused by the labels used
by the ATMS. When using the ATMS, the problem solver has no effective control
on the number of contexts maintained by the ATMS. The XFRMS provides significantly extended functionality for managing contexts, including one called
focus that represents the current context of the problem solver, by allowing
the problem solver to state explicitly which contexts it is interested in. By
making context management an RMS task, the XFRMS can use a new label
structure that avoids the resource and performance problems of the ATMS.
The new label structure also lays the foundation for making improved context
deletion facilities feasible.

The ideas and techniques developed for XFRMS to improve multiple context
assumption-based reason maintenance in single agents prove to be important
steps towards the development of adequate reason maintenance support for
multiagent systems. However, as illustrated in Figure 1.4), even these improvements to standard RMS technology are not sufficient to yield systems

---

[20]See e.g. [Geisler, 1994] for examples that illustrate how quickly the size of ATMS labels
can explode.

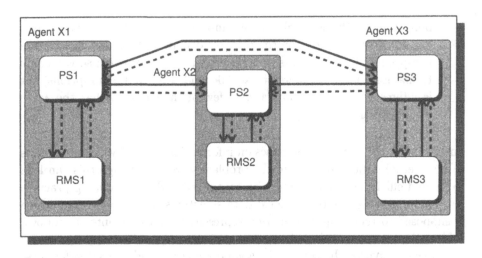

Figure 1.4: Multiagent system using standard RMS technology.
The thorough lines between PS and RMS modules are normal, local interactions, while thorough lines between the problem solver modules indicate application-dependent communication between the agents. Dotted lines illustrate communication necessary for communicating beliefs and updating such communicated beliefs.

capable of adequately solving the distributed context determination and distributed belief revision problems.

As pointed out earlier, agents often have to communicate and to exchange information relevant to their problem solving. This information may be about an agent's beliefs. Whenever beliefs are communicated, the problem of updating and revising them occurs. As standard, single agent RMS systems do not automatically determine necessary belief updates for beliefs that have been communicated to other agents, the problem solver must take care of all processing and communication necessary for such belief updates. This violates the two-level-architecture idea as depicted in Figure 1.3, which was invented to improve the infrastructure of an agent and to free the problem solver from the burden of updating and revising beliefs: Although the problem solver does not have to update its own beliefs, it must provide means to inform other agents having received information about its beliefs whenever these beliefs are changed. This makes problem solvers unnecessarily complex and leads to code that is difficult to design and maintain. Significant modifications and extensions to existing reason maintenance systems must be made to yield systems useful for multiagent settings. Thus, distributed reason maintenance systems are needed that are capable of communicating with each other directly.

Because there are few distributed reason maintenance systems known,[21] notably for *multiple-context, assumption-based* reasoning, a thorough analysis

---

[21]See e.g. [Fuhge, 1993] and Chapter 7 of [Beckstein, 1994].

is in order first. The analysis yields several main results: First, a multiagent reason maintenance support module associated with a particular problem solver should be able to locally represent beliefs communicated from other agents. Next, the multiagent reason maintenance module should allow to distinguish between the agent's local beliefs and beliefs communicated from other agents. Also, it should support formulating dependencies that include such communicated beliefs. Finally, the problem solver should be able to specify whether communicated beliefs are to be taken into account for determining contexts or not; this requirement especially applies to deciding whether contexts are consistent or not.

Meeting the above requirements is essential for achieving *belief autonomy*, which means that an agent's beliefs cannot be manipulated by other agents without the agent's consent. Belief autonomy is an important aspect in making agents autonomous; one can hardly consider an agent autonomous if it determines its actions on the basis of beliefs which can be arbitrarily manipulated by other agents. Autonomy itself is commonly considered a characterizing feature of agents [Foner, 1993].

An interesting question arising here is how to adequately formalize multiagent multiple-context assumption-based reasoning and notions like belief autonomy. In the single agent case, a very simple propositional Horn clause logic was sufficient to formally describe the kind of assumption-based reasoning we are interested in. Modal logics,[22] which are most often used in formal work about knowledge and belief in multiagent systems, appeared to be more complex than necessary while not adequately capturing our intuitive notion of multiagent assumption-based reasoning. Therefore, we developed FHPL (Facetted Horn Propositional Logic) as a formal tool for describing the kind of multiagent reasoning investigated in this text. FHPL extends propositional Horn clause logic by introducing two operators for each agent: one is used as to uniquely assign a formula to a facet (which is the logical equivalent of an agent's database), the other one is used by other agents to refer to beliefs of the agent. FHPL, including its semantics, calculus, and logical consequence and derivability relations, is discussed in some detail.

Based on the analysis and formalization of multiagent assumption-based reasoning the functionality desirable for distributed reason maintenance systems is specified. This specification still leaves a lot of freedom regarding architecture and implementation of such systems. Two extreme alternatives for *distributed reason maintenance system architectures* are:

- The centralized server approach (see Figure 1.5) follows ideas from database systems and client/server architectures. A multiagent system according

---

[22]For an introduction, see [Hughes and Cresswell, 1968], or [Chellas, 1980]. An overview on the application of modal logics to knowledge and belief can be found e.g. in [Wooldridge and Jennings, 1995] or [Halpern and Moses, 1992].

to this approach will feature a single agent (comparable to a central DBMS), called Centralized RMS (CRMS), that provides reason maintenance services for all other agents. The problem solving agents have an appropriate interface (called virtual RMS) to interact with the central RMS server, e.g. based on function calls, remote procedure calls, the TCP/IP protocol, or email messages.

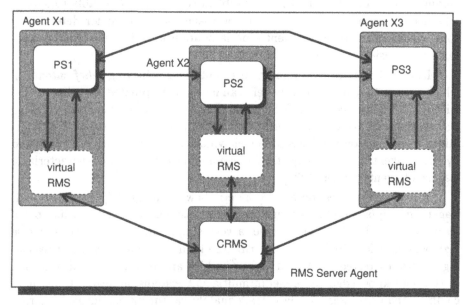

Figure 1.5: Multiagent system using centralized RMS technology.

A central server, tagged CRMS, provides all reason maintenance services. Each agent has an interface, tagged *virtual RMS*, to access the server functionality. Thorough lines within an agent represent the usual interaction between a problem solver and its associated (virtual) RMS. Thorough lines between problem solvers of different agents indicate application-dependent communication, while dotted lines between virtual RMS modules and the CRMS represents communication related to belief exchange and update.

- In the distributed system approach (see Figure 1.6) each agent has its own reason maintenance module. These modules communicate with each other to provide coherent RMS services. When speaking of a distributed reason maintenance system (DRMS), we actually mean such a set of communicating RMS modules.

A compromise between these two extremes is a *mixed approach*: The multiagent system uses several communicating RMS modules, each of which may provide RMS services to several agents.

All previously existing systems, notably the DATMS [23] and DARMS [24], take

---

[23]See [Mason and Johnson, 1989].
[24]See [Fuhge, 1993], [Beckstein et al., 1993], [Beckstein et al., 1994], and Chapter 7 of [Beckstein, 1994].

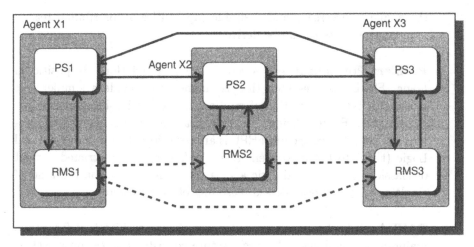

Figure 1.6: Multiagent system using multiagent RMS technology.
Thorough lines between agents indicate application-dependent communication between the problem solver modules of the agents. Dotted lines indicate communication related to belief exchange and updates.

the distributed systems approach. Neither one, however, can fully meet all requirements as outlined above. Therefore, we developed the system MXFRMS. Like DATMS and DARMS, it follows the distributed approach as outlined above and can be viewed as multiagent variant of XFRMS. However, the extended expressive power requires more complex labels and modified label propagation procedures. Nevertheless, MXFRMS exhibits basically the same advantageous characteristics as its single agent counterpart XFRMS: it gives the problem solvers full control on the number of contexts under consideration and provides means to explicitly construct and delete relevant environments.

1.5   Contributions and Results

The main contributions and results presented in this book can be grouped into the four areas problem analysis, problem formalization, RMS architectures, and RMS systems.

- **Problem Analysis:** An in-depth analysis (and formalization) of multi-agent assumption-based reasoning is performed. This analysis uncovers a number of subtle issues that seem to have been neglected by former attempts to build distributed reason maintenance systems.[25] Based on

---

[25]See especially [Bridgeland and Huhns, 1990], [Horstmann, 1991], [Mason and Johnson, 1989], [Fuhge, 1993], [Beckstein et al., 1993].

the analysis, necessary and desirable capabilities of distributed reason maintenance systems can be derived.

- **Problem Formalization:** A new logic, Facetted Horn Propositional Logic (FHPL), is presented that is claimed to provide a simpler, yet more intuitive formalization of multiagent assumption-based reasoning. In particular, FHPL provides syntactic means to express belief update relationships between agents. FHPL is an extension of Horn Propositional Logic (HPL) to the multiagent case. HPL itself is a restricted variant of classical propositional logic and is sufficient to describe the kind of single-agent assumption-based reasoning of interest here.

- **RMS Architecture:** We present a new generic architecture for reason maintenance modules. This architecture consists of three units each of which fills a well-defined role: The dependency net unit (DNU) maintains a dependency net and is — with some exceptions — quite similar to a classical RMS like the ATMS. The context management unit (CMU) has to manage contexts. The communication and control unit (CCU) is responsible for all communication between these three units, with other reason maintenance modules, and with the associated problem solver(s). Furthermore, the CCU maps problem solver data into internal data structures and vice versa. This new architecture is particularly well-suited for application in distributed reason maintenance systems.

- **RMS Systems:** Two new reason maintenance systems are presented and described in detail. While XFRMS is a single agent RMS, the MXFRMS is a hybrid system that can serve several problem solving agents and can communicate with other MXFRMS modules. Both systems provide the ability to maintain multiple contexts with great computational efficiency. The functionality of each system is formally specified — an aspect of RMSs that has often been neglected.[26] Architecture and design are discussed in detail for both systems. In particular, the structure of the labels used in each system, the constraints that must hold for the labels, and the label update procedures that ensure that constraints are always met are presented. Correctness and complexity considerations are made for both systems.

These results build a solid foundation for developing more sophisticated tools that provide computational support for multiagent planning and scheduling and PEDE problems.

---

[26] For some notable exceptions see [Beckstein, 1994], [Geisler, 1994], and [McAllester, 1990].

1.6 Outline of the Book

This introductory chapter (Chapter 1) motivated the research described in this book (Section 1.1), set it into perspective of the PEDE research project (Section 1.2), gave a brief, informal sketch of the problem (Section 1.3), described the solution approach (Section 1.4), and summarized the major contributions and results (Section 1.5).

The remainder of the text is structured into the following five chapters:

- *Single Agent Reason Maintenance* (Chapter 2),

- *XFRMS: A Single Agent Focus-Based Reason Maintenance System* (Chapter 3),

- *Multiagent Reason Maintenance* (Chapter 4),

- *MXFRMS: A Multiagent Focus-Based Reason Maintenance System* (Chapter 5), and

- *Conclusions* (Chapter 6).

The *Bibliography* is appended at the end. My thesis is supplemented by two technical reports ([Kraetzschmar, 1996b] and [Kraetzschmar, 1996a]) which describe the implementations of XFRMS and MXFRMS.[27]

Chapter 2 starts with an analysis of assumption-based reasoning in single agent systems (Section 2.1). The reasoning of a secretary performing meeting scheduling is presented in some detail (Section 2.1.1) in order to later on derive a set of tasks (Section 2.1.2) that must commonly be performed by an agent applying assumption-based reasoning techniques. The next section, Section 2.2, deals with the formalization of assumption-based reasoning. After giving a few arguments for the use of logics to formalize assumption-based reasoning (Section 2.2.1), we introduce Horn Propositional Logic (HPL, Section 2.2.2). HPL is an extremely simple and restricted propositional logic that is sufficient to describe the kind of multiple-context, assumption-based reasoning and to formally characterize the functionality of the reason maintenance systems we are interested in, e.g. de Kleer's basic ATMS [de Kleer, 1986a]. For illustration, we present a formalization of the meeting scheduling example from Section 2.1.1 in terms of HPL in Section 2.2.3. Section 2.3 provides then an informal specification of the functionality of an RMS that is suitable for single agent planning and scheduling applications. Standard reason maintenance technology for the single agent case is briefly reviewed in Section 2.4, before the whole chapter is summarized in Section 2.5.

---

[27]Initially, I planned to have the material on implementation details as two appendices. Due to their substantial length and technical detail, it was recommended to publish them as two separate technical reports.

Chapter 3 is oncerned with the presentation and discussion of XFRMS, which is done in six steps: An informal overview at the beginning (Section 3.1) provides a road map for the remainder. Section 3.2 contains the formal specification of XFRMS, including all its interface functionality. The next two sections discuss the generic RMS architecture used for the implementation of XFRMS (Section 3.3) and the structure of the implementation (Section 3.4), in particular, the format of the labels used to represent belief state and the procedures used to update the labels. Complexity considerations are discussed in the section thereafter (Section 3.5). The final section of Chapter 3, Section 3.6, summarizes the central features of the XFRMS system.

Chapter 4, which is structured quite similar to Chapter 2, then turns the discussion towards multiagent reason maintenance. Again, the analysis of assumption-based reasoning, although this time for multiagent systems, is done first in Section 4.1. A multiagent variant of the example used in the single agent case is used in the case study of Section 4.1.1: the meeting scheduling scenario now considers the reasoning of several secretaries that face the problem of setting up several meetings for their managers. This case study is quite detailed for two reasons: First, it clearly exhibits the desirability of reason maintenance support for multiagent assumption-based reasoning (Section 4.1.2). And second, it allows to illustrate some of the more fine-grained problems of multiagent assumption-based reasoning (Section 4.1.3). The problem analysis section concludes with a review, modification and extension of the (single agent) reason maintenance tasks in a multiagent context (Section 4.1.4). Section 4.2 investigates the formalization of multiagent multiple-context, assumption-based reasoning. Section 4.2.1 briefly surveys the classical approaches for the formalization of intentional notions of (single or multiple) agents: modal logics and first-order syntactic theories and summarizes some of their deficiencies. In our view, the combined impact of several of these arguments renders these approaches more or less inappropriate for the problem on hand. Therefore, Section 4.2.2 introduces the new, though much simpler logic FHPL which is just expressive enough to capture the problem with sufficient detail, but has by far simpler and much more intuitive semantics than e.g. typical modal logics for knowledge and belief. The application of FHPL to the meeting scheduling problem presented in Section 4.1.1 is demonstrated in Section 4.2.3. Based on the problem analysis and formalization the desirable (minimal) functionality of a DRMS which is suitable to support the construction of multiagent planning and scheduling applications is informally described in Section 4.3. Although there is, of course, much less "standard" reason maintenance technology for multiagent systems, we review what was available and known to us in Section 4.4. This review includes the system DARMS [Beckstein et al., 1993], an attempt on solving the problem that was undertaken in early stages of this work. The review of these systems exhibits their weaknesses and where they do not meet the requirements set forth in

Section 4.3. Section 4.5 summarizes the chapter on multiagent reason maintenance.

In order to remedy the unsatisfactory situation regarding adequate distributed reason maintenance technology, the system MXFRMS is presented as a solution in Chapter 5, which is structured in a way similar to the chapter on XFRMS: The introductory section (Section 5.1) provides an informal road map. Because of the strongly entwined relationship between architectral issues and functionality, the next section (5.2) first discusses several alternatives for the overall MXFRMS system architecture and introduces the generic concept of the facet module as common grounds for several of these implementation alternatives. Then, the MXFRMS is formally specified (Section 5.3). The architecture of a facet module turns out to require only a minor modification of the generic XFRMS architecture; this is discussed in Section 5.4. Then, the structure of an MXFRMS implementation is outlined, including representation of belief state via labels and the procedures necessary to keep these labels up to date (5.5). Some complexity considerations are taken in Section 5.6.

The final chapter (Chapter 6) contains a brief history of how the work described here developed (Section 6.1), reviews the major contributions and results (Section 6.2), sets these results into perspective with other systems and approaches (Section 6.3), outlines directions for future work (Section 6.4), and summarizes the book (Section 6.5).

Chapter 2

Single Agent Reason Maintenance

In this chapter, single agent reason maintenance is discussed. Because the main topic of our work is distributed reason maintenance, the chapter is kept short where possible and contains a number of references to more elaborate discussions of single agent reason maintenance (see especially [Beckstein, 1994] and [Forbus and de Kleer, 1993]). The reasons for including a chapter on single agent reason maintenance are that it provides a sound basis for the discussion of multiagent reason maintenance, that some of the techniques used in multiagent reason maintenance systems are much easier understood in a single agent setting, and that it prepares the ground for the system XFRMS, presented in the next chapter, which is a valuable tool in its own right and represents a major contribution of this text.

2.1 Analysis of Assumption-Based Reasoning

We present a small though elaborate example for assumption-based reasoning.

Due to its limited scope, it contains only few data dependencies and few contexts. However, the example suffices to illustrate the principle problem we want to solve and to derive a general characterization of the tasks that a support module for assumption-based reasoners should be able to perform. Also, it should be quite obvious that any realistic, practical example is of much larger scale and renders the "toy" problem discussed here a real practical difficulty.

2.1.1   The Lonely Secretary's Nightmare

Appointment scheduling[1] is a typical example for a problem-solving task that
involves assumption-based reasoning. We present the single agent variant of
an appointment scheduling problem which served as the common theme for
the CAIA-94[2] Workshop on Coordinated Design and Planning.[3]

EXAMPLE 2.1.1 (SINGLE AGENT MEETING SCHEDULING)
*The Domain: The example is about Patricia Perfect, secretary of a much-
stressed manager named Tom Tough. Patricia's task is to schedule Tom's
appointments (or meetings) at various places and times. The task is not always
easy, because Patricia often does not know well in advance where a meeting
is to take place and which time (*"meeting must be before next Thursday"*)
or ordering (*"this meeting must be before that meeting"*) constraints must be
met.*

*Besides scheduling the meetings, Patricia has to make all necessary ar-
rangements, e.g. booking flights and making hotel reservations, such that Tom
can successfully follow his appointment schedule.[4] Patricia knows that Tom
always takes early morning flights, which means that Tom needs flights always
on days with meetings scheduled in a city other than the city he was in the
day before. Tom lives in Boston; together with his policy on taking flights it
follows that he needs hotel room reservations for all days with meetings taking
place away from Boston.*

*Often, Patricia has to make last minute changes to Tom's schedule because
Tom or his business partners request the meeting to be held at other places or
dates. In such cases Patricia must also rearrange flights and hotel reservations.*

*Tasks and Constraints: Patricia's meeting scheduling problem is solved,
if all meetings have been scheduled such that Tom has to be neither at two
places nor in two meetings the same day, and if all necessary arrangements
are made.*

*Problem Solving Situation: A particular problem solving situation, that
Patricia Perfect (the Lonely Secretary) has to master, is given as follows: For
next week, Patricia has to schedule five meetings, creatively named $m_1, \ldots, m_5$.
As all of Tom's meetings take up the whole day, Patricia only needs to determine one of the days of the week. Tom told Patricia that meetings m_3 and m_4*

---

[1]See for instance [Haddadi and Bussmann, 1994], [Lux and Schupeta, 1994],
[Park and Birmingham, 1994], [Sen, 1994], and [Liu and Sycara, 1994].

[2]CAIA is an abbreviation for Conference on Artificial Intelligence Applications.

[3]The CAIA-94 Workshop on Coordinated Design and Planning was an international workshop organized by Charles Petrie, Marty Tenenbaum and Michael
Huhns. Information on the workshop is available via World Wide Web at URL
http://cdr.stanford.edu/html/people/petrie/caia.html. All papers are available via
anonymous ftp from URL ftp://cdr.stanford.edu/pub/caia-wrkshp/.

[4]Another example is to arrange phone call forwarding.

have to be in Seattle, but said nothing about the others. Unfortunately, Tom currently is on an important trip to Europe and cannot be asked to provide further information until he is back. However, Patricia knows that meetings will usually be in Boston unless Tom instructs her otherwise. Only meeting m_5 troubles Patricia to some extent: although Tom said nothing about where the meeting should be, in which case Patricia assumes Boston, she knows from previous meetings of Tom with this particular business partner, that all these meetings happened to be in Seattle.

Initial Solution Generation: *Patricia's line of reasoning in order to solve her scheduling problem looks as follows: Patricia starts with scheduling the first meeting. As Tom said nothing about where it should take place, Patricia assumes that it is held in Boston on Monday. Neither flight nor hotel reservation are necessary for Monday, because Tom spends the weekend as well as Monday night at his home in Boston. With a similar line of reasoning, Patricia schedules the second meeting for Tuesday in Boston. Again, no flight or hotel arrangements are necessary. Both the third and fourth meeting must take place in Seattle, and Patricia schedules them for Wednesday and Thursday. Because Tom is in Boston on Tuesday and must be Seattle on Wednesday, he needs a flight from Boston to Seattle on Wednesday morning. He also needs a hotel room in Seattle for Wednesday and Thursday, because he is away from his home in Boston. The only meeting remaining is m_5, which Patricia schedules for Friday. As she has no information on where the meeting is going to take place, Patricia works out two alternatives and makes the respective arrangements for both of them (it is easier to cancel reservations than to get flights or hotel rooms on short notice). Alternative 1 assumes the meeting will be in Seattle like all the previous meetings of Tom with this customer. Thus, Tom needs his hotel room in Seattle for another night. And he needs a flight from Seattle to Boston on Staruday morning to meet his family for the weekend. In alternative 2, Patricia assumes the meeting must be in Boston and schedules a flight from Seattle to Boston on Friday morning. No further hotel arrangements are necessary in this case.*

The schedule Patricia worked out is summarized in Table 2.1. The two alternatives, named $A1$ and $A2$, are described by the first two columns, where + in the column means that the respective line is part of that alternative and − means the opposite. Both alternatives themselves are marked with a + symbol to indicate that both are complete schedules satisfying all scheduling constraints.

The above scheduling problem is obviously not a very difficult one. It does not involve constraints that are very hard to meet or exhibit severe goal conflicts, like two meetings required to be held the same day. The uncertainty regarding meeting m_5, which arises from incomplete knowledge about the domain and the problem specification, is accounted for by working out two

Alternatives		Schedule Data			Arrangements	
A1+	A2+	Date	Meeting	Place	Flight	Hotel
+	+	Monday	m_1	Boston	—	—
+	+	Tuesday	m_2	Boston	—	—
+	+	Wednesday	m_3	Seattle	Boston → Seattle	Seattle Hilton
+	+	Thursday	m_4	Seattle	—	Seattle Hilton
+	−	Friday	m_5	Seattle	—	Seattle Hilton
−	+	Friday	m_5	Boston	Seattle → Boston	—
+	+	Saturday	—	Boston	Seattle → Boston	—

Table 2.1: Patricia's first schedule.

alternative schedules.

However, the Lonely Secretary's nightmare is about to begin ...

EXAMPLE 2.1.2 (THE NIGHTMARE: SCHEDULE REVISION REQUESTS)
After Patricia successfully arranged all flights and hotel rooms as necessary, she informs Tom about his schedule for next week by sending him a fax to his hotel in Europe. Tom agrees with the schedule so far, but cannot remember any specific agreements with Mark Moneymaker, his business partner in meeting m_5. Tom instructs Patricia to call Mark's secretary and check out the details for this meeting. Mark's secretary confirms Patricia's earlier assumption that the meeting is to be held in Seattle, but tells her that it must be held no later than Tuesday. Furthermore, the secretary of Carlo Capone, whom Tom is scheduled to see in meeting m_4, has called and asked the meeting to be held on Wednesday.

Patricia has to modify Tom's schedule such that it reflects the changed situation. If possible, Patricia wants to reuse parts of the previous schedule alternatives. Her reasoning could be similar to the following: The changed requests require meetings m_4 and m_5 to be rescheduled. Patricia chooses to schedule m_5 on Tuesday and m_4 on Wednesday, both in Seattle. This will give Tom some time to prepare for the meetings. As a consequence of these decisions, conflicts with the scheduling decisions for meetings m_2 and m_3 occur. These meetings will have to be rescheduled towards the end of the week. In order to minimize Tom's travel time Patricia schedules meeting m_3 for Thursday in Seattle and meeting m_2 in Boston on Friday. This makes schedule alternative A3 complete.

Patricia is a very good secretary and knows most of the pecularities about Tom's business partners. She knows that Bernie Business, whom Tom meets in meeting m_2, likes to go golfing in Florida on Fridays and therefore prefers not to have business meetings on Fridays. Thus, she works out yet another alternative that accommodates more to Bernie's tastes, but requires Tom to do more travel. Patricia leaves the final decision about which schedule alternative *to choose for execution to Tom.*

Invalidating the previous two schedule alternatives and creating two new ones has also consequences on flight and hotel arrangements. For alternative A3, a flight from Boston to Seattle must be scheduled for Tuesday morning. The hotel room in Seattle must be booked for Tuesday night already. Tom can use the existing reservation for a flight from Seattle to Boston on Friday morning to get back to Boston. In this case, no hotel room is needed for Friday night in Seattle. Alternative A4 requires Tom to fly back to Boston on Thursday; thus an appropriate flight must be booked for that day and no hotel room in Seattle is necessary. Tom must again fly to Seattle on Friday, and thus needs another flight. The existing flight reservation for Saturday takes care of bringing him back home for the weekend. As neither one of the complete alternatives requires Tom to fly from Boston to Seattle on Wednesday, the reservation for the flight on Wednesday is cancelled by Patricia.

The modified schedule as worked out by Patricia Perfect is illustrated in Table 2.2. The first four columns represent the alternatives. Again, the

Alternatives				Schedule Data			Arrangements	
A1−	A2−	A3◇	A4+	Date	Meeting	Place	Flight	Hotel
+	+	+	+	Monday	m_1	Boston	−	−
+	+	−	−	Tuesday	m_2	Boston	−	−
−	−	+	+	Tuesday	m_5	Seattle	B→S	SH
+	+	−	−	Wednesday	m_3	Seattle	B→S	SH
−	−	+	+	Wednesday	m_4	Seattle	−	SH
+	+	−	−	Thursday	m_4	Seattle	−	SH
−	−	+	−	Thursday	m_3	Seattle	−	SH
−	−	−	+	Thursday	m_2	Boston	S→B	−
+	−	−	−	Friday	m_5	Seattle	−	SH
−	+	−	−	Friday	m_5	Boston	S→B	−
−	−	+	−	Friday	m_2	Boston	S→B	−
−	−	−	+	Friday	m_3	Seattle	B→S	SH
+	−	−	+	Saturday	−	Boston	S→B	−

Table 2.2: Patricia's second schedule.

symbols + and − are again used to indicate that a line is part of an alternative or not. The alternatives themselves are marked +, −, or ◇, which indicates whether an alternative represents a complete schedule meeting all constraints (+) or not (−) and which one is the alternative currently selected for execution (◇). Flights from Boston to Seattle and the other way round have been abbreviated with B→S and S→B, respectively, while room reservation at the Seattle Hilton are indicated by SH.

2.1.2   Tasks in Assumption-Based Reasoning

It is quite obvious that Patricia Perfect's meeting scheduling problem is getting increasingly complex as the number of

- meetings to be scheduled,

- possible conflicts,

- revisions due to changes in the environment, and

- decisions dependent on (other) scheduling decisions

increases. Keeping track of all decisions and their consequences while ensuring that no conflicts occur becomes more and more difficult. For these reasons, we assume that Patricia Perfect maintains Tom's meeting schedule with the help of IMSA (the Intelligent Meeting Scheduling Assistant), some imaginary piece of software running on Patricia's workstation. We assume IMSA to be implemented as a single agent system that aids in maintaining Tom's schedule. In particular, it should keep a record of scheduled meetings, allow the representation of several alternative schedules, identify conflicts, determine consequences of scheduling decisions like necessary flights and hotel rooms, and support the identification of incompletely scheduled meetings. The question is how the construction of a software system such as IMSA can be supported. One of the goals of the PEDE project is to provide the technology for constructing software such as IMSA. Building such applications is greatly facilitated by application-independent, general-purpose software modules that provide some reasonably self-contained functionality in an efficient manner and can be used as off-the-shelf components in large software systems. Thus, the following question arises:

What kind of functionality would be helpful

- for planning and scheduling applications in general, and

- in particular for a scheduling assistant such as IMSA?

In principle, the answer to both questions is that functionality is needed for *representing* and for (assumption-based) *reasoning* with planning and scheduling data and knowledge. However, considering the wealth of approaches in automated or computer-supported planning and scheduling,[5] constructing a general purpose tool that is useful for all these approaches does not seem to be feasible at the moment. It seems to be more useful to adopt a layered architecture approach, where a small, but very general functionality with wide applicability is provided at a base layer, while larger, but more specialized

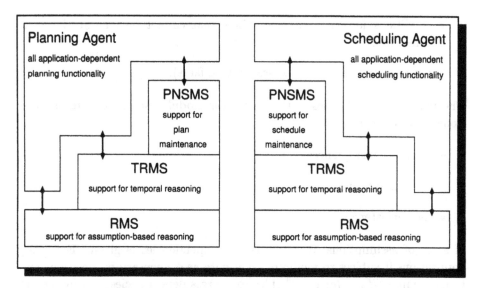

Figure 2.1: The layered architecture approach.

The base layer is provided by a reason maintenance system (RMS), which supports multiple context, assumption-based reasoning by providing functionality to maintain assumptions and dependencies. On top of the RMS layer, a temporal reason maintenance system (TRMS, see e.g. the ATTMS [Geisler, 1994]) supports both qualitative (ordering relationships) as well as quantitative (e.g. time points and intervals on a reference timeline) temporal reasoning. Yet another layer, the plan network and schedule maintenance system PNSMS, could then provide facilities to manage plans and schedules, e.g. through operations to insert or remove operations or partial plans, and to ease control of execution, e.g. by retrieving all currently executable operations.

functionality is provided by higher layers (see Figure 2.1). Examples for the wide-spread use of this approach throughout computing are the architecture of the X11 Windows Systems or the ISO/OSI architecture for communication protocols.

Following the layered architecture idea, we will concentrate our efforts on a particular kind of base layer that supports a simple form of multiple context assumption-based reasoning.[6] Such a base layer module should permit to represent

- relevant data (representing facts in the planning and scheduling domain),

- assumptions (facts that are assumed to be true),

- dependencies between data (in our case restricted to definite Horn clauses),

---

[5]See for instance [Allen et al., 1990], [Sycara, 1990], [Allen et al., 1991], [Hendler and McDermott, 1992], [Zweben and Fox, 1994], and [Hammond, 1994].

[6]See also [Beckstein, 1994].

- conditions for inconsistencies (facts that cannot be true at the same time), and

- premises (representing necessarily true facts).

The reasoning capabilities of the base layer module should encompass functionality to determine

- singular consequences,

- the context, and

- the consistency

of a set of assumptions, if a database of dependencies is given. For many applications it suffices to model relevant data as elementary propositions and to use simple *"if ... then ... "* rules to express dependencies. An important practical aspect is that planners and schedulers will construct and maintain databases consisting of the above mentioned information in an incremental manner, i.e. a support module should allow to

- build and update the database incrementally and to

- revise contexts after incremental updates.

In order to construct software components providing this functionality, we need to describe it in a formal manner. This is done in the next section.

2.2   Formalization of Assumption-Based Reasoning

The goal of this section is to provide a formal framework for describing the form of assumption-based reasoning, e.g. as used in Patricia Perfect's case and in planning and scheduling in general. After a brief discussion of approaches to formalize reasoning, we define HPL, a rather weak and restrictive logic that is nevertheless sufficiently expressive to capture the propositional variant of multiple-context assumption-based reasoning. A formalization of Patricia Perfect's example in HPL is provided in the last subsection.

2.2.1   Logics for Formalizing Reasoning

In the past three decades, many different approaches to formalize knowledge and reasoning have been developed in Artificial Intelligence.[7] Some examples

---

[7]See e.g. [Bench-Capon, 1990] or [Stoyan, 1988] and [Stoyan, 1991].

are production rules[8], semantic nets[9], frames[10], and constraints[11]. The by far largest variety of approaches have been developed in logics[12]. The use of logics has been strongly advocated by John McCarthy, Nils Nilsson and many others for a long time.[13] Some of the more often cited reasons in support for using logics in AI are the following:

- Logic has by far the strongest foundation, mainly because of its very long tradition in mathematics and philosophy, which reaches back to the ancient Greeks. There is a wealth of theoretical results and practical systems to build upon.

- Of all approaches mentioned, logics have the best understood semantics.

- Logic is a good tool for formal analysis of various types of reasoning.

- Logic can be used to model most of the other representation approaches.

- For many logics, we have well-established complexity results.

Thus, we will use logics to formalize representation of and reasoning with assumptions and justifications. The question then is, which logic is best suited for our purposes? The requirements a suitable logic should meet are as follows:

- The logical language should have syntax powerful enough such that we can express all relevant problem solving knowledge using this language.

- The logical language should have a simple, intuitive semantics, a well-defined notion of logical consequence, and a consistency criterion that is easy to test.

- The calculus should be sound and complete. If the calculus is not complete, a reasonably simple, formal characterization of its power should be given. The calculus should be easy to implement such that derivations can be generated efficiently.

One easily notices, that the more computationally oriented of these requirements, like simple consistency test and efficient theorem prover, are at odds with the more logically oriented requirements, like expressive power or completeness. And indeed, for most of the classical logics (propositional logic, first-order predicate logic), efficient implementations of complete theorem provers

---

[8]See e.g. [Forgy, 1981], and [Brownston et al., 1985].

[9]See e.g. [Findler, 1979] and [Brachman and Schmolze, 1985].

[10]See e.g. [Minsky, 1975].

[11]See e.g. [Waltz, 1975].

[12]See e.g. [Genesereth and Nilsson, 1987], [Davies, 1992], and [Ginsberg, 1993]; more general texts are e.g. [Enderton, 1972] or [Abramsky et al., 1992].

[13]For instance, in [McCarthy and Hayes, 1969], [Nilsson, 1991], and [Giunchiglia and Serafini, 1994].

are not known and even testing consistency of a set of formulas is computationally expensive. Fortunately, in many situations these classical logics are more powerful than necessary. In this case, a weaker logic with less expressive power but better computational characteristics can be defined. Examples for such an approach are database query languages [Gray and Reuter, 1993], DATALOG ([Maier and Warren, 1988], [Maier, 1983]) and KL-ONE-type concept languages in knowledge representation [Lakemeyer and Nebel, 1994].

For the above reasons, we take a similar approach and define the logics HPL and FHPL for assumption-based reasoning in single agent systems and multiagent systems, respectively. Both are propositional logics and just powerful enough to express the kind of reasoning we want our agents to perform, but with consistency criteria and proof procedures that are reasonable efficient and simple to implement.

Note, that the notions of *logic, (logical) language, calculus*, etc. are used in many slightly different ways by different authors. In this text, we adopt the following use of these notions:

- A **logic** consists of a *language* and a *calculus*.

- A (logical) **language** is defined by *syntax* and *semantics*.

- A (logical) **calculus** consists of *axioms* and *deduction rules*.

The definition of a calculus is, of course, meaningful only if the language has been previously fixed; thus, the language is implicitly assumed. Also, it is possible to view axioms as deduction rules with empty preconditions.

2.2.2   Horn Propositional Logic

Horn Propositional Logic (HPL) is a restricted variant both of classical propositional logic (also: sentential logic; see. e.g. [Ginsberg, 1993], [Davis, 1990], [Genesereth and Nilsson, 1987]) and of general (e.g. first order) Horn clause logic, which plays an important role in the logic programming community (see e.g. [Maier and Warren, 1988]). Like any other logic, a Horn Propositional Logic HPL consists of a propositional language $\mathcal{L}_{HPL}$ and a calculus $\mathcal{C}_{HPL}$.

DEFINITION 2.2.1 (HPL WELL-FORMED FORMULAS)
The language $\mathcal{L}_{HPL}$ is based on an alphabet Λ_{HPL} which consists of a set $\Sigma = \{p_1, p_2, \dots\}$ of atomic symbols that serve as propositional variables, the two special symbols $\top$ and $\bot$, the two logical connectives $\wedge$ and $\rightarrow$, and a pair of parentheses ().

The set of literals Γ_{lit} is defined to be the set Σ of propositional variables. The extended set of literals Γ_{lit*} also contains $\top$ and $\bot$. The only complex formulas in $\mathcal{L}_{HPL}$ are definite clauses. Definite clauses have the structure

$(p_1 \wedge \ldots \wedge p_k \rightarrow q)$, where $p_1, \ldots, p_k, q$ are literals from Γ_{lit}. The $p_1, \ldots, p_k$ are called antecedents, q the consequent of the clause. A shortcut notation for clauses is $(\Phi \rightarrow q)$ where $\Phi = \{p_i \mid 1 \leq i \leq k\}$ represents the conjunction of all literals in the set of antecedents. The set of Horn clauses Γ_{Horn} consists of all clauses that can be constructed by using literals from Γ_{lit} as antecedents and consequent. Thus, Γ_{Horn} contains only clauses where neither $\top$ nor $\bot$ occur in either the antecedent or the consequent of the clause. The set of premise clauses Γ_{prem} contains all clauses that have $\top$ as their single antecedent. The set of nogood clauses Γ_{nogood} contains all clauses with $\bot$ as their consequent. The set $\Gamma_{cl} =_{def} \Gamma_{Horn} \cup \Gamma_{prem} \cup \Gamma_{nogood}$ denotes the set of all well-formed clauses.

The set of well-formed formulas of language $\mathcal{L}_{HPL}$ consists just of all literals and all well-formed clauses. Formally:

$$\mathcal{L}_{HPL} =_{def} \Gamma_{lit} \cup \Gamma_{cl}$$

The language $\mathcal{L}_{HPL}$ obviously is a subset of the language of any standard propositional logic, e.g. of CPL as defined in [Farwer et al., 1993]. Standard propositional semantics defines a notion of logical consequence $\models_{HPL}$ between subsets of the language and language elements, i.e.

$$\models_{HPL} \quad \subseteq \quad \mathfrak{P}(\mathcal{L}_{HPL}) \times \mathcal{L}_{HPL}$$

The logical consequence relation of HPL, $\models_{HPL}$, is a subset of the logical consequence relation of the classical propositional logic CPL, $\models_{CPL}$, i.e.

$$\models_{HPL} \quad \subseteq \quad \models_{CPL}$$

Many of the properties of $\models_{CPL}$ apply also to $\models_{HPL}$, e.g. monotonicity (see e.g. [Beckstein, 1992]):

$$\Gamma \models_{HPL} \phi \quad \Longrightarrow \quad \Gamma \cup \Gamma' \models_{HPL} \phi$$

We now define a calculus for the language. A calculus consists of a set of axioms and a set of inference rules.[14] Both axioms and inference rules are specified as schemata.

DEFINITION 2.2.2 (HPL CALCULUS)
Let $\mathcal{L}_{HPL}$ be a language as in Definition 2.2.1. The calculus $\mathcal{C}_{HPL}$ consists of the single axiom $\top$ (the **verum**) and the single inference rule (schema) **modus ponens**: $MP[X,Y] \frac{X,(X \rightarrow Y)}{Y}$

Note, that the schema variable X may be substituted by a set of HPL *literals* (respectively, the conjunction of the set of literals in the antcedent of the implication), while Y may be substituted by a single HPL literal only.

---

[14]Note that axioms can also be viewed as inference rules with empty precondition.

The calculus $\mathcal{C}_{HPL}$ defines the usual derivability relation (also: deductive consequence relation) $\vdash_{HPL}$ as follows:

DEFINITION 2.2.3 (HPL DERIVABILITY)
*Let Γ be a set of HPL formulas and ϕ an arbitrary HPL formula. ϕ is **derivable from** Γ (or: **deductive consequence of**), denoted by*

$$\Gamma \vdash_{HPL} \phi,$$

if there exists a finite sequence $S = \langle \Gamma_1, \ldots, \Gamma_n \rangle$ of sets of formulas, where for each i in $1, \ldots, n-1$ the set Γ_{i+1} consists of Γ_i plus all formulas that are derivable by a single application of modus ponens to formulas from Γ_i, until a set Γ_n results that contains ϕ. Formally, the sequence S must meet the following conditions:

$$\Gamma_1 = \Gamma \tag{2.1}$$
$$\Gamma_{i+1} = \Gamma_i \cup \{\, \psi \mid \exists_{(\Phi \to \varphi) \in \Gamma_i} : [\, \psi = \varphi \text{ and } \forall_{\phi_i \in \Phi} : [\phi_i \in \Gamma_i] \,] \,\} \tag{2.2}$$
$$\phi \in \Gamma_n \tag{2.3}$$

Consecutive sets in the above sequence are constructed by applying all possible instances of the modus ponens inference rule to the respective previous set. Obviously, $\vdash_{HPL}$ is a subset of $\vdash_{CPL}$, the derivability relation of (full) classical propositional logic CPL. Hence, as CPL is sound, HPL must be sound as well. HPL is, however, **incomplete**. The following simple example demonstrates this fact:

EXAMPLE 2.2.1 (INCOMPLETENESS OF HPL)
Let $\Gamma = \{p, q\}$. $(p \to q)$ is a logical, but not a deductive consequence, i.e.

$$\Gamma \models_{HPL} (p \to q) \qquad but \qquad \Gamma \nvdash_{HPL} (p \to q)$$

Hence, $\mathcal{C}_{HPL}$ is not complete.

Reasons for the incompleteness of $\mathcal{C}_{HPL}$ include the use of only simple modus ponens (instead of its generalized form), the absence of axioms like $X \to (Y \to X)$, and the restricted syntactic expressiveness of $\mathcal{L}_{HPL}$ (which prevents us to formulate e.g. the previously mentioned axiom).

However, it is possible to define a restricted notion of completeness as follows:

DEFINITION 2.2.4 (LITERAL COMPLETENESS)
*Let PL be a propositional logic with language $\mathcal{L}$ and some calculus C. Let Γ_{lit} be the set of literals in language $\mathcal{L}$. A calculus is **literal complete** if and only if for any set of formulas Γ all literals that are logical consequence of Γ are also derivable from Γ, formally:*

$$\forall_\Gamma \forall_{p_i \in \Gamma_{lit}} : \quad \Gamma \models p_i \quad \Longrightarrow \quad \Gamma \vdash p_i \tag{2.4}$$

Literal completeness[15] means that although the calculus may not be able to derive complex formulas it guarantees derivability at least for atomic sentences. Using the above definition, we can make a statement about the completeness of HPL. Let HPL be a Horn propositional logic with language $\mathcal{L}_{HPL}$ as defined in Definition 2.2.1 and calculus $\mathcal{C}_{HPL}$ as defined in Definition 2.2.2:

THEOREM 2.2.1 (HPL LITERAL COMPLETENESS)
$\mathcal{C}_{HPL}$ is literal complete.

PROOF 2.2.1 (HPL LITERAL COMPLETENESS)
The proof is by contradiction. We show that the negation of the literal completeness condition,

$$\Gamma \models_{HPL} \phi \quad\text{and}\quad \Gamma \not\vdash_{HPL} \phi \tag{2.5}$$

cannot hold for any pair of Γ and ϕ.

For the proof, the following lemma (see [Thayse and Gochet, 1988] and [Thayse, 1989]) is useful.

LEMMA 2.2.1
A literal is logical consequence of a consistent set of formulas if and only if the literal is in the set of formulas or if there exists a clause with the literal as consequent and all antecedents of that clause are logical consequences of the set of formulas. Formally:

$$\Gamma \models_{HPL} \varphi \iff \begin{cases} \varphi \in \Gamma \\ \text{or} \\ \exists_{(\Phi \to \psi) \in \Gamma} : [\, \psi = \varphi \text{ and } \forall_{\phi_i \in \Phi} : \Gamma \models_{HPL} \phi_i \,] \end{cases} \tag{2.6}$$

Assume the condition in Equation 2.5 holds. With Lemma 2.2.1, there must exist a clause with ϕ as consequent and all its antecedents are logical consequences of Γ. But then we can apply modus ponens and derive ϕ, which leads to a contradiction to condition 2.5. Hence,

$$\Gamma \vdash_{HPL} \phi$$

holds and $\mathcal{C}_{HPL}$ is literal complete. □

The value of literal completeness is illustrated by the following scenario: Assume the problem solver has stated some set Γ of clauses representing data dependencies and wants to find out whether it must believe some proposition, represented by φ, if it believes a set of other propositions, represented by $\Phi = \{\phi_1, \ldots, \phi_n\}$. Expressed in HPL, this means that $(\phi_1 \wedge \ldots \wedge \phi_n \to \varphi)$

---

[15]Literal completeness is also mentioned in [Forbus and de Kleer, 1993].

must be a logical consequence of the propositions represented by Γ. Thus, the problem solver wants to know whether

$$\Gamma \models_{\mathsf{HPL}} (\Phi \to \varphi)$$

holds or not. As HPL is not complete, it cannot directly decide that. Applying the deduction theorem (see e.g. [Genesereth and Nilsson, 1987]) reduces the above decision problem to

$$\Gamma \cup \Phi \models_{\mathsf{HPL}} \varphi$$

Because $\mathcal{C}_{\mathsf{HPL}}$ is literal complete, this can be easily decided by assuming the formulas in Φ, i.e. we temporarily put the assumptions into the clause database and then decide the above problem.

2.2.3   A HPL Formalization of The Lonely Secretary's Nightmare

It is now briefly shown, how Patricia Perfect's Intelligent Meeting Scheduling Assistant IMSA could represent the relevant scheduling data and the dependencies between them in HPL. Several steps need to be performed:

- First, the propositional variables, i.e. the elementary propositions Patricia uses in her meeting scheduling microworld, must be fixed.

- Then, the dependencies must be formulated.

- Finally, it must be shown how the resulting clause database is used to help Patricia to accomplish her task.

Conceptualization: Fixing the propositional variables.   Patricia uses simple propositions about meetings, dates, and places, like *"Meeting m1 is scheduled for Monday in Boston"*. In order to keep the syntax reasonably short, propositions are denoted in Prolog-like syntax, e.g. by

$$\mathsf{decision}(m1, boston, mon).$$

Note, however, that in terms of HPL, and later on by reason maintenance systems, the whole expression is viewed as an atom with no internal structure. Using this syntactic convention, Patricia's problem can then be expressed by using the following set of propositional variables, where *Meeting*, *Date*, and *Place* are used as metavariables that have to be substituted with all relevant instance values (in our example: $m1, \ldots$ for Meetings, $mon, tue, \ldots$ for Dates, and *seattle* or *boston* for Places):

- decision($Meeting, Place, Date$) expresses Patricia's decision to schedule Meeting on Date at Place.

- scheduled($Meeting$) expresses that a scheduling decision regarding Meeting has been taken.

- place-of($Meeting, Place$) is used to express that Meeting is held at Place.

- date-of($Meeting, Date$) expresses that Meeting is held on Date.

- at($Place, Date$) expresses that Tom is at Place on Date.

- doing($Meeting, Date$) is used to say that Tom has Meeting on Date.

- flight($Place, Date$) expresses that Tom needs a flight to Place on Date.[16]

- hotel($Place, Date$) says that Tom needs a hotel reservation in Place on Date.

- complete is used to express that the schedule is complete, i.e. that all meetings have been successfully scheduled.

Domain Theory: Formulating Data Dependencies. Between the relevant propositions, dependencies as follows must be formulated:[17]

$$\text{decision}(Meeting, Place, Date) \rightarrow \text{at}(Place, Date)$$
$$\text{decision}(Meeting, Place, Date) \rightarrow \text{doing}(Meeting, Date)$$
$$\text{decision}(Meeting, Place, Date) \rightarrow \text{place-of}(Meeting, Place)$$
$$\text{decision}(Meeting, Place, Date) \rightarrow \text{date-of}(Meeting, Date)$$
$$\text{decision}(Meeting, Place, Date) \rightarrow \text{scheduled}(Meeting)$$
$$\text{at}(Place1, PrevDate) \wedge \text{at}(Place2, Date) \rightarrow \text{flight}(Place2, Date)$$
$$\text{at}(AwayPlace, Date) \rightarrow \text{hotel}(AwayPlace, Date)$$

The metavariables in the above clause schemata take value as suggested by their names; in Patricia's example *PrevDate* and *Date* must be consecutive days, and *AwayPlace* has as its only instance *seattle*.

---

[16]We do only use the flight destination in our conceptualization and assume it always starts from the right place. This is a strong oversimplification, of course, because ensuring that flights are always booked such that they start from the correct airport is a nontrivial task for secretaries. However, this simplification was made intentionally in order to keep the example reasonably small.

[17]Metavariables, like *Meeting, Place*, and *Date* are used as in the conceptualization; it is further assumed that differently named metavariables take different values.

Consistency and completeness of scheduling decisions is ensured by the following set of clauses:

$$\text{at}(Place1, Date) \wedge \text{at}(Place2, Date) \rightarrow \bot$$
$$\text{doing}(Meeting1, Date) \wedge \text{doing}(Meeting2, Date) \rightarrow \bot$$
$$\text{place-of}(Meeting, Place1) \wedge \text{place-of}(Meeting, Place2) \rightarrow \bot$$
$$\text{date-of}(Meeting, Date1) \wedge \text{date-of}(Meeting, Date2) \rightarrow \bot$$
$$\text{scheduled}(Meeting1) \wedge \ldots \wedge \text{scheduled}(MeetingN) \rightarrow \text{complete}$$

Note, that in order to ensure that Tom always spends his weekends with his family in Boston, Patricia simply introduces a meeting f (for family) on all Saturdays and Sundays in Boston. This will ensure that Tom always gets a flight back to Boston on Saturday mornings, if he had a business meeting away from Boston on Friday.

Using the conceptualization and clauses as described above, a representation of Patricia's initial schedule as displayed in Table 2.1 looks roughly as follows (see also the graphical illustration in Figure 2.2):

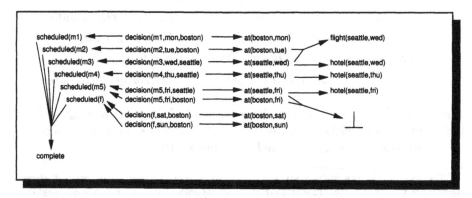

Figure 2.2: Graphical illustration of some dependencies in Patricia's initial schedule.

Arrows illustrate simple dependencies of the form $p \rightarrow q$. Arrows with multiple origins are used to represent the conjunction of several antecedents.

The relevant instances of clause schemata for necessary flights and hotel rooms are:

$$1\text{at}(boston, sun) \wedge \text{at}(seattle, mon) \rightarrow \text{flight}(seattle, mon)$$
$$\text{at}(boston, mon) \wedge \text{at}(seattle, tue) \rightarrow \text{flight}(seattle, tue)$$

$$\cdots$$

$$\text{at}(seattle, sun) \wedge \text{at}(boston, mon) \rightarrow \text{flight}(boston, mon)$$
$$\text{at}(seattle, mon) \wedge \text{at}(boston, tue) \rightarrow \text{flight}(boston, tue)$$

$$\cdots$$

$$\text{at}(seattle, sun) \rightarrow \text{hotel}(seattle, sun)$$
$$\text{at}(seattle, mon) \rightarrow \text{hotel}(seattle, mon)$$

$$\cdots$$

The relevant instances of clauses for ensuring consistency are:

$$\text{at}(boston, sun) \wedge \text{at}(seattle, sun) \rightarrow \perp$$
$$\text{at}(boston, mon) \wedge \text{at}(seattle, mon) \rightarrow \perp$$

$$\cdots$$

$$\text{place-of}(m_1, boston) \wedge \text{place-of}(m_1, seattle) \rightarrow \perp$$
$$\text{place-of}(m_2, boston) \wedge \text{place-of}(m_2, seattle) \rightarrow \perp$$

$$\cdots$$

$$\text{doing}(m_1, sun) \wedge \text{doing}(m_2, sun) \rightarrow \perp$$
$$\text{doing}(m_1, sun) \wedge \text{doing}(m_3, sun) \rightarrow \perp$$

$$\cdots$$

$$\text{date-of}(m_1, sun) \wedge \text{date-of}(m_1, mon) \rightarrow \perp$$
$$\text{date-of}(m_1, sun) \wedge \text{date-of}(m_1, tue) \rightarrow \perp$$

$$\cdots$$

That Tom spends his weekend with his family in Boston is expressed by:

$$\text{decision}(f, sat, boston) \rightarrow \text{at}(boston, sat)$$
$$\text{decision}(f, sat, boston) \rightarrow \text{doing}(f, sat)$$
$$\text{decision}(f, sat, boston) \rightarrow \text{place-of}(f, boston)$$
$$\text{decision}(f, sat, boston) \rightarrow \text{date-of}(f, sat)$$
$$\text{decision}(f, sat, boston) \rightarrow \text{scheduled}(f)$$
$$\text{decision}(f, sun, boston) \rightarrow \text{at}(boston, sun)$$
$$\text{decision}(f, sun, boston) \rightarrow \text{doing}(f, sun)$$
$$\text{decision}(f, sun, boston) \rightarrow \text{place-of}(f, boston)$$
$$\text{decision}(f, sun, boston) \rightarrow \text{date-of}(f, sun)$$
$$\text{decision}(f, sun, boston) \rightarrow \text{scheduled}(f)$$

The necessity to schedule all meetings is expressed by the following single clause:

$$\text{scheduled}(m_1) \wedge \ldots \wedge \text{scheduled}(f) \rightarrow \text{complete}$$

Finally, Patricia's scheduling decisions for the five meetings will add the following clause schemata instances:

$$\text{decision}(m_1, mon, boston) \rightarrow \text{at}(boston, mon)$$
$$\text{decision}(m_1, mon, boston) \rightarrow \text{doing}(m_1, mon)$$
$$\text{decision}(m_1, mon, boston) \rightarrow \text{place-of}(m_1, boston)$$
$$\text{decision}(m_1, mon, boston) \rightarrow \text{date-of}(m_1, mon)$$
$$\text{decision}(m_1, mon, boston) \rightarrow \text{scheduled}(m_1)$$
$$\text{decision}(m_2, tue, boston) \rightarrow \text{at}(boston, tue)$$
$$\text{decision}(m_2, tue, boston) \rightarrow \text{doing}(m_2, tue)$$
$$\text{decision}(m_2, tue, boston) \rightarrow \text{place-of}(m_2, boston)$$
$$\text{decision}(m_2, tue, boston) \rightarrow \text{date-of}(m_2, tue)$$
$$\text{decision}(m_2, tue, boston) \rightarrow \text{scheduled}(m_2)$$
$$\text{decision}(m_3, wed, seattle) \rightarrow \text{at}(seattle, wed)$$
$$\text{decision}(m_3, wed, seattle) \rightarrow \text{doing}(m_3, wed)$$
$$\text{decision}(m_3, wed, seattle) \rightarrow \text{place-of}(m_3, seattle)$$
$$\text{decision}(m_3, wed, seattle) \rightarrow \text{date-of}(m_3, wed)$$
$$\text{decision}(m_3, wed, seattle) \rightarrow \text{scheduled}(m_3)$$
$$\text{decision}(m_4, thu, seattle) \rightarrow \text{at}(seattle, thu)$$
$$\text{decision}(m_4, thu, seattle) \rightarrow \text{doing}(m_4, thu)$$
$$\text{decision}(m_4, thu, seattle) \rightarrow \text{place-of}(m_4, seattle)$$
$$\text{decision}(m_4, thu, seattle) \rightarrow \text{date-of}(m_4, thu)$$
$$\text{decision}(m_4, thu, seattle) \rightarrow \text{scheduled}(m_4)$$
$$\text{decision}(m_5, fri, seattle) \rightarrow \text{at}(seattle, fri)$$
$$\text{decision}(m_5, fri, seattle) \rightarrow \text{doing}(m_5, fri)$$
$$\text{decision}(m_5, fri, seattle) \rightarrow \text{place-of}(m_5, seattle)$$
$$\text{decision}(m_5, fri, seattle) \rightarrow \text{date-of}(m_5, fri)$$
$$\text{decision}(m_5, fri, seattle) \rightarrow \text{scheduled}(m_5)$$
$$\text{decision}(m_5, fri, boston) \rightarrow \text{at}(boston, fri)$$
$$\text{decision}(m_5, fri, boston) \rightarrow \text{doing}(m_5, fri)$$
$$\text{decision}(m_5, fri, boston) \rightarrow \text{place-of}(m_5, boston)$$
$$\text{decision}(m_5, fri, boston) \rightarrow \text{date-of}(m_5, fri)$$
$$\text{decision}(m_5, fri, boston) \rightarrow \text{scheduled}(m_5)$$

It should be noted, that the problem solver does not need to declare all possible instances of the dependencies in domain theory as relevant propositions. As an example, as long as Tom being in Boston on Thursday — at(boston,thu) — is not a relevant problem solver proposition, none of the clauses involving that proposition needs to be added to the clause database.

Reasoning: Checking schedules.   Given the above representation of Patricia Perfect's meeting scheduling problem in a database Γ of HPL clauses, a schedule is determined by a set Γ_D of scheduling decisions. For example, schedule alternative $A1$ of Table 2.1 is represented by the set of scheduling decisions

$$\Gamma_{A1} = \{\ \text{decision}(m_1, boston, mon), \text{decision}(m_2, boston, tue),$$
$$\text{decision}(m_3, seattle, wed), \text{decision}(m_4, seattle, thu),$$
$$\text{decision}(m_5, seattle, fri), \text{decision}(f, boston, sat)\ \}.$$

Patricia can apply an HPL proof procedure to check consistency and completeness of schedules by determining whether

$$\Gamma \cup \Gamma_{A1} \vdash_{\mathsf{HPL}} \bot \quad \text{and} \quad \Gamma \cup \Gamma_{A1} \vdash_{\mathsf{HPL}} \text{complete}$$

hold or not and to determine consequences of scheduling decisions, like whether Tom needs a flight to Seattle on Wednesday or hotel room in Seattle on Thursday, by determining whether

$$\Gamma \cup \Gamma_{A1} \vdash_{\mathsf{HPL}} \text{flight}(seattle, wed) \quad \text{and} \quad \Gamma \cup \Gamma_{A1} \vdash_{\mathsf{HPL}} \text{hotel}(seattle, thu)$$

hold or not. If Patricia wants to check whether certain meeting requirements, e.g. meeting m_4 to be held in *seattle*, are met by her scheduling decisions, she can simply include the respective propositions into Γ_{A1}. The clauses for checking consistency will then ensure that a conflict is discovered.

Representing several alternative schedules is obviously no problem: the problem solver simply uses different sets Γ_{A_i} of scheduling decisions. It is similarly easy to "modify" schedules: The problem solver makes new scheduling decisions, adds all new relevant data dependencies as clauses to Γ, and uses a different set Γ_{A_j} of scheduling decisions.

2.3   Generic Single Agent Reason Maintenance

After the analysis and formalization of the problem, it is now possible to give an informal specification of the functionality needed to provide adequate support for multiple context assumption-based reasoning in planning, scheduling and control applications. A formal version of the functionality specified here is given later on (Section 3). The purpose of this informal specification is to fix the desirable functionality, which may be specialized and implemented in several different ways. In particular, it is discussed in the next section how far standard reason maintenance systems match this desired functionality.

As outlined previously (Section 1.4), we assume a problem solving architecture consisting of problem solver (PS) and a reason maintenance system (RMS). The RMS is a facility that can represent some aspects of a world the PS is interested in and can be viewed as a partial implementation of $\mathcal{C}_{\mathsf{HPL}}$. The PS specifies relevant information, expressed in the propositional language $\mathcal{L}_{\mathsf{HPL}}$ of the propositional Horn logic HPL, to the RMS. The PS may pose queries to retrieve information from the RMS. The RMS maintains a *partial* representation of the derivability relation $\vdash_{\mathsf{HPL}}$, i.e. it can e.g. determine whether $\Gamma \vdash_{\mathsf{HPL}} p$ holds or not. The representation is partial, because the RMS usually restricts for which Γ and p it can provide this service. Some examples for typical restrictions are:

- Only the relevant part of the language $\mathcal{L}_{\mathsf{HPL}}$ is represented. The relevant part is defined by formulas that have been declared relevant by the PS. Thus, the RMS will decide the derivability relation only for literals p that have been declared relevant.

- Most systems also restrict Γ such that all clauses in Γ must have been declared relevant. Often, the set of clauses can only be changed by adding clauses. This restriction, together with a monotonic derivability relation of the underlying logic, makes an RMS a monotonic RMS (see [Beckstein, 1994]).

- Assuming the previous restriction regarding Γ, the only degree of freedom left for specifying different sets Γ in queries are the literals used as assumptions. If the RMS's representation is such that it is restricted to a single set of assumptions at any point of time (in this case, Γ is fixed), then it is called a single context RMS.

The specification of an RMS should explicitly state such restrictions. Furthermore, the specification should include any restrictions on the applicability of functions and define the domain for parameter and argument values.

2.3.1 Components of Single Agent RMS Specifications

A single agent RMS specification consists of four components:

- A **logical state**, which fixes the language used by the problem solver to express relevant information and defines a representation of the information the PS has communicated to the RMS. In particular, a precise characterization of which arguments are allowed in calls to interface functions should be possible in terms of the logical state. From a logical perspective, an RMS always has a (i.e. exactly one) well-defined logical state.

- A **logical query interface**, which allows to retrieve information that requires to access the partial implementation of the logical consequence relation represented by the logical state.

- A **state change interface**, which allows to manipulate the logical state, e.g. by adding logical formulas representing dependencies.

- A **state query interface**, which allows to retrieve information represented in the logical state. The main difference between the state query interface and the logical query interface is that in order to provide the functionality for the latter the logical consequence relation must be accessed while this is not the case for the former.

These components are discussed in the next few sections.

2.3.2   Generic RMS Logical State

The logical state of a single agent RMS is a structure consisting of several components, which together serve the following three main purposes:

- Fix the language the problem solver uses to state its problem.

- Give a precise description of the part of the language which has been declared relevant by the problem solver; in particular, this must include a representation of the problem solver's data dependencies.

- Provide the means to precisely characterize the permissable arguments for the interface functions described later on.

Within this text, the language is assumed to be $\mathcal{L}_{\mathsf{HPL}}$ for the single agent case. A more expressive language may be used in the specification of more powerful systems.

The description of the relevant part of the language is usually done by specifying a set of relevant propositions (only these can be used to formulate dependencies and as arguments in queries) and a set of clauses describing dependencies between such propositions. Usually, $\top$ and $\bot$ (the *verum* and the *falsum*) are assumed to be implicitly known by the RMS; they can be used in premise and nogood implication clauses.

Characterizing permissable arguments for interface functions, which require queries like $\Gamma_e \vdash_{\mathsf{HPL}} \phi$ to be decided, is done in terms of the set of relevant propositions, the subset of propositions that are considered as assumptions, and a specific set of environments to be used in such queries. A very useful feature is the maintenance of an explicit problem solver focus, a specific environment that describes the set of assumptions currently made by the problem solver.

2.3.3   Generic RMS Logical Query Interface

The query interface of an RMS allows the problem solver to retrieve information, which is represented by the RMS but requires the use of the derivability relation. The logical query interface includes functions for

- determining whether a proposition is logical consequence of a given set of assumptions (called an *environment*),

- determining whether a given environment is consistent,

- determining the set of *all* logical consequences (called the *context*) of a given environment.

A set of logical query functions useful for solving PEDE problems should at least include the following:

- A function follows-from?, which takes an environment e and a proposition ϕ as arguments and determines whether the proposition is derivable from the justifications Γ and the environment, i.e. it returns T iff

$$\Gamma \cup e \vdash_{\mathsf{HPL}} \phi$$

holds. Note, that for this function the consistency of the environment e is irrelevant.

- A function holds-in?, which takes an environment e and a proposition ϕ as arguments (just like follows-from) and determines whether the environment is consistent and the proposition is derivable in it, i.e. the function returns T iff

$$\Gamma \cup e \not\vdash_{\mathsf{HPL}} \bot \quad \text{and} \quad \Gamma \cup e \vdash_{\mathsf{HPL}} \phi$$

both hold.

- A function context-of?, which takes an environment e as its single argument and returns the set of all relevant propositions for which holds-in returns T for the environment e.

In preference for a compact description of the RMSs we will present, all the standard single agent RMS functionality for generating explanations is omitted. However, it is usually straightforward to provide two functions justified-by? and justifies?, which allow to determine the set of clauses which reference a given proposition in their consequent part or their antecedent part, respectively, as part of the RMS state query interface. These functions allow to retrieve information about the justification structure represented in the RMS. By using these functions in combination with the logical query interface functions, it is possible to build functionality for generating explanations. Of course, an actual implementation may choose to directly provide more specific explanation generation functions for reasons of efficiency.

2.3.4   Generic RMS State Change Interface

The change interface provides facilities to update the information represented in the logical state, i.e. executing functions of the change interface will usually result in a *new logical state*. In particular, functions for enlarging the relevant part of the language and for modifying the permissable arguments in queries must be provided. A set of useful update functions include

- A function add-proposition!, which takes an arbitrary proposition p as argument and declares it relevant.

- A function add-justification!, which takes a clause (Horn, premise, or nogood) as argument and adds it to the clause database.

- A function add-assumption! to indicate that a relevant proposition is to be used as assumption.

- A function add-environment! to declare a particular set of assumptions (provides as argument) as relevant environment.

Additional functions may be provided to manipulate environments (extending them with additional assumptions, retracting them altogether) or to modify the problem solver focus (shifting it to another environment).

2.3.5   Generic RMS State Query Interface

The state query interface provides functions that retrieve information about the logical state per se. These functions do not refer to the logical consequence relation. They allow the problem solver to find out whether it has already declared a proposition as relevant, whether a data dependency is already known to the RMS, etc. All these functions either return a component of the logical state or perform simple element tests. Obviously, the state query interface is quite trivial. Like the logical query functions, they leave the logical state unchanged.

2.3.6   Relaxation of Protocol Assumptions

Previously, we made some assumptions about the PS/RMS protocol and stated that all error checking has been left out to make the specification more concise. Summarized, these restrictions are that the problem solver must

- declare a proposition prior to making it an assumption,

- declare all antecedents and the consequent as propositions prior to using them in justifications,

- declare all assumptions before using them in environment arguments, and

- declare a proposition before using it in queries.

An actual implementation may relax these constraints and offer a slightly more elaborate interface without these restrictions. Such an interface provides functions that perform the appropriate checks first before actually performing the core function. It can easily be implemented on top of the above interface. An example is the following:

PROCEDURE 2.3.1 (SAFE-ADD-ASSUMPTION!)

1 safe-add-assumption!(ϕ) $\equiv$
2   **if** $(\neg(\text{is-proposition?}(\phi)))$ **then** add-proposition!(ϕ) **fi**
3   add-assumption!(ϕ)

The above procedure assumes the availability of a total function is-proposition?, which is usually provided as part of the generic RMS state query interface.

2.4   Standard Single Agent Reason Maintenance Technology

In this section, we review standard reason maintenance technology for single agent systems. First the principal design tradeoffs and the commonly used implementation architecture are presented. Then, major classes of reason maintenance systems are overviewed, before de Kleer's ATMS and some of its descendants are discussed. The final subsection summarizes this review. A more detailed and complete review and formal treatment of standard single agent reason maintenance technology can be found in [Beckstein, 1994]. Readers interested in implementational issues are referred to [Forbus and de Kleer, 1993].

2.4.1   Design Tradeoffs

A variety of possibilities exist for providing the services of the generic RMS functionality as informally specified in Section 2.3. A fundamental space versus time tradeoff underlies this spectrum of alternatives. This tradeoff is best described by illustrating the two extreme positions:

- The *theorem proving* approach trades time (efficiency of executing interface functions) for space (size of database to represent the logical state). The database contains the relevant propositions and justifications. A simple flag (attribute) suffices to mark propositions being used as assumptions. Also, a list of assumptions representing the focus is stored.

Obviously, updating the representation in the theorem proving approach is quite easy. Answering queries, however, requires to construct proofs in HPL. If a lot of such proofs are requested by the problem solver, this can get very inefficient for large logical states (i.e. for large numbers of propositions, assumptions, and justifications.

- The *pure database* approach, on the contrary, uses space in order to maximize performance. As an example, we assume that two tables are used to represent the relevant part of the logical consequence relation. The first table represents all possible environments and contains tuple consisting of an environment identifier and an assumption. The second table represents contexts and contains tuples consisting of environment identifiers and propositions. These tables are used in addition to the explicit representation of relevant propositions and justifications. It is then possible to provide very fast implementations of functions like follows-from?. However, the tables quickly become very large; each additional assumption doubles the number of possible environments (and thus, environment identifiers), which has tremendous effect on the size of the two tables. Thus, in the above example, the database size grows exponentially with the number of assumptions. Furthermore, adding a single justification can potentially require to modify the complete table. Thus, the pure database approach makes an efficient implementation of the update interface difficult.

These two extreme positions of the spectrum also show that the space/time tradeoff is reflected by the problem solver interface functions and imposes a performance tradeoff on the generic functionality between fast query and fast update functions. We cannot implement both the query and the update interface the most efficient way at the same time. A compromise must be found. This compromise should be influenced by the *typical pattern of interface usage*. For planning and scheduling applications, it is important for an agent to exactly know the context (i.e. all the consequences) of a particular plan/schedule alternative which is determined by a particular set of underlying assumptions. Adding a single clause to the clause database may have dramatic effect on the context. In order to determine the new context after such a change to the clause database, the theorem proving approach may have to construct a proof for *all* relevant propositions. In general, planning and scheduling applications may have to execute a substantial number of queries after each single update to the database. Thus, an approach that favors fast query response while allowing for reasonably fast update procedures seems to be suited best.

2.4.2   RMS Architecture

All one can say about the architecture of single agent RMSs is that there is not much architecture. This remark is substantiated e.g. by looking into [Forbus and de Kleer, 1993], a book which is devoted to building problem solvers based on reason maintenance systems, but contains — aside of the standard two-level PS/RMS architecture picture as given in Figure 1.3 — not a single figure about the (internal) architecture of the RMS and little information on architectural issues in roughly 700 pages of text.[18] In this book, which discusses all major single agent reason maintenance systems, the typical implementation strategy becomes obvious: The RMS is implemented as a module (with no further internal architecture), which maintains a set of internal data structures (nodes, justifications). The module exports a set of functions used by the problem solver to make new propositions and justifications known and to pose queries.

A noteworthy point about standard RMS implementations is the fact, that most implementations return a pointer to an RMS node data structure if the problem solver makes a new proposition relevant. Whenever the problem solver wants to use that proposition in justifications or in queries, it is expected to provide that pointer to the RMS (see e.g. de Kleer's code for the basic ATMS as provided with the book [Forbus and de Kleer, 1993]). This approach requires a tight integration of problem solver and RMS and allows for efficient PS/RMS interaction (once problem solver data and data dependencies have been "translated" into RMS nodes and lists of RMS nodes, no further translation between problem solver data and RMS data is necessary). However, using the same approch in multiagent reason maintenance systems poses a difficult problem: as pointers to an agent's internal RMS data structures are menaningless for all other agents, the question is what RMSs and problem solver are to communicate. Having later extensions to multiagent systems in mind, it seems more appropriate to base PS/RMS communication on some standardized language for expressing knowledge, e.g. $\mathcal{L}_{\mathsf{HPL}}$ as defined in Section 2.2 or a subset of KIF [Neches et al., 1991b], and to let the RMS itself do the mapping into internal data structures.

2.4.3   RMS Families

Several classes or families of reason maintenance systems have been developed. RMSs can be classified along two major dimensions:

- expressive power to formulate constraints and

---

[18]This is not at all meant to discredit the book [Forbus and de Kleer, 1993]; the authors' intention simply is a different one: to teach the reader *how to apply* RMS techniques in actual problem solvers. Nevertheless, considering the extensive discussion of implementational issues of RMSs, the absence of an architecture remains astonishing.

- number of contexts that are simultaneously maintained.

As illustrated in Figure 2.3 (adapted from [Forbus and de Kleer, 1993]), both

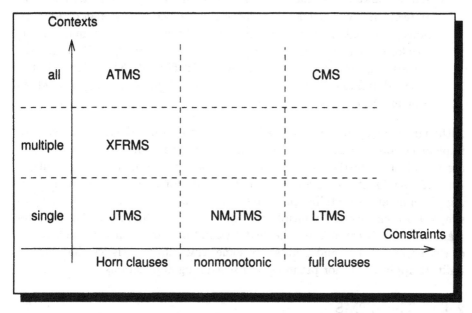

Figure 2.3: Families of reason maintenance systems.

The two dimensions are number of contexts and expressive power for formulating constraints. The latter dimension is divided into the three categories *definite Horn clauses*, *nonmonotonic justifications*, and *full propositional clauses*. Likewise, the number of contexts dimension is divided into the three categories *single context systems*, *multiple context systems*, and *all context systems*.

dimensions are divided into three categories. The three categories for the kind of constraints used are the same as in [Forbus and de Kleer, 1993]: Horn clauses, nonmonotonic justifications (see Doyle's original paper [Doyle, 1979]), and full (in the sense of general) clauses. For the other dimension — number of contexts here (versus label complexity in [Forbus and de Kleer, 1993]) — we use the three categories single, multiple and all contexts as follows:

- **Single context** RMSs can maintain for the problem solver only a single set of assumptions, and thus, a single context, at any time. Examples are the JTMS (a TMS a la Doyle using only monotonic justifications, see e.g. [Forbus and de Kleer, 1993], Chapters 7 and 8), the NMJTMS (Doyle's original TMS [Doyle, 1979]), and the LTMS ([McAllester, 1990], see also [McDermott, 1991]).

- **Multiple context** RMSs maintain several contexts for the problem solver, but only those that the problem solver has *explicitly* declared relevant. None of the classical systems falls into this category, but a new system of this type — XFRMS— is presented later on.

- **All context** RMSs maintain all possibly interesting contexts, based on all relevant environments that can be constructed from the set of assumptions. Relevant environments are usually those that are minimal. Examples for systems in this category are de Kleer's ATMS ([de Kleer, 1986a], see also the extended ATMS [de Kleer, 1986b], [de Kleer, 1986c]), the CMS ([Kean and Tsiknis, 1992], [Kean and Tsiknis, 1993]), and ARMS [Dotzel, 1994].

Although single context reason maintenance systems like the JTMS are easy to implement and to use and provide their services at reasonable efficiency, they are not of much further interest for our work, because maintaining multiple contexts was identified as an essential capability for multiagent systems solving planning and scheduling problems. Thus, when constraints are limited to simple Horn clauses and multiple contexts must be maintained, the ATMS remains as the only candidate. The next section summarizes the central features of the basic ATMS [19] and points out some ATMS characteristics that severly limit its applicability for planning and scheduling applications.

2.4.4   The ATMS

De Kleer's basic ATMS (see [de Kleer, 1986a]) is *the* standard multiple-context assumption-based reason maintenance system. The ATMS uses a labelled dependency network representation of the logical state to provide fast response to problem solver queries.

The dependency network can be described as a directed bipartite graph consisting of two types of nodes and directed arcs (links) between them. One kind of nodes represents propositions, the other kind justifications. The directed arcs between nodes always link two nodes of different type, An arc from a proposition node to a justification node means that the proposition is an antecedent of the respective justification, while an arc between a justification node and a proposition node means that the proposition is the consequent of the justification.

The proposition nodes carry labels that describe *all minimal and consistent sets of assumptions that allow to derive the proposition* represented by the node. Thus, labels are sets of sets of assumptions and have the form

$$\{\{A, B\}, \{C, D\}, \dots\};$$

---

[19]In his — by now classical — three *Artificial Intelligence* journal articles in 1986 ([de Kleer, 1986a], [de Kleer, 1986b], [de Kleer, 1986c]), de Kleer describes both a *basic* ATMS and an *extended* ATMS. While the former is limited to Horn clauses, the latter provides additional features, e.g. CHOOSEs for representing choices.

each element of the ATMS label represents a minimal consistent environment
(i.e. set of assumptions) that allows to derive the node. De Kleer has specified
the following four constraints the ATMS labels must meet: (Let E denote environments in the label $lab(n_\phi)$ of some node n representing a proposition ϕ, Γ_A
denote the set of all assumptions, Γ_J denote the set of all ATMS justifications
provided by the problem solver, and N denote elements of nogoods, the set of
all minimal environments that are inconsistent.

Consistency: $\forall_{E \in lab(n_\phi)} \forall_{N \in nogoods} :$ $[\, N \not\subseteq E \,]$

Soundness: $\forall_{E \in lab(n_\phi)} :$ $[\, \Gamma_J \vdash E \to \phi \,]$

Completeness: $\forall_{E \subseteq \Gamma_A} \forall_{N \in nogoods} :$ $[\, (N \not\subseteq E \wedge \Gamma_J \vdash E \to \phi)$

$$\implies \exists_{E' \in lab(n_\phi)} : [\, E' \subseteq E \,] \,]$$

Minimality: $\forall_{E, E' \in lab(n_\phi)} :$ $[\, E \subseteq E' \implies E = E' \,]$

Assuming a correct labelling of the ATMS dependency network, the ATMS can
obviously very quickly provide responses to queries pertaining to the consequence determination problem: in order to decide

$$\Gamma_J \vdash E \to \phi$$

the ATMS only has to perform subset tests; if any environment of the label
is a subset of the argument environment, and if the argument environment is
consistent, then the proposition is a logical consequence and in the context.
Determining the complete context requires some more work, because the above
question must be decided for each relevant proposition.

It is obvious that the ATMS labels must change, if new dependencies are
added to the clause database, or if propositions are turned into assumptions. If
a new justification is added, one can imagine the labels of the antecedent nodes
to flow to the justification node, where the labels are appropriately combined.
The combined label is then propagated (flows on) to the consequent node,
where it merges with the previously existing label of the consequent node
and is then propagated further to all justifications that refer the consequent
node. Turning a proposition into an assumption has a similar effect. Thus,
the direction of the links coincides with the direction of label propagation.

De Kleer has provided quite efficient incremental label update procedures
that, according to de Kleer's claims, ensure that all ATMS labels meet the four
constraints listed above after an update to the clause database. However, to
our knowledge de Kleer never provided a proof for the correctness (in the sense
of ensuring that labels meet the four constraints) of his ATMS label update
procedures. Beckstein has closed this gap in [Beckstein, 1994] and provided
a formal correctness proof for the incremental label propagation procedures
used by the ATMS.

Despite the effort that has been spent to make the propagation of ATMS-type labels efficient, the use of the ATMS is quite limited for many applications. The resource demands of the ATMS may grow exponentially, if the number of assumptions to be maintained is increased linearly. This is due to the fact that ATMS labels contain always *all* minimal and consistent environments that allow to derive a proposition. Whether exponentially growing label size is actually encountered in a particular application depends solely on the justification structure, i.e. the set of Horn clauses expressing data dependencies. There are certainly cases where this justification structure is favourable and ATMS labels remain small, but cases where the opposite is true can easily be constructed (see e.g. [Geisler, 1994] or [Beckstein, 1994]). In most cases, the ATMS is useful only for comparatively small numbers of assumptions (less than 1000), while planning and scheduling applications are expected to use far larger numbers of assumptions (more than 10000). The problem with the ATMS is that the number of environments represented in the ATMS is determined by the ATMS itself and not under control of the problem solver. Aside of severely restricting the freedom of the problem solver to formulate constraints, e.g. to at most one justification per proposition (which appears to be an inadequate approach to solve that problem), there are few other possibilities to improve the ATMS performance such that it looks like a promising tool for (large) planning and scheduling applications. A few attempts to achieve such improvements are discussed in the next section.

2.4.5   Some ATMS Derivates

Collins and DeCoste [Collins and DeCoste, 1991], [DeCoste and Collins, 1991] introduce a technique to compactify labels that uses c-subsumption instead of the usual set subsumption for label comparison in their systems CATMS.

Kelleher and van der Gaag [Kelleher and van der Gaag, 1993] apply the lazy evaluation technique to the propagation of ATMS labels in their system LazyRMS.

Dressler and Farquhar [Dressler and Farquhar, 1991] introduce a problem solver focus that differs from the one used here. Their focus is a subset of all assumptions and limits the problem solver to investigate only those environments that consist exclusively of assumptions in the focus.

Tatar developed the 2vATMS [Tatar, 1994], which combines the focusing techniques by de Kleer and others with the lazy evaluation technique of Kelleher and van der Gaag.

A technique that does not use some lazy evaluation techniques or compromise on completeness are bulk updates, which are extensively discussed in [Geisler, 1994] and [Beckstein, 1994]. Instead, bulk updates attempt to make the propagation process itself more efficient by exploiting topological information about the dependency net.

2.5   Review of Single Agent Reason Maintenance

Before we proceed and present a new single agent RMS in the next chapter, a short review is in order. In Section 2.1, we have used a practical example to study assumption-based reasoning in planning and scheduling. This analysis showed that multiple contexts and explicit representation of assumptions are of central importance, because several alternative plans and schedules must commonly be maintained. The most important tasks we identified were *consequence determination, context determination,* and *belief revision.*

The formalization of the kind of assumption-based reasoning performed by planners and schedulers and a precise characterization of the problems mentioned above were done in Section 2.2. A very simple type of logic, Horn Propositional Logic or HPL, was demonstrated to be sufficient for this purpose. This was demonstrated using the example from the analysis section.

The third section of this chapter (Section 2.3) provided then an informal description of the functionality required of a single agent reason maintenance system suitable for large planning and scheduling applications.

Single agent reason maintenance technology is well researched and developed field. Several systems are available for practical use. However, the review of existing single agent reason maintenance technology in Section 2.4 showed that none of the available systems provides the right combination of characteristics — the right mixture of expressive power and performance — desirable for reason maintenance systems to be used in planning and scheduling applications. A similar conclusion has been drawn by Petrie in [Petrie, 1991], who evaluated single agent reason maintenance systems with respect to their applicability for planning and replanning. Petrie, however, concentrates in his thesis on support for single context reasoning, while one of our main requirements was the capability for representing multiple contexts. Single context RMSs provide sufficient performance characteristics, but the restriction to a single problem solver context is unacceptable even for single agent planners/schedulers that must maintain several plan/schedule alternatives. Multiple context RMSs like the ATMS provide the capability to maintain multiple contexts, but are likely to exhibit unacceptable performance, if very large numbers of assumptions and justifications must be represented.

Thus, there is a need for a tool that is somewhat a compromise between the two extremes JTMS and ATMS and offers a suitable compromise between expressive power and convenient functionality on one side and performance and resource demands on the other. Such a tool is XFRMS, which is presented in the next section.

Chapter 3

XFRMS:
A Single Agent Focus-Based
Reason Maintenance System

3.1 Overview on XFRMS

The main purpose of the eXtended Focus-Based Reason Maintenance System
(XFRMS) is to overcome the complexity problem of ATMS-type systems and to
develop a useful concept and functionality for supporting multiple-context
assumption-based reasoning in planning and scheduling applications. Special
attention is paid to develop techniques that are suitable for extending them
to distributed scenarios like multiagent systems.

    The main idea underlying the XFRMS are as follows: In order to get around
the complexity problem and achieving significant performance improvements
some of the ATMS functionality must be given up or changed. Because we
are mainly interesting in a tool that *maintains contexts* based on a set of
underlying dependencies and *solves the consequence determination, context
determination*, and *belief revision* problems, we neglect ATMS capabilities like
explanation generation or interpretation construction, if we gain significantly
more control on resource use instead. The main reason for the complexity
problems of the ATMS is that the size of ATMS labels can grow exponentially
with the number of assumptions, regardless of the number of contexts the PS
is actually interested in. To generate an exponential number of contexts must
be considered inappropriate for all application systems, for which the PS never
wants to investigate all — or even a substantial portion — of these contexts.
For any practical planning and scheduling system, the PS will be able to investigate only a comparatively small number of contexts (e.g. several dozens
or hundreds). In such a case the RMS should not generate environments (and

contexts) that the PS does not consider relevant. It should maintain only those that the PS explicitly declares as relevant. Also, it is better to accept a predictable, limited performance penalty for declaring new environments as relevant than to have completeness (with respect to all contexts!), but combinatorial explosion. Thus, the XFRMS provides functionality for the problem solver to explictly state which environments (and their associated contexts) are of interest. Knowing which contexts the problem solver is interested in allows the XFRMS to reduce the relevant part of the logical consequence relation (and thus, the derivability relation) to just those environments that have been explicitly declared relevant, and thus, in general allows to use labels that are significantly smaller and simpler to manipulate.

Another ATMS feature that causes problems in multiagent scenarios is that the ATMS gives to the PS references to ATMS-internal data structures (so-called *tms nodes*). This may be efficient in the single agent case, but is not meaningful in multiagent scenarios, because pointers to internal data structures do not make any sense to other agents. Furthermore, it must be considered bad programming practice, because nothing prevents the PS from manipulating these internal data structures such that the internal consistency of the RMS is threatened.[1] The RMS needs to have an interface based on the language used for formulating propositions and dependencies. If several agents use the same language for that, or if their languages can be unambiguously translated back and forth, then these agents may communicate in terms of this language. The problem solver interface of the XFRMS is based on such a language (for simplicity, we simply use HPL). Thereby, the XFRMS improves information hiding.

The extension of RMS functionality by explicit context management and a language-based problem solver interface suggests a better structured internal RMS architecture, which is presented and proposed as a new generic RMS architecture in the next section.

3.2   XFRMS Specification

The specification of XFRMS follows the scheme given in Section 2.3: first, the logical state of an XFRMS module is defined, then the logical query, state change, and state query interfaces are specified.

3.2.1   XFRMS Logical State

The logical state of an XFRMS is specified by the following definition:

---

[1]Applying this approach to a database system would mean that the database system returns physical storage addresses of newly created tuples, which the problem is supposed to use as (secondary) keys in other tuples.

DEFINITION 3.2.1 (XFRMS LOGICAL STATE)
Let HPL *be a Horn propositional logic and the function* lits, *defined on all possible sets of clauses* $(\mathfrak{P}(\Gamma_{cl}))$, *be a function that maps a set of clauses* Γ *to the set* Γ_l *of all its literals* $(\Gamma_l \subseteq \Gamma_{lit*})$ *occurring in the clauses* Γ. *The logical state of an* XFRMS *module is a structure*

$$\mathfrak{s} = \langle \mathcal{L}_{\mathsf{HPL}}, \Gamma_P, \Gamma_J, \Gamma_A, \Delta_E, \Gamma_f \rangle,$$

where $\Gamma_P, \Gamma_A, \Gamma_f \subseteq \Gamma_{lit}$ *with* $\Gamma_f \subseteq \Gamma_A \subseteq \Gamma_P$, $\Delta_E \subseteq \mathfrak{P}(\Gamma_A)$, *and* $\Gamma_J \subseteq \Gamma_{cl}$ *with* lits$(\Gamma_J) \subseteq \Gamma_P$. $\mathfrak{S}$ *denotes the set of all possible logical RMS states* $\mathfrak{s}$.

The sets used in the definition above have the following intuitive meaning:

- Γ_P is a set of positive[2] literals that represents a set P of relevant propositions.

- Γ_J is a set of clauses (containing Horn, premise, and nogood clauses) that represents a set J of dependencies between the propositions represented by the literals occurring in the clauses. These dependencies are also called justifications. Only literals that have been declared relevant can be used in justifications, i.e. lits$(\Gamma_J) \subseteq \Gamma_P$ must hold.

- Γ_A is a set of literals representing a set of propositions A that the problem solver wants to use as assumptions in queries to XFRMS. Γ_A must be a subset of Γ_P. Subsets of Γ_A are referred to as *environments*.

- Δ_E is a particular set of (relevant) environments that may actually be used by the problem solver as arguments in queries to XFRMS. The use of the Δ_E logical state component can vary: Some XFRMS implementations may provide their query services only for queries referring to one of the environments in Δ_E, while others may provide their query services in principle for all possible environments from $\mathfrak{P}(\Gamma_A)$, but can do so much faster for queries related to environments which have already explicitly been declared relevant.

- Γ_f is a set of literals that represent the *current* environment or *focus* f, which is a set of assumptions that the problem solver currently makes. The focus uniquely determines the *current context*.

Let $\mathfrak{s} = \langle \mathcal{L}_{\mathsf{HPL}}, \Gamma_P, \Gamma_J, \Gamma_A, \Delta_E, \Gamma_f \rangle$ be the logical state of an RMS and $\Gamma_e \in \Delta_E$ be an environment. The following abbreviations are used below:

$$\Gamma_{\mathfrak{s}} = \Gamma_J \cup \{\top\}$$
$$\Gamma_{\mathfrak{s}}(e) = \Gamma_{\mathfrak{s}} \cup \Gamma_e$$
$$\Gamma_{\mathfrak{s}}(f) = \Gamma_{\mathfrak{s}} \cup \Gamma_f$$

---

[2] As HPL does not permit negative literals, we will from now on simply say literals.

A Note on RMS Interface Function Specifications   In Section 2.3, we emphasized the importance of clearly stating the applicability and any additional constraints relevant for functions specified in the interfaces. This poses indeed the following minor problem for an RMS specification: Any interface function that takes arguments defined in terms of the logical state is a "moving target" to some extent: as long as the arguments are not defined in the state, the query function should be considered undefined for these arguments; after the arguments are contained in the logical state, they are valid arguments for such function calls, which should produce a well-defined result. As an example, consider some arbitrary atomic proposition from $\mathcal{L}_{\mathsf{HPL}}$. As long as it is not declared relevant by the problem solver, the XFRMS query functions should produce an error, if such a proposition is used as an argument. After declaring the proposition relevant, it may occur as argument in queries and other interface functions. The problem for the specification is that either we must make all such error handling explicit in the specification (which we do not want in order to keep the specification simple), or we must find some other means to characterize the applicability of functions. In the specifications following below, we use the following convention: Each function specifies *i)* a mapping from some set to another set and *ii)* how the return value or side effect of the function is determined based on the input arguments and the logical state. The former is always kept as general as possible, but the latter is usually constrained by quantifications, which refer to components of the current logical state and thereby precisely characterize the applicability of a particular interface function in a particular logical state.

3.2.2   XFRMS Logical Query Interface

Logical query interface functions require the use of the derivability relation. The following definition specifies a base set of such functions for XFRMS.[3] All logical query interface functions leave the state unchanged.

DEFINITION 3.2.2 (XFRMS LOGICAL QUERY INTERFACE)
The basic logical query interface of an XFRMS *module provides the following functions:*

$$
\begin{aligned}
\text{follows-from?}\ : \quad & \mathfrak{S} \times \mathfrak{P}(\Gamma_{lit}) \times \Gamma_{lit} \longmapsto \{T, F\} \\
\text{holds-in?}\ : \quad & \mathfrak{S} \times \mathfrak{P}(\Gamma_{lit}) \times \Gamma_{lit} \longmapsto \{T, F\} \\
\text{context-of?}\ : \quad & \mathfrak{S} \times \mathfrak{P}(\Gamma_{lit}) \longmapsto \mathfrak{P}(\Gamma_{lit})
\end{aligned}
$$

Because the logical state is implicitly known by an RMS implementation, it does not need to be provided as an explicit argument. For a current logical

---

[3]The definition follows similar approaches by [Beckstein, 1994] and [McAllester, 1990].

state $s = \langle \mathcal{L}_{\text{HPL}}, \Gamma_P, \Gamma_J, \Gamma_A, \Delta_E, \Gamma_f \rangle \in \mathfrak{S}$ of the generic RMS, these functions are then defined as follows:

$\forall_{\Gamma_e \in \Delta_E} \forall_{\phi \in \Gamma_P}$:

$$\text{follows-from?}(\Gamma_e, \phi) = \begin{cases} T & \text{iff } \Gamma_s(e) \vdash_{\text{HPL}} \phi \\ F & \text{otherwise} \end{cases}$$

$\forall_{\Gamma_e \in \Delta_E} \forall_{\phi \in \Gamma_P}$:

$$\text{holds-in?}(\Gamma_e, \phi) = \begin{cases} T & \text{iff } \Gamma_s(e) \vdash_{\text{HPL}} \phi \text{ and } \Gamma_s(e) \nvdash_{\text{HPL}} \bot \\ F & \text{otherwise} \end{cases}$$

$\forall_{\Gamma_e \in \Delta_E}$:
$$\text{context-of?}(\Gamma_e) = \{ \phi \mid \phi \in \Gamma_P \text{ and holds-in?}(\Gamma_e, \phi) = T \}$$

Furthermore, as XFRMS explicitly maintains a focus for the problem solver, the following variants of the functions above are useful:

$$\begin{aligned}
\text{follows-from-focus?} &: & \mathfrak{S} \times \Gamma_{lit} &\longmapsto \{ T, F \} \\
\text{holds-in-focus?} &: & \mathfrak{S} \times \Gamma_{lit} &\longmapsto \{ T, F \} \\
\text{context-of-focus?} &: & \mathfrak{S} &\longmapsto \mathfrak{P}(\Gamma_{lit})
\end{aligned}$$

$$\begin{aligned}
\forall_{\phi \in \Gamma_P} : && \text{follows-from-focus?}(\phi) &= \text{follows-from?}(\Gamma_f, \phi) \\
\forall_{\phi \in \Gamma_P} : && \text{holds-in-focus?}(\phi) &= \text{holds-in?}(\Gamma_f, \phi) \\
&& \text{context-of-focus?}() &= \text{context?}(\Gamma_f)
\end{aligned}$$

All the above functions return an error, if the arguments do not meet the conditions of the specified quantifications.

Note, that the logical query interface already provides some support for solving certain instances of the belief revision problem: if two contexts are characterized by two different sets of assumptions, but the same clause database, the problem solver can compute the effect of switching between these two sets of assumptions simply by comparing the contexts of the respective environments.

3.2.3 XFRMS State Change Interface

The set of procedures for updating the XFRMS logical state is specified in the following definition. As all the functions are called for their effect (updating the logical state), the return value is not of interest and therefore omitted from the specification.

DEFINITION 3.2.3 (XFRMS STATE CHANGE INTERFACE)

The change interface of an XFRMS module can roughly be divided in functions for extending the relevant part of the language and in functions for manipulating environments. The former category includes the following functions:[4]

$$
\begin{aligned}
\text{add-proposition!} &: & \mathfrak{S} \times \Gamma_{lit} &\longmapsto \mathfrak{S} \\
\text{add-justification!} &: & \mathfrak{S} \times \Gamma_{cl} &\longmapsto \mathfrak{S}
\end{aligned}
$$

For any current logical state $\mathfrak{s} = \langle \mathcal{L}_{\mathsf{HPL}}, \Gamma_P, \Gamma_J, \Gamma_A, \Delta_E, \Gamma_f \rangle \in \mathfrak{S}$ *of the generic RMS, these functions are defined as follows:*

$$\forall_{\phi \in \Gamma_{lit}, \phi \notin \Gamma_P} :$$
$$\text{add-proposition!}(\phi) \;=\; \langle \Gamma_P \cup \{\phi\}, \Gamma_J, \Gamma_A, \Delta_E, \Gamma_f \rangle$$

$$\forall_{(\Phi \to \varphi) \in \Gamma_{cl}, (\Phi \to \varphi) \notin \Gamma_J, \mathit{lits}(\Phi \cup \{\varphi\}) \subseteq \Gamma_P} :$$
$$\text{add-justification!}((\Phi \to \varphi)) \;=\; \langle \Gamma_P, \Gamma_J \cup \{(\Phi \to \varphi)\}, \Gamma_A, \Delta_E, \Gamma_f \rangle$$

The functions for manipulating environments include the following:

$$
\begin{aligned}
\text{add-assumption!} &: & \mathfrak{S} \times \Gamma_{lit} &\longmapsto \mathfrak{S} \\
\text{add-environment!} &: & \mathfrak{S} \times \mathfrak{P}(\Gamma_{lit}) &\longmapsto \mathfrak{S} \\
\text{extend-environment!} &: & \mathfrak{S} \times \mathfrak{P}(\Gamma_{lit}) \times \mathfrak{P}(\Gamma_{lit}) &\longmapsto \mathfrak{S} \\
\text{remove-environment!} &: & \mathfrak{S} \times \mathfrak{P}(\Gamma_{lit}) &\longmapsto \mathfrak{S} \\
\text{set-focus!} &: & \mathfrak{S} \times \mathfrak{P}(\Gamma_{lit}) &\longmapsto \mathfrak{S}
\end{aligned}
$$

which, again for any current logical state $\mathfrak{s} = \langle \mathcal{L}_{\mathsf{HPL}}, \Gamma_P, \Gamma_J, \Gamma_A, \Delta_E, \Gamma_f \rangle \in \mathfrak{S}$ *of the generic RMS, is defined as follows:*

$$\forall_{\phi \in \Gamma_P, \phi \notin \Gamma_A} :$$
$$\text{add-assumption!}(\phi) \;=\; \langle \Gamma_P, \Gamma_J, \Gamma_A \cup \{\phi\}, \Delta_E, \Gamma_f \rangle$$

$$\forall_{\Gamma_e \in \mathfrak{P}(\Gamma_A), \Gamma_e \notin \Delta_E} :$$
$$\text{add-environment!}(\Gamma_e) \;=\; \langle \Gamma_P, \Gamma_J, \Gamma_A, (\Delta_E \cup \{\Gamma_e\}), \Gamma_f \rangle$$

$$\forall_{\Gamma_e \in \Delta_E, \Gamma_e^+ \in \mathfrak{P}(\Gamma_A)} :$$
$$\text{extend-environment!}(\Gamma_e, \Gamma_e^+) \;=\; \langle \Gamma_P, \Gamma_J, \Gamma_A, ((\Delta_E \smallsetminus \{\Gamma_e\}) \cup \{\Gamma_e \cup \Gamma_e^+\}), \Gamma_f \rangle$$

$$\forall_{\Gamma_e \in \Delta_E} :$$
$$\text{remove-environment!}(\Gamma_e) \;=\; \langle \Gamma_P, \Gamma_J, \Gamma_A, (\Delta_E \smallsetminus \{\Gamma_e\}), \Gamma_f \rangle$$

$$\forall_{\Gamma_e \in \Delta_E} :$$
$$\text{set-focus!}(\Gamma_e) \;=\; \langle \Gamma_P, \Gamma_J, \Gamma_A, \Delta_E, \Gamma_e \rangle$$

If any of constraints set forth by the above quantifications are not met, an error is returned.

---

[4]The logical state is implicitly known by any RMS implementation and does not need to be provided as an explicit argument.

Like most other well-known single agent reason maintenance systems, XFRMS is a monotonic RMS and allows only for addition of relevant propositions and justifications, i.e. its clause database is incrementally growing. An exception in XFRMS is the set of relevant environments, which does not grow monotonically: relevant environments can also be *extended*, which means that additional assumptions are included (from a logical point of view, the old environment is discarded and a new one used instead) or removed altogether.

As described more detailed in [Beckstein, 1994], the effect of retracting a justification can be simulated by using a special assumption (which does not occur as consequent in any justification) that is included in the antecedent of that justification: unless the assumption is explicitly assumed in a particular environment, the justification cannot contribute anything to a context; the assumption functions like an explicit switch for the justification. However, this approach becomes unwieldy if extensively used. If the problem solver can guarantee a cycle-free justification stucture (which may be difficult in general), an extension of XFRMS to include functions for retracting justifications, assumptions, and propositions is comparatively easy (see implementation notes for XFRMS in [Kraetzschmar, 1996b]). The section on implementation of XFRMS will exhibit later on, that the correct handling of retraction requests, especially of justifications, in the presence of cyclic justification structures requires more elaborate processing facilities in most typical reason maintenance systems designs, which favor compilation of belief state into labels in order to optimize average query time. There are two main implementation alternatives, if retraction functionality is required: The first requires the temporary deletion of all environments in which the consequent of a proposition follows and to reinstantiate them after deletion of the justification. This could be a viable approach if the number of relevant environments is limited, but in other cases it can easily result in a substantious label propagation effort in the dependency net maintained by a typical RMS. The alternative is to use more complex data structures in the dependency net in order to maintain information about justification cycles (see e.g. the techniques used for JTMS or LTMS as described in [Forbus and de Kleer, 1993] or [Beckstein, 1994]). However, the more complex data structures need to be maintained and increase the computational effort to be expended even for operations like the addition of justification. As a result, the necessary effort can easily outweigh the advantages gained, if retraction is used scarcely.

3.2.4   XFRMS State Query Interface

The functionality of the XFRMS state query interface is determined by structure of the logical state and made up of functions for retrieving logical state components or testing membership in such components, where appropriate.

DEFINITION 3.2.4 (XFRMS STATE QUERY INTERFACE)
The state query interface of an XFRMS *module consists of the following functions:*

$$
\begin{aligned}
\text{is-proposition?} &: & \mathfrak{S} \times \Gamma_{lit} &\longmapsto \{T, F\} \\
\text{is-justification?} &: & \mathfrak{S} \times \Gamma_{cl} &\longmapsto \{T, F\} \\
\text{is-assumption?} &: & \mathfrak{S} \times \Gamma_{lit} &\longmapsto \{T, F\} \\
\text{is-environment?} &: & \mathfrak{S} \times \mathfrak{P}(\Gamma_{lit}) &\longmapsto \{T, F\} \\
\text{all-propositions?} &: & \mathfrak{S} &\longmapsto \mathfrak{P}(\Gamma_{lit}) \\
\text{all-assumptions?} &: & \mathfrak{S} &\longmapsto \mathfrak{P}(\Gamma_{lit}) \\
\text{all-justifications?} &: & \mathfrak{S} &\longmapsto \mathfrak{P}(\Gamma_{cl}) \\
\text{all-environments?} &: & \mathfrak{S} &\longmapsto \mathfrak{P}(\mathfrak{P}(\Gamma_{lit})) \\
\text{focus?} &: & \mathfrak{S} &\longmapsto \mathfrak{P}(\Gamma_{lit})
\end{aligned}
$$

For any current logical state $\mathfrak{s} = \langle \mathcal{L}_{\text{HPL}}, \Gamma_P, \Gamma_J, \Gamma_A, \Delta_E, \Gamma_f \rangle \in \mathfrak{S}$ *of the generic RMS, these functions are defined as follows:*

$$
\text{is-proposition?}(\phi) = \begin{cases} T & \text{iff } \phi \in \Gamma_P \\ \mathit{NIL} & \text{otherwise} \end{cases}
$$

$$
\text{is-justification?}((\Phi \rightarrow \varphi)) = \begin{cases} T & \text{iff } (\Phi \rightarrow \varphi) \in \Gamma_J \\ \mathit{NIL} & \text{otherwise} \end{cases}
$$

$$
\text{is-assumption?}(\phi) = \begin{cases} T & \text{iff } \phi \in \Gamma_A \\ \mathit{NIL} & \text{otherwise} \end{cases}
$$

$$
\text{is-environment?}(\Gamma_e) = \begin{cases} T & \text{iff } \Gamma_e \in \Delta_E \\ \mathit{NIL} & \text{otherwise} \end{cases}
$$

$$
\begin{aligned}
\text{all-propositions?} &= \Gamma_P \\
\text{all-justifications?} &= \Gamma_J \\
\text{all-assumptions?} &= \Gamma_A \\
\text{all-environments?} &= \Delta_E \\
\text{focus?} &= \Gamma_f
\end{aligned}
$$

Note, that the protocol assumptions made in Section 2.3.6 apply for all specification given above.

3.3   XFRMS Architecture

The XFRMS is based on a three-unit architecture (see Figure 3.1) consisting of a dependency net unit (DNU), a context management unit (CMU), and a communication and control unit (CCU).

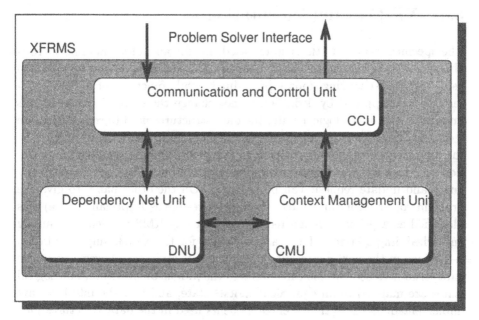

Figure 3.1: A generic reason maintenance system architecture.

- The **dependency net unit** (DNU) is comparable to a ATMS-like dependency net. It uses nodes and links to represent relevant propositions and justifications in a bipartite graph. Nodes are structured objects carrying a variety of information, including labels, that aid the XFRMS in providing its services in an efficient manner.

- The **context management unit** (CMU) takes care of managing environments and their associated contexts. In particular, it maintains a problem solver *focus*, which is an environment that describes the current set of assumptions made by the problem solver.

- The **communication and control unit** (CCU) provides the problem solver interface. It parses data provided by the problem solver, translates it into some normal form, if necessary, and keeps hash tables to map PS data to internal data structures.

We propose this architecture as a general architecture for reason maintenance systems; it is especially suited for application in distributed reason maintenance systems (see Chapter 4).

3.4   XFRMS Implementation

The specification of XFRMS is state-based, i.e. for an XFRMS module there is always a well-defined logical state defined. The logical state can be modified using the state-changing update procedures, while functions of the query interfaces are supposed by definition to not change the state. Because of this important role of the logical state, the data structures used to represent it are a central design issue for any XFRMS implementation. As outlined previously, the data structures should provide for the representation of sufficient information such that a reasonable tradeoff with respect to the efficiency of processing query and update requests can be achieved. On the other hand, to give the problem solver tight control over the use of resources (especially space) was identified as a primary design requirement for any RMS applied in planning and scheduling systems. The tradeoff chosen for the XFRMS implementation is outlined in the next paragraph, which presents an informal overview on the data structures used by the three units in the XFRMS architecture, how logical states are mapped to an equivalent XFRMS state, and how the interfaces are implemented. Because the label components used in the data structures play an essential role in achieving a satisfying resource/performance tradeoff, these labels are discussed in more detail in the second paragraph. The constraints that must hold for labels, the use of labels to provide fast query response, and the procedures used to update them are discussed in the paragraph thereafter.

3.4.1   Representation: Mapping Logical State to XFRMS State

In Section 3.3 we presented the general architecture of an XFRMS module. This architecture is reflected by the top level structure of the XFRMS state (see Figure 3.2), which is composed of

- the state of the dependency net unit,

- the state of the context management unit,

- and the state of the communication and control unit.

Both DNU and CMU use so-called *nodes* — which are structured data objects like C **structs** or CLOS objects — to represent some relevant piece of problem solver data (propositions, justifications, environments) in a concise manner. The node does not only store the problem solver datum itself, but is augmented with additional information, which is computed internally by the XFRMS and speeds up query processing. Such additional information includes simple flags (e.g. to indicate the inconsisteny of an environment), (sets or lists of) pointers to other nodes, and *labels* (discussed below).

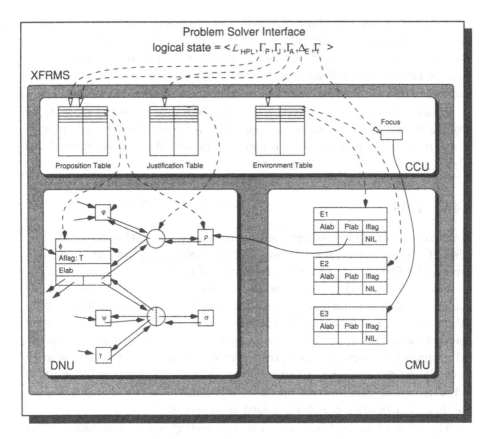

Figure 3.2: Mapping a logical state to a (refined) XFRMS architecture.

In the DNU, propositions are represented by rectangular nodes, while justifications are represented by circular nodes. Arrows illustrate pointers. Similarly, environments in the CMU are represented by rectangular nodes. For proposition nodes and environment nodes, some important parts of their internal structure is shown. The bidirectional hash tables in the CCU implement the mapping between problem solver data and XFRMS internal data.

The DNU uses *proposition nodes* and *justification nodes* to represent the respective components (Γ_P, Γ_J) of the logical state.[5] These nodes are suitably linked together to form a dependency net. The dependency net is utilized by the label propagation procedures (described below) to propagate changes by traversing a graph instead of repeatedly performing data retrieval, data update, and data storage operations. The subset of propositions which can be used as assumptions (Γ_A) is represented by introducing a flag Aflag for proposition nodes, which is set if the proposition is an assumption.

---

[5]Note, that the *verum* $\top$ and the *falsum* $\bot$ are always explicitly represented in the XFRMS state.

The CMU uses a third kind of node — *environment nodes* — to represent the set of relevant environments (Δ_E) and their associated contexts. The flag lflag indicates that the environment is inconsistent. Environment nodes are appropriately interlinked with proposition nodes, again to ensure fast query responses.

Finally, the CCU uses bidirectional hash tables to provide fast mapping of problem solver data into nodes and vice versa. A variable containing a pointer to a particular environment node is used to represent the problem solver focus (Γ_f).

3.4.2   Labels

Both proposition nodes and environment nodes have a label component. The label of a proposition node representing ϕ is called environment label and denoted by Elab(ϕ). It describes the subset of all relevant environments Γ_e, for which $(\Gamma_J \cup \{\top\} \cup \Gamma_e) \vdash_{HPL} \phi$ holds.[6] Conceptually, we introduce a unique marker for each relevant environment (see also the discussion of label propagation and Figure 3.3 below). The labels of all proposition nodes representing assumptions of an environment are assigned the respective marker. The label propagation procedures must then ensure that the marker is also assigned to the labels of all other proposition nodes that represent propositions which follow from the environment the label represents. In the implementation, pointers to environment nodes are used as unique markers.

The label of an environment node representing some environment Γ_e is called proposition label (because it stores pointers to proposition nodes) and denoted by Plab(Γ_e). It describes the context associated with the environment (therefore, it is also called context label), i.e. the set of all propositions that are derivable from that environment (all propositions for which $\Gamma_J \cup \{\top\} \cup \Gamma_e \vdash_{HPL} \phi$ holds). Environment node labels are constructed and maintained as a side effect of propagating proposition node labels. The implementation uses sets of pointers to propositions nodes as context labels in environment nodes. The set of proposition node labels and environment node labels are actually dual representations of the same concept: the relevant part of the derivability relation.

3.4.3   Integrity Constraints

Obviously, any constraint that has been defined for logical states (see Definition 3.2.1) must have an equivalent constraint on XFRMS states. However, because of the additional information represented by the various nodes, ad-

---

[6]Note, that the environment is not required to be consistent; checking consistency is done by different means. For details, see [Kraetzschmar, 1996b].

ditional constraints must be defined, e.g. ones that ensure correct linking of proposition and justification nodes or a unique and complete representation of the logical state. A complete set of these constraints is formally given in a technical report; here, we only present the constraints pertaining to labels.

DEFINITION 3.4.1 (XFRMS LABEL CONSTRAINTS)
Let $\mathfrak{s} = \langle \Gamma_P, \Gamma_A, \Gamma_J, \Gamma_f \rangle \in \mathfrak{S}$ be a logical RMS state with $\Gamma_{\mathfrak{s}} = \Gamma_J \cup \{\top\}$ and $\Gamma_{\mathfrak{s}}(e) = \Gamma_{\mathfrak{s}} \cup \Gamma_e$.

The following constraints must be met by proposition node labels and environment node labels in any XFRMS state:[7]

C1	$\forall_{\phi \in \Gamma_P} \forall_{\Gamma_e \in \Delta_E}$:	$[\, \Gamma_e \in Elab(\phi) \implies \Gamma_{\mathfrak{s}}(e) \vdash_{\mathsf{HPL}} \phi \,]$
C2	$\forall_{\phi \in \Gamma_P} \forall_{\Gamma_e \in \Delta_E}$:	$[\, \Gamma_{\mathfrak{s}}(e) \vdash_{\mathsf{HPL}} \phi \implies e \in Elab(\phi) \,]$
C3	$\forall_{\phi \in \Gamma_P} \forall_{\Gamma_e \in \Delta_E}$:	$[\, \phi \in Plab(\Gamma_e) \implies \Gamma_{\mathfrak{s}}(e) \vdash_{\mathsf{HPL}} \phi \,]$
C4	$\forall_{\phi \in \Gamma_P} \forall_{\Gamma_e \in \Delta_E}$:	$[\, \Gamma_{\mathfrak{s}}(e) \vdash_{\mathsf{HPL}} \phi \implies \phi \in Plab(\Gamma_e) \,]$

Constraints C1 and C2 ensure soundness and completeness of proposition node labels, while C3 and C4 ensure soundness and completeness of environment node labels.

3.4.4 Exploiting Labels in Query Processing

The XFRMS is inactive unless it must process a problem solver request. Processing such requests works as follows:

- The CCU receives a request and tries to map the problem solver data supplied as arguments into internal data structures of the XFRMS. If the CCU cannot perform this mapping, an error is reported and the problem solver request is discarded.

- Otherwise, the CCU calls the appropriate internal functions of the CMU or DNU to process the query or update request.

- The CCU takes the results provided by the internal functions of the DNU and CMU, maps them into problem solver data, and returns.

The logical query functions follows-from? and holds-in? are usually processed by the DNU. The following two function definitions illustrate how this is done:[8]

---

[7]Because the XFRMS data objects are not yet formally defined, the specification of these constraints refers to entities of the logical state, although they actually constrain the nodes representing these entities.

[8]The functions and procedures are specified in *mathematical pseudocode*. The pseudecode is tagged mathematical, because we sometimes use mathematical notation for parts that are obviously easy to implement, e.g. set union, element tests, or subset tests. Pseudocode keywords are underlined. Words set in sans serif font are function, procedure, or data structure attribute names.

FUNCTION 3.4.1 (FOLLOWS-FROM?)

```
1  function follows-from?(Γₑ, φ) ≡
2          if [ Γₑ ∈ Elab(φ) ]
3              then return(T)
4                else return(NIL)
5          fi
6  end
```

Function follows-from? performs a simple element test: it checks whether the environment is contained in the proposition node's label. Depending on the number of environments actually used, an implementation of labels based on bit vectors may be advisable in order to make the element test fast.

FUNCTION 3.4.2 (HOLDS-IN?)

```
1  function holds-in?(Γₑ, φ) ≡
2          if [[ lflag(Γₑ) == NIL ] ∧ [ Γₑ ∈ Elab(φ) ]]
3              then return(T)
4                else return(NIL)
5          fi
6  end
```

Query function holds-in? first tests the **lflag** flag of the environment node in order to find out whether the environment is consistent. The remainder is equivalent to follows-from?.

The logical query functions follows-from? and holds-in? can actually be processed both by the DNU and the CMU; usually the DNU will provide the response faster, unless the average number of environments in a proposition node label exceeds the average number of proposition nodes in an environment node label.

The answer to the logical query function context-of? is always provided by the context management unit:

FUNCTION 3.4.3 (CONTEXT-OF?)

```
1  function context-of?(Γₑ) ≡
2          if [ lflag(Γₑ) == T ]
3              then return(∅)
4                else return(Plab(Γₑ))
5          fi
6      end
```

Function context-of? simply returns the (proposition) label of the respective environment node, if the environment is consistent. Otherwise, it returns the empty set.

The three focus-related variants of the above query functions do not take an explicit environment argument, but use the known problem solver focus instead. As an example the function follows-from-focus? is given:

FUNCTION 3.4.4 (FOLLOWS-FROM-FOCUS?)

```
1 function follows-from-focus?(φ) ≡
2        if [ Γ_f ∈ Elab(φ) ]
3            then return(T)
4                else return(NIL)
5        fi
6 end
```

The state query functions are obviously trivial to implement and not further discussed. They are, however, included in the appendix.

3.4.5   Label Propagation

Label propagation is the means an XFRMS uses to compute the deductive closure of an environment. In the logic underlying the XFRMS, the only rule of inference is (the simplest form of) modus ponens, which says that the consequent of a clause is derivable, if the clause and all its antecedents are derivable. In the dependency net of the XFRMS DNU, the derivability of a proposition in a particular environment is represented by the presence of the marker used for the environment in the environment label of the proposition node. Also, all clauses in the database (i.e. all justifications) are derivable by definition. Then, applying modus ponens to the dependency net means that a marker must be propagated across a justification node to the label of its consequent, if the marker appears in the labels of all antecedent nodes of the justification. Thus, for a single marker a justification behaves similar to a logical AND gate. For arbitrary sets of markers in antecedent node labels, this means that we have to take the intersection of the antecedent node labels to yield the (partial) label of the consequent node, which is contributed by a single justification (see also Figure 3.3).

For constructing the deductive closure, it does not matter how a proposition is derived, i.e. which of several clauses with the same consequent is used in an instance of modus ponens to derive a proposition. For label propagation this means that a marker can (and must) be included into the environment label of a proposition node, if any of its justifications propagates it to the node. Thus, for a single marker several justifications for the same proposition are treated like a logical OR gate. For arbitrary sets of markers produced by several justifications, all markers must be included in the proposition node's label, i.e. the label is constructed by building the union of the labels produced by the justifications.

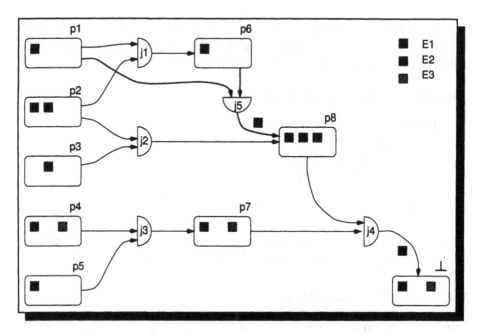

Figure 3.3: Illustration of XFRMS Label Propagation.

A small dependency net with eight proposition nodes (large, rounded rectangle), five justifications (shaped like logical AND gate), and three environments (small pattern-filled boxes, black represents $E1 = \{p_1, p_2, p_4, p_5\}$, dark grey represents $E2 = \{p_2, p_3\}$, and light grey represents $E3 = \{p_4, p_7, p_8\}$,) is shown. The effect of adding justification $j5$ is illustrated. The environment gets propagated across $j5$ to node p_8, and from there across justification $j4$ to the falsum node.

The functionality of XFRMS has been chosen such that XFRMS is monotonic. Propositions, assumptions, and justifications cannot be retracted once declared as such by the problem solver. The logical consequence relation of the underlying logic HPL (and the derivability relation of the logic's calculus) is also monotonic. This allows for very efficient incremental label propagation procedures without threatening the constraints specified above. The only exception to the monotonicity principle is that environments can be retracted. However, because the environment is totally removed, this can be easily implemented without danger for the constraints.

Only two procedures are used to implement the incremental label update procedures: xfrms-propagate and xfrms-update-label. Let us assume the label of some node representing ϕ_i has just been extended by the non-empty incremental label Δ_E^+ and $(\Phi \rightarrow \varphi)$ is a justification with $\phi_i \in \Phi$. Then xfrms-propagate will get called as follows:

$$\text{xfrms-propagate}(\varphi, \Phi \setminus \{\phi_i\}, \Delta_E^+)$$

The procedure xfrms-propagate ensures the propagation of the label increment over such a justification by executing the following steps:

PROCEDURE 3.4.5 (PROPAGATE)

```
1  procedure xfrms-propagate(φ, Φ, Δ_E^+) ≡
2        if [ Δ_E^+ = ∅ ]
3            then Δ_E^{+'} ← ⋂_{φ_i ∈ Φ} Elab(φ_i)
4            else Δ_E^{+'} ← Δ_E^+ ∩ ⋂_{φ_i ∈ Φ} Elab(φ_i)
5        fi
6        if [ Δ_E^{+'} ≠ ∅ ]
7            then xfrms-update-label(φ, Δ_E^{+'})
8        fi
9  end
```

Provided that Δ_E^+ is non-empty[9] as assumed above, the procedure xfrms-propagate constructs the intersection of the incremental label Δ_E^+ and all environment labels of the antecedent nodes in Φ. The result is propagated to the φ by calling the procedure xfrms-update-label, which is defined as follows:

PROCEDURE 3.4.6 (UPDATE-LABEL)

```
1   procedure xfrms-update-label(φ, Δ_E^+) ≡
2         Δ_E' ← Elab(φ)
3         Δ_E^{+'} ← Δ_E^+ ∖ Δ_E'
4         if [ Δ_E^{+'} ≠ ∅ ]
5             then Elab(φ) ← Δ_E' ∪ Δ_E^{+'}
6                 foreach [ Γ_{e_j} ∈ Δ_E^{+'} ] do
7                     Plab(Γ_{e_j}) ← Plab(Γ_{e_j}) ∪ {φ}
8                 od
9                 if [ φ == ⊥ ]
10                    then foreach [ Γ_{e_i} ∈ Δ_E^{+'} ] do
11                        Iflag(Γ_{e_i}) ← T
12                    od
13                fi
14                foreach [ (Φ→φ) ∈ Γ_J where φ ∈ Φ ] do
15                    Φ' ← Φ ∖ {φ}
16                    xfrms-propagate(φ, Φ', Δ_E^{+'})
17                od
18            fi
19  end
```

The xfrms-update-label procedure first checks whether an update is actually necessary: environments propagated in the label increment may already be in

---

[9]Calls to xfrms-propagate with an empty incremental label are covered in the next section.

the label of the node which is updated. In this case, label propagation stops and returns, because there is nothing further to do. Otherwise, the node's new environment label is created by constructing the union of the old label and the label increment. Next, the proposition labels of the environments in the incremental label are updated. After that, xfrms-update-label checks whether the node which is curently updated is the *falsum*. In this case, all environments in the label increment become inconsistent and the appropriate flag is set in each of them. Finally, the label increment must be propagated across all justifications which contain the node in the antecedents.

When applied as outlined above, xfrms-propagate and xfrms-update-label carry out a complete incremental label update in the dependency network of the DNU in a depth-first manner.[10] As a side effect, the proposition labels of the environment nodes are updated as well. Thus, after propagation stops, all labels are updated and meet the constraints C1 to C4 as specified above. This claim is now substantiated in the next paragraph.

3.4.6   Updating XFRMS States and Correctness of Label Propagation

Label propagation must be initiated whenever a state change interface procedure modifies the XFRMS state such that the constraints C1 to C4 would be violated. In order to ensure correct labels, the state changing procedures themselves call the appropriate label update procedures. The relationship between state change interface procedures and label update procedures can be described as follows:

- A call to add-proposition! adds an isolated proposition node without any links to justification nodes in the dependency net. Two conclusions can be drawn from this fact: Firstly, the label of the newly added proposition node must be empty, because the proposition can be neither in any of the relevant environments (it is not even an assumption yet) nor can it be derived via a justification. Secondly, the labels of all other proposition nodes cannot change, because this node cannot occur in any derivation for such a proposition. Therefore, the label of the new proposition node must be appropriately initiated to the empty set, but no label propagation occurs.

- Turning a proposition into an assumption is done by setting a flag in the proposition node, which means that future update requests are allowed to include this proposition into environments. However, executing add-assumption! does not modify any of the existing environments nor

---

[10]See [Beckstein, 1994] for details and a description of ways (like bulk updates) to further improve efficiency.

create new ones, nor modify the dependency net. Thus, no label constraints can be violated and, hence, no label propagation must be done.

- Adding a justification ($\Phi \rightarrow \varphi$) by calling add-justification! introduces a new justification node and links it with the antecedent and consequent nodes. Label propagation must be done because new derivations are possible for the consequent of the justification and (iteratively) for all its consequences. The label update is initiated by calling the (incremental) label propagation procedure xfrms-propagate with an empty incremental label as follows:

$$\text{xfrms-propagate}(\varphi, \Phi, \varnothing).$$

The correctness of this call is discussed below.

- Adding an environment Γ_e creates a new environment node. The environment node's proposition label is initiated to the empty set and will be correctly updated as a side effect of propagating a new marker (a pointer to the environment node) through the dependency net. Because the assumptions of an environment are by definition derivable in that environment, the label of each of the assumption nodes must be updated, which is done by executing the following call for each ϕ_i of the assumptions in the environment:

$$\text{xfrms-update-label}(\phi_i, \{\Gamma_e\})$$

That this is sufficient to ensure a complete update of the labels in the dependency net is also outlined below.

- The state change procedure extend-environment! is just a variant of creating a new environment: the environment node already exists and for all assumptions already previously declared, the respective node has been updated with the appropriate environment marker. The newly added assumptions remain to be updated, which is done by calling

$$\text{xfrms-update-label}(\phi_i, \{\Gamma_e\})$$

for each assumption newly added to the environment.

- Setting the focus means replacing one pointer to an environment node by another, but does not necessitate any label updates.

- Finally, the procedure remove-environment completely discards an environment Γ_e, which may no longer occur in any proposition node label. Because the proposition label Plab of an environment node contains pointers to all nodes which reference the environment in their environment label, this operation can be very easily performed by executing

$$\mathsf{Elab}(\phi_i) \leftarrow \mathsf{Elab}(\phi_i) \smallsetminus \{\Gamma_e\}$$

for all $\phi_i \in \mathsf{Plab}(\Gamma_e)$. Thus, no label propagation in the usual sense is necessary.

In order to complete the discussion of XFRMS label propagation correctness with respect to the integrity constraints C1 to C4 specified above, the following steps remain to be done:

1. Show the correctness of an incremental xfrms-propagate step.

2. Verify that the (incremental) xfrms-propagate step, which is initiated by add-justification!, correctly computes a full label for the new justification.

3. Show the correctness of an incremental xfrms-update-label step.

4. Demonstrate termination of the propagation process.

Correctness of an incremental xfrms-propagate step   Let us assume, the label of some node ϕ has just been extended by the non-empty incremental label Δ_E^+, which is now propagated across a justification $(\Phi \rightarrow \varphi)$ with $\phi \in \Phi$ via the call

$$\mathsf{xfrms\text{-}propagate}(\varphi, \Phi \smallsetminus \{\phi\}, \Delta_E^+).$$

xfrms-propagate must compute an incremental label for φ that is contributed by the justification $(\Phi \rightarrow \varphi)$ and contains all environments that now allow to derive φ by using the justification. This incremental label $\Delta_E^{+'}$ for φ is a subset of the incremental label Δ_E^+. It contains only those environments from Δ_E^+, which allow to derive all remaining antecedents of the justifications, i.e. which are an element of $\bigcap_{\phi_i \in (\Phi \smallsetminus \{\phi\})} \mathsf{Elab}(\phi_i)$. Thus, the incremental label is

$$\Delta_E^{+'} = \Delta_E^+ \cap \bigcap_{\phi_i \in (\Phi \smallsetminus \{\phi\})} \mathsf{Elab}(\phi_i),$$

which is just what is computed by line 4 of procedure xfrms-propagate. If the resulting incremental label (over justification $(\Phi \rightarrow \varphi)$) is empty (none of the environments added to the label of the recently updated antecedent node occurs in all other antecedent node labels as well), then no new derivations involving this justification are possible, and propagation stops. Otherwise, the incremental label must be merged into the consequent node's label, which is achieved by calling xfrms-update-label in line 7 of procedure xfrms-propagate.

Correctness of xfrms-propagate **after adding justifications** The previous step showed that xfrms-propagate works correctly for existing justifications, if an incremental label produced by updating one of the justification's
antecedents needs to be propagated across a justification. This situation is,
however, different from adding a new justification ($\Phi \rightarrow \varphi$), where all its antecedents Φ already have a well-formed label. The label for the consequent
must be the intersection of the labels of all antecedents, because only if an
environment allows to derive all antecedents, it also allows to derive the consequent via the justification on hand. Above (see3.4.6), calling

$$\text{xfrms-propagate}(\varphi, \Phi, \varnothing)$$

was claimed to correctly produce the required label increment for updating
φ. Note, that the second argument encompasses now *all* antecedents of the
justification, while in the incremental xfrms-propagate step discussed above
the second argument contained all antecedents *except* the antecedent that has
just been updated and which initiates the incremental xfrms-propagate step
across the justification. Of course, we have to prevent that xfrms-propagate
builds the intersection with the incremental label argument, which is empty
in the case of xfrms-propagate after adding a justification. The procedure
definition for xfrms-propagate given above takes this into account: If Δ_E^+, the
third argument, is empty, then the intersection of all antecedent labels is built
in line 3. Otherwise, the intersection of the labels of all antecedents given
as the second argument is built, and this is intersected with the incremental
label Δ_E^+ in line 4. Thus, in the case of adding justifications, xfrms-propagate is
called such that it correctly computes a full candidate label for the consequent,
which can then be merged into the consequent label by xfrms-update-label.

Correctness of xfrms-update-label **steps** The procedure xfrms-update-label
must merge (incremental) labels, which are supplied either by xfrms-propagate
(which propagated some label update across a justification) or directly by
state update procedures like add-environment! or extend-environment!, into the
labels of proposition nodes. Only those environments not already contained
in an environment label $\text{Elab}(\phi)$ must actually be included and propagated
further through the dependency net. This subset $\Delta_E^{+'}$ of the label increment
Δ_E^+ is obtained by

$$\Delta_E^{+'} = \Delta_E^+ \setminus \text{Elab}(\phi),$$

which is what xfrms-update-label computes in lines 2 and 3. If this set is empty,
all environments in the incremental label were already present and nothing
further needs to be done (line 4). Otherwise, the label increment $\Delta_E^{+'}$ is merged
into the proposition node's environment label (line 5) and the proposition
node is added to the proposition label Plab of all environment nodes referred

in $\Delta_E^{+'}$ (lines 6 to 8). If the currently updated node represents the *falsum*, all environments in the incremental label allow to derive a contradiction and therefore become inconsistent (lines 9 to 13). Adding an environment to a proposition node's environment label represents that the node has become derivable in that environment. Any justification, which refers the recently updated proposition node, may now allow to derive further propositions in that environment. Therefore, ensuring that the XFRMS always maintains the deductive closure of an environment (see the label constraints C1 to C4) means that the label increment must be propagated to all such justifications. This is exactly what the remaining lines in xfrms-update-label achieve.

Termination of Label Propagation   So far, we only considered single propagation steps involving xfrms-propagate and xfrms-update-label. These steps are, however, tightly linked and mutually call each other, even multiple times in a single step, such that the number of propagation and update steps seems to increase infinitely. We must ensure, that this process always finishes after a finite number of steps; in particular, if cycles are present in the dependency net. Recalling several facts immediately allows to follow that incremental label updates in XFRMS terminates:

1. The size of the labels, and thus, the size of the label increment, is bounded by the number of relevant environments.

2. The size of proposition node environment labels is montonically ascending.

3. The propagation process itself does not create any new environments.

4. The size of the label increment is descending during propagation.

5. The propagation step stops whenever the label increment becomes empty during propagation.

Some more details about termination are provided by the discussion of complexity considerations in the next section.

3.5   XFRMS Complexity Considerations

As we claim the XFRMS to be significantly more efficient than the ATMS, especially for large numbers of assumptions, a look at space and runtime complexity is in order. In the following, let $\|S\|$ denote the cardinality of a set S. Let $c_1, c_2,$ and c_3 denote the number of all relevant propositions, justifications, and environments, respectively, c_4 denote the maximum number of antecedents of all justifications, and c_5 be the maximum number of justifications for any particular proposition:

$$c_1 \quad =_{\text{def}} \quad \|\Gamma_P\|$$

$$c_2 \quad =_{\text{def}} \quad \|\Gamma_J\|$$

$$c_3 \quad =_{\text{def}} \quad \|\Delta_E\|$$

$$c_4 \quad =_{\text{def}} \quad \max_{(\Phi\to\varphi)\in\Gamma_J} \{ \|\text{ANset}((\Phi\to\varphi))\| \}$$

$$c_5 \quad =_{\text{def}} \quad \max_{\phi\in\Gamma_P}\{ \|\{(\Phi\to\varphi) \mid (\Phi\to\varphi) \in \Gamma_J \text{ and } \varphi = \phi\}\| \}$$

3.5.1   Space Complexity

The purpose of the XFRMS is to represent a logical state, which describes a finite subset of the logical consequence relation of a Horn propositional logic (HPL). It is obvious, and therefore not further discussed, that the representation of such a logical state as outlined above can be done with a finite and linear (related to the size of the logical state represented in XFRMS) number of (proposition, justification, and environment) node objects used by the DNU and the CMU. The actual space requirements are largely determined by the size of these node objects. The space necessary to represent the dependency net structure, including all cross-links between proposition nodes and justification nodes, requires no more than $O(c_1 \times c_2)$ space (for details, see [Kraetzschmar, 1996b]). Environment label size of proposition nodes is $O(c_3)$, while the size of proposition labels in environment nodes is $O(c_1)$. Thus, space requirements grow *linearly* both with the number of relevant propositions and environments. This is one of the central advantages of the XFRMS. The space required by the CCU to implement the mappings between problem solver data and internal XFRMS data structures depends on the particular technique used for implementation. Usually, B-trees or hash tables are used and their space requirements do not grow with more than $O(n \times \log(n))$; with hashing, space requirements can be reduced to $O(n)$ while still having average access time of $O(1)$ [Cormen et al., 1990], where n is the number of relevant propositions, justifications, or environments, respectively.

3.5.2   Runtime Complexity

All query interface functions of the XFRMS are very efficient: Aside of the time necessary to perform the mapping to and from problem solver data to internal data structures, which is no more than $O(\log(n))$ for B-trees and $O(n)$ for hashing (for the worst case, but with $O(1)$ for the average case), only simple membership tests, flag tests, or simple value assignments are performed.

The state update functions also have very reasonable performance characteristics. Except for invoking label propagation, the runtime of all other operations performed by these functions depends linearly on the size of the arguments provided (e.g. the number of assumptions in an environment). The runtime requirements for incremental label propagation is more difficult, but can be estimated by taking a global view and finding boundaries for the maximum number of possible calls to the procedures xfrms-propagate and xfrms-update-label.

A single environment is the smallest label increment, that xfrms-update-label can add to the label $\mathsf{Elab}(\phi)$ for a particular proposition node ϕ. A particular environment cannot be added to a label more often than there are proposition nodes; thus, this event can, for a particular environment, occur at most c_1 times. Because no new environments are created by label propagation procedures, at most c_3 environments can be added to a node's label. The request to add an environment to a particular node's label can occur at most $(c_3 + c_5)$ times: c_3 times caused by add-environment! or extend-environment!, c_5 times caused by propagating it across a justification. Of course, only the very first attempt is successful and causes further updates; once the node's label contains the environment, propagation ends at all other attempts. In particular, this holds for cycles: if an environment is propagated through a cycle and propagation arrives at a previously traversed node in the dependency net, the environment must already be in the label and propagation stops. Thus, cycles can be traversed at most once for each environment. Altogether, in order to generate a particular logical state, the overall number of possible calls to xfrms-update-label is at most $O(c_1 \times c_3 \times (c_3 + c_5))$, and $O(c_1 \times c_3)$ of these calls an environment can actually have been added to the label and further label propagation could have been invoked, while in all other cases label propagation stops.

The procedure xfrms-propagate can, for each justification, be called at most $c_3 \times c_4$ times (each time a single environment has been added to the label of any of its antecedent nodes). Again, at most c_3 times the call to propagate will actually result in a call to xfrms-update-label (no more than all relevant environments can be propagated across a justification), while for all others propagation stops. Altogether, the overall number of calls to xfrms-propagate in order to generate a particular logical state is $O(c_2 \times c_3 \times c_4)$, and $O(c_2 \times c_3)$ of these calls can have resulted in calls to xfrms-propagate.

Note, that these boundaries describe the sum of all calls to xfrms-propagate and xfrms-update-label that occurred to produce a particular logical state. A single state update operation has far smaller complexity: adding or extending an environment can at most result in adding that environment to all node labels, while adding a justification can produce at most all known environment markers in the label of the consequent and all its consequences.

3.6 Summary of XFRMS

We have presented XFRMS, a very simple and easy to implement RMS that allows to represent and reason efficiently with multiple contexts and large numbers of assumptions and dependencies. We buy this advantage by giving up some ATMS functionality, like the automatic computation of all consistent and minimal environments. However, the requirements set forth by the analysis of the application domain, in particular, the large numbers of assumptions and justifications to be maintained, suggest that this kind of functionality is less important and that for reasons of efficiency the ATMS is not suited for such domains. Similar arguments have been given by others (see e.g. [Petrie, 1991], [Lindner, 1992] and [Tatar, 1994]), who tried to apply the ATMS to planning and scheduling or other domains with similar requirements. XFRMS gives up some ATMS functionality, in order to gain performance. The main idea is to make context management an explicit task of XFRMS and to provide functions in the problem solver interface such that the problem solver can explicitly declare its interest in particular environments. XFRMS employs a more structured internal RMS architecture and new, much simpler labels to efficiently implement its functionality. The basic implementation idea was to use labels made up from several indexed JTMS-like labels. These labels allow for the representation of multiple contexts, while the propagation procedures required to maintain the labels are significantly simpler than those of the ATMS.

Which of the various RMSs is best suited for an application depends on the particular requirements. We intent to apply the XFRMS mainly as a means to represent and maintain several, large plans and/or schedules (involving many assumptions, many dependencies). Different plans/schedules are assumed to be represented as different contexts (with different sets of underlying assumptions). In comparison to the number of *all possible* contexts (plans/schedules), our problem solvers are assumed to be interested in *comparatively small* numbers of contexts, while the vast majority of contexts is never investigated. For this kind of application, XFRMS is claimed to be a useful tool. It does not, of course, provide much help, if a problem solver indeed must investigate almost all contexts. For these kind of applications, systems based on focusing techniques, lazy evaluation, and bulk updates (see [Beckstein, 1994]) may offer much better functionality.

Nevertheless, the XFRMS system is considered a solid basis to build upon more advanced functionality for supporting planning and scheduling tasks. In particular, support for temporal reasoning and functionality to represent and maintain schedules (insert actions into plans, schedule and unschedule jobs) are desirable, but left for future work. XFRMS is also a cornerstone in tackling multiple-context assumption-based reasoning problems in multiagent systems, because it provides significant levy for some complexity problems of the ATMS.

Chapter 4

Multiagent Reason Maintenance

After single agent reason maintenance has been discussed and the respective technology has been improved, the remainder of this book focuses on reason maintenance in multiagent systems. The principle approach to the topic is similar to that used in the single agent case: we start from an analysis of the problem, formalize it, derive a generic framework for a suitable functionality and discuss existing technology (this chapter), before we finally arrive at the specification, design, and implementation of a system to solve the problems of distributed context determination and distributed belief revision in a multiagent setting (next chapter).

4.1 Analysis of Multiagent Assumption-Based Reasoning

Like in the single agent case, we study the problem using a small example. Despite the brevity and simplicity of the example used, it should be obvious that realistic examples are of significantly larger scale and complexity, such that the necessity for appropriate tools is much stronger.

4.1.1 The Secretaries' Nightmare

Appointment scheduling was presented as an example for a single agent problem solving task that involves assumption-based reasoning. Usually, however, several human agents have to attend meetings, and the agents responsible for arranging a meeting (secretaries) have to communicate and coordinate in order to work out an appointment that suites all participants. An example for such a situation was used as the common problem to work on for all

participants of the CAIA-94 Workshop on Coordinated Design and Planning
(see [Petrie et al., 1993] and [Petrie et al., 1994b]).[1] The following example
is an adapted variant of the workshop scenario. The original workshop scenario makes some implicit assumptions regarding global knowledge available
to the person or agent performing meeting scheduling. The modifications are
intented to remove or weaken these assumptions.

EXAMPLE 4.1.1 (MULTIAGENT MEETING SCHEDULING)
General Setting and Agents Involved: *Wanda, Xynthia, Yvonne, and
Zarah are the secretaries of the four managers Axel, Brigitt, Carl, and Dirk.
The managers work for four different companies doing a joint project, for
which Carl's company is a subcontractor to Dirk's company. Axel is based in
New York City, Brigitt in Palo Alto, Carl in Los Angeles, and Dirk in Austin.*

    Tasks and Constraints: *The tasks of the four secretaries are similar to
those of Patricia Perfect (see Example 2.1.1): scheduling meetings, maintaining (possibly several alternative) schedules, booking flights and hotel rooms for
their managers. In contrast to Patricia's situation, however, the four secretaries must perform these tasks in cooperation and agreement with each other,
if their respective managers participate in a meeting. The secretaries may have
to negotiate to find acceptable compromises. Care must be taken by the secretaries to not reveal confidential information: For example, any information*
regarding the *reasons* and *consequences* of a manager being available or not
at certain dates is considered confidential.[2] *Also, secretaries are not supposed
to reveal more availability information than necessary.[3] It is assumed that for
each meeting one of the secretaries is assigned the role of coordinator. The
coordinator has the prime opportunity to suggest dates and locations, but must
also execute all coordination activities. In addition to the date of the meeting,
the secretaries must also determine a location for it. Meetings have no a priori
fixed location as assumed in the single agent scenario, although constraints or
preferences regarding meeting locations may be given. Otherwise, secretaries
will attempt to schedule meetings locally in order to minimize travel, which is
an important schedule quality criterion. The attempt to keep meetings local
will usually be given up if overall travel by all managers can be reduced by
scheduling a meeting in a different location. Of course, the usual scheduling*

---

[1]For further reference to this workshop, see Section 2.1.1.

[2]Availability information itself is very hard to maintain confidential: if one suggests a
date and the other person declines to accept it, the other person must be considered not
available (whatever the reason). By common business practices, however, one will usually
not be able to find out the (real) reason except for something like "Mr. X is out of the office
that day."

[3]This excludes solutions based on an initial exchange of complete availability information.
Although such an approach simplifies the problem and has been taken by several papers presented at the CAIA-94 Workshop ([Liu and Sycara, 1994], [Haddadi and Bussmann, 1994]),
it is not very realistic and incompatible with common business practices.

constraints (avoiding scheduling conflicts like two meetings at the same time or being in two different places) must be observed. A meeting is considered scheduled, if it has been locally scheduled and the scheduling decision is accepted by all other parties involved in the meeting. A secretary has solved her local scheduling problem, if all meetings requiring her manager to attend have been scheduled.

A Typical Problem Solving Situation: *(See Figure 4.1) Axel, Brigitt,*

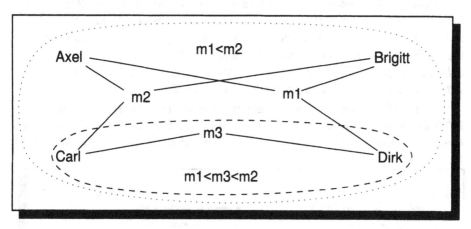

Figure 4.1: A typical multiagent meeting scheduling situation.

Lines from meetings to persons indicate the participants of meetings. The dotted line describes who knows about meetings m_1 and m_2, while the dashed line indicates who knows about the (secret) third meeting. The precedence relations describe knowledge of temporal orderings for meetings.

and Dirk, the managers of the prime contractors in this project, agree to hold a meeting m_1 concerning general business agreements and marketing issues. Furthermore, they agree that Axel, Brigitt, and Carl should have another meeting, m_2, in order to discuss various strategic technical issues. Axel's secretary is supposed to coordinate scheduling of the first meeting, while Dirk agrees to inform Carl about the second meeting and to ask Carl's secretary to arrange the second meeting. All agree that both meetings m_1 and m_2 must be scheduled on weekdays during April 1994. The faster the meetings can take place, the better. Travel should be minimized by scheduling two days in a row if possible. The meetings can be either in Austin or Los Angeles, but it is preferable for the second meeting to be in Los Angeles because of the availablility of a demonstration. If the meetings are back-to-back in the same city, Los Angeles is preferable.

When Dirk calls Carl to tell him about the meetings, they agree that Dirk must inform Carl about the results of meeting m_1, such that the technical designs to be proposed by Carl in meeting m_2 reflect the marketing decisions agreed upon in the first meeting. Although they might be able to exchange this *information on a phone call, Dirk and Carl prefer to meet in person. If the two meetings are held back-to-back, then Carl and Dirk can meet in the evening of the first day. Otherwise, an optional (possibly secret) meeting m_3, which must be held between the other two meetings, should be scheduled if possible. Because Carl's secretary Yvonne (by default) need not be informed about the date of the first meeting and can, therefore, hardly ensure that the third meeting is possible, Dirk's secretary Zarah is supposed to arrange the third meeting.*

Because all managers are involved in several other projects, they already have several meetings in their respective schedules. Presuming that these meeting constraints are to be observed (see also Table 4.1), Axel is available in April the week of the 4th, the 18th and 19th, and the 25th and 26th, Brigitt is available the 7th, 8th, 19th, and the week of the 25th, Carl is available on the 7th, 19th, and 26th, and Dirk is available on the 7th, 8th, 18th, and 25th.

Initial Knowledge of a Secretary/Scheduling Agent: *Each manager informs the secretary about the meetings to be scheduled and the role the secretary is supposed to take (see Figure 4.2). Note, that at least initially not all of*

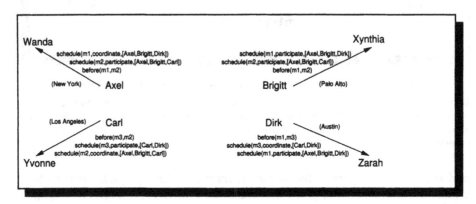

Figure 4.2: Initial information given to the secreatries by their managers.
The arrows illustrate communication between the managers and their secretaries; arrows are annotated with the information conveyed to secretaries by their respective managers (all in a Prolog-like notation).

the above information is known by every secretary. Each secretary is informed only about those meetings that her manager is supposed to participate in. For example, only Yvonne and Zarah know of Dirk and Carl's intention to have a third meeting and are supposed to keep this meeting secret. Each secretary knows only the availability constraints of her own manager. Also, the preferences for meeting locations are different for each manager: Brigitt and Carl prefer Los Angeles, while Axel and Dirk prefer Austin. Table 4.1 summarizes the secretaries' initial knowledge about availability.

Generation of Initial Schedule Alternatives: *(See Figure 4.3. Numbers in parenthesis in the following text refer to message numbers in the figure.)*

Agent	Person	Availability on date					Preference
		1	4 5 6 7 8	11 12 13 14 15	18 19 20 21 22	25 26 27 28 29	
Wanda	Axel	n	y y y y y	n n n n n	y y n n n	y y n n n	Austin
	Brigitt						
	Carl						
	Dirk						
Xynthia	Axel						
	Brigitt	n	n n n y y	n n n n n	n y n n n	y y y y y	L. A.
	Carl						
	Dirk						
Yvonne	Axel						
	Brigitt						
	Carl	n	n n n y n	n n n n n	n y n n n	n y n n n	L. A.
	Dirk						
Zarah	Axel						
	Brigitt						
	Carl						
	Dirk	n	n n n y y	n n n n n	y n n n n	y n n n n	Austin

Table 4.1: Overview on initial availability knowledge.

Wanda starts to schedule meeting m_1 by checking Axel's availablility and sug-

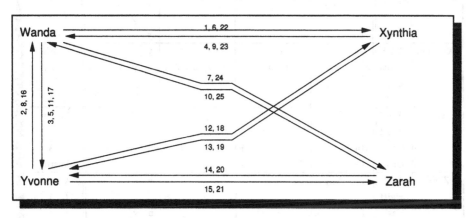

Figure 4.3: Generation of two initial schedule alternatives.

gesting the 4th to Xynthia (1). At about the same time Yvonne suggests the 7th, which is the first date Carl is available, for meeting m_2 (2). Wanda responds by saying the 7th would be okay (3) just before she receives Xynthia's answer that Brigitt is not available on the 4th and the first possible date for Brigitt is the 7th (4). This forces Wanda to resign her acceptance of the 7th for m_2 (5) and to suggest the 7th as the date for m_1 to both Xynthia and Zarah

(6, 7), who both accept (9, 10). Because Wanda requested a change to the proposed date for m_2, Yvonne simultaneously suggests the 19th, which is the next date Carl is available, first to Wanda (8) and later on to Xynthia (12). Both accept (11, 13). Under this first scheduling alternative A1, m_1 would be in Austin and m_2 in L.A. Wanda and Xynthia locally consider this alternative a complete solution. Zarah tries to schedule the secret meeting m_3 and suggests to hold m_3 on the 8th in Austin (14), but Yvonne responds that Carl cannot make the 8th or any other date before the 19th (15). Thus, Wanda asks Yvonne to reschedule m_2, which results in the acceptance of the 26th as an alternative date for m_2 (16, 17, 18, 19). However, this does not allow a third meeting either, because the only date Dirk is available between the 19th and the 26th is the 25th, where Carl is tied up (20, 21). As holding the meetings back-to-back is considered more fruitful anyway, Zarah also approaches Wanda and suggests to reschedule meeting m_1. This rescheduling effort results in the 25th as an alternative to the 7th (22, 23, 24, 25). Thus, a second schedule alternative A2 has been generated, which would allow Dirk and Carl to meet in the evening of the 25th. Tables 4.2 and 4.3 summarize the four secretaries local knowledge and scheduling alternatives at this point.

Agent	Person	Availability on date																					Preference
		1	4	5	6	7	8	11	12	13	14	15	18	19	20	21	22	25	26	27	28	29	
Wanda	Axel	n	y	y	y	y	y	n	n	n	n	n	y	y	n	n	n	y	y	n	n	n	Austin
	Brigitt		n	n	n	y												y					L. A.
	Carl				y														y				L. A.
	Dirk				y													y					Austin
Xynthia	Axel		y		y													y					Austin
	Brigitt	n	n	n	n	y	y	n	n	n	n	n	n	y	n	n	n	y	y	y	y	y	L. A.
	Carl				y										y				y				L. A.
	Dirk																						L. A.
Yvonne	Axel				y								y					y					Austin
	Brigitt												y					y					L. A.
	Carl	n	n	n	n	y	n	n	n	n	n	n	n	y	n	n	n	n	y	n	n	n	L. A.
	Dirk				y													y					Austin
Zarah	Axel				y													y					Austin
	Brigitt																						L. A.
	Carl				n													n	y				L. A.
	Dirk	n	n	n	n	y	y	n	n	n	n	n	y	n	n	n	n	y	n	n	n	n	Austin

Table 4.2: Local knowledge after the initial solution generation stage.

Problem Solving Dynamics: *(See Figure 4.4 and Table 4.4.) Each secretary presents the current solution to her manager. Dirk and Carl are not satisfied, however, because it is really important to meet as soon as possible.*

| | Wanda | | Xynthia | | Yvonne | | Zarah | |
	m_1	m_2	m_1	m_2	m_2	m_3	m_1	m_3
A1	7, Austin	19, L. A.	7, Austin	19, L. A.	19, L. A.	?	7, Austin	?
A2	25, L. A.	26, L. A.	25, L. A.	26, L. A.	26, L. A.	25, L. A.	25, L. A.	25, L. A.

Table 4.3: Local scheduling alternatives after the initial solution generation stage.

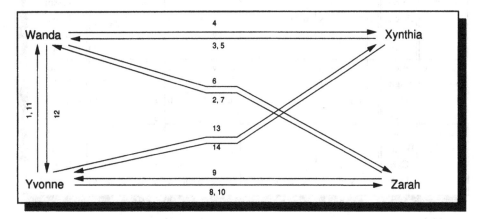

Figure 4.4: Reactions to rescheduling requests and changes in availability.

They request another try to schedule the meetings earlier and both offer to reschedule other meetings in their schedules such that they become available on the 5th and 6th (1, 2). However, it turns out that this does not permit any new scheduling options, because Wanda already knows that Brigitt cannot meet on any date before the 7th. Then Brigitt offers to change her plans for the 18th and to make that date available. Xynthia offers that date for the first meeting to Wanda (3), who takes the opportunity to generate an alternative A3, with m_1 on the 18th (4, 5, 6, 7) and m_2 on the 19th. Under these circumstances, both meetings would be held in L.A. Finally, Carl's plans change and he becomes available on the 8th (8). This change permits Zarah to schedule the third meeting in Austin on the 8th (9, 10), which completes alternative A1 and makes it acceptable to Carl and Dirk. It also allows Yvonne to generate an alternative A4 for meeting m_2 to be held in L.A. on the 8th (11, 12, 13, 14). However, Wanda has now already made other plans for Axel based on the assumption that he is in L.A. on the 19th. Thus, the previous alternative (A3) is chosen as the final plan. Again, Tables 4.4 and 4.5 summarize local knowledge and scheduling alternatives of the four secretaries.

Agent	Person	Availability on date																				Preference
		1	4	5	6	7	8	11	12	13	14	15	18	19	20	21	22	25	26	27	28	29	
Wanda	Axel	n	y	y	y	y	y	n	n	n	n	n	y	y	n	n	n	y	y	n	n	n	Austin
	Brigitt		n	n	n	y							y					y					L. A.
	Carl		y	y	y	y													y				L. A.
	Dirk		y	y	y								y					y					Austin
Xynthia	Axel	y		y														y					Austin
	Brigitt	n	n	n	n	y	y	n	n	n	n	n	y	y	n	n	n	y	y	y	y	y	L. A.
	Carl			y	y									y				y					L. A.
	Dirk																						L. A.
Yvonne	Axel			y	y								y					y					Austin
	Brigitt			y									y					y					L. A.
	Carl	n	n	y	y	y	y	n	n	n	n	n	n	y	n	n	n	n	y	n	n	n	L. A.
	Dirk			y	y													y					Austin
Zarah	Axel			y														y					Austin
	Brigitt																						L. A.
	Carl				y													n	y				L. A.
	Dirk	n	n	y	y	y	y	n	n	n	n	n	y	n	n	n	n	y	n	n	n	n	Austin

Table 4.4: Local knowledge after the final solution generation stage.

	Wanda		Xynthia		Yvonne		Zarah	
	m_1	m_2	m_1	m_2	m_2	m_3	m_1	m_3
A1	7, Austin	19, L. A.	7, Austin	19, L. A.	19, L. A.	8, Austin	7, Austin	8, Austin
A2	25, L. A.	26, L. A.	25, L. A.	26, L. A.	26, L. A.	25, L. A.	25, L. A.	25, L. A.
A3	18, L. A.	19, L. A.	18, L. A.	19, L. A.	19, L. A.	18, L. A.	18, L. A.	18, L. A.
A4	7, L. A.	8, L. A.	7, L. A.	8, L. A.	8, L. A.	7, L. A.	7, L. A.	7, L. A.

Table 4.5: Local scheduling alternatives after the final solution generation stage.

4.1.2   Desirability of Multiagent Assumption-Based Reasoning Support

The example in the previous section exhibits striking similarities to the situation encountered in single agent meeting scheduling. Each agent must solve its local scheduling problems. The agent may have to maintain a (usually small) number of alternative schedules. Each schedule alternative must be conflict-free. An agent may be forced to revise its schedule due to changes in the environment or the task specification. When schedules are revised, care must be taken to ensure schedule consistency, i.e. the introduction of conflicts must be avoided and decisions (e.g. booking flights and hotel rooms) that depend on previous scheduling decisions must be revised as well.

Agents that are faced with the above tasks could use IMSA, the hypothetic Intelligent Meeting Scheduling Assistant of Patricia Perfect. Each secretary's IMSA system would then allow to represent local propositions and dependencies and to solve some of the problems related to belief updates. However, in multiagent problem-solving scenarios the situation is more difficult: assumptions, propositions, and dependencies are often communicated between agents and used by receiving agents in their decision making. Whenever the agent providing such information somehow changes its state, any agent that received such information should be notified. As an example, we consider Wanda and Xynthia. We assume that Wanda has proposed the 7th as meeting date and Xynthia has accepted. If Xynthia has to change Brigitt's schedule such that Brigitt cannot make the 7th any more, everybody would expect Xynthia to inform Wanda about this change and to ask Wanda to reschedule the meeting. Ensuring that all such notifications will always be executed is quite difficult, even if scheduling assistants based on single agent reason maintenance technology (such as IMSA) are used: The IMSA problem solver first has to keep track of what information has been communicated to whom. Next, whenever an update of the RMS database may result in a change of the belief state of such information, the IMSA problem solver must explicitly check this possibility with the RMS. Finally, if the belief status of such information has indeed changed, the IMSA problem solver must communicate that change to all other agents that have received that information.

It is quite obvious, that such an approach would result in an unnecessarily complex problem solver architecture, which would be difficult to build and maintain and probably exhibit unsatisfactory performance. Because communication between problem solvers related to belief updates becomes necessary due to activities of an agent's RMS, the RMS is the module that should handle such communication. Thus, in a multiagent system consisting of RMS-based problem solvers, the agents' RMS modules should be able to communicate directly and take care of all communication necessary due to the exchange and update of beliefs. (A set of) RMS modules with such capabilities are called distributed reason maintenance systems (DRMSs). Thus, in order to provide adequate support for multiagent problem solving, in particular for multiagent planning and scheduling, we need to provide a distributed variant of the XFRMS system presented in Chapter 2.

4.1.3 Subtle Issues in Multiagent Assumption-Based Reasoning

Before actually undertaking an effort to implement a distributed reason maintenance system, a more careful analysis of the problem and the desirable features of a multiagent or distributed RMS is in order. For the single agent case, we argued that a system such as XFRMS supports (single agent) planning and scheduling, because it provides generally useful capabilities for representing and reasoning with planning and scheduling data and knowledge. In particular, XFRMS allows to represent relevant problem solving data — such as propositions, assumptions, and premises — and logical dependencies between them (including conditions for inconsistencies) in the logical language HPL, and its reasoning capabilities included the ability to determine singular consequences, complete contexts, and the consistency of contexts. The update interface of XFRMS also ensured that, whenever the problem solver added dependencies or modified environments, all necessary changes in the XFRMS database were performed. We now need to review and, if necessary, adopt both the logical language used to represent relevant data and dependencies and the reasoning to be performed during query and update operations such that they are suited for multiagent scenarios.

The first issue is to determine what should be considered a proposition in the presence of multiple agents ("believers"). As system developers, we clearly want to be able to distinguish between an agent x's belief in some proposition p (later denoted as $x.p$) and an agent y's belief in p ($y.p$). However, if agents communicate propositions which are stored locally by the receiver and used in its further decision making, then agents themselves should have the ability to distinguish between their own beliefs ($x.p$) and (local representations of) beliefs communicated from other agents (agent x's belief of agent y's belief of p, later denoted as $x:y.p$ and referred to as *communicated beliefs*). If this capability is not provided, strong assumptions about the (global) consistency of the agents' local databases of dependencies must be made. A situation where an agent x believes p to be a premise ($(\top \rightarrow p)$), while another agent y believes p to be a contradiction ($(p \rightarrow \bot)$) and queries x about p, would lead to an inconsistency, which can neither be treated nor resolved. The assumption that all local databases of beliefs and dependencies of all agents that ever communicate with each other can always be merged into a single, global, consistent database seems extremely strong and unjustified for many potential multiagent applications. Thus, a logic is asked for that allows to adequately formalize such situations and still to perform useful reasoning.

It must also be determined whether and how agents can use local representations of communicated beliefs to formulate dependencies. The ability to reference such beliefs in the antecedents of Horn clauses is a must, if agents base their local decision making on such communicated information. In contrast, it seems to make not much sense to permit an agent to formulate clauses with a communicated belief as consequent. Formulating such a clause means changing the conditions for which the consequent is believed. The idea of an agent being able to locally change when another agent is supposed to belief some proposition seems ill-conceived. Thus, this possibility will be excluded from all further discussions.

Next, the influence of communication on an agent's set of relevant propositions and assumptions needs to be investigated. If agents communicate — consider a request that is answered with an appropriate response —, propositions are exchanged (e.g. because they are referred to as assumptions in the environment of a particular query or because they occur in labels exchanged between RMS modules). It is possible, if not likely, that the RMS status of a proposition for the sending and receiving agents do not match. As an example, an assumption used in the environment of a query may not be even known as a relevant proposition by the receiving agent. We refer to this problem as the **congruence problem**. For illustration, Figure 4.5 and Table 4.6 are provided, that summarize all possible situations. If we want to provide a

Figure	Agent X		Agent Y	
Element	relevant?	assumption?	relevant?	assumption?
p1	no	no	yes	no
p2	no	no	yes	yes
p3	yes	no	yes	no
p4	yes	no	yes	yes
p5	yes	yes	yes	no
p6	yes	yes	yes	yes
p7	yes	yes	no	no
p8	yes	no	no	no

Table 4.6: Summary of possible constellations in the congruence problem.

clean formalization for multiagent assumption-based reasoning later on, and in particular, if we want to precisely describe the functionality of a multiagent or distributed reason maintenance system, we need to determine how the various cases illustrated in the figure are handled. Two main approaches are possible:

1. **Denial of Service:** In the first approach, an agent that receives in-

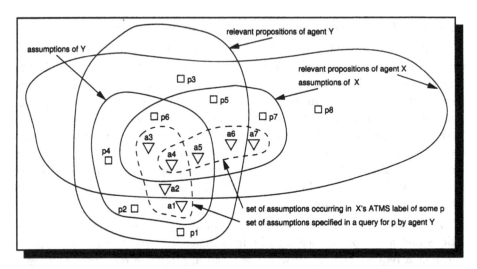

Figure 4.5: Graphical illustration of the congruence problem.

Solid lines refer to relevant propositions and — as subsets — to assumptions of two arbitrary agents. Small rectangles represent arbitrarily chosen elements from the respective sets. Dashed lines illustrate the situation in a scenario based on ATMS-like labels and queries. One dashed line represents assumptions occurring in the label of some proposition, the other the set of assumptions specified by the other agent in its query. The triangles represent arbitrary assumptions from these sets.

formation that has different (metalogical) state simply denies to accept that information. However, the agent should notify the provider of such information about its way of handling it. For instance, if agent x receives a query from agent y specifying some assumption p in the environment that is not considered an assumption by x, it responds by saying something like "*query '....' denied; reason: p not an assumption.*" This would be considered appropriate cooperative behavior in a multiagent system. In Figure 4.5, which illustrates (in dashed lines) the query situation for a distributed RMS using ATMS-like labels and queries, denial of service would occur if y specifies assumptions of type $a1$ and $a2$ in the query. Even if y provides only assumptions of type $a3$ and $a4$, it will get a positive response only, if some subset of $a4$-type assumptions happens to make up an environment in the agent x's label of the proposition.

The denial of service approach prevents the agents' local databases from growing in a way that is not under control of their local problem solvers, and therefore, seems to be very simple. However, it also has a few subtle problems. The first is the situation, where the querying agent specifies assumptions that are just relevant propositions for the queried agent. Recall that we consider making a proposition an assumption to mean nothing else than allowing it in the environments of queries. Being an assumption has no object-level logical meaning. Thus, it may well be that the queried agent is able to derive a proposition, if it considers some of its propositions as additional assumptions, but it would simply deny this service under the first approach.

Another problem is that the resulting query behavior could be extremely dependent on race and timing conditions in communications. Just after denying the service for a query, the local problem solver may initiate RMS updates that result in a situation where the previous query could be processed. If communication conditions and timing had been a little different, these updates may have been already performed when the query arrived and it would have been serviced without complaint. Informing an agent having sent an unsuccessful query later on could solve this problem. However, there is no mechanism to inform the sender of the previous request that answering its request is now possible. Implementing such a mechanism would severely complicate system design: the RMS has to record all denied queries and to keep track of their servicability. This can be very complex and costly.

Of course, the response of an RMS to a query will always be based on its current state of information. Thus, the problem described in the previous paragraph is intrinsic to any RMS as well as any database-like approach. In order to avoid a major portion of queries posed by other agents to be denied, some mechanism would be useful which ensures that the agents' local databases are sufficiently congruent to allow queries be reasonably answered. This idea is somewhat taken up and extended by the second approach.

2. **Assimilation of New Information:** The alternative approach is based on the idea that the (metalogical) state of propositions can change due to communication. Thus, an agent would understand the occurrence of propositions or assumptions in communication as implicit requests to accept their metalogical state and to adopt its local metalogical state accordingly. Figure 4.6 summarizes the possible meta-logical states of an proposition in the context of assumption-based reasoning.

If the queried agent encounters a previously unseen proposition, then this will usually be quite trivial to handle: it cannot occur in any logical dependencies or — as assumption — in environments. The situation is different, however, for already relevant propositions which another agent requires to treat as assumptions in its query ($a2$-type assumptions in Figure 4.5), and great care must be taken to not provoke undesired effects. In a system using ATMS-like labels and label propagation, turning a relevant proposition into an additional assumption can — in the worst case — double the number of environments in the labels, and thereby have dramatic effect on the performance of the overall system. Thus, the

prohibitive computational cost in the case of ATMS-type label exclude
this approach for such systems. Note, though, that the XFRMS system
is not based on ATMS-like labels and seems to fit well with this second
approach.

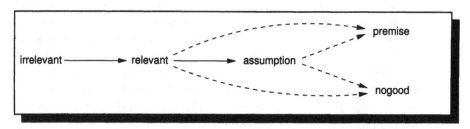

Figure 4.6: The possible metalogical states of a proposition.
Arrows indicate possible state changes.

Agent Autonomy   Another important issue to be considered is agent autonomy. Autonomy is considered a characteristic and desirable property for
agents; some researchers consider it even a defining property [Foner, 1993].
Autonomy is endangered, if communication between the RMS modules of
agents may modify an agent's beliefs in an unexpected way. For example,
if an agent looks only at its own relevant propositions (in contrast to communicated beliefs) and dependencies, there should be no influence whatsoever
from other agents' communicated beliefs. Furthermore, agents should be able
to increase dependence on other agents' beliefs in an autonomous and incremental manner. This allows for the inclusion of beliefs from "trusted" agents,
while beliefs from agents whose database of beliefs seems to be inconsistent
with the agent's local one can be excluded. A useful idea to let an agent keep
track of the above distinction is to tie the set of trusted agents to contexts, or
to explicitly represent the set of trusted agents in contexts. As an example, if
we have a system consisting of ten agents x_1 to x_{10}, then x_1 should be able
to build a context where it trusts (besides itself) agents x_2, x_5, and x_7, while
in another it trusts agents x_3 and x_4. If such a context becomes inconsistent,
i.e. a contradiction is derivable, this could be interpreted as trust in all agents
associated with the context not being justified any more.

4.1.4   Tasks in Multiagent Assumption-Based Reasoning

It was already shown in Chapter 2, that assumption-based reasoning is a difficult problem even for single agent planning and scheduling applications. The
previous sections strongly indicate that the problem is much more difficult

in multiagent assumption-based reasoning, which is ubiquious in multiagent
planning and scheduling. While all the basic planning and scheduling tasks
also occur in the multiagent scenario (often in a more complex form), the
need for a substantial amount of communication between agents in order to
coordinate plans and to keep track of any changes, adds another dimension
of application system complexity. In order to deal with this complexity, we
suggest to adopt the layered architecture approach to multiagent systems as
shown in Figure 4.7. The architecture suggests to implement multiagent plan-

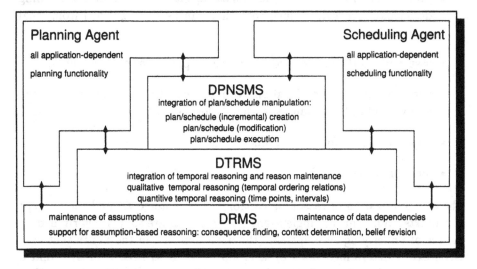

Figure 4.7: The layered architecture approach for multiagent systems.

The base layer is provided by a distributed reason maintenance system (DRMS), which supports multiagent, multiple context, assumption-based reasoning by providing functionality
to reason with assumptions and to maintain dependencies that cross agent boundaries. On
top of the DRMS layer, distributed versions of a TRMS and PNSMS (see Figure 2.1), a
distributed temporal reason maintenance system (DTRMS) and a distributed plan network
and schedule management system (DPNSMS) must be built to provide adequate support for
multiagent planning and scheduling applications. The latter two levels, however, are left for
future work.

ning and scheduling systems based on several layers of general utilities, which
provide common functionality needed for planning and scheduling in a distributed (multiple modules, one for each agent), yet coherent and efficient
fashion. In this book, only the base layer can be handled, where we — in
analogy to the single agent case — suggest a distributed reason maintenance
system (DRMS). As illustrated in the figure, the DRMS can be viewed as a
single module from an architectural perspective, although it can (and often
will) be implemented in a distributed fashion. Each agent has its own DRMS
module, which can communicate with other DRMS modules. However, this
communication is to be kept transparent such that the set of all DRMS modules look like a single system to each of the problem solvers. The specific

capabilities of the DRMS basically encompass those of a single agent RMS
(see 2.1.2), but must take into account the additional requirements arising
from the multiagent scenario. Thus, each DRMS module (to be used by a
particular agent) must be able to represent

- the agent's own relevant propositions (facts representing local planning
  and scheduling decisions),

- propositions from other agents (those agents' planning and scheduling
  decisions) in a fashion such that they can be distinguished from local
  propositions,

- assumptions (facts assumed to be true in particular environments)

- dependencies between local and communicated propositions (restricted
  to a variant of Horn clauses, with only local propositions as consequents)

- local conditions for inconsistencies, and

- local premises.

The characterization of reasoning capabilities is centered around the concept
of contexts. While in the single agent case, contexts are simply determined by
the set of underlying assumptions (the environment), in the multiagent case
a context is determined both by a group (a set of trusted agents)   and a
set of assumptions (assumed by all agents simultaneously). Based on such a
group/environment pair, the reasoning capabilities should include functionality to determine

- single local consequences,

- all local consequences (the local context), and

- the consistency

of the context.

As usual, whenever an agent updates its local database, all necessary dependent modifications to the local database must be performed. In addition,
the DRMS should take over various communication tasks. First, whenever
an agent considers another agent's proposition as relevant, the DRMS module should be able to take care of requesting it from the other agent's DRMS
module and properly add it to the local database. Furthermore, local database
updates that result in modifications concerning other agents as well require
communication to these agents' DRMS modules, all of which should be automatically handled by the local DRMS module.

4.2 Formalization of Multiagent Assumption-Based Reasoning

Similar to our approach in the single agent case, we will first provide a formalism for describing problem solving situations as outlined in the previous section. The logic used here, called FHPL, is one we define specifically for our purposes. The next subsection motivates the need for FHPL by outlining very briefly why existing logics used for reasoning about multiagent systems are considered inadequate for our purposes. The second subsection then formally introduces the FHPL language and calculus, while the third subsection sketches an exemplary formalization of *The Secretaries' Nightmare* example from the previous section.

4.2.1 Logics for Formalizing Multiagent Reasoning

Given the comparatively short history of Distributed AI, the number of formal logics for representing and reasoning about various central aspects of multiagent systems — like knowledge, belief, intentions, goals, and communication — seems astonishingly large.[4] However, many of these aspects are also relevant for single intelligent agent, such as an autonomous mobile robot, which has to take into account other agents in its environment. Therefore, there has been a lot of interest in these aspects in many other subfields of AI as well.

Wooldridge [Wooldridge, 1992] classifies and reviews most of these logics into various categories along syntactic and semantic dimensions. For our purposes, it suffices to apply a rough categorization into modal logics approaches and syntactic theories (metalanguage approaches). Despite of their theoretical appeal, most of these logics in both categories exhibit major problems when applied to practical problems of representing and reasoning about multiagent systems.

Modal Logics of Knowledge and Belief The first kind of logics handles intentional notions by introducing *modal operators*, e.g. K or *Knows* for knowledge and B or *Bel* for belief. For examples, see [Hintikka, 1962], [Halpern and Moses, 1985], [Halpern, 1986], or [Halpern, 1990].[5] When ex-

---

[4]Some examples for formal theories of intentional notions include [Hintikka, 1962], [Moore, 1977], [Moore, 1990], [Konolige, 1982], [Konolige, 1986], and [Cohen and Levesque, 1990a]. Aspects of communication among agents are treated by various speech act theories, e.g. [Searle, 1969], [Appelt and Konolige, 1988], [Cohen and Perrault, 1979], [Cohen and Levesque, 1990b], [Singh, 1991], and [Werner, 1988]. For a short overview, see [Wooldridge and Jennings, 1995]; a more in-depth review is [Wooldridge, 1992]. More introductory texts can be found in [Davis, 1990], chapters 8 to 10, and [Genesereth and Nilsson, 1987], chapters 9, 10, and 13.

[5]For a general introduction into modal logics see [Hughes and Cresswell, 1968], [Chellas, 1980] and [Fitting, 1993].

plicitly dealing with multiple agents, the modal operators are often indexed
with agent identifiers (often just small integers), as for instance in

$$B_x(K_y(\text{location\_of\_ball}))$$

which expresses that agent x believes that agent y knows where the ball is
located. Possible worlds semantics, introduced by Kripke ([Kripke, 1963b],
[Kripke, 1963a]), are commonly applied.

In modal logics, a number of logical axioms are usually required to hold,
which have some far-reaching consequences. Examples for such axioms (from
[Davis, 1990]) for modal operators $\Box, \Diamond$ include the following:

M1	$\phi \to \Box\phi$	knowledge axiom, ϕ
		for all non-modal logical axioms ϕ
M2	$(\Box\phi \wedge \Box(\phi \to \psi)) \to \Box\psi$	consequential closure
M3	$\Box\phi \to \phi$	veridicality
M4	$\Box\phi \to \Box\Box\phi$	positive introspection
M5	$\neg\Box\phi \to \Box\neg\Box\phi$	negative introspection

One problem caused by these axioms[6] is the *logical omniscience problem*.
When substituting $\Box$ with *Bel* or *Knows*, a consequence of the two axioms
M1 and M2 is that an agent must believe/know all logical and mathematical
axioms, including all their consequences. Ernest Davis comments this fact as
follows:

> *This principle is plausible for operators like "Necessarily ϕ" or
> "At all times, ϕ"; all logical truths are necessarily true, and true
> at all times. It is not plausible for operators "I know that ϕ" or "I
> believe that ϕ"; people do not know all the logical consequences of
> their knowledge and they do not know all mathematical theorems.*
> [Davis, 1990, p. 63]

Ernest Davis continues with

> *Despite this implausibility, axioms ...[M1] and [M2]... are part
> of virtually every modal logic, since it seems to be impossible to
> get either interesting logical conclusions or a coherent semantics
> without them.* [Davis, 1990, p. 63]

---

[6]Axiom **M2** is also known as axiom **K** (in honour of Saul Kripke), axiom **M3** as axiom
T, axiom **M4** simply as axiom **4**, and axiom **M5** as axiom **5**, various modal logics are then
often referred to by names like KT45 (e.g. in [Wooldridge, 1992]) indicating which axioms
are included.

and Hector Levesque comments on the logical omniscience problem:

> *Any one of these* [problems] *might cause one to reject a possible-worlds formalization as unintuitive at best and completely unrealistic at worst.* [Levesque, 1984]

Given Davis' opinion on the above axioms M1 and M2, it is somewhat surprising that he finds nothing curious about M3. Applied to a modal operator *Always*, M3 says that what is always true must be true at the current moment, which we can unanimously accept. For the modal operator *Knows*, M3 says that everything an agent "knows" must actually be true. This was — and probably still is — generally accepted by most logicians, although some recent papers [Moses and Shoham, 1993] indicate that there exist different views on what "knowing" is supposed to mean exactly. From a practical perspective, M3 has certainly its problems and is not generally acceptable. For a modal operator *Bel*, even most logicians will concede that M3 is not generally acceptable. Axioms M4 and M5 for modal operators *Knows* or *Bel* together imply that an agent has perfect knowledge/beliefs about what it does and does not know or believe, which is another quite debatable feature of such modal logics, especially to more practically oriented people. Nonetheless, the majority of more well-known modal logics described in the literature include the above axioms.

Aside of the axioms, there are also problems arising from the inference rules commonly used in proof theories for modal logics. In particular, the inference rule of necessitation

$$\frac{\phi}{\Box\phi}$$

raises problems, some of which are related to the logical omniscience problem. Only two issues involving the necessitation rule are briefly mentioned here: *material* axioms, i.e. the base sentences of a theory closed under logical consequence, and applying necessitation to *intentional* modal operators. Regarding material axioms, called "proper" axioms in [Davis, 1990], Davis notes (interpreting $\Box$ as *Necessary*)

> *The inference rule of necessitation, ... is rather curious. The intention is, essentially, to replace axiom ..[M1].. with a slightly stronger statement; all logical theorems are necessarily true. In a theory without proper axioms, ϕ can be inferred as true only if it is a logical theorem, so this rule will be legitimate. It is not, of course, legitimate in a theory with proper axioms; we do not want to infer "Necessarily, John is bald", from the proper axiom, "John is bald". Modal logics are often formulated without considering proper axioms; AI, however, is primarily concerned with theories that do have proper axioms.* [Davis, 1990, p. 64f]

If necessitation already poses problems when used with well-studied operators like *Necessary* or *Always*, this is even more so (including for logical axioms, as pointed out in the discussion of M1 above) for intentional modal operators. In most practical applications, one simply cannot infer that an agent believes or knows a fact if that fact is true.

Although most logicians view the logical omniscience problem as the most significant argument against modal logics of beliefs, there is another quite difficult barrier that prevents their wide-spread practical use. This barrier is an argument related to the possible-worlds semantics that are typically used for intentional modal logics. A (possible-worlds) model for a normal propositional modal logic based on a set P of propositional variables is a so-called *Kripke structure*, typically defined as a triple $\langle W, R, \pi \rangle$, where W is a set of worlds (possible worlds, hence the name), $R \subseteq W \times W$ is a binary relation (known as *accessibility relation*), and π is a valuation function that maps worlds into subsets of P:

$$\pi : W \quad \longrightarrow \quad \mathfrak{P}(P)$$

Kripke structures provide a theoretically appealing model theory for modal logics, in particular, because it has been shown that there is a close correspondence between the axioms and mathematical properties of the accessibility relation R. For example, the **T** axiom requires R to be reflexive, axiom **4** requires R to be transitive, and so on. Correspondence theory studies such relationships between axioms and properties of R. Despite its theoretical nicety, possible-worlds semantics poses a severe practical problem: the ontological status of possible worlds and of the accessibility relation are far from being clear or intuitive when intentional modal logics are used to formalize specific practical problems. Put in Seel's words:

> *The ontology of possible worlds and accessibility relations ... is frankly mysterious to most practically minded people, and in particular has nothing to say about agent architectures.* [Seel, 1989]

Interestingly, this problem has certain similarities to the well-known *(physical symbol) grounding problem* in AI and connectionism.

Finally, there is another disadvantage on top of all the other problems: although Halpern and Moses [Halpern and Moses, 1992] have shown for the most common modal logics[7] that provability is decidable, they also established that the computational complexity of deciding satisfiability and validity is PSPACE-complete.

All the previous comments should not be mistaken as arguments to dismiss modal logics as useless in general; they certainly have their uses (see e.g.

---

[7]$\mathbf{K}_n, \mathbf{T}_n, \mathbf{S4}_n$, weak-$\mathbf{S5}_n$, and$\mathbf{S5}_n$.

[Halpern, 1987]), and they had significant influence and a leading role in the research of intentional notions of agents. However, one must carefully investigate their properties, especially the implications of certain axioms and the consequences for the proof theory, before applying them to practical problems.

In our specific case, none of the common modal logics presents itself as a suitable candidate to formalize multiple-context, assumption-based reasoning in multiagent systems. Almost none of the standard axioms are acceptable in our setting. Giving them all up, poses great difficulties to get useful proof theories and semantics. Not the least of the arguments substantiating the above statement is the argument of grounding semantics.

Syntactic Theories   The main alternatives to modal logics of knowledge and belief are first-order metalanguage logics that model intentional notions as metalanguage predicates, i.e. they treat them as syntactic modalities (see e.g. [Konolige, 1982]). In such a logic, the base formulas to be represented are formulas of a (first-order) object language. These formulas are then, often via some quoting mechanism, treated as terms of another first-order language — the metalanguage —, which provides predicates for modeling intentional notions. For example, the modal logic formula

$$Knows_x(\text{location\_of\_ball})$$

would be represented in a metalanguage logic by a formula similar to

$$Knows(x, \text{location\_of\_ball}).$$

The major advantage of the metalanguage approach seems to be additional expressive power, because certain quantified metalanguage formulas cannot be expressed by an equivalent modal logic formula, e.g. the formulas (following [Wooldridge, 1992])

$$\exists_\phi : B_x(\phi) \qquad \text{x believes something}$$
$$\forall_\phi : [B_x(\phi) \rightarrow B_y(\phi)] \qquad \text{y believes everything x believes}$$

Another advantage often claimed for metalanguage approaches is computational tractability. Wooldridge notes

> *Meta-languages are just many-sorted first-order languages, for which automated theorem provers exist. It should therefore be possible — in principle at least — to use existing theorem provers for meta-languages. However, this claim has yet to be satisfactorily demonstrated.* [Wooldridge, 1992, p. 28]

The main disadvantages of metalanguage approaches is that is quite easy to run into inconsistency, especially in self-referential metalanguage logics, where a single language is used both as object language and metalanguage.[8] This problem is closely related to the truth predicate paradox. An alternative to self-referential languages are hierarchical languages, where a different language is used on each hierarchical level, and higher-level languages may use as terms only formulas of lower-level languages. However, these languages have their own difficulties, e.g. expressional deficiencies: In such languages, it is usually not possible to formally state the following sentence:

x believes that everything y believes is true.

Both self-referential and hierarchical languages often suffer from cumbersome notation, being complex and unintuitive [Konolige, 1986, p. 111].

As for modal logics, neither one of the common metalanguage approaches seems to be directly suited for formalizing multiple-context, assumption-based reasoning in multiagent systems. Compared to the rather simple approach used to define the well-suited and sufficiently rich logic FHPL in the next section, reformulating FHPL as a metalanguage logic was not a primary goal of this work. However, the metalanguage approach seems to pose by far less problems with grounding the semantics. We take this as the main argument to consider metalanguage approaches the more viable path for investigating more powerful scenarios in the future.

Other Approaches Numerous attempts to avoid the disvantages of modal logics or syntactic theories are described in the literature. For example, Moore has presented an approach in which a modal logic is translated into a first-order logic over possible worlds [Moore, 1980]. Another attempt to avoid some of the problems of modal logics and syntactic theories are situation logics; see e.g. [Barwise and Perry, 1983]. A more complete review of these can be found in [Wooldridge, 1992]. At the bottom line, however, none of these attempts really helps us to overcome the major difficulties with the respective approaches as outlined above.

Altogether, the situation can be summarized as follows: Intentional logics are powerful and theoretically appealing, but so far they have not been routinely applied to large problems in practice. Despite of their expressive power, not all practical problem solving aspects can be easily formalized and their semantics are not very intuitive for the practitioner.

When looking closely at our specific problem, formalizing communication and multiple-context assumption-based reasoning in multiagent system, we encounter many of the problems outlined above. For example, when using

---

[8]Don Perlis has extensively treated self-reference in logic in [Perlis, 1985], [Perlis, 1988a], [Perlis, 1988b].

modal logics we are forced to formulate proper axioms to express belief update relationships between agents; furthermore, the problem of defining useful accessibility relations for Kripke structures and finding intuitive interpretations for them must be considered unsolved.

Because there is no suitable logic presenting itself as the ideal candidate for formalizing the kind of reasoning we are interested in, defining a new, specialized logic is advisable. As in the single agent case, where suitable but more powerful than necessary logics already existed and defining a specialized logic was more a formal exercise, we strive for a logic that is as simple as possible and provides just enough power such that we can formalize the kind of reasoning problems we are interested in. Such a logic is presented in the next section.

4.2.2 Facetted Horn Propositional Logic

In this section, we introduce Facetted Horn Propositional Logic, abbreviated FHPL, as the logic being used to formalize the kind of multiagent, multiple context assumption-based reasoning problems presented previously. Because the completeness and cleanliness of the FHPL presentation require some detail that could opaque the central ideas, we present them very shortly beforehand in form of a road map to FHPL. After that, FHPL language syntax and semantics as well as the FHPL calculus are presented in detail.

4.2.2.1 Basic Idea: A Road Map for FHPL

The logic FHPL allows to abstract from some details that we do not want to consider at the logical level in our discussion, e.g. time and synchronization. But it also allows to make explicit relevant notions like distributed representation and concurrent and simultaneous deduction in *multiple, distributed* (logically separated) *reasoning spaces*, which we call *facets*.

- View HPL as defining an imaginary, abstract reasoning space.

- Now imagine several such abtract spaces. We call them *facets* and name them $x_1, x_2, \ldots$, and so forth.

- We extend the syntax such that we can

  1. distinguish between formulas in different facets,
  2. reference atomic formulas from other facets,
  3. use such references in antecedents of clauses, and
  4. write formulas expressing relationships between atomic formulas and references to them.

These extensions are very limited, but we will demonstrate that they suffice for our purposes.

- We define two different semantics for FHPL. One is a straightforward extension of standard semantics for propositional logics, but this turns out to be too restrictive (it makes too many sets of formulas inconsistent). The other one allows more freedom. The latter semantics weakly resembles a Kripke structure. Our semantics are truth-functional.

- The notion of logical consequence must be discussed in-depth. We have the notions of *local*, *group*, and *global* logical consequence. They all use the common notions of *group coherence* and *group consistency*.

- A calculus is defined for FHPL, which uses an additional type of inference rule similar to *Modus Ponens* to model inter-facet communication.

- Several notions of derivability can be defined that match the notions of logical consequence: *local*, *group*, *global* derivability.

- Several important properties must be discussed: *soundness, completeness, base belief* or *literal completeness, deduction theorem, facet theorem*.

Note, that we have a global notion of derivability, which eliminates some intricate problems we encountered in the distributed notion of derivability formerly used for DARMS (see Section 4.4.6).

4.2.2.2   FHPL: Language Syntax

DEFINITION 4.2.1 (FHPL ALPHABET)
The alphabet $\Lambda[\Upsilon, \Sigma]$ of a facetted Horn propositional logic FHPL is determined by two sets $\Upsilon = \{x_1, x_2, \dots\}$ and $\Sigma = \{p_1, p_2, \dots\}$ of atomic symbols. The alphabet $\Lambda_{\mathsf{FHPL}}[\Upsilon, \Sigma]$ consists of the following pairwise disjoint sets of symbols:

1. *a set Σ of propositional variables,*

2. *a set Υ of facet constants,*

3. *the set $\{\top, \bot\}$ of special symbols which represent **verum** and **falsum**,*

4. *the set $\{\wedge, \rightarrow\}$ of logical connectives,*

5. *the set $\{., :, \rightsquigarrow\}$ of facet connectives, and*

6. *the pair of parenthesis ().*

If there is no ambiguity, we abbreviate $\Lambda[\Upsilon, \Sigma]$ to Λ. Vice versa, if it is not clear from the context what type of logic an alphabet is for, we write $\Lambda_{\mathsf{FHPL}}[\Upsilon, \Sigma]$ to distinguish an FHPL alphabet from alphabets of other logics. In order to avoid the necessity to use a lot of parenthesis, we introduce a precedence order $\prec$ on the connectives as follows[9]:

$$\boxed{\,.\,} \;\prec\; \boxed{\,:\,} \;\prec\; \boxed{\rightsquigarrow} \;\prec\; \boxed{\wedge} \;\prec\; \boxed{\rightarrow}$$

The extended alphabet allows for a richer set of formulas in FHPL. Along the way towards the definition of FHPL, a few additional specific subsets of formulas are introduced for reference in later chapters and definitions.

Just like HPL, formulas in FHPL can be divided into two main categories: literals and clauses. First, literals are defined.

DEFINITION 4.2.2 (FHPL LITERALS)
Let $\Lambda[\Upsilon, \Sigma]$ be an alphabet.

1. *The set Γ_{blit} of **base literals** is defined by*

$$\Gamma_{blit} =_{\text{def}} \{x_i.p_j \mid x_i \in \Upsilon \text{ and } p_j \in \Sigma\}.$$

   A literal $x_i.p_j$ is pronounced as "proposition p_j in facet x_i".

2. *The extended set of base literals, denoted by Γ_{blit*}, is defined by*

$$\Gamma_{blit*} =_{\text{def}} \Gamma_{blit} \cup \{x_i.\top \mid x_i \in \Upsilon\} \cup \{x_i.\bot \mid x_i \in \Upsilon\}.$$

3. *The set Γ_{lref} of **base literal references**, sometimes also called remote literals, is defined by*

$$\Gamma_{lref} =_{\text{def}} \{x_i{:}x_j.p_k \mid x_i, x_j \in \Upsilon \text{ and } x_i \neq x_j \text{ and } p_k \in \Sigma\}.$$

   A base literal reference $x_i{:}x_j.p_k$ is pronounced "The facet x_j reference of proposition p_j in facet x_i".

4. *The extended set Γ_{lref*} of base literal references is defined by*

$$\Gamma_{lref*} =_{\text{def}} \Gamma_{lref} \cup \{x_i{:}x_j.\top \mid x_i, x_j \in \Upsilon\} \cup \{x_i{:}x_j.\bot \mid x_i, x_j \in \Upsilon\}.$$

5. *The set Γ_{lit} of **literals** and the extended set of literals are then defined as follows:*

$$\Gamma_{lit} =_{\text{def}} \Gamma_{blit} \cup \Gamma_{lref} \qquad \text{and} \qquad \Gamma_{lit*} =_{\text{def}} \Gamma_{blit*} \cup \Gamma_{lref*}$$

---

[9]Connectives are boxed for better readability.

Note, that the outermost facet constant of any literal uniquely associates that literal to a facet, if we view facets as abstract reasoning spaces. For use in later definitions, two functions for accessing the facet and the proposition of a literal are defined as follows:

$$\text{facet} : \Gamma_{\text{lit}*} \longmapsto \Upsilon \qquad\qquad \text{prop} : \Gamma_{\text{lit}*} \longmapsto \Sigma$$

$$\text{facet}(\phi) = \begin{cases} x_i & \text{iff } \phi = x_i.p_k \\ x_j & \text{iff } \phi = x_j{:}x_i.p_k \end{cases} \qquad \text{prop}(\phi) = \begin{cases} p_k & \text{iff } \phi = x_i.p_k \\ p_k & \text{iff } \phi = x_j{:}x_i.p_k \end{cases}$$

Literals are the atomic formulas in FHPL. Like in HPL, the only complex formulas in FHPL are clauses. For FHPL four distinct sets of clauses are defined. The first three sets are Horn, premise, and nogood clauses, almost as in HPL, except that FHPL has different kind of literals. In addition, Horn and nogood clauses in FHPL may refer to base literal references in their antecedents:

DEFINITION 4.2.3 (FHPL FACET CLAUSES)
Let $\Lambda[\Upsilon, \Sigma]$ be an alphabet and Γ_{blit} and Γ_{lit} be sets of literals.

1. *The set Γ_{Horn} of **Horn clauses** is defined by*

$$\Gamma_{Horn} =_{\text{def}} \{ (\Phi \to \varphi) \mid \varphi \in \Gamma_{blit}$$
$$\text{and } \forall_{\phi_i \in \Phi} : [\phi_i \in \Gamma_{lit} \text{ and } \text{facet}(\phi_i) = \text{facet}(\varphi)] \}.$$

2. *The set Γ_{prem} of **premise clauses** is defined by*

$$\Gamma_{prem} =_{\text{def}} \{ (x_i.\top \to \varphi) \mid \varphi \in \Gamma_{blit} \text{ and } \text{facet}(\varphi) = x_i \}.$$

3. *The set Γ_{nogood} of **nogood clauses** is defined by*

$$\Gamma_{nogood} =_{\text{def}} \{ (\Phi \to x_i.\bot) \mid \forall_{\phi_i \in \Phi} : [\phi_i \in \Gamma_{lit} \text{ and } \text{facet}(\phi_i) = x_i] \}.$$

*The set Γ_{fcl} of **intra-facet clauses**, or briefly **facet clauses**, contains all Horn, nogood and premise clauses, i.e.*

$$\Gamma_{fcl} =_{\text{def}} \Gamma_{Horn} \cup \Gamma_{prem} \cup \Gamma_{nogood}$$

Note, that each Horn, premise, or nogood clause can refer to literals of a single facet only. Thus, such clauses can be uniquely assigned to a facet, just like literals, by extending the function facet as follows:

$$\text{facet} : \Gamma_{fcl} \cup \Gamma_{\text{lit}*} \longmapsto \Upsilon$$

$$\text{facet}(\phi) = \begin{cases} \text{facet}(\phi) & \text{iff } \phi \in \Gamma_{\text{lit}*} \\ \text{facet}(\varphi) & \text{iff } \phi = (\Phi \to \varphi) \in \Gamma_{fcl} \end{cases}$$

Additionally, we define a function propset for retrieving all propositional variables from a facet clause as follows:

$$\text{propset} \; : \; \Gamma_{\text{fcl}} \cup \Gamma_{\text{lit}*} \longmapsto \mathfrak{P}(\Sigma)$$

$$\text{propset}(\phi) = \begin{cases} \{\text{prop}(\phi)\} & \text{iff } \phi \in \Gamma_{\text{lit}*} \\ \{\text{prop}(\varphi)\} \cup \{\text{prop}(\phi_i) \mid \phi_i \in \Phi\} & \text{iff } \phi = (\Phi \rightarrow \varphi) \in \Gamma_{\text{fcl}} \end{cases}$$

Furthermore, we sometimes use functions cons and antes to retrieve the consequent and the set of antecedents of a clause.

The fourth kind of clauses in FHPL are clauses that allow to express links between literals in different facets. Such clauses are called contract clauses.

DEFINITION 4.2.4 (FHPL CONTRACT CLAUSES)
Let $\Lambda[\Upsilon, \Sigma]$ be an alphabet and Γ_{blit*} and Γ_{lref*} be sets of literals.
*The set Γ_{ccl} of **inter-facet clauses** or **contract clauses** is defined by*

$$\Gamma_{ccl} =_{\text{def}} \{ (x_i.\phi \rightsquigarrow x_j:x_i.\phi) \mid x_i.\phi \in \Gamma_{blit*} \text{ and } x_j:x_i.\phi \in \Gamma_{lref*} \}.$$

For a contract clause $(x_i.\phi \rightsquigarrow x_j:x_i.\phi)$, the base literal $x_i.\phi$ is called *contract source object*, x_i is called *contractor* or *sender*, the base literal reference $x_j:x_i.\phi$ is also called *contract delivery object*, and x_j is called the *subscriber* or *receiver*. Occasionally, the functions source and dest are used to retrieve the contract source object and the contract delivery object, respectively, of a contract clause.

Note, that contract clauses cannot be assigned to a single facet. Rather, one can imagine such clauses as facet connectors that link a base literal in one facet to a base literal reference in the other facet. The name contract clauses has been chosen to capture and illustrate the intented use of such clauses: to express that a contract exists between the two facets involved to the effect that whenever the local base literal of the contractor holds, then the base literal reference of the subscriber should hold as well. This intuition will be supported by the semantics defined for FHPL later on.

Before completing the definition of the language, we first introduce the function facetset and extend and complete the definitions of prop and propset to cover contract clauses as well.

$$\text{facetset} \; : \; \mathcal{L}_{\text{FHPL}} \longmapsto \mathfrak{P}(\Upsilon)$$

$$\text{facetset}(\phi) = \begin{cases} \{\text{facet}(\phi)\} & \text{iff } \phi \in \Gamma_{\text{lit}*} \text{ or } \phi \in \Gamma_{\text{fcl}} \\ \{\text{facet}(\text{source}(\phi)), \text{facet}(\text{dest}(\phi))\} & \text{iff } \phi \in \Gamma_{\text{ccl}} \end{cases}$$

For contract clauses, prop is extended as follows:

$$\text{prop} \; : \; \Gamma_{\text{ccl}} \cup \Gamma_{\text{lit}*} \longmapsto \Sigma$$

$$\text{prop}(\phi) = \begin{cases} \text{prop}(\phi) & \text{iff } \phi \in \Gamma_{\text{lit}*} \\ \text{prop}(\text{source}(\phi)) & \text{iff } \phi \in \Gamma_{\text{ccl}} \end{cases}$$

Then, the propset function is also easily extended to cover contract clauses:

$$\text{propset} : \mathcal{L}_{\text{FHPL}} \longmapsto \mathfrak{P}(\Sigma)$$

$$\text{propset}(\phi) = \begin{cases} \{\text{prop}(\phi)\} & \text{iff } \phi \in \Gamma_{\text{lit}*} \text{ or } \phi \in \Gamma_{\text{ccl}} \\ \{\text{prop}(\varphi)\} \cup \{\text{prop}(\phi_i) \mid \phi_i \in \Phi\} & \text{iff } \phi = (\Phi \rightarrow \varphi) \in \Gamma_{\text{fcl}} \end{cases}$$

Natural extensions of the facetset and propset functions to *sets of formulas* $\Phi \subseteq \mathcal{L}_{\text{FHPL}}$ are the functions facetset* and propset*:

$$\text{facetset}* : \mathfrak{P}(\mathcal{L}_{\text{FHPL}}) \longmapsto \mathfrak{P}(\Upsilon)$$

$$\text{facetset}*(\Phi) = \bigcup_{\phi_i \in \Phi} \text{facetset}(\phi_i)$$

$$\text{propset}* : \mathfrak{P}(\mathcal{L}_{\text{FHPL}}) \longmapsto \mathfrak{P}(\Sigma)$$

$$\text{propset}*(\Phi) = \bigcup_{\phi_i \in \Phi} \text{propset}(\phi_i)$$

Based on the above definitions, the language for FHPL can be fixed as follows:

DEFINITION 4.2.5 (FHPL WELL-FORMED FORMULAS)
Let $\Lambda[\Upsilon, \Sigma]$ be an alphabet and Γ_{lit*}, Γ_{fcl}, and Γ_{ccl} be sets of literals and clauses. The set of all well-formed formulas of a facetted Horn propositional language $\mathcal{L}_{\text{FHPL}}$ is defined as follows:

$$\mathcal{L}_{\text{FHPL}} =_{\text{def}} \Gamma_{wff} =_{\text{def}} \Gamma_{lit*} \cup \Gamma_{fcl} \cup \Gamma_{ccl}$$

For reference in later sections, we now define the reduction of a set of FHPL formulas to a group of facets as follows:

DEFINITION 4.2.6 (GROUP REDUCTION)
*Let Γ be an arbitrary set of formulas from $\mathcal{L}_{\text{FHPL}}$ and $g = \{x_1, \ldots, x_k\} \subseteq \Upsilon$ be a set of facet constants called a **facet group** or simply **group**. The **reduction of Γ to the facet group g**, or briefly g reduction of Γ, is defined as follows:*

$$\Gamma_{\lceil g \rceil} =_{\text{def}} \Gamma_{\lceil x_1, \ldots, x_k \rceil} =_{\text{def}} \{\phi \mid \phi \in \Gamma \text{ and } \text{facetset}(\phi) \subseteq g\}$$

Thus, $\Gamma_{\lceil g \rceil}$ contains just all facet clauses of Γ that belong into one of the facets in group g and all contract clauses between the facets of the group.

Obviously, the following property holds:

$$\text{facetset}*(\Gamma_{\lceil g \rceil}) = \text{facetset}*(\Gamma_{\lceil x_1, \ldots, x_k \rceil}) \subseteq \{x_1, \ldots, x_k\} = g$$

This concludes the definition of syntactic concepts. The next section is devoted to assign meaning to sentences of FHPL. In order to have an example available for discussions of semantic concepts, we provide one here.

EXAMPLE 4.2.1 (A SMALL DOMAIN THEORY)
Let Γ be the following set of formulas:

$(x.\top \to x.t)$		$(x.s \to x.\bot)$
$(x.a \to x.p)$		
$(x.b \to x.q)$		$(y.b \to y.\bot)$
$(x.c \to x.u)$	$(x.u \rightsquigarrow y\!:\!x.u)$	$(y.d \to y.v)$
$(x.u \wedge x\!:\!y.v \to x.w)$	$(y.v \rightsquigarrow x\!:\!y.v)$	$(y.v \wedge y\!:\!x.u \to y.r)$

All formulas in the left column are facet x formulas $(= \Gamma_{\lceil x \rceil})$, all formulas on the right are facet y $(= \Gamma_{\lceil y \rceil})$ formulas. The contract clauses in the middle are only in the reduction to group $g = \{x, y\}$, which is in this case equal to all formulas of the given set: $\Gamma_{\lceil x,y \rceil} = \Gamma$.

In later discussions, the following three formulas will be referred to:

$$(x.\top \to x.s)$$
$$(y.t \to y.\bot)$$
$$(y.q \to y.\bot)$$

4.2.2.3   FHPL: Language Semantics

Having defined the language, the task on hand is now to define an appropriate semantics for it. There are basically two approaches:

1. **ω-semantics** assigns truth values to propositional constants and disregards all facet constants: a literal ($x_i.p$ or $x_j\!:\!x_i.p$ is assigned the truth value $\top$ iff its propositional constant p is assigned the value $\top$. In effect, ω-semantics "strips off" all facet constants, thereby reducing any set of FHPL formulas to a set of HPL formulas, and applies standard propositional semantics to the resulting set.

2. **α-semantics** consists of two relations that can be understood as truth tables for the facet connectives . and :. One relation serves to directly assign truth values to base literals; an alternative interpretation is that each facet gets its own interpretation function and that this relation is just the union of all local interpretation functions. The other relation defines the truth value of base literal references in terms of the truth value of the base literals. It can be interpreted as a set of proposition-specific update contracts between the facets.

The following definitions formally define these two semantics.

DEFINITION 4.2.7 (ω-INTERPRETATION OF FHPL)
Let $\mathcal{L}_{\mathsf{FHPL}}$ be a facetted Horn propositional language over an alphabet $\Lambda[\Upsilon, \Sigma]$.

An ω-interpretation of $\mathcal{L}_{\mathsf{FHPL}}$, denoted by I_ω, is a structure

$$I_\omega =_{\text{def}} \langle \mathcal{L}_{\mathsf{FHPL}}, \omega \rangle$$

where ω is mapping

$$\omega : \Sigma \longmapsto \{T, F\}$$

that assigns a truth value to each propositional variable in Σ.
*For a given I_ω-interpretation, a **truth assignment function** ν_ω,*

$$\nu_\omega : \mathcal{L}_{\mathsf{FHPL}} \longmapsto \{T, F\}$$

is uniquely defined on $\mathcal{L}_{\mathsf{FHPL}}$ as follows:

1. *In any facet, the special symbol $\top$ is always true and the special symbol $\bot$ is always false:*

$$\nu_\omega(x_i.\top) = T \text{ and } \nu_\omega(x_i.\bot) = F$$

2. *Base literals are assigned the value that ω assigns to the propositional variable of that literal:*

$$\nu_\omega(x_i.p_j) = \omega(x_i.p_j)$$

3. *Base literal references are assigned the same value that is assigned to the base literal:*

$$\nu_\omega(x_i{:}x_j.p_k) = \nu_\omega(x_j.p_k)$$

4. *Intra-facet clauses are true if and only if the consequent literal is true or one of the antecedent literals is false :*

$$\nu_\omega((\Phi{\to}\varphi)) = \begin{cases} T & \text{iff } \nu_\omega(\varphi) = T \text{ or exists } \phi_k \in \Phi \; : \; \nu_\omega(\phi_k) = F \\ F & \text{otherwise} \end{cases}$$

5. *Contract clauses are true if and only if the contract source object and contract delivery object are assigned the same truth value*

$$\nu_\omega((\phi{\rightsquigarrow}\varphi)) = \begin{cases} T & \text{iff } \nu_\omega(\phi) = \nu_\omega(\varphi) \\ F & \text{otherwise} \end{cases}$$

Note, that ω-semantics is very restrictive: only sets of formulas that are consistent in HPL are consistent in FHPL under these semantics. The set of formulas in Example 4.2.1, for instance, is material inconsistent. This is often too restrictive, because this amounts to a global consistency criterion in multiagent systems.

DEFINITION 4.2.8 (α-INTERPRETATION OF FHPL)
*Let $\mathcal{L}_{\mathsf{FHPL}}$ be a facetted Horn propositional language over an alphabet $\Lambda[\Upsilon, \Sigma]$.
An α-**interpretation** of $\mathcal{L}_{\mathsf{FHPL}}$, denoted by I_α, is a structure*

$$I_\alpha =_{\text{def}} \langle \mathcal{L}_{\mathsf{FHPL}}, \alpha, \kappa \rangle$$

where α is a binary relation

$$\alpha \subseteq \Upsilon \times \Sigma$$

providing a truth table for the facet connective . and κ is a ternary relation

$$\kappa \subseteq \Upsilon \times \Upsilon \times \Sigma$$

*providing a truth table for the facet connective :.
For a given I_α-interpretation, a **truth assignment function** ν_α,*

$$\nu_\alpha : \mathcal{L}_{\mathsf{FHPL}} \longmapsto \{T, F\}$$

is uniquely defined on $\mathcal{L}_{\mathsf{FHPL}}$ as follows:

1. *In any facet, the special symbol $\top$ is always true and the special symbol $\bot$ is always false:*

$$\nu_\alpha(x_i.\top) = T \quad \text{and} \quad \nu_\alpha(x_i.\bot) = F$$

2. *Base literals are true if the pair consisting of its facet constant and propositional variable is in the relation α:*

$$\nu_\alpha(x_i.p_j) = \begin{cases} T & \text{iff} \langle x_i, p_j \rangle \in \alpha \\ F & \text{otherwise} \end{cases}$$

3. *Base literal references are true, if the referred base literal is true and the triple consisting of subscriber, contractor and propositional variable is in the relation κ:*

$$\nu_\alpha(x_i{:}x_j.p_k) = \begin{cases} T & \text{iff} \ \nu_\alpha(x_j.p_k) = T \text{ and } \langle x_i, x_j, p_k \rangle \in \kappa \\ F & \text{otherwise} \end{cases}$$

4. *Facet clauses are true if and only if the consequent literal is true or one of the antecedent literals is false:*

$$\nu_\alpha((\Phi{\rightarrow}\varphi)) = \begin{cases} T & \text{iff} \ \nu_\alpha(\varphi) = T \text{ or exists } \phi_k \in \Phi : \nu_\alpha(\phi_k) = F \\ F & \text{otherwise} \end{cases}$$

5. *Contract clauses are true if and only if the contract source object and contract delivery object are assigned the same truth value and the triple consisting of subscriber, contractor and propositional variable is in the relation κ:*

$$\nu_\alpha((\phi \leadsto \varphi)) = \begin{cases} T & \text{iff } \nu_\alpha(\phi) = \nu_\alpha(\varphi) \text{ and } \langle x_i, x_j, p_k \rangle \in \kappa \\ F & \text{otherwise} \end{cases}$$

The two semantics can be illustrated using the example presented in the syntax section:

EXAMPLE 4.2.2 (SEMANTICS OF THE EXAMPLE DOMAIN THEORY)
Let Γ be the set of FHPL formulas defined in Example 4.2.1. An ω-interpretation I_ω that makes all formulas in Γ true and, thus, is a model for Γ, is given by the following interpretation function ω:

$$\omega : \text{FHPL} \longmapsto \{T, F\}$$

$$\omega(\phi) = \begin{cases} T & \text{iff } \phi \in \{a, c, d, p, q, r, t, u, v, w\} \\ F & \text{iff } \phi \in \{b, s\} \end{cases}$$

Note, that under ω-semantics, there exists no model for Γ with $\omega(b) = T$.

Using α-semantics such models can be easily constructed. An example would be the α-interpretation I_α based on relation α and κ as follows:

$$\alpha = \{ \langle v, \sigma \rangle \mid v \in \{x, y\} \text{ and } \sigma \in \Sigma \smallsetminus \{s\} \}$$
$$\kappa = \{ \langle x, y, v \rangle, \langle y, x, u \rangle \}$$

ω-semantics reduces all FHPL formulas to their HPL or classical logic equivalent, thereby discarding all interesting information about agents and enforcing each clause as a global consistency constraint. α-semantics is better suited for situations where global consistency of the local beliefs of all agents cannot be guaranteed. Here, each facet representing an agent can be viewed to provide its own local interpretation for the base literals in that facet and to accept the base literal interpretations of all other facets for interpreting any base literal reference. Most of the notions discussed below can be defined for ω-semantics as well, although the restriction regarding global consistency stated above always applies. In our further discussion, however, we concentrate on α-semantics, because it seems much more appropriate for the multiagent domain.

A formula ϕ is said to be α-satisfiable, iff there exists an I_α-interpretation with $\nu_\alpha(\phi) = T$. In this case, I_α is said to be an α-model or simply a model for the formula ϕ. If no such α-model exists, ϕ is said to be α-unsatisfiable or simply unsatisfiable. An interpretation I_α is said to be a α-model or just model of a set Γ of FHPL formulas iff I_α is a α-model for every formula $\phi \in \Gamma$. In this case, Γ is called consistent in I_α. If no such model exists, then Γ is said to be inconsistent. A formula ϕ is called a logical consequence of a set of formulas Γ, denoted by

$$\Gamma \models_{\mathsf{FHPL}} \phi$$

iff every model of Γ is also a model of ϕ. Note, that the logical consequence relation trivially holds for any formula ϕ if Γ is inconsistent, i.e. if Γ has no model (*ex falso quod libet*). In particular, any falsum literal is a logical consequence of an inconsistent set of formulas:

$$\Gamma \;\; \text{(globally) inconsistent} \quad \Longrightarrow \quad \Gamma \models_{\mathsf{FHPL}} x_i.\bot \;\; \text{for all } x_i \in \Upsilon$$

Thus, the latter property is often used to characterize inconsistency.

The notions of consistency and logical consequence can be supplemented with more fine-grained variants as follows:

DEFINITION 4.2.9 (GROUP CONSISTENCY AND GROUP CONSEQUENCE)
Let $\Gamma \subseteq \mathcal{L}_{\mathsf{FHPL}}$ be an arbitrary set of FHPL formulas and the set

$$g = \{x_1, \dots, x_k\} \subseteq facetset*(\Gamma) \subseteq \Upsilon$$

*be a set of facets called a **group**.*

1. *The set Γ is called **g-consistent** iff there exists a model for $\Gamma_{\lceil g \rceil} = \Gamma_{\lceil x_1, \dots, x_k \rceil}$*

2. *A formula $\phi \in \mathcal{L}_{\mathsf{FHPL}}$ is called a **g-consequence** of Γ, denoted by $\Gamma \models_g \phi$, iff every model of $\Gamma_{\lceil g \rceil}$ is also a model for ϕ:*

$$\Gamma \models_g \phi \quad \Longleftrightarrow \quad \Gamma_{\lceil g \rceil} \models_{\mathsf{FHPL}} \phi$$

Group consistency is a form of *common* or *shared* consistency in a group of agents in the sense, that none of the agents can locally derive a contradiction from a common or shared set of assumptions. Group consequence is also tagged as *joint* consequence, because the justifications of a group, distributed across the group agents, contribute all to the consequence relation. To illustrate these concepts, we provide a few examples related to the previously defined domain theory Γ:

EXAMPLE 4.2.3 (GROUP CONSISTENCY AND GROUP CONSEQUENCE)
We assume the set Γ of FHPL formulas as defined in Example 4.2.1 and the I_α-interpretation as defined in Example 4.2.2. The set $\Gamma' = \Gamma \cup \{x.a, y.a\}$ is g-consistent for any of the groups

$$g_1 = \{x\} \qquad\qquad g_2 = \{y\} \qquad\qquad g_3 = \{x, y\}$$

and $x.p$ is g-consequence of Γ' for all three groups. In contrast, the set $\Gamma'' = \Gamma \cup \{x.b, y.b\}$ is g-consistent only for group g_1, but neither for g_2 nor for g_3. Note, that if y would contain the formula $(y.q \rightarrow y.\bot)$ instead of $(y.b \rightarrow y.\bot)$, then Γ'' would be g-consistent for all three groups! Due to the definition of g-consequence, $x.q$ is g-consequence of Γ'' for all three groups. Finally, the set $\Gamma''' = \Gamma \cup \{x.c, y.d\}$ is g-consistent for all three groups. Both $x.w$ and $y.r$ are g-consequence of Γ''' for group g_3, but neither for g_1 nor for g_2.

LEMMA 4.2.1 (GROUP CONSISTENCY)
A set Γ is g-consistent iff $\forall_{x_i \in g} : \Gamma_{\lceil g \rceil} \not\models_{\textsf{FHPL}} x_i.\bot$.

The lemma states that in order to determine group consistency, we need to look only at facet formulas of the facets in the group and the contract clauses between facets of the group. We sometimes abbreviate the condition stated in Lemma 4.2.1 to $\Gamma_{\lceil g \rceil} \not\models_{\textsf{FHPL}} g.\bot$.

PROOF 4.2.1 (GROUP CONSISTENCY)
i) If Γ is g-consistent, then by definition there exists at least one model for $\Gamma_{\lceil g \rceil}$. In any model, all falsum literals must be valued F. In particular, this holds for all falsum literals of the group, and thus, for none of them can hold the right side.

ii) The other direction is done by diagonalization. Assume the right hand side of the lemma holds, i.e. $\exists_{x_i \in g} : \Gamma_{\lceil g \rceil} \models_{\textsf{FHPL}} x_i.\bot$. It directly follows, that there can be no model for $\Gamma_{\lceil g \rceil}$, and thus, Γ cannot be g-consistent. □

THEOREM 4.2.1 (MONOTONICITY OF GROUP CONSEQUENCE)
The group consequence relation is monotonic in g and Γ. Formally: for arbitrary sets Γ, Γ' of formulas and arbitrary groups g, g' the following condition holds:

$$\Gamma \models_g \phi \quad \Longrightarrow \quad \Gamma \cup \Gamma' \models_{g \cup g'} \phi \tag{4.1}$$

PROOF 4.2.2 (MONOTONICITY OF GROUP CONSEQUENCE)
Using the definition of group consequence, (4.1) can be rewritten as

$$\Gamma_{\lceil g \rceil} \models_{\textsf{FHPL}} \phi \quad \Longrightarrow \quad \Gamma \cup \Gamma'_{\lceil g \cup g' \rceil} \models_{\textsf{FHPL}} \phi,$$

which is fulfilled especially in the case that the set of models $\mathcal{M}'$ for $\Gamma \cup \Gamma'_{\lceil g \cup g' \rceil}$ is no larger than the set of models $\mathcal{M}$ for $\Gamma_{\lceil g \rceil}$, i.e. if

$$\mathcal{M}' \subseteq \mathcal{M}$$

Because of

$$\Gamma_{\lceil g \rceil} \quad \subseteq \quad \Gamma \cup \Gamma'_{\lceil g \cup g' \rceil}$$

every interpretation that satisfies all formulas of $\Gamma \cup \Gamma'_{\lceil g \cup g' \rceil}$ is necessarily also a model for $\Gamma_{\lceil g \rceil}$, thus $\mathcal{M}' \subset \mathcal{M}$. □

For $\Gamma \subseteq \Gamma''$ and $g \subseteq g''$, the following two conditions are specialization of the previous theorem:

$$\Gamma \models_g \phi \quad \Longrightarrow \quad \Gamma'' \models_g \phi$$
$$\Gamma \models_g \phi \quad \Longrightarrow \quad \Gamma \models_{g''} \phi$$

Both the notion of g-consistency as well as g-consequence are based on the reductions of a formula set to a group. The reduction mechanism provides a very flexible mechanism to consider only a subset of the facets defined by a group. Varying the group under consideration provides a flexible means to take into account more or less facets. For singletons $g = \{x_i\}$, g-consistency and g-consequence reduce to *local consistency* (there exists a model at least for the set of all intra-facet formulas of facet x_i) and *local consequence* (a formula is logical consequence already of a set of intra-facet formulas in facet x_i). If the group g encompasses all facets, then g-consistency for a set Γ of formulas (i.e. there exists a model for Γ) only means that an interpretation exists that makes all formulas in Γ true, and g-consequence only means that possibly all formulas in Γ can contribute to ϕ being a logical consequence. It does not at all imply that any two agents agree on the truth of some proposition, i.e. assign the same truth value to it (see the example below). This is desirable, however, at least for propositions to be treated as assumptions, i.e. a mechanism is required that guarantees the agreement of agents on the truth of certain propositions. This concept is group coherence, which is defined as follows:

DEFINITION 4.2.10 (GROUP COHERENCE)
Let $\Gamma \subseteq \mathcal{L}_{\mathsf{FHPL}}$ be an arbitrary set of formulas in FHPL *and $g \subseteq facetset*(\Gamma) \subseteq \Upsilon$ be a group. Γ is called **g-coherent** iff the following condition holds:*

$$\forall_{x_i \in g} \forall_{\phi \in \Sigma} : [\, x_i.\phi \in \Gamma \quad \Longrightarrow \quad \forall_{x_j \in g} : [\, x_j.\phi \in \Gamma \,]\,]$$

Thus, if a set of formulas is g-coherent, then a propositional variable occurring in a base literal of an arbitrary facet in the group must also occur as base literal in all other facets of the group. This limits the models of that set to those interpretations where all agents of the group assign the same truth value to a proposition. If we view the base literals of a set of formulas Γ as assumptions, then Γ being g-coherent means that all agents make the same assumptions in terms of propositional variables, and that the set of base literals represents a *common* or *shared* environment.

From an assumption-based reasoning perspective, an interesting situation obviously is

$$\Gamma \models_g \phi \quad \text{and} \quad \Gamma \not\models_g g.\bot$$

i.e. a formula is g-consequence of Γ and Γ is g-consistent. An even more interesting situation is one where, in addition to the previous condition, the set Γ is g-coherent.

4.2.2.4   FHPL: Calculus

A calculus is now defined for FHPL, which is sound and literal complete with respect to α-semantics. The calculus uses two variants of modus ponens as deduction rules. The first is the usual modus ponens, now called local modus ponens (LMP). It allows to derive formulas only *within* a facet. The second kind of inference rule is called contract modus ponens (CMP) and introduces inference steps that *cross* facet boundaries.

DEFINITION 4.2.11 (FHPL CALCULUS)
Let $\mathcal{L}_{\mathsf{FHPL}}$ be a facetted Horn propositional language. The calculus $\mathcal{C}_{\mathsf{FHPL}}$ is a structure

$$\mathcal{C}_{\mathsf{FHPL}} \ =_{\text{def}} \ \langle \Theta, \Xi \rangle$$

where Θ is the following set of axioms

$$\Theta \ =_{\text{def}} \ \{ \ x_i.\top \ | \ x_i \in \Upsilon \ \}$$

and $\Xi \ =_{\text{def}} \ \Xi_{LMP} \cup \Xi_{CMP}$ is the union of the two sets of inference rule schemas Ξ_{LMP} and Ξ_{CMP} that are defined as follows:

$$\Xi_{LMP} \ =_{\text{def}} \ \left\{ \ LMP[x, \phi_1, \ldots, \phi_k, \varphi] \frac{x.\phi_1, \ldots, x.\phi_k, (x.\phi_1 \wedge \ldots \wedge x.\phi_k \to x.\varphi)}{x.\varphi} \ \right\}$$

$$\Xi_{CMP} \ =_{\text{def}} \ \left\{ \ CMP[x, y, \phi] \frac{x.\phi, (x.\phi \rightsquigarrow y{:}x.\phi)}{y{:}x.\phi} \ \right\}$$

The calculus $\mathcal{C}_{\mathsf{FHPL}}$ defines a derivability relation as follows:

DEFINITION 4.2.12 (DERIVABILITY AND GROUP DERIVABILITY)
Let FHPL be a facetted Horn propositional logic with language $\mathcal{L}_{\mathsf{FHPL}}$ and calculus $\mathcal{C}_{\mathsf{FHPL}}$. The calculus uniquely defines a derivability relation $\vdash_{\mathsf{FHPL}}$ as follows:

$$\vdash_{\mathsf{FHPL}} \ \subseteq \ \mathfrak{P}(\mathcal{L}_{\mathsf{FHPL}}) \times \mathcal{L}_{\mathsf{FHPL}}$$

*A formula ϕ is **derivable** from a set Γ (the pair $\langle \Gamma, \phi \rangle$ is in the relation), denoted by*

$$\Gamma \vdash_{\mathsf{FHPL}} \phi$$

iff there exists a finite sequence $\langle \Gamma_1, \ldots, \Gamma_m \rangle$ of sets of formulas as follows:

$$1\Gamma_1 \ = \Gamma$$
$$\Gamma_{i+1} \ = \Gamma_i \cup \{ \ \varphi \ | \ \exists_{(\Phi \to \varphi) \in \Gamma_{fcl}} : \forall_{\phi \in \Phi} : \phi \in \Gamma_i \ \}$$
$$\cup \{ \ \varphi \ | \ \exists_{(\phi \rightsquigarrow \varphi) \in \Gamma_{ccl}} : \phi \in \Gamma_i \ \}$$
$$\phi \in \Gamma_m$$

*A formula ϕ is said to be **g-derivable** (also: g-provable or g-inferable) from a set Γ of formulas iff it is derivable from the reduction of Γ to group g:*

$$\Gamma \vdash_g \phi \qquad \Longleftrightarrow \qquad \Gamma_{\lceil g \rceil} \vdash_{\mathsf{FHPL}} \phi$$

Whenever a logical calculus has been defined, the question arises whether it is sound, complete, etc. The following few theorems clarify these issues.

THEOREM 4.2.2 (SOUNDNESS)
$\mathcal{C}_{\mathsf{FHPL}}$ *is sound.*

PROOF 4.2.3 (SOUNDNESS OF THE FHPL CALCULUS)
Let $\mathcal{C}_{\mathsf{FHPL}} = \langle \Theta, \Xi \rangle$ be a FHPL calculus.

1. *Θ is consistent by definition of I_α-interpretation.*

2. *Every inference rule $LMP[x, \phi_1, \ldots, \phi_k, \varphi]$ from Ξ is sound. We only need to consider models that satisfy all of $x.\phi_1, \ldots, x.\phi_k$. Any such model can then satisfy $(x.\phi_1 \wedge \ldots \wedge x.\phi_k \rightarrow x.\varphi)$ iff it also satisfies $x.\varphi$ by definition of α-semantics. Thus, every model satisfying all preconditions also satisfies the postcondition, and thus, the inference rule is sound.*

3. *Every $CMP[x, y, \phi]$ from Ξ is consistent. The proof is analogous to the previous case.*

$\square$

An argument similar to the single agent case shows that FHPL as defined above is incomplete:

EXAMPLE 4.2.4 (INCOMPLETENESS OF FHPL CALCULUS)
$\mathcal{C}_{\mathsf{FHPL}}$ *is incomplete. Let $\Gamma = \{x.p, x.q\}$. The formula $(x.p \rightarrow x.q)$ is logical, but not deductive consequence, i.e.*

$$\Gamma \models_{\mathsf{FHPL}} (x.p \rightarrow x.q) \qquad but \qquad \Gamma \not\vdash_{\mathsf{FHPL}} (x.p \rightarrow x.q)$$

The reasons are quite similar to those of the incompleteness of HPL: use of only simple modus ponens, absence of logical axioms, and restricted syntax. However, just as for HPL, one can define the notion *literal completeness* for FHPL, which simply says that all literals (base literals *and* literal references) that are logical consequence of a set of formulas are also derivable.

THEOREM 4.2.3 (LITERAL COMPLETENESS)
$\mathcal{C}_{\mathsf{FHPL}}$ *is literal complete, i.e.*

$$\forall_\Gamma \forall_{\phi \in \Gamma_{lit}} : \quad \Gamma \models_{\mathsf{FHPL}} \phi \qquad \Longrightarrow \qquad \Gamma \vdash_{\mathsf{FHPL}} \phi \qquad (4.2)$$

The proof is basically analogous to the HPL case, but we need to cover the additional case of derivations using contract clauses. First, we provide a FHPL variant of Lemma 2.2.1, page 37, which is useful in proving $\mathcal{C}_{\mathsf{FHPL}}$ of literal complete.

LEMMA 4.2.2

An FHPL *literal is logical consequence of a consistent set of formulas if and only if i) the literal is in the set of formulas, or ii) if there exists a facet clause with the literal as consequent and all antecedents of that clause are logical consequences of the set of formulas, or iii) if there exists a contract clause with the literal as contract delivery object and the contract source object is logical consequence of the set of formulas. Formally:*

$$
\Gamma \models_{\mathsf{FHPL}} \psi \iff
\begin{cases}
\psi \in \Gamma \\
\text{or} \quad \exists_{(\Phi \to \varphi) \in \Gamma} : [\, \psi = \varphi \text{ and } \forall_{\phi_i \in \Phi} : \Gamma \models_{\mathsf{FHPL}} \phi_i \,] \\
\text{or} \quad \exists_{(x.p \leadsto y:x.p) \in \Gamma} : [\, \psi = y{:}x.p \text{ and } \Gamma \models_{\mathsf{FHPL}} x.p \,]
\end{cases}
$$

PROOF 4.2.4 (LEMMA 4.2.2)

The proof for direction right to left is trivial: if the right side is given, than any model satisfying Γ must also satisfy ψ by definition of α-semantics.

The proof in the reverse direction is by diagonalization. We assume that ψ is satisfied by every model that satisfies Γ (at least one such model exists, because Γ is consistent), but the right side does not hold, which means that either does ψ occur only as antecedent/source of facet/contract clauses or not at all.

i) If ψ does not occur at all in any formula, then one can construct a model satisfying Γ but not ψ, simply by taking any model of Γ and replacing the truth assignment for ψ with $\nu_\alpha(\psi) = \mathsf{F}$. Contradiction!

ii) If ψ occurs in formulas and is a base literal reference ($\psi = y{:}x.p$), it can by definition of $\mathcal{C}_{\mathsf{FHPL}}$ only occur in antecedents of facet clauses. Removing the tripel $\langle y, x, p \rangle$ from the κ relation of a model yields a model that still satisfies all formulas in Γ, but not ψ. Contradiction!

iii) If ψ occurs in formulas of Γ and is a base literal ($\psi = x.p$), then a model satisfying Γ but not ψ can be constructed by removing the tuple $\langle x, p \rangle$ from the α relation of an arbitrary model of $(\Gamma \cup \{\psi\})$: as a consequence, ψ plus any references to that base literal will be valued F; according to the assumption, ψ occurs only in antecedents of facet clauses and contract clauses; the former are obviously satisfied by the modified model, the latter are also satisfied because all references are valued F as well; the base literal references themselves can — aside of a single contract clause — only occur in antecedents, which are therefore still satisfied. Contradiction!

Hence, there is no model for which the assumption holds, and thus, the lemma holds. □

PROOF 4.2.5 (LITERAL COMPLETENESS OF FHPL CALCULUS)
The proof is by diagonalization and induction on the length of proofs. We show that the negation of the literal completeness condition

$$\Gamma \models_{\mathsf{FHPL}} \phi \quad \text{and} \quad \Gamma \not\vdash_{\mathsf{FHPL}} \phi \tag{4.3}$$

cannot hold for any pair of Γ and ϕ.

Assume condition 4.3 holds. With Lemma 4.2.2, there must exist a facet or contract clause with ϕ as consequent and all its antecedents or its source object are logical consequences of Γ. But then we can apply modus ponens — LMP or CMP — and derive ϕ, which leads to a contradiction to condition 4.3. Hence,

$$\Gamma \vdash_{\mathsf{FHPL}} \phi \tag{4.4}$$

holds and C_{FHPL} is literal complete. □

At this point, two theorems, that are the FHPL analogon to the deduction theorem in HPL or some standard propositional logics, are provided in order to complete the discussion of FHPL. They can be proved in a similar fashion as the deduction theorem for HPL. However, because in the following we do not rely on these theorems, we only present the theorems and omit their proofs here.

THEOREM 4.2.4 (DEDUCTION THEOREM FOR FHPL)
Let Γ be a set of FHPL formulas and $(\Phi \to \varphi)$ a FHPL facet clause, on which the following relationship holds:

$$facetset_*(\Gamma \cup \{(\Phi \to \varphi)\}) \subseteq g$$

Then the following holds:

$$\Gamma \models_g (\Phi \to \varphi) \quad \Longleftrightarrow \quad \Gamma_{\lceil g \rceil} \cup \Phi_{\lceil g \rceil} \models_{\mathsf{FHPL}} \varphi \tag{4.5}$$

The following theorem is the analog to the deduction theorem but for contract clauses:

THEOREM 4.2.5 (FACET THEOREM)
Let Γ be a set of FHPL formulas and $(\phi \leadsto \varphi)$ a FHPL contract clause, on which the following relationship holds:

$$facetset_*(\Gamma \cup \{(\phi \to \varphi)\}) \subseteq g$$

Then the following holds:

$$\Gamma \models_g (\phi \leadsto \varphi) \quad \Longleftrightarrow \quad \Gamma_{\lceil g \rceil} \cup \phi_{\lceil g \rceil} \models_{\mathsf{FHPL}} \varphi \tag{4.6}$$

The value of having a literal complete calculus is similar to the single agent case. We assume a set of problem solvers, each of which has stated a local set of facet clauses expressing data dependencies and which have established a set of belief update contracts for communicated base beliefs; all formulas together denoted by Γ. We further assume that a problem solver wants to decide whether it should believe a certain (local) proposition (a base literal φ) given a set of assumptions (Φ) and on the basis of the clauses of a particular group of facets (agents) g, i.e. it wants to know whether

$$\Gamma \models_g (\Phi \rightarrow \varphi)$$

holds or not. Because FHPL is incomplete, this cannot be directly decided. However, because of the deduction theorem the above problem can be reduced to deciding whether

$$\Gamma_{\lceil g \rceil} \cup \Phi_{\lceil g \rceil} \models_{\mathsf{FHPL}} \varphi$$

holds or not. This can be easily achieved by a literal complete theorem prover for FHPL.

4.2.2.5   Discussion: Some Properties of FHPL

It is worthwhile to review and discuss a few properties of FHPL. First of all, it provides a logical language which allows to formalize assumption-based reasoning problems in a multiagent setting. In particular, on can distinguish syntactically between an agent x's belief in some proposition p ($x.p$), another agent y's belief in proposition p ($y.p$), and agent x's belief about agent y's belief in proposition p ($x{:}y.p$) and vice versa.

The concepts introduced allow for belief autonomy: there is no way that some other facet can force an agent to adopt some local belief.

The group-related concepts introduced and defined above (g-reduction, g-consistency, g-consequence, g-derivability, g-coherence) provide a sound formal basis for discussing multiple-context assumption-based reasoning in multiagent settings. Contexts are determined by an environment *and* a group of facets. This also provides a conceptualization for *distributed proofs* and a localization of proof steps: applications of local modus ponens (LMP) are facet-local derivation steps, while applications of contract modus ponens (CMP) involve cross-facet proof steps.

It should be noted that under g-derivability local modifications to a database of clauses can have non-local effects, i.e. if some agent represented by a facet x adds a local facet clause, the literals derivable in some other facet y may be affected.

It is easy to see, that FHPL encompasses HPL and the expressive power of the basic ATMS.

Note also, that the model of communication is directed: a contract between two facets x (as sender) and y (as receiver) regarding some proposition p does not necessitate a contract in the reverse direction.

It is possible to model *belief merge*: An agent x, which has some local facet clauses with p as consequent can force itself to believe p also in all situations, where y believes p by first establishing a contract for the base belief $y.p$ via the base literal reference $x{:}y.p$ and the according contract clause $(y.p \leadsto x{:}y.p)$, and then by locally adding the facet clause $(x{:}y.p \to x.p)$.

If two or more agents (facets) apply the previous scheme for belief merge for a particular proposition p, the resulting dependency structure ensures that all agents will believe p in the very same contexts. This way, somewhat higher-level concepts like shared beliefs [Bridgeland and Huhns, 1990] can be easily modeled.

4.2.3   A FHPL Formalization of The Secretaries' Nightmare

In analogy to our approach in the single agent case, we want to present an example for the application of the chosen logic — now FHPL— to a practical example. The example is the one already used in the analysis section: the multiagent meeting scheduling problem of Axel, Brigitt, Carl, and Dirk and their four secretaries. The formalization of the problem consists of three major steps:

- Fixing the FHPL language, in particular the sets Σ and Υ which determine the alphabet $\Lambda[\Upsilon, \Sigma]$.

- Formulating the dependencies used by the secretaries to record decision making and reasoning steps.

- Demonstrating how the secretaries can use the resulting problem formalizations in their local problem solving tasks.

Because of the example's length, we do present neither a complete nor a very detailed formalization of the problem; instead, we present the general structure of a very simple formalization. In particular, we restrict the definition of Σ and of the dependencies to schematic characterizations plus a few examples and neglect the explicit representation of status information regarding the negotiation between two agents. Also, all dependencies regarding hotel and flight reservations are left out of consideration. (They are quite similar to the single agent meeting scheduling example; please refer to Section 2.2.3.) A complete formalization can be easily derived, but requires too much space to be represented here.

Conceptualization: Fixing the alphabet. In order to determine the alphabet $\Lambda[\Upsilon, \Sigma]$, the set Υ of facets and the set Σ of propositional constants must be defined.[10] The set of facets — representing the (reasoning) agents under consideration — is defined as follows:

$$\Upsilon = \{wanda, xynthia, yvonne, zarah\}$$

The set of propositional variables Σ is a little bit larger. We first define the following (possibly indexed) schema variables and their associated sets of possible values:

$$Man \in \{axel, brigitt, carl, dirk\}$$
$$Sec \in \{wanda, xynthia, yvonne, zarah\}$$
$$Meet \in \{m_1, m_2, m_3\}$$
$$Place \in \{austin, l\_a\}$$
$$Date \in [1, \dots, 30]$$
$$Asit \in \{s_1, \dots\}$$
$$Csit \in \{c_1, \dots\}$$

The values of the latter two variables are used to denote different manager availability and scheduling completeness situations to easily model changes to the available dates of a manager and to the set of meetings that must be scheduled.[11] Using these schema variables, ground instances of the following schemas are defined as propositional variables contained in Σ:

- avail($Man_i, Date_j$) expresses that manager Man_i is available at some date $Date_j$.

- avec($Man_i, Asit_j$) is used to refer to a particular availability situation $Asit_j$ of manager Man_i.

---

[10] As usual, a Prolog-like syntax and schematic definitions are used, where words starting with a lowercase letter are constants and words starting with a capital letter are (schema) variables (in term schemas), which are to be instantiated with constants to form ground terms, which are then considerd the propositional constants of the logical language. Note also, that the internal structure of such a term is totally opaque to our calculus (and thereby the DRMS); it is just helpful for the reader to better understand what a particular proposition is intented to represent.

[11] Changes to availability do not include the effects of scheduling a meeting; the dependencies take care of making a date de facto unavailable if a meeting is scheduled for that date (unless the agent decides to reschedule the other meeting). The availability situation is used to model the exclusion or inclusion of dates for which the reason is not under control of the application (here: meeting scheduling by the secretary). If availability of a manager is exclusively determined by the meeting scheduling application, or if meetings must be scheduled by agents that do not concern the group under investigation, the availability situation should be replaced by a decision situation, which takes a quite similar role and determines availability.

- decision($Meet_i, Place_j, Date_k$) represents the decision to hold meeting $Meet_i$ on date $Date_k$ at some place $Place_j$.

- lsched($Sec_i, Meet_j$) expresses the fact that secretary Sec_i has locally scheduled meeting $Meet_j$.

- sched($Meet_i$) expresses the fact that meeting $Meet_i$ has been (completely, i.e. by all participants) scheduled.

- cvec($Sec_i, Csit_j$) refers to a secretary Sec_i's completeness situation $Csit_j$, i.e. to a particular set of meetings the secretary must have scheduled.

- place_of($Meet_i, Place_j$) says that meeting $Meet_i$ is at place $Place_j$.

- date_of($Meet_i, Date_j$) says that meeting $Meet_i$ is held at date $Date_j$.

- doing($Man_i, Meet_j, Date_k$) expresses that manager Man_i is involved in meeting $Meet_j$ at date $Date_k$.

- at($Man_i, Place_j, Date_k$) expresses that manager Man_i is in place $Place_j$ at date $Date_k$.

These definition suffice to fix the alphabet.

Domain Theory: Formulating data dependencies. The dependencies represented by the agents can divided into several categories as listed below. Examples from Wanda's clause database are provided in a smaller font.

- **Representation of local availability:** A secretary Sec_i represents every availability situation $Asit_j$ of her manager Man_k by the appropriate instances of the following Horn clause schemas:

$$(Sec_i.\text{avec}(Man_k, Asit_j) \rightarrow Sec_i.\text{avail}(Man_k, Date_l))$$
$$(Sec_i.\text{avec}(Man_k, Asit_j) \wedge Sec_i.\text{avail}(Man_k, Date_l) \rightarrow Sec_i.\bot)$$

  Wanda's representation of Axel's initial availability situation s_1 consists of the following clauses:

$$(wanda.\text{avec}(axel, s_4) \rightarrow wanda.\text{avail}(axel, 4))$$
$$\dots \text{also for dates } 5, \dots, 8, 18, 19, 25, 26$$
$$(wanda.\text{avec}(axel, s_1) \wedge wanda.\text{avail}(axel, 1) \rightarrow wanda.\bot)$$
$$\dots \text{also for dates } 11, \dots, 15, 20, \dots, 22, 27, \dots, 29$$

- **Representation of non-local availability:** A secretary Sec_i represents the availability situation $Asit_l$ of another secretary Sec_j's manager Man_k by *base literal references* as follows:

$$Sec_i:Sec_j.\text{avec}(Man_k, Asit_l)$$

In order to ensure that secretary Sec_i is kept informed about avec(Man_k) by secretary Sec_j, both secretaries must include the facet clause

$$(Sec_j.\text{avec}(Man_k, Asit_l) \leadsto Sec_i{:}Sec_j.\text{avec}(Man_k, Asit_l))$$

In our modelling approach, *no explicit local* dependencies involving these literals must be formulated by a secretary. However, the problem solvers need to inform each other about changes to availability (there will be a mechanism to support the automatic exchange of such changes to availability), and the other agents' availability situation should always be included as an assumption into the relevant environments. For details, see below.

Wanda declares the following literal references as relevant:

$$wanda{:}xynthia.\text{avec}(brigitt, s_1)$$
$$wanda{:}yvonne.\text{avec}(carl, s_1)$$
$$wanda{:}zarah.\text{avec}(dirk, s_1)$$

A necessary requirement for the derivability of these literal references is the representation of the following facet clauses:

$$(xynthia.\text{avec}(brigitt, s_1) \leadsto wanda{:}xynthia.\text{avec}(brigitt, s_1))$$
$$(yvonne.\text{avec}(carl, s_1) \leadsto wanda{:}yvonne.\text{avec}(carl, s_1))$$
$$(zarah.\text{avec}(dirk, s_1) \leadsto wanda{:}zarah.\text{avec}(dirk, s_1))$$

- **Representation of local scheduling decision consequences.** The local consequences for a manager Man of a secretary Sec's scheduling decision must be represented by appropriate instances of the following Horn clause schemas:

$$(Sec.\text{decision}(Meet, Place, Date) \rightarrow Sec.\text{at}(Man, Place, Date))$$
$$(Sec.\text{decision}(Meet, Place, Date) \rightarrow Sec.\text{doing}(Man, Meet, Date))$$
$$(Sec.\text{decision}(Meet, Place, Date) \rightarrow Sec.\text{place\_of}(Meet, Place))$$
$$(Sec.\text{decision}(Meet, Place, Date) \rightarrow Sec.\text{date\_of}(Meet, Date))$$

As an example, Wanda adds the following clauses in response to Yvonne's suggestion of holding meeting m_2 on the 7th:

$$(wanda.\text{decision}(m_2, l\_a, 7) \rightarrow wanda.\text{at}(axel, l\_a, 7))$$
$$(wanda.\text{decision}(m_2, l\_a, 7) \rightarrow wanda.\text{doing}(axel, m_2, 7))$$
$$(wanda.\text{decision}(m_2, l\_a, 7) \rightarrow wanda.\text{place\_of}(m_2, l\_a))$$
$$(wanda.\text{decision}(m_2, l\_a, 7) \rightarrow wanda.\text{date\_of}(m_2, 7))$$

- **Representation of local schedule consistency.** The local consistency of scheduling decisions for a local manager Man is ensured by his secretary Sec as follows (instances of differently indexed schema variables must be different):

$$(Sec.\mathsf{at}(Man, Place_i, Date) \wedge Sec.\mathsf{at}(Man, Place_j, Date) \rightarrow Sec.\bot)$$
$$(Sec.\mathsf{doing}(Man, Meet_i, Date) \wedge Sec.\mathsf{doing}(Man, Meet_j, Date) \rightarrow Sec.\bot)$$
$$(Sec.\mathsf{place\_of}(Meet, Place_i) \wedge Sec.\mathsf{place\_of}(Meet, Place_j) \rightarrow Sec.\bot)$$
$$(Sec.\mathsf{date\_of}(Meet, Date_i) \wedge Sec.\mathsf{date\_of}(Meet, Date_j) \rightarrow Sec.\bot)$$

The clauses for ensuring local schedule consistency are quite similar to those of the single agent meeting scheduling scenario. A few examples in FHPL notation from Wanda's database are

$$(wanda.\mathsf{at}(axel, austin, 4) \wedge wanda.\mathsf{at}(axel, l\_a, 4) \rightarrow wanda.\bot)$$
$$(wanda.\mathsf{doing}(axel, m_1, 4) \wedge wanda.\mathsf{doing}(axel, m_2, 4) \rightarrow wanda.\bot)$$
$$(wanda.\mathsf{place\_of}(m_1, austin) \wedge wanda.\mathsf{place\_of}(m_1, l\_a) \rightarrow wanda.\bot)$$
$$(wanda.\mathsf{date\_of}(m_1, 4) \wedge wanda.\mathsf{date\_of}(m_1, 5) \rightarrow wanda.\bot)$$

Note, that Wanda has the option of formulating all possible such clauses beforehand (resulting in an unnecessarily large database with lots of useless clauses) or just *on demand*, i.e. whenever a new meetings, dates or places are considered.

- **Representation of local acceptability of scheduling decisions.**
  Scheduling decisions are locally acceptable, if the manager is available. This kind of dependency is represented by an instance of the clause schema

$$(Sec.\mathsf{avail}(Man, Date) \wedge Sec.\mathsf{decision}(Meet, Place, Date)$$
$$\rightarrow Sec.\mathsf{lsched}(Sec, Meet))$$

As an example, we provide Wanda's clause for her acceptance of the 7th as meeting date for m_1:

$$(wanda.\mathsf{avail}(axel, 7) \wedge wanda.\mathsf{decision}(m_1, austin, 7) \rightarrow wanda.\mathsf{lsched}(wanda, m_1))$$

- **Representation of group acceptability of scheduling decisions.**
  The secretary Sec, who is taking the role coordinator for scheduling a particular meeting $Meet$, is also responsible for representing the group acceptance of a scheduling decision. Assuming that aside of Sec's manager the managers of secretaries Sec_1 to Sec_k are involved in meeting $Meet$, Sec represents a dependency as follows:

$$(Sec{:}Sec_1.\mathsf{lsched}(Sec_1, Meet) \wedge \ldots \wedge Sec{:}Sec_k.\mathsf{lsched}(Sec_k, Meet)$$
$$\wedge Sec.\mathsf{lsched}(Sec, Meet) \rightarrow Sec.\mathsf{sched}(Meet))$$

In order to have Sec_i kept informed about $Sec{:}Sec_i.\mathsf{lsched}(Sec_i, Meet)$, both Sec and Sec_i must include the facet clauses

$$(Sec_i.\mathsf{lsched}(Sec_i, Meet) \rightsquigarrow Sec{:}Sec_i.\mathsf{lsched}(Sec_i, Meet))$$

As coordinator for meeting m_1, Wanda must include the following clause to represent the acceptance of her scheduling decisions by Xynthia and Zarah, the secretaries of the other managers involved in the meeting:

$$(wanda{:}xynthia.\mathsf{lsched}(xynthia, m_1) \wedge wanda{:}zarah.\mathsf{lsched}(zarah, m_1)$$
$$\wedge wanda.\mathsf{lsched}(wanda, m_1) \rightarrow wanda.\mathsf{sched}(m_1))$$

Both Wanda and Xynthia must include the facet clause

$$(xynthia.\mathsf{lsched}(xynthia, m_1) \rightsquigarrow wanda{:}xynthia.\mathsf{lsched}(xynthia, m_1))$$

while both Wanda and Zarah must include the facet clause

$$(zarah.\mathsf{lsched}(zarah, m_1) \rightsquigarrow wanda{:}zarah.\mathsf{lsched}(zarah, m_1))$$

- **Representation of schedule completeness.** Each secretary must know when she has successfully scheduled all meetings for her manager. Because the set of meetings may change over time, we introduce propositional variables for modelling different completeness situations, which are determined by different sets of meetings being successfully scheduled. For each such completeness situation $Csit$, comprising a set of meetings m_1 to m_n, a secretary Sec must include a clause

$$(\phi_1 \wedge \ldots \wedge \phi_n \rightarrow Sec.\mathsf{cvec}(Sec, Csit))$$

where

$$\phi_i = Sec.\mathsf{sched}(m_i) \qquad \text{if } Sec \text{ is coordinator for } m_i$$
$$\phi_i = Sec{:}Sec_j.\mathsf{sched}(m_i) \qquad \text{if } Sec_j \text{ is coordinator for } m_i$$

For Wanda, the completeness situation c_1 we considered consisted of scheduling meetings m_1 (as coordinator) and m_2 (as participant). This is represented in her clause database as follows:

$$(wanda.\mathsf{sched}(m_1) \wedge wanda{:}yvonne.\mathsf{sched}(m_2) \rightarrow wanda.\mathsf{cvec}(wanda, c_1))$$

A partial graphical illustration of the four secretaries' clause databases is provided in Figure 4.8. The figure focuses on the structure of inter-agent dependencies, while most local dependencies have been left out.

Reasoning: Checking Availability and Schedule Completeness. Given the above representation, the four secretaries can now use this formalization to reason about various problem solving aspects.

In the single agent case, any query to the RMS had to specify an environment; the query was answered relative to the specified set of assumptions. In the multiagent case, a query must additionally include the specification of a group, i.e. queries are answered relative to a group *and* a set of assumptions. We continue to specify as an evironment e a set of *propositional variables*

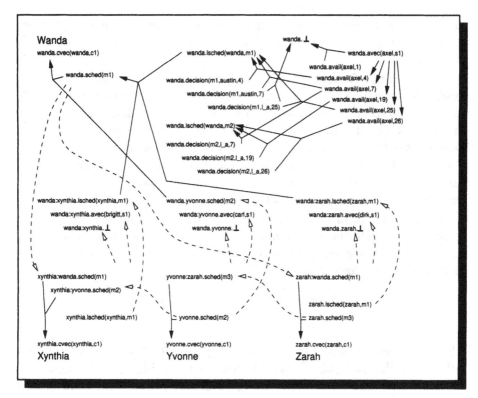

Figure 4.8: Graphical illustration of initial schedule dependencies.

A major portion of Wanda's clause database plus the dependencies to the other agents are shown. The local databases are surrounded by a dotted line. Dashed lines with a hollow arrow represent facet clauses, while straignt lines and filled arrows represent local Horn clauses.

and introduce the convention, that all possible base literals $x.p$ with $x \in g$ and $p \in e$ — the set of all such base literals is abbreviated $g.e$ — are made relevenat and assumed, i.e. the propositional variables are always assumed in all facets of a group. This also means, that we consider only *coherent* sets of formulas; the particular specification mechanism in queries just ensures this property.

Turning to our particular example, the question which facet groups and environments are useful arises. The answer is that this varies from agent to agent. As an example, we look at Wanda's reasoning. The groups useful for her include at least the following:

$$g_1 = \{wanda\} \qquad\qquad g_2 = \{wanda, xynthia, zarah\}$$
$$g_3 = \{wanda, xynthia, yvonne\} \quad g4 = \{wanda, xynthia, yvonne, zarah\}$$

Group g_1 is used to determine purely local things, while groups g_2 and g_3

are useful for checking propositions related to meetings m_1 and m_2 respectively. Group g_4 is useful to determine certain global properties, e.g. schedule completeness.

Environments for queries basically consist of two kinds of assumptions: availability situations and scheduling decisions. Due to the structure of the dependencies specified above, an agent will not be able to derive much without including the availability situation; this is especially true for communicated beliefs (base literal references). Thus, a useful environment for some group g will include at least the availability situations of all group members as assumptions. Note, that there must be an additional mechanism that ensures that the *current* availability situation is included.

For a given set of dependencies and contracts Γ and each group g, an agent z can decide the consistency of an environment e (more exactly: the consistency of the group g reduction of Γ extended by $g.e$) by deciding for every $x \in g$ the following query

$$\Gamma_{\lceil g \rceil} \vdash_{\mathsf{FHPL}} x.\bot \qquad\qquad \text{if } z = x$$

$$\Gamma_{\lceil g \rceil} \vdash_{\mathsf{FHPL}} z{:}x.\bot \qquad\qquad \text{if } z \neq x$$

The environment is consistent for the group only if all of the above queries fail. The ability to locally decide the consistency is, of course, based on the assumption that agents communicating with each other always include a contract regarding $\bot$, which we will make a convention.

Based on the previously specified representation (manifested in a set of formulas Γ) and the above assumptions and conventions, queries of the following kind can be answered:

- An agent x can check whether it has locally scheduled a meeting m_i by deciding whether

$$\Gamma = \Gamma_{\lceil x \rceil} \cup \{x.\mathsf{avec}(\dots), x.\mathsf{decision}(m_i, \dots), \dots\}$$
$$\Gamma \vdash_{\mathsf{FHPL}} x.\mathsf{lsched}(x, m_i)$$

  holds or not.

- A scheduling agent x, taking the role as coordinator for a particular meeting m_i, can determine whether

  - a participating agent y has locally scheduled the meeting by deciding whether

$$\Gamma = \Gamma_{\lceil x, y \rceil} \cup \{\{x, y\}.\{\mathsf{avec}(\dots), \mathsf{decision}(m_i, \dots)\}\}$$
$$\Gamma \vdash_{\mathsf{FHPL}} x{:}y.\mathsf{lsched}(y, m_i)$$

    holds or not, and whether

– the meeting is completely scheduled by all agents involved by checking whether

$$\Gamma = \Gamma_{\lceil x,y,\dots \rceil} \cup \{\{x, y, \dots\}.\{\mathsf{avec}(\dots), \mathsf{decision}(m_i, \dots)\}\}$$
$$\Gamma \vdash_{\mathsf{FHPL}} x.\mathsf{sched}(m_i)$$

holds or not.

- An agent can check whether all meetings have been scheduled by deciding
whether

$$\Gamma = \Gamma_{\lceil x,y,\dots \rceil} \cup \{\{x, y, \dots\}.\{\mathsf{avec}(\dots), \mathsf{decision}(m_i, \dots), \mathsf{decision}(m_j, \dots)\}\}$$
$$\Gamma \vdash_{\mathsf{FHPL}} x.\mathsf{cvec}(x, \dots)$$

holds or not.

Assuming the environment specified to the last query is consistent and contains the actual availability situations for all involved agents, the query still
only ensures that the scheduling decisions specified as assumptions represent
a solution that is possible and conflict-free for all involved agents. It does
not enforce this set of decisions as the solution to be taken, because the other
agents involved may not assume the same set of decisions. Agreeing on such
a set of decisions is still left to the problem solvers.

4.3   Generic Multiagent Reason Maintenance

A review of the previous two sections indicates that multiple-context assumption-
based reasoning in multiagent systems differs more from the single agent case
than on first sight. The logics we developed, FHPL, allows for the clear and
intuitive representation of several agents' propositional data — including the
logical dependencies between these data and of the exchange of such data
via communication between agents — from a global perspective and — based
on facet group-oriented concepts of consistency, coherence, consequence, and
derivability — provides flexible reasoning mechanisms. Given these rich possibilities, a careful evaluation of what functionality is desirable to have in a
multiagent reason maintenance system is advisable before actually designing
and implementing a system. This is the purpose of this section. As becomes
obvious later on, the generic functionality specified here may be specialized
and implemented in several different ways. In particular, it is useful to have a
generic functionality available when reviewing and evaluating available RMSs
for multiagent systems, in particular, distributed RMSs (DRMSs), in the next
section. Before such a generic functionality is identified and informally specified, however, some basic modelling assumptions have to be made explicit.

We assume a problem solving architecture consisting of set $\mathcal{PS} = \{PS_1, \dots, PS_k\}$ of k problem solver modules (PSs) and a multiagent reason maintenance system (MRMS). Currently, no particular assumptions are made on how the MRMS may be implemented, e.g. as a central RMS server with a virtual RMS interface for each agent, as a set of distributed communicating modules that together make up a DRMS, or some hybrid form between these two extremes (see sections 1.4 and 5.2). The MRMS is, for now, simply viewed as a facility that can represent a set of FHPL formulas and provides reasoning services. The problem solvers represent information in the MRMS using a facetted Horn propositional language $\mathcal{L}_{\mathsf{FHPL}}$. Every problem solver PS_i is uniquely assigned a facet constant x_i (occasionally denoted by $\mathsf{rep}(PS_i) = x_i$). Each problem solver x_i specifies

- a set $\Gamma_P(x_i)$ of base literals, which represent relevant local propositions,

- a set $\Gamma_Q(x_i)$ of relevant base literal references, which are locally relevant representations of propositions communicated from other agents, and

- a set $\Gamma_J(x_i)$ of intra-facet clauses, which represent logical dependencies between locally relevant data (the agent's own propositions or communicated ones).

All these formulas together make up the set of formulas relevant to the MRMS. In contrast to the single agent scenario, this set is now specified in a distributed fashion by a set of agents. Note, that the global concept of a set of all relevant formulas is introduced purely for reasons of simplicity; the set of formulas relevant to any particular agent consists only of formulas from the facet representing the agent.

While making a base literal relevant or entering a facet clause is an act that is local to a facet, declaring a base literal reference as relevant is more complex and may even fail to succeed. We assume roughly the following procedure:

1. An agent x requests the MRMS to make relevant a base literal reference $x{:}y.p$.

2. Depending on the particular implementation, the MRMS may have to request permission for providing the above base literal reference from agent y. Especially, if the requested base literal has not yet been considered relevant by agent y, a decision about making it relevant or not must be made.[12] The policy applied here has a strong influence on how the congruence problem (see Section 4.1.3) is dealt with.[13]

3. If permission to communicate the base literal is denied by agent y, the request fails.

---

[12] A similar question arises regarding the use of literals as assumptions.
[13] Belief autonomy vs. relevance autonomy.

4. If y agrees, the MRMS adds the respective contract clause $(y.p \rightsquigarrow x{:}y.p)$
   to its database and provides the requested base literal reference.

Note, that we do not further consider whether and how permission to communicate information is granted. This is completely left open to a particular implementation, or the agents involved. From a logical perspective, the request to make a base literal reference relevant either succeeds, in which case the respective contract clause is automatically added, or it fails, which means that the requesting agent will not be able to use the base literal reference in any way, e.g. in local facet clauses.

The problem solvers may pose queries to retrieve information from the MRMS. The MRMS maintains a suitable partial representation of the derivability relation $\vdash_{\mathsf{FHPL}}$, which means it can e.g. determine whether

$$\Gamma \vdash_{\mathsf{FHPL}} \phi$$

holds or not. A more general query variant, which exploits the group concepts of FHPL, is to determine whether

$$\Gamma \vdash_{\mathsf{g}} \phi$$

holds or not for some group g. Note, that the latter is equivalent to

$$\Gamma_{\lceil g \rceil} \vdash_{\mathsf{FHPL}} \phi$$

Like in the single agent case, the representation of $\vdash_{\mathsf{FHPL}}$ will be partial, because the MRMS usually restricts for which Γ and ϕ it can provide the above service. Assuming Γ is composed of a set of clauses Γ_{cl} and a set of literals Γ_{lit} (i.e. $\Gamma = \Gamma_{cl} \cup \Gamma_{lit}$), some typical restrictions are:

- ϕ must be a literal ($\mathcal{C}_{\mathsf{FHPL}}$ is only literal complete!) and must have been declared relevant before it can be used in queries.

- A useful restriction increasing locality is to provide the service of answering the above query only to the agent that is represented by the facet of the literal specified in the query, i.e. $\mathsf{facet}(\phi) = x_i = \mathsf{rep}(PS_i)$. That is, an agent may query the MRMS only about its locally relevant literals. Note, that this restricts an agent only from getting knowledge about the communicated beliefs of another agent, and thus, prevents agents from passing on communicated beliefs. An agent can still get knowledge about any other agent's local beliefs. Put differently, this restriction ensures that communicated information is first-hand information, not second-hand information.

- All clauses of Γ_{cl} must have been declared relevant. Usually, the only modifications to Γ_{cl} permitted by the MRMS will be additions of clauses. This makes the MRMS a monotonic RMS, because $\vdash_{\mathsf{FHPL}}$ is monotonic.

- Assuming a monotonic MRMS as above, there are two degrees of freedom left for specifying different sets Γ in queries: the set of literals Γ_{lit} used as assumptions and the group g used to specify the scope of the proof to be constructed. The group can basically be chosen freely by the problem solver, although the calculus requires that the group contains the agent's own facet.[14] Γ_{lit}, however, is usually required to meet the following two conditions:

$$\text{facetset}*(\Gamma_{lit}) = g \qquad (4.7)$$

$$\Gamma_{lit} \quad \text{is g-coherent} \qquad (4.8)$$

A MRMS specification should explicitly state which restrictions of the above kind are made. Furthermore, any constraints on the applicability of problem solver interface functions must be made explicit, which includes a precise characterization of the domains for parameter and argument values.

4.3.1   Components of Multiagent RMS Specifications

A MRMS specification consist at least of the following components:

- A **multiagent logical state**, which fixes the language used by the problem solvers in the multiagent system to express relevant information and defines a representation of the information the problem solvers have communicated to the MRMS. Aside of a *global* logical state it should be possible to identify a *local logical (sub)state* for each agent/facet. The local logical state of an agent/facet should suffice to allow a precise characterization of arguments permissable in the agent's functions calls of the interfaces described below.

- A **logical query interface**, which allows an agent's problem solver to retrieve information from the MRMS. The retrieval of information via the logical query interface usually requires access to the DRMS's partial representation of the derivability relation as represented by the logical state.

- A **state change interface** that allows to manipulate the logical state, e.g. by making additional formulas relevant or by adding clauses that represent logical dependencies or update contracts for communicated beliefs. The state change interface should include a *basic facet interface* for defining new facets.

- A **state query interface** which allows to retrieve information directly represented in the logical state, i.e. producing an answer to such a query

---

[14] For the practical consequences of this limitation, see the discussion of MXFRMS later on.

can be done by looking up the logical state and does not require access to the derivability relation.

As pointed out previously, we will not explicitly consider the intricacies of setting up an update contract for communicated beliefs between two agents. For our discussion, only the final outcome of a request to make a base literal reference relevant is of interest: if it fails, nothing has or is changed; if it succeeds, then the respective update contract — represented by the contract clause — is assumed to be successfully established. For instance, a particular implementation could assume liberal agents that provide free access to all their relevant data and make literals relevant if necessary. In this case, the MRMS can establish the update contract on its own and requests for base literal references will always succeed. The opposite end of the spectrum is marked by a MRMS that has no competence whatsoever about establishing update contracts and always has to ask the problem solver. A practical compromise would probably provide additional functionality such that problem solvers can inform the MRMS about how to deal with their local data, e.g. by declaring certain data public or private or exporting it to a well-defined group of agents only. If the MRMS employs anything else than the liberal approach described above, then the specification should include the following additional components:

- An **extended facet interface**, which specifies data structures plus access and manipulation functions for the representation of information about the accessibility of local information by other agents.

- A **callback interface**, which specifies functions to be provided *by the problem solvers* and that are called by the DRMS to clarify the accesibility of local data by other agents.

As practiced already in the single agent case, simplifying assumptions about the protocol used for communication between problem solvers and the MRMS will be made, e.g. that problem solvers always declare data relevant before using them in queries or in logical dependencies. Functions return an error and leave the logical state unchanged, if this is not the case.

4.3.2   Generic Multiagent RMS Logical State

The logical state of a multiagent RMS is a structure consisting of several components, which together serve the following purposes:

- Fix the common language the problem solvers use to formulate their problems.

- Give a precise description of the part of the language which has been declared relevant by the problem solvers.

- Provide sufficient means to precisely characterize the permissable arguments for the interface functions described later on.

The language used by the problem solvers will usually be $\mathcal{L}_{\mathsf{FHPL}}$; the specification should fix the language by specifying the sets Σ and Υ, which determine the alphabet, and thus, the syntax.

The components specifying the relevant part of the language are more elaborate than in the single agent case: First of all, for each facet we need to specify a set of relevant other facets (sometimes referred to as *acquaintances* of the agent), which have some kind of relationship to the facet on hand. Such a relationship is given in three cases:

- With each facet that have requested base literals from the local facet, if the request was satisfied and the information supplied (supply-based relationship).

- With each facet the local facet has requested base literals from and the request has been satisfied by the other facet (request-based relationship).

- With each facet the local facet wants to use in group specifications of queries (focus-based relationship).

Aside of the propositions and dependencies locally relevant in a facet (base literals and facet clauses), the communicated beliefs (base literal references) and the according update relationships (contract clauses) need to be described. Together, these sets just make up a set of FHPL formulas. The verum and falsum literals are always assumed to be implicitly known. Furthermore, it must be represented what propositions an agent wishes to use as assumptions, which can simply be done by specifying the according set of base literals; the facet identifiers an agent intents to use in groups is usually assumed to be the set of facets that has been declared relevant by an agent.

Because most multiagent RMSs will limit an agent's query capabilities to what has been declared relevant previously by the agent, the characterization of permissable arguments for interface functions usually calls for an appropriate characterization of an agent's local logical substate. This should be easily derivable from the global state. Characterizing permissable function arguments may also require additional logical state components, such as sets of relevant focus structures or the identification of an agent's *current focus*.

4.3.3   Generic Multiagent RMS Logical Query Interface

Functions of the logical query interface retrieve information from the multiagent RMS which it usually was not directly told, i.e. in order to provide such information the logical consequence relation must be consulted. In the single agent case, we were interested in determining whether propositions $\phi \in \Sigma$ are logical consequences of a fixed set of clauses Γ and a variable set of assumptions e, expressed formally as

$$\Gamma \cup e \vdash_{\text{HPL}} \phi.$$

In the multiagent systems case, the basic type of questions to be answered is whether literals are logical consequences of the dependencies formulated by a group of agents. This means, that we want to determine, for an agent x, whether literals (base literals *or* base literal references) are logical consequences of a coherent set of formulas, which consists of a fixed set of clauses Γ, reduced to a group g, and a coherent set of assumed literals $g.e$, which is determined by the group g and a set of assumed propositions e. Put shortly, one can say that in the single agent case logical interface query functions determine logical consequence relationships of literals relative to e, while in the multiagent case they perform this functionality for some agent x with $\text{facet}(\phi) = x$, relative to a pair $\langle g, e \rangle$ which determines the context and is referred to as *focus*. This difference kept in mind, the desirable functionality is quite similar to the single agent case:

- Functions that determine whether a particular literal is derivable from a focus.

- Functions that determine whether a particular focus is consistent.

- Functions that determine the (local) context of a focus.

If the agents maintain a special *current focus*, functions that implicitly assume the use of this current focus increase usability and comfort. Furthermore, functionality for generating explanations may be added, but is not further considered here.

A minimal set of logical query functions for solving PEDE problems should at least consist of:

- A function follows-from?, which takes a focus structure $f = \langle g, e \rangle$ and a literal ϕ as arguments and returns the boolean value T if ϕ is g-derivable in facet x from the MRMS clause database Γ and the focus, i.e. it returns T iff (with Γ denoting the set of all clauses known to the MRMS)

$$\Gamma_{\lceil g \rceil} \cup g.e \vdash_{\text{FHPL}} \phi$$

  where ϕ is either a base literal $x.p$ or a base literal reference $x{:}y.p$.

- A function holds-in?, which takes the same arguments as follows-from? and determines whether the context specified by the focus structure is g-consistent *and* the literal is g-derivable, i.e. it returns T iff

$$\Gamma_{\lceil g \rceil} \cup g.e \vdash_{\text{FHPL}} \phi \qquad \text{and} \qquad \Gamma_{\lceil g \rceil} \cup g.e \nvdash_{\text{FHPL}} g.\bot$$

- A function context-of?, which takes a focus structure $f = \langle g, e \rangle$ as argument and computes, for facet x, the set of all in facet x locally relevant literals, for which holds-in? returns T.

Additional or specialized logical query functions may be provided by a particular implementation.

4.3.4   Generic Multiagent RMS State Change Interface

Problem solvers must use the state change interface functions to inform the MRMS about relevant local propositions, assumptions and clauses. Furthermore, non-local propositions (communicated beliefs, expressed as base literal references in FHPL), may be declared relevant with the effect that they can be used in queries afterwards. An often desirable side effect of declaring a communicated belief relevant (at least in distributed implementations of a MRMS) is that information about its derivability should be communicated, stored locally, and kept up to date. The facet interface functionality has already been mentioned above; the minimum security measure here is to require a problem solver to explicitly declare all relevant facets.

An exemplary, though rather minimalistic state change interface consists of the following functions:

- The function add-proposition!, which declares a base literal as relevant.

- The function add-reference!, which declares a base literal reference as relevant. Depending on the particular approach of implementation, this call may result in communication between the MRMS modules representing the provider and the subscriber of the communicated belief.

- The function add-justification! adds clauses expressing dependencies between an agent's local data. Base literal references may only occur in the antecedents of a clause, if FHPL is used.

- The function add-assumption!, which takes as argument a base literal that has previously been declared relevant and tells the MRMS, that the propositional variable will be used as assumption.

- Finally, the function add-focus! takes an environment and a group as arguments and informs the MRMS, that the respective focus structure is relevant for the agent calling the function.

As part of the basic facet interface, the following function should be provided:

- The function add-facet!, which takes as argument a facet constant (and possible a few other arguments with communication-related information such as IP addresses as well), must be used by problem solvers to tell the MRMS that an information update relationship of some kind exists between the two facets.

An implementation may provide additional functionality, such as functions that allow certain modifications of focus structures, or functions for shifting a problem solvers current focus. Furthermore, if the system uses a more complex scheme for handling the congruence problem than the one described here, state changing functions for manipulating appropriate data structures of an extended facet interface must be provided. Also, the extended facet interface, if provided, will be changing the state.

4.3.5 Generic Multiagent RMS State Query Interface

Similar to the single agent case, a MRMS should provide functionality that allows problems solvers to find out what they have told the MRMS. In contrast to the logical query interface functions, the state query interface functions can be answered simply by investigating the logical state and do not require the logical consequence relation to be consulted. An actual set of functions is trivial to generate and, therefore, omitted here. An actual implementation may be forced to restrict the functionality provided in the state query interface due to security and performance reasons. System designers may consider it inappropriate that an agent can get knowledge of what other agents consider relevant information. The policy enforced here must be adapted to the policy chosen for dealing with the congruence problem mentioned earlier (see Section 4.1.3, page 92). Even if this policy is very liberal, extensive use of this functionality may lead to significant costs in distributed implemenations.

4.3.6 Relaxation of Protocol Assumptions

We already mentioned previously that certain assumptions about the interface between problem solvers and MRMS are made and assumed to be followed by the problem solvers. Summarized, the problem solvers must

- declare a facet relevant before making a reference to one of this facet's base literals relevant,

- declare a facet relevant before requests from this facet for base literals are handled,

- declare facets relevant before using them in groups of focus structures,

- declare facets relevant before other agents are allowed to us

- declare all antecedents and the consequent of a justification as relevant literals before adding the justification to the clause database,

- declare literals relevant before using them in queries,

- declare base literals as assumptions before using the base literal's propositional variable in environments of focus structures

Under these assumptions, the specification of error conditions and ways to handle them is usually omitted or significantly scaled down. An actual implementation, however, should not rely on problem solvers always following these assumptions. Instead, the multiagent RMS should explicitly check for situations violating these assumptions. There are basically two approaches to deal with such situations:

1. The system simply signals an error and rejects the execution of the interface function, i.e. the unsuccessful attempt to execute the interface function is treated like an unsuccessful database transaction. In this case, the system must ensure that the logical state is the same as before the interface functions was attempted.

2. The system tries to repair the situation by initiating the execution of an appropriate sequence of other interface function prior to actually handling the request on hand. For example, if a problem solver tries to declare a base literal reference relevant, which refers to the base literal of a yet undeclared facet, the system could automatically declare the facet relevant.

The latter approach can be demonstrated by using the example of a safe add-justification! procedure as follows:

PROCEDURE 4.3.1 (SAFE-ADD-JUSTIFICATION)

```
 1  procedure safe-add-justification!((Φ→φ))  ≡
 2          foreach [ φᵢ ∈ Φ ] do
 3              if [ is-literal?(φᵢ) = F ]
 4                  then if [ φᵢ = x.p ] then add-proposition!(φᵢ)
 5                      elsif [ φᵢ = y:x.p ] then safe-add-reference!(φᵢ)
 6                                          else error
 7                  fi
 8              fi
 9              if [ is-proposition?(φ) = F ] then add-proposition!(φ)
10              fi
11          od
12          add-justification!((Φ→φ))
13  end
```

In the above example, safe-add-justification refers to the functionality as specified previously. In order to be on the safe side, the add-justification! function should be made an internal function of the MRMS module and all problem solvers should (be forced to) use the exported **safe-add-justification!** function.

Another issue in the PS/multiagent RMS protocol is reduction of syntactic complexity. Because each agent is restricted to specify only FHPL formulas of its own facet (i.e. the outermost facet specifier of a formula is always the same as the facet representing the agent that calls the interface function), it can be omitted in argument specifications, if the multiagent RMS has a means to find out the caller of an interface function. Thus, instead of

$$\text{add-proposition!}(x.\phi)$$
$$\text{add-reference!}(x{:}y.\phi) \qquad \text{and}$$
$$\text{add-justification!}((x.\phi_1 \wedge \ldots \wedge x{:}y.\phi_n \rightarrow x.\varphi))$$

one could just write

$$\text{add-proposition!}(\phi)$$
$$\text{add-reference!}(y.\phi) \qquad \text{and}$$
$$\text{add-justification!}((\phi_1 \wedge \ldots \wedge y.\phi_n \rightarrow \varphi))$$

Providing this capability in a multiagent RMS reduces its interface complexity and significantly increases its usability.

4.4 Standard Multiagent Reason Maintenance Technology

In the chapter on single agent reason maintenance, we discussed standard single agent reason maintenance technology at this point in order to give a summarized overview on the state of the art. In comparison to the vast amount of work that has been done in single agent reason maintenance, there is relatively little work in distributed reason maintenance. Nevertheless, the basic scheme we used in Chapter 2 works well for the multiagent case and allows to relate the relevant issues to those of the single agent case. Thus, we will first outline some major design tradeoffs for multiagent reason maintenance systems. Next, a few alternative architectures for multiagent reason maintenance systems are outlined and the major families of DRMSs are surveyed. Two systems claiming to provide multiagent, multiple context, assumption-based reason maintenance functionality — DATMS by [Mason and Johnson, 1989] and DARMS by [Beckstein et al., 1993] — are then outlined in some more detail. The final section summarizes the state of the art in multiagent reason maintenance technology.

4.4.1   Design Tradeoffs

The generic functionality specified in the previous section already uncovered several hints to major tradeoffs. These and a few others are briefly summarized in the following list:

- The first tradeoff is the language used by the problem solvers to formulate the relevant propositions and data dependencies. FHPL is a rather restricted language and does not allow, for example, to formulate passing on communicated beliefs to a third party. Also, we do not explicitly distinguish between knowledge and belief (although the notion of communicated belief is used widely) or deal with uncertainty. Future work may pick up the handle from here and carry it on to more powerful logics.

- The second tradeoff is between belief autonomy and relevance autonomy (see below). It is buried in the protocol used to acquire communicated beliefs and, thus, in the way the congruence problem is dealt with, i.e. how agents handle communication containing data that was not yet relevant. It is obvious that, in order to be useful, an agent should not simply neglect all data it is told by other agents but does not consider relevant yet. On the contrary, arbitrarily making all such data relevant opens opportunities for malevolent agents to swamp the local agent's RMS facility by huge amounts of data and dependencies that are completely irrelevant to the agent's problem solving. As outlined in the previous section, a useful approach should provide an extended facet interface which allows an agent to provide policies for dealing with such situation to the RMS component.

- A tradeoff related to the previous one is that of agent autonomy vs. global coherence. Complete agent autonomy can be viewed as being comprised of *belief autonomy* and *relevance autonomy*. Relevance autonomy allows each agent to decide completely on its own, what data and data dependencies it considers relevant, and which propositions it wants to use as assumptions. This includes, of course, all data occurring in communication as mentioned by the previous point. The less overhead making communicated beliefs relevant incurs, the easier it will be to give up relevance autonomy. Belief autonomy means that the agent can decide on its own which assumptions it currently makes and which contexts (respectively environments) are important for its problem solving.[15] Giving up belief autonomy is a very hard thing to do and reasonable only in exceptional cases, e.g. in a closed multiagent system, where agents are

---

[15] By determining the context, all beliefs are determined; hence the name for the concept.

strictly hierarchically organized, communicate only with other agents of the system and are designed by a single person or development group.

Total agent autonomy would allow agents to believe completely the opposite of each others beliefs; such a situation must be adequately handled by an appropriate multiagent RMS.[16] In contrast, global coherence would require agents to always agree on a globally consistent set of beliefs; requiring this property must be considered unrealistic for all but the simplest applications, including all real-world applications.

- Another tradeoff is concerned with optimizing (i.e. minimizing) the communication overhead related to reason maintenance tasks. If the requesting agent often repeats queries regarding a communicated belief — either explicitly in a query or implicitly via a context — and the belief is updated by the provider only occasionally, storing the communicated belief locally at the requester and updating it makes sense. On the contrary, if a belief is updated very often and queried only seldomly, the updating of local copies of communicated beliefs may require significant communication bandwidth. We usually assume that queries occur much more often than updates and opt for local copies of communicated beliefs to provide fast response to queries.

- The previous issue is ultimately related to the last tradeoff, which involves the classical space/time tradeoff and was already discussed in the single agent case. The comments in Section 2.4.1 apply directly to the multiagent case. It should be noted that under a pure theorem proving approach the communication overhead may be much higher than in a more database-oriented approach (even if communicated beliefs need to updated very often), if a substantial number of queries involves communicated beliefs.

In general, there is no single correct answer to the questions raised by the above issues. The specific requirements of a system's intented application area must be investigated. Based on these requirements, the correct design decisions must be made such that the system shows satisfactory overall performance.

4.4.2   Multiagent RMS Architectures

Because there has been relatively little work in multiagent reason maintenance systems, it is difficult to identify something like a standard architecture. For

---

[16]In order to deal with such situations, the logical language used to specify the problem must allow to formalize the two agents' beliefs in a set of formulas that is consistent in the logic used but is possibly considered inconsistent from an application point of view. In FHPL, these two views are made explicit by the two alternative semantics.

this reason, we include a brief discussion of the principle architectural alternatives and of some issues connected to them. The decision for chosing a particular architecture is, of course, highly influenced by the design tradeoffs discuused in the previous section.

Basically, there are two focal points regarding a multiagent RMS architecture. The first is the structure of an agent, in particular, the way multiagent reason maintenance services are integrated with the agents' problem solving capabilities. Here, most systems more or less stick to the two-level agent architecture as discussed for the single agent case (see Figure 4.9).

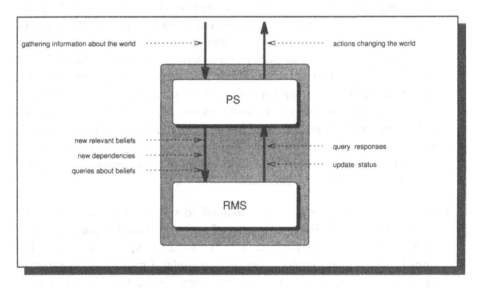

Figure 4.9: The basic two-level software architecture of each agent.

Each problem solving agent is structured into a core problem solver (PS) and a reason maintenance module (RMS). Interaction between PS and RMS is as usual. In a multiagent setting, however, both PS and RMS module communicate with other agents' PS and RMS modules.

The second critical point deals with the implementation structure of the multiagent reason maintenance system itself. Here, there are three principle alternatives:

- The **centralized server approach** employs the basic idea of (centralized) database management systems and will usually be implemented using a client/server architecture (see Figure 4.10). The multiagent RMS services are tightly integrated into a single monolithic RMS server system. The problem solving agents are the clients that use the RMS services by communicating with the RMS server via a standardized protocol, which is provided by a library of RMS interface functions (called a *virtual RMS* module). Note, that a central RMS server has no need to perform reason maintenance-related communication with some other RMS module, but must be able to handle requests from many different problem solvers. Therefore, the PS/RMS protocol must ensure that the RMS server can determine the identity of the agent that submitted a request for some service.

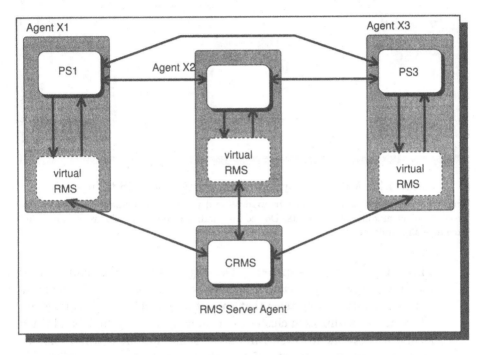

Figure 4.10: Multiagent system using centralized RMS technology.

A central server, tagged CRMS, provides all reason maintenance services. Each agent has an interface, tagged *virtual RMS*, to access the server functionality. Thorough lines within an agent represent the usual interaction between a problem solver and its associated (virtual) RMS. Thorough lines between problem solvers of different agents indicate application-dependent communication, while dotted lines between virtual RMS modules and the CRMS represents communication related to belief exchange and update.

- The **distributed system approach** (see Figure 4.11) is based on a distributed implementation of the RMS across all agents in the multiagent system. Each agent features its own local multiagent RMS module, which provides all the services requested by its problem solver. In contrast to a central RMS server, each RMS module deals only with a single problem solver. Usually, the identity of the associated problem solver is assumed to be implicitly known by the RMS module, and there is little need to include identitfication information in messages between the PS and the RMS module. However, each RMS module must be able to communicate with other RMS modules to perform vital reason maintenance operations.

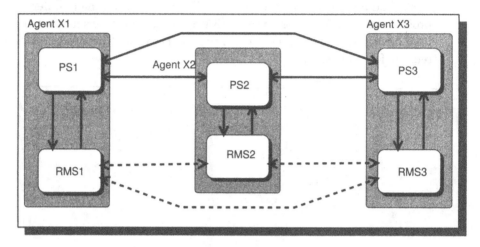

Figure 4.11: Multiagent system using multiagent RMS technology.

Thorough lines between agents indicate application-dependent communication between the problem solver modules of the agents. Dotted lines indicate communication related to belief exchange and updates.

- The **hybrid system approach** (see Figure 4.12) is a combination of the previous two approaches. This architecture would useful to employ in bigger multiagent systems that consist of multiple clusters of agents, where agents within each cluster can communicate via a high bandwidth local area network (or even run on the same machine), while communication between agents of different clusters must use e.g. a wide area network with a much lower effectively available bandwidth. In this variant, RMS modules must both be able to serve multiple problem solvers and to communicate with several other RMS modules. For simplicity, we will assume that each agent is uniquely assigned to an RMS module, i.e. a problem solver cannot interact with two RMS modules (of the same multiagent RMS) simultaneously. An important conceptual advantage of the hybrid approach is that it encompasses the two other approaches: a hybrid multiagent reason maintenance system can also be applied both in a centralized server and a distributed system architecture.

Two important aspects in the discussion of multiagent RMS architectures are synchronization and distribution of control. A central RMS server approach enforces the synchronization of RMS activities by its design. Similarly, distribution of control is not an issue. Therefore, a centralized server aproach is the easiest to implement. However, depending on the number of problem solvers and how intensely they use the RMS services, the RMS server can easily become a significant performance bottleneck. For the distributed systems

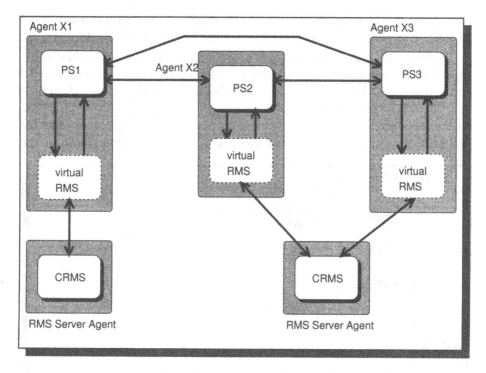

Figure 4.12: Multiagent system using hybrid multiagent RMS technology.

The multiagent system is structured into several clusters, which could be built using features such as locality or degree of interaction and cooperation. Each agent cluster features a local RMS server, which may comunicate in order to provide global RMS services. Again, thorough lines between agents indicate application-dependent communication between the problem solver modules of the agents. Dotted lines indicate communication related to belief exchange and updates.

approach it is assumed that PS/RMS interaction can be completely concurrent. The execution of RMS services — in particular, of label updates — is however, much more difficult to control in a distributed manner. As shown later on, all of the few existing systems seem to employ update algorithms that at least partially require global (and synchronous) control. Although this somewhat simplifies the effort to make qualified statements about the global system state, it must be considered a very drastic measure that can easily prove to be another performance bottleneck.

4.4.3   Multiagent RMS Families

The existing multiagent reason maintenance systems are constructed as extensions of a single agent counterpart. Based on this observation, a first, but simple attempt to classify multiagent reason maintenance systems would be to divide them in JTMS-based systems and ATMS-based systems. However, given the significant degree of design freedom for multiagents RMSs (as discussed in the previous sections), this classification must be considered insufficient.

A more fine-grained classification scheme for multiagent RMSs can be designed as a three-dimensional extension of the classification scheme presented in Section 2.4.3. In addition to the basic two dimensions *number of contexts* maintained by the RMS and *expressive power* of the language to formulate logical dependencies, we take into account the *level of consistency* enforced by the RMS as a third dimension (see Figure 4.13). The categories for the

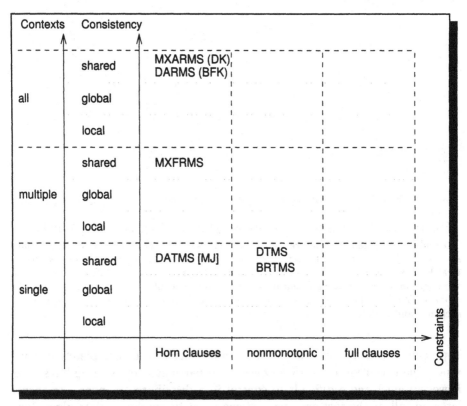

Figure 4.13: Families of multiagent reason maintenance systems.

Three dimensions with three categories each are used for classification: i) number of contexts with categories single, multiple, and all, ii) expressive power of the language for expressing logical dependencies with categories Horn clauses, nonmonotonic clauses, and full clauses, and iii) level of consistency with categories local, shared, and global.

various dimensions are defined as follows:

- **Expressive Power:** Horn clauses, nonmonotonic clauses, full clauses

- **Number of Contexts:** single, multiple, all

- **Level of Consistency:** local, shared, global

The categories of the first two dimensions have already been explained in Section 2.4.3. The three categories for level of consistency can more precisley be characterized as follows:

- **Local Consistency** means that the beliefs of each agent are locally consistent.

- **Shared Consistency** (also referred to as local-and-shared consistency by some authors) means that agents have locally consistent belief databases *and* agree on *all communicated beliefs.*

- **Global Consistency** means that all agents agree on all beliefs, or — more precisely — that the agents' local belief databases could be merged into a global one without conflict.

The latter level of consistency is, of course, the hardest to achieve. As pointed out earlier, achieving global consistency is unrealistic for any practical multiagent system, and therefore none of the existing systems tries to achieve it.

Several systems supporting distributed reason maintenance have been described in the literature. The next few sections contain brief descriptions of their main ideas and functionality. The following list classifies them into the schema just described:

- The DTMS [Bridgeland and Huhns, 1990], developed by David Bridgeland and Michael Huhns at MCC, is a single context RMS, that allows to formulate nonmonotonic dependencies and tries to achieve shared consistency.

- The BRTMS [Horstmann, 1991], developed by Tilo Horstmann in Donald Steiner's group at DFKI, is also a single context RMS with nonmonotonic clauses and shared consistency. The main difference to the DTMS seems to be its integration with a backward reasoning Prolog engine.

- The DATMS was developed by Cindy Mason in Rowland Johnson's group at Lawrence Livermore Laboratory[Mason and Johnson, 1989]. The DATMS is claimed to be an extension of de Kleer's ATMS and to provide ATMS-style multiple context reasoning (i.e. *all* context reasoning) for multi-agent systems. As is shown below, this claim must be seriously questioned. In our categorization scheme, we believe the DATMS should be classified as a single context RMS with Horn clauses. A classification along the consistency dimension is also quite difficult, because maintenance of consistency is, in principle, left to the problem solver; we classified it as a shared consistency, because it is at least possible to actually achieve it with the mechanisms provided. See the section on the DATMS below for a more detailed explanation and discussion of this design decision.

- Another system, unfortunately called DATMS as well, has recently been presented by Malheiro, Jennings and Oliveira. Unfortunately, the only information available to us was [Malheiro et al., 1994], and it is not possible to classify their system based on this paper.

- The DARMS system, presented in detail by [Fuhge, 1993][17], was an early development in our group. It is a serious attempt to provide full ATMS functionality in a multiagent domain and is therefore classified as all contexts, shared consistency. Horn clause-based multiagent RMS. DARMS described in more detail below.

- The MXARMS system is a follow-up development effort to DARMS and tries to resolve some of the more intricate problems of DARMS. It is classified into the same category as DARMS. Because the problem solver functionality is not that much different from DARMS, it is not further discussed here; the interested reader is referred to [Dotzel, 1994].

The MXFRMS system presented in the next chapter has already been included in Figure 4.13 in order to indicate where we are heading to.

4.4.4   The DTMS and the BRTMS

The DTMS [Bridgeland and Huhns, 1990] and the BRTMS [Horstmann, 1991] are distributed extensions of the JTMS [Doyle, 1979]. Therefore, each agent's RMS can maintain only one context at a time. If information represented by RMS-nodes is communicated, they are tagged as so-called *shared nodes*. Agents can have only one node for some piece of information p, and thus, cannot distinguish between what some other agent believes and what they themselves believe about p. *Local-and-shared consistency* is strived for on the global system level, meaning that each agent's RMS must keep its dependency net locally consistent and all shared nodes representing a particular proposition p must have the same belief state in all agents that communicated about p. Thus, shared nodes link the dependency nets of communicating agents together, as shared nodes are treated as if they were identical. A *global label update algorithm* ensures local-and-shared consistency by propagating label updates of shared nodes to all other agents[18]. Local-and-shared consistency means, that all agents that share (communicate about) some piece of information must agree on its belief state, i.e. these agents share a common partial context consisting of all the propositions they communicated about. The more agents communicate, the bigger the shared part will be. In the worst case this will

---

[17]Shorter presentations were published in [Beckstein et al., 1993] and [Beckstein et al., 1994].

[18]The DTMS achieves this by first finding a consistent labelling of all shared nodes and then completing local relabelling.

end up in all agents sharing one huge shared context. Another problem arises, if agents disagree on the belief state of shared nodes. A global relabelling process, which is controlled by more or less blind backtracking, is specified by [Bridgeland and Huhns, 1990] as the means to resolve this conflict. This is not only extremely expensive, but also subject to serious termination problems. As conflict resolution caused by some other agent's reasoning may change the belief state of a shared node, further updates may be necessary in order to maintain local consistency. Thus, an agent's beliefs could be changed without the PS getting notice of it. The agent cannot even prevent this effectively.

Neither the DTMS nor the BRTMS can be considered well-suited for the PEDE domain[19], because they do not support multiple contexts, have a notion of non-local control in their label propagation and conflict resolution algorithms, and compromise on the autonomy of agents by establishing a level of global consistency that is too strong for the PEDE domain.

4.4.5 The DATMS

The DATMS [Mason and Johnson, 1989] is claimed to be a distributed version of deKleer's ATMS. Indeed, the DATMS provides data structures for representing facts, assumptions, and justifications. This data can be interpreted as a dependency net. The DATMS architecture assumes the existence of a rule engine, which performs both problem solver reasoning steps as well as reason maintenance tasks. Thus, the DATMS does not help very much in maintaining such a clear-cut separation between problem solver and reason maintenance (both in terms of control as well as the underlying knowledge) as we were arguing for previously. Problem solver inference steps are performed by applying inference rules. The execution of an inference rule creates a new node representing the newly derived fact, establishes a justification for the new node corresponding to the inference rule, and once and for all computes a single set of assumptions as the node's label. The latter is possible, because facts are restricted to have one justification only. Therefore, no real reason maintenance in the common sense (updating labels of nodes in a dependency net) is performed. The only thing that can happen to a node after its initial label has been computed is that the single environment it contains is discovered to be inconsistent. In such a case, the node label is tagged accordingly and cannot ever be changed again. However, restricting nodes to have at most one justification makes reasoning in multiple contexts virtually impossible, at least for practical matters: It is not totally impossible, but for each additional justification an additional node is required to represent some fact p. Also, all logical dependencies the fact p is involved in need to be represented by multiple justifications, creating additional nodes for all facts that depend on

---

[19]Of course, this is neither a surprise nor a deficiency of these systems. They simply have been designed for a different purpose.

p, and so on. For example, given the logical dependencies $(A \rightarrow p)$, $(B \rightarrow p)$, $(C \rightarrow q)$, $(D \rightarrow q)$, and $(p \wedge q \rightarrow r)$, the DATMS needs two nodes each for p and q and four nodes for r. Thus, although label size is bounded to one environment per label, the number of nodes and justifications necessary to express a set of logical dependencies tends to grow exponentially. Because the problem solver would have to keep track of how many nodes are needed to represent a particular fact and would also have to ensure that all justifications necessary to represent a particular logical dependency are given to the DATMS, this possibility must be considered completely unpractical. Therefore, we classify the DATMS as a single context RMS.

After each application of an inference rule, a set of *TMS rules* and a set of *communication rules* are applied to the dependency net. The antecedents of TMS rules are used to detect inconsistent situations. The consequent action CONTRADICT allows to declare a set of assumptions as inconsistent and to propagate this information to other agents as well. There is no built-in functionality to handle inconsistency, and relying on the TMS rule mechanism it is difficult and completely up to the user to implement a reasonable notion of consistency. Communicating revisable information is done by *communication rules*. An action is provided which effectively transmits a DATMS node to another agent, together with its corresponding assumption set. The receiving agent creates a new node in its own DATMS, thus keeping its own belief about some proposition apart from communicated beliefs. However, it is completely up to the PS to find out that a local node and a node representing a communicated fact actually do represent the same proposition. Another restriction is that only facts that do not depend on communicated information may be sent to other agents. Agents may use communicated facts in their own reasoning process and derive new information, but this information can never be communicated to other agents.

To summarize the arguments above, the DATMS can neither be considered to be upward compatible with the ATMS nor does it effectively support multiple contexts (much to our own surprise). The use of various kinds of rules and the dependence on an external rule engine, which is not described in [Mason and Johnson, 1989], does not allow a clear statement about how control is distributed among the agents' DATMS modules. Some features are only vaguely described in the paper and it seems unlikely, that the system could be easily and well adapted to the problems at hand in the PEDE domain.

4.4.6   The DARMS

When we started to work on PEDE problems and looked for multiagent reason maintenance tools, the only three systems that were described in the literature were those described in the previous two sections. Both the DTMS and the BRTMS were ruled out early, because they provided only single context reasoning, which was felt to be inadequate for the PEDE domain. It was therefore a big disappointment, that our analysis of the DATMS revealed a number of design decisions and features that rendered the DATMS effectively useless for our purposes. Therefore, we started to develop multiagent RMS technology on our own. An initial system, called DARMS and developed jointly with Clemens Beckstein and Robert Fuhge, was defined and described in detail in [Fuhge, 1993]. The main purpose of the DARMS system was to provide a multiagent RMS that is downward compatible with de Kleer's ATMS. The next few pages contain a description of DARMS, which is a revised and abbreviated version of [Beckstein et al., 1993]. The description of DARMS is more detailed than those of the other systems. This detail is necessary, because at the end of this section, we will analyze and review some critical DARMS features, which ultimately led to the development of the family of focus-based reason maintenance systems, to which both the XFRMS (Chapter 3) and the MXFRMS (Chapter 5) belong.

4.4.6.1 Multiagent RMS Requirements

To solve the distributed belief revision problem in PEDE domains, we decided to apply mechanisms based on RMS technology. However, as previously shown, RMSs designed for single-agent systems need to be extended for multiagent scenarios. A definite requirement for an extended, distributed RMS is support for the two-level architecture described above (Figure 4.9). The question is, what additional features we expect from a RMS for multiagent systems. The answer is difficult in general; a closer analysis of PEDE problems revealed some additional requirements for the PEDE domain:

- **Multiple contexts:** Reasoning in multiple contexts is needed. Therefore, JTMS-type systems seem less attractive than ATMS-type RMSs.

- **ATMS compatibility:** The full expressiveness of the ATMS should be provided. The functional interface should be (upward) compatible with the ATMS interface.

- **Local control:** Updates in the distributed RMS should be done separately by each agent's own RMS module. There should be no necessity for any global update or conflict resolution algorithms, i.e. algorithms that force the whole agent system to stop temporarily and recompute belief states.

- **Autonomy of agents:** Agents should be able to distinguish between own derivations and information received from other agents, i.e. they can recognize that dependencies involve external information. Also, agents should not be forced to change their beliefs or their context, if they merely handle information provided to or received from others (*belief autonomy*).

- **Flexibility and extendability:** The distributed RMS should impose few restrictions and limitations on a multiagent environment and yet provide basic, powerful functionality that supports the implementation of higher-level protocols for inter-agent communication.

As illustrated in the previous section, there exist only few distributed versions of RMSs and none of them provides the functionality required by our application domain, e.g. effective support for managing multiple contexts. Therefore, we developed a distributed, assumption-based reason maintenance system, called DARMS, which has the basic machinery necessary for the PEDE domain and is flexible enough to allow for easy implementation of higher-level inter-agent protocols.

A Note on Representation Language   An important assumption underlying the DARMS approach is that all agents basically use the same representation language (syntax *and* semantics) for beliefs (assumptions, propositions, justifications). If communication is supposed to make sense, i.e. if agents are supposed to be able to correctly interpret and use information received from other agents, this assumption simply makes sense[20]. Furthermore, we require all agents to agree on a common notion of normal form for propositions, i.e. they all map a (potentially large) number of logically equivalent propositions into the same syntactic form. These restrictions ensure that communicating agents know what they are talking about, and that they have a common "understanding" of the propositions they exchange. Note, that FHPL was not yet available at the time DARMS was developed. This explains the use of slightly different logical syntax in the description of DARMS.

4.4.6.2   Key Ideas

Before describing architecture and functionality of DARMS in detail, we briefly introduce the key ideas for DARMS:

- **Two-level architecture support:** The DARMS approach assumes that agents are structured into a problem solving (PS) component and a DARMS module. Once a belief has been communicated initiated by PS ↔PS interaction, all further communication necessary to update belief states should be handled by DARMS ↔DARMS communication.

---

[20]Other approaches to distributed reason maintenance have more or less neglected this issue.

- **Remote belief query capability:** In order to maximize the amount of inter-agent communication that can be handled on the DARMS module level, the PS ↔DARMS interface is extended by a *remote belief query* capability, i.e. an agent's PS asks its associated DARMS module, if it wants to find out what some other agent believes about some proposition.

- **Context management:** As a DARMS module is supposed to answer queries (like "Does your PS currently believe p?") from other DARMS modules that involve the PS's current context (*focus*), the functionality of DARMS modules include a *context management* facility. The PS ↔DARMS interface has been extended to include functions for managing the focus.

- **Communicated nodes:** DARMS modules use a new node type – *communicated nodes* – to represent other agents' beliefs, i.e. beliefs are kept separate and are not automatically merged into the the agent's own belief structures.

- **Update contract:** An *update contract* is established between a DARMS module providing information (the belief state of a proposition) and the DARMS module receiving information. It ensures that the communicated node created by the receiving DARMS module will be updated whenever a change to the original node occurs.

- **Directed communication:** Communication is asymmetric, i.e. a *mutual exchange of belief states is not performed automatically*. Receiving a proposition from another DARMS module does not require the recipient to send information on that proposition the other way around.

- **Sharing inconsistency:** As all agents use the same representation language, there is a *common notion of inconsistency* also. Whenever agents detect inconsistent situations, the DARMS modules exchange the corresponding NOGOODs, if they believe the NOGOODs to be relevant to each other. NOGOODs relevant to an agent involve one or more assumptions occuring in labels of nodes communicated to that agent. Also, NOGOODs which make an environment of a communicated node inconsistent must be communicated to the sender of that node.

4.4.6.3 Architecture of DARMS Modules

Each DARMS module is structured into three sub-modules

- dependency net management,

- context management and

- communication and control.

For the following discussion, we introduce two agents X_i and X_j. Also, we assume X_i and X_j each have declared a proposition p to be relevant, that X_i believes p if the assumptions A and B hold, and that X_j has asked its DARMS module whether X_i believes p.[21]

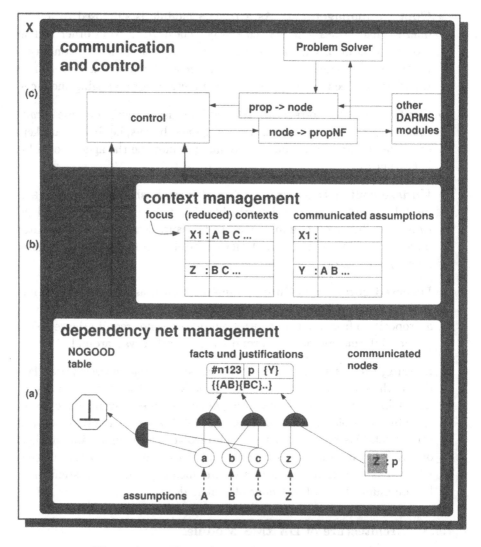

Figure 4.14: The architecture of DARMS modules

Dependency Net Management   The dependency net module is very similar to that of an ATMS. A new node type – *communicated nodes* – is used to locally represent communicated information. A communicated node also stores the identifier of the agent it was received from, e.g. $X_i{:}p$. Communicated nodes may be used in the antecedent of justifications, but not in the consequent. The DARMS module also ensures, that any unknown assumptions contained in the label of a communicated node will be locally represented[22]. There is no mechanism to automatically link a communicated node $X_i{:}p$ with the node p representing the agent's own belief about the proposition at hand. Higher level protocols can easily provide such functionality in order to implement shared belief (see below) or various mechanisms for trust, for example. The data structure for DARMS nodes has been extended to include *receivers*, a representation of the set of agents the node has been communicated to ($\{X_j\}$ in node p of X_i's DARMS module). This set serves to find out, which agents are to be informed in case of label updates to the node. At present, we assume that communicated information is not passed on to other agents, i.e. an agent does provide other agents only with locally derived information[23]. Thus, *receivers* of communicated nodes will usually be empty.

Context Management   The context management facility manages an agent's own current context $focus_{X_i}$ and two tables of assumption sets. The first is a *reduced context table*, which is indexed by agents. For each agent that X_i has received information from, the DARMS module maintains an entry in the table that represents the other agent's *reduced focus*, written as $cont_{X_i}(X_j)$. Simply speaking, the reduced focus contains only those assumptions in $focus_{X_j}$, which occur at least once in a label of any communicated node X_i received from X_j. By using the reduced focus of X_j, X_i can determine for any communicated node received from X_j by *local* label lookup, whether X_j currently believes the data represented by the node or not. This is possible because whenever X_j modifies its focus, it determines whether any other agents, e.g. X_i, are affected and sends a message to update the reduced focus. In order to provide this capability, DARMS modules must keep track of the set of assumptions relevant to some other agent, which are exactly those assumptions that occur in nodes that have been communicated to this agent. We denote this set of *communicated assumptions* by $comm\text{-}ass_{X_j}(X_i)$. In the example above, agent X_i needs to know that assumptions A and B are relevant to agent X_j. This information is stored in a *communicated assumptions table*, which is indexed by agents.

---

[22]However, the local system is not forced to include any of these new assumptions in its focus.

[23]Note, however, that in contrast to the DATMS, we allow any locally derived information to be communicated, even if it depends on communicated information. Also, passing on communicated nodes is not strictly forbidden; it simply does not make much sense.

Communication and Control   Finally, the communication and control unit coordinates dependency net management module and context management facility, provides the necessary functional interface (adding data to the net, changing the focus, etc.) to the problem solver, and handles all communication with other DARMS modules. It also provides translation of propositions to normal form, which is used whenever propositions must be passed back to the problem solver or to other DARMS modules.

4.4.6.4   Functional Interface and DARMS Behavior

DARMS extends traditional ATMS functionality mainly in two ways: it provides functions to manage the focus and functions with an additional agent parameter. The former allows us – as DARMS maintains the agent's focus – to provide query functions without an assumption set parameter; they can be viewed as traditional ATMS queries with the focus as default assumption set. The latter provides remote belief query capability, because the problem solver can ask its own DARMS about other agents beliefs and the DARMS module handles all necessary communication.

The functionality of the problem solver interface of DARMS is specified in [Fuhge, 1993] and cannot be fully described here. To illustrate the behavior of DARMS modules we describe

- how a remote belief query is handled and

- how inconsistency is dealt with.

Remote Belief Query   Let us suppose the above example involving DARMS modules X_i and X_j and their associated problem solver PS_{X_i} and PS_{X_j}, but without p already being communicated. Suppose PS_{X_j} asks X_j, whether PS_{X_i} currently believes p. X_j checks its dependency net, finding out that it does not have a communicated node $X_i{:}p$ yet. It sends a *sp-request* message[24] to X_i. Without interrupting PS_{X_i}, X_i looks up it's node representing p, adds X_j to *receivers* of node p, retrieves the label of p, and sends it via a *sp* message to X_j. Furthermore, X_i checks it's communicated assumptions table, finding no entry *comm-ass*$_{X_i}(X_j)$ for X_j yet. Thus, a new entry is created, which is a list representing the union of all environments in p's label. Finally, it produces a reduced focus by intersecting *comm-ass*$_{X_i}(X_j)$ with its own current context, *focus*$_{X_i}$, and sends it to X_j using a *update-context* message. On receiving the *sp* message from X_i, X_j creates a communicated node $X_i{:}p$ using the label provided in the message. It also checks all the assumptions in the label received and creates any new assumption it has not seen before. On receiving the *update-context* message, it adds an entry to the reduced context table.

---

[24]sp = sufficient preconditions

This entry is used to locally determine the result of the problem solver's query whether X_i currently believes p by checking whether some environment in the label is a subset of the reduced context.

In X_i has been established all information necessary to provide X_j with update information if local changes occur: If the node is relabelled, it can look up the node's set of *receivers* and send all of them an *update-sp* message. Also, it needs to update the communicated assumptions entries for all agents in *receivers*, if relabelling causes any new assumptions to occur in the node. If the problem solver changes its focus, the entries in the communicated assumptions table are used to find out, which agents must be informed via an *update-context* message. In X_j a local representation for PS_{X_i}'s belief state of p and for the relevant part of PS_{X_i}'s focus have been established.

Inconsistency   The previous discussion neglects how inconsistent situations (NOGOODs) are dealt with. If an agent detects a NOGOOD that is inconsistent with an environment in the label of a communicated node $X_j{:}p$, then this NOGOOD must be communicated to X_j. As discussed previously, NOGOODs relevant for another agent are also communicated to that agent. A NOGOOD of agent X_i is relevant for an agent X_j if it involves one or more assumptions occuring in the label of any node communicated from X_i to X_j. X_i can efficiently find the NOGOODs $ng\text{-}comm_{X_i}(X_j)$ relevant for X_j by intersecting each known NOGOOD with $comm\text{-}ass(X_j)$. Any NOGOOD resulting in a non-empty intersection is relevant and must be communicated to X_j. To summarize: an agent X_i communicates a NOGOOD to X_j in the following situations:

- After communication from X_i to X_j, agent X_i recomputes the vector of communicated assumptions $comm\text{-}ass_{X_i}(X_j)$. This may give rise to new NOGOODs relevant for X_j.

- Whenever X_i updates the label of a node communicated to X_j, it must check for new NOGOODs relevant for X_j.

- If X_i detects a NOGOOD in the label of a communicated node $X_j{:}p$, then this is a NOGOOD relevant for X_j.

- Whenever X_i locally derives a new NOGOOD, it checks whether it is relevant for another agent or occurs in the label of any communicated node.

- Agents also check the reduced context table for NOGOODs, because a NOGOOD could be in a reduced focus, but not occur in any communicated label.

In contrast to the usual approach of striving for various degrees of shared consistency, the above measures impose a strict notion of inconsistency. Although agents may arbitrarily disagree otherwise (how propositions are justified, what assumptions to make) they may not do so when it comes to inconsistent information. If an agent actually derives a set of assumptions to be inconsistent, basically all others have to accept the corresponding NOGOOD.

4.4.6.5   Formal Specification of DARMS

This section provides a formal specification for DARMS, which consists of two definitions. The first one formally specifies the functionality by defining the derivability relation for a communicating, assumption-based reasoner. This derivability relation is very similar to the derivability relation for a simple assumption-based reasoner (see deKleer[de Kleer, 1986a]), but accounts for communication by introducing modal operators. The second definition specifies a set of integrity constraints, which the data structures used by DARMS must meet in order to correctly implement the derivability relation.

Derivability in Communicating Agents   The basic question an assumption-based reasoner is supposed to answer is whether a given proposition holds wrt. a given context represented by a set of assumptions (also called environment). In order to produce an answer, the reasoner must compute a derivability relation $\vdash$. In a simple, non-communicating, assumption-based reasoner as assumed e.g. in de Kleer's ATMS, the derivability relation is defined as follows:

DEFINITION 4.4.1 (SINGLE-AGENT DERIVABILITY RELATION $\vdash$)
Let $\mathcal{P}$ be the set of propositions in some language L and X be an agent with a set of justifications $\mathcal{JUST}$ of the form $(x_1, \ldots, x_k \Rightarrow y)$ with $y \in \mathcal{P}$ and $x_r \in \mathcal{P}$ for $1 \leq r \leq k$.

X can derive a proposition p from a set of assumptions U (characterizing a context), written

$$\mathcal{JUST} \vdash U \rightarrow p,$$

if there is a sequence of sets $S_1, \ldots, S_m$ such that

$$S_1 = U$$
$$S_{l+1} = S_l \cup \{\, y \mid \exists_{(x_1,\ldots,x_k \rightarrow y) \in \mathcal{JUST}} \forall_{r,1 \leq r \leq k} : [\, x_r \in S_l \,] \,\}$$
$$p \in S_m$$

In the distributed case, we must take account for communication. We do this by introducing a modal operator X_j for each agent. Thus, $X_j{:}p$ is used to represent agent X_j's belief of p (*communicated belief*). Justifications may refer to communicated beliefs in their antecedents, but not in their consequent. The derivability relation of a communicating, assumption-based reasoner X_i, written $\vdash_{X_i}$, is given by the following definition.

DEFINITION 4.4.2 (MULTIAGENT DERIVABILITY RELATION $\vdash_{X_i}$)
*Let $\mathcal{P}$ be the set of propositions in some language L. Let $\mathcal{X} := \{X_i \mid 1 \leq i \leq n\}$
be a set of n agents, each of which is described by a tuple $\langle COMM_{X_i}, JUST_{X_i}\rangle$,
where $COMM_{X_i}$ is a set of communicated beliefs $X_j{:}p$ with $X_j \in \mathcal{X}, j \neq i$ and
$p \in \mathcal{P}$, and $JUST_{X_i}$ is a set of local justifications of the form $(x_1, \ldots, x_k \Rightarrow y)$
with $y \in \mathcal{P}$ and $[x_r \in \mathcal{P} \vee x_r \in COMM_{X_i}]$ for $1 \leq r \leq k$.*

*An agent X_i with local justifications $JUST_{X_i}$ and communicated beliefs
$COMM_{X_i}$ can locally derive a proposition p from a set of assumptions U,
written*

$$(COMM_{X_i}, JUST_{X_i}) \vdash_{X_i} U \to p,$$

if there is a sequence of sets $S_1, \ldots, S_m$ such that

$$S_1 = U \cup \{\, X_t{:}q \mid X_t{:}q \in COMM_{X_i} \wedge ((COMM_{X_t}, JUST_{X_t}) \vdash_{X_t} U \to q) \,\}$$
$$S_{l+1} = S_l \cup \{\, y \mid \exists_{(x_1,\ldots,x_k \to y) \in JUST_{X_i}} \forall_{r,1 \leq r \leq k} : [x_r \in S_l] \,\}$$
$$p \in S_m$$

Hence, a proposition p holds wrt. a given context, if it is derivable from this
context, the currently known local justifications and those propositions known
from other agents that these agents are able to derive from the given context.
The above definition also specifies the condition for an agent X_i to derive
a communicated belief $X_j{:}p$, which is stated more explicit in the following
lemma (without proof).

LEMMA 4.4.1 (DERIVABILITY OF A COMMUNICATED BELIEF)
An agent X_i can derive a communicated belief $X_j{:}p$, written

$$(COMM_{X_i}, JUST_{X_i}) \vdash_{X_i} U \to X_j{:}p$$

iff agent X_j can derive p, i.e.

$$(COMM_{X_j}, JUST_{X_j}) \vdash_{X_j} U \to p$$

In a naive approach, one could compute the derivability relation every time a
query is posed. However, this would require substantial computational effort
and a full-fledged theorem prover that would have to construct a proof tree for
each query. Furthermore, in the distributed case substantial communication
overhead would be necessary and a simple query could invoke proof procedures
in several reasoners.

An (ATMS-type) RMS can do this much more efficiently by maintaining a
dependency net and performing label propagation; it can answer the query
by simply checking subset relationships (if any environment in the node's
label is a subset of the context, the answer to the query is positive). For the

labels used in the ATMS, deKleer has specified four integrity constraints that guarantee well-formedness of labels. DARMS uses equivalent constraints by extending them to communicated nodes. Furthermore, DARMS must ensure certain inter-agent constraints between the DARMS modules, which is achieved by another four integrity constraints.

DEFINITION 4.4.3 (DARMS INTEGRITY CONSTRAINTS)
Let $\mathcal{P}$ be the set of propositions in some language L. Let $\mathcal{X} := \{X_i \mid 1 \leq i \leq n\}$ be a set of n agents, each of which is described by a tuple $\langle COMM_{X_i}, JUST_{X_i} \rangle$, where $COMM_{X_i}$ is a set of communicated beliefs $X_j{:}p$ with $X_j \in \mathcal{X}, j \neq i$ and $p \in \mathcal{P}$, and $JUST_{X_i}$ is a set of local justifications of the form $(x_1, \ldots, x_k \Rightarrow y)$ with $y \in \mathcal{P}$ and $[x_j \in \mathcal{P} \lor x_j \in COMM_{X_i}]$ for $1 \leq j \leq k$. Let $\mathcal{A} \subseteq \mathcal{P}$ be all the assumptions known to any agent in $\mathcal{X}$. Also, for X_i, let $lab_{X_i}(p)$ be the label of the node representing p (consisting of a set of environments $U \subseteq \mathcal{A}$), $nogoods_{X_i}$ be X_i's nogood table, and $focus_{X_i}$ be its current context. Furthermore, for any two agents X_i and X_j, let $sp\text{-}comm_{X_i}(X_j)$ be the set of propositions that X_i transmitted to X_j, $comm\text{-}ass_{X_i}(X_j)$ be the set of relevant assumptions that X_i transmitted to X_j, $ng\text{-}comm_{X_i}(X_j)$ be the set of relevant NOGOODs that X_i transmitted to X_j and $cont_{X_i}(X_j)$ be X_i's reduced focus of X_j.

Then, the following integrity constraints must hold for a set of DARMS modules:

1. *Consistency:*

$$\forall U \in lab_{X_i}(p) \forall_{N \in nogoods_{X_i}} : [N \not\subseteq U]$$

2. *Soundness:*

$$\forall U \in lab_{X_i}(p) : [(COMM_{X_i}, JUST_{X_i}) \vdash_{X_i} U \to p]$$

3. *Completeness:*

$$\forall_{U \subseteq \mathcal{A}} : [\forall_{N \in nogoods_{X_i}} : [N \not\subseteq U] \land (COMM_{X_i}, JUST_{X_i}) \vdash_{X_i} U \to p)]$$
$$\implies \exists_{U' \in lab_{X_i}(p)} : [U' \subseteq U]]$$

4. *Minimality:*

$$\forall U_1, U_2 \in lab_{X_i}(p) : U_1 \subseteq U_2 \longrightarrow U_1 = U_2$$

5. *Correctness of communicated node labels:*

$$\forall p \in sp\text{-}comm_{X_i}(X_j) : lab_{X_i}(p) = lab_{X_j}(X_i{:}p)$$

6. *Exchange of relevant context information:*

$$\forall A \in comm\text{-}ass_{X_i}(X_j) : (A \in focus_{X_i} \longleftrightarrow A \in cont_{X_j}(X_i))$$

7. *Correctness of communicated contexts:*

$$\forall N \in nogoods_{X_i} : N \nsubseteq focus_{X_i} \land N \nsubseteq cont_{X_i}(X_j)$$

8. *Exchange of relevant* NOGOODs *:*

$$\forall N \in ng\text{-}comm_{X_i}(X_j) : (\exists N' \in nogoods_{X_j} \land N' \subseteq N)$$

Consistency ensures, that no environment in the label is inconsistent. Soundness ensures, that a node can be derived from every environment in its label. Completeness ensures that for any context, which allows to derive a node, there is an environment representing this context in the node's label. Minimality ensures that the environments of a node label do not contain assumptions that could be left out and still allow to derive the node from the environment. Strictly speaking, minimality is not a necessary requirement, but it is useful for efficiency reasons. The correctness of communicated labels ensures that the label of a communicated node is always the same as the label of the original node. Exchange of relevant context information ensures that an agent receiving information always knows the relevant part of the sending agent's focus. All assumptions occurring in any environment of any label communicated from the sending to the receiving agent are relevant. Correctness of communicated contexts ensures, that the discovery of inconsistencies in a communicated context is propagated to the agent which owns this context. The focus of the own problem solver is also checked for NOGOODs to prevent the PS from reasoning in an inconsistent focus. Finally, exchange of relevant NOGOODs ensures, that all NOGOODs relevant for another agent are communicated to this agent.

If the DARMS data structures as described in the previous sections meet these eight integrity constraints, the subset test in DARMS effectively computes the derivability relation for a communicating, assumption-based reasoner $\vdash_{X_i}$. The formal specification of DARMS allows us to conclude the following propositions:

PROPOSITION 4.4.1 (ATMS EXPRESSIVENESS) DARMS *has at least the expressive power of an* ATMS.

PROOF 4.4.1 *The proof is trivial: Assume a single* DARMS-*based agent* X_i *that does not communicate at all, i.e.* $\mathcal{COMM}_{X_i} = \emptyset$. *The first four integrity constraints are equivalent to deKleer's constraints for* ATMS *labels. Thus,* DARMS *is at least as restrictive as the* ATMS. *The other four constraints are trivially met, as the sets of communicated propositions, communicated assumptions, communicated contexts and reduced focus are all empty. Hence,* DARMS *is no more restrictive than the* ATMS. *Thus, any* DARMS *is at least* ATMS-*expressive.*□

Often, agents want to merge beliefs received from other agents. A simple way to (unconditionally) believe p whenever some agent X_j believes p is to create a justification from node $X_j{:}p$ to node p. In this case, we can conclude the following proposition:

PROPOSITION 4.4.2 (BELIEF MERGE) *If an agent X_i has a communicated node $X_j{:}p$ and adds the justification $X_j{:}p \Rightarrow p$, then it will believe p at least in all contexts, in which agent X_j believes p.*

PROOF 4.4.2 $\forall p \in sp\text{-}comm_{X_j}(X_i) : U \in lab_{X_j}(p) \implies (\exists U' \in lab_{X_i}(p) \wedge U' \subseteq U)$ □

We can now state the following proposition about cycles in communication of propositions.

PROPOSITION 4.4.3 (CYCLIC COMMUNICATION) *Let p be a proposition and $\langle X_i \rangle_{0 \le i \le n-1}$ with $n \ge 2$ be a sequence of agents such that for all $0 \le i \le n-1$: $X_{i \bmod n}$ has communicated p to $X_{(i+1) \bmod n}$ and $X_{(i+1) \bmod n}$ has recorded a justification $X_{i \bmod n}{:}p \Rightarrow p$, i.e. there is cyclic communication wrt. p, then all these agents completely agree on p: for all $0 \le i, j \le n-1$: $lab_{X_i}(p) = lab_{X_j}(p)$*

PROOF 4.4.3 *The proof is by induction on the length n for sequences of agents. Since X_0 and X_1 are merging their communicated beliefs, we have for $n = 2$: $\forall U \in lab_{X_0}(p) : (\exists U' \in lab_{X_1}(p) \wedge U' \subseteq U)$ and $\forall U' \in lab_{X_1}(p) : (\exists U \in lab_{X_0}(p) \wedge U \subseteq U')$. Therefore $lab_{X_0}(p) = lab_{X_1}(p)$.*

Hence, cyclic communication of a proposition p in DARMS is essentially the same as establishing a shared node for p in the DTMS.

4.4.6.6   Applying DARMS

This section outlines the use of DARMS for improving the integration of planning, scheduling, and control. Due to space limitations, the examples must be very short, and may seem trivial at first glance. However, they illustrate the basic mechanisms used to support replanning and contingency planning in the transmission job shop scenario.

As an example, consider some workpiece B to be manufactured. Its process plan contains some operation p to be executed on some machine (which is not of interest here) using one of two possible tools $A1$ or $A2$, which require different NC programs and have different duration. Normally, using $A1$ is more efficient, and this option is preferred to using $A2$. However, $A1$ breaks every now and then, it takes considerable time to replace it, and $A2$ is used in such cases.

We consider two scenarios. Both assume, that the job for workpiece B has been scheduled under the assumption that tool $A1$ would be available, but the executer detects the contrary at some time between scheduling and execution. The first scenario shows how to dynamically react in such a situation, the second one shows how the scheduler may plan ahead and provide contingencies, especially if $A1$ breaks really often.

Both scheduler and executer use a DARMS module to represent their planning and scheduling data. Assumptions are used to represent that the the workpiece is okay, and that a tool can be configured. An executable operation is represented as a fact that is justified by the belief in other facts, e.g. the underlying assumptions.

Handling Failure Situations In the first scenario (see Figure 4.15, the scheduler X creates a schedule for performing operation p using tool $A1$. In its DARMS module, it will have the assumptions $A1$ and B, the fact p and a justification $A1, B \implies p$. Thus, p holds (p is executable), if both $A1$ and B can be assumed at the same time. Since there is no knowledge to the contrary, the scheduler does actually assume both $A1$ and B and includes these assumptions in its focus. It then tells executer Y about the newly created schedule, which will add assumptions $A1$ and B as well as the communicated node $X{:}p$ with label $\{\{A1, B\}\}$. Some time later, the executer detects that $A1$ cannot be used for some reason and tells its DARMS the corresponding NOGOOD $\{A1\}$. The NOGOOD results in label propagation in Y's DARMS (giving p the empty label) and in a low-level communication from Y's DARMS module to X's DARMS module about this NOGOOD. This triggers label propagation in X's DARMS as well, which gives p the empty label and yielding X's focus inconsistent. X must take $A1$ out of its focus and notices that there is a scheduled operation with an empty label, which means the machine cannot execute it as scheduled. The scheduler can now back up on its second alternative and decide on the use of tool $A2$. It creates an assumption for $A2$ and a new justification for p. The label update performed at p will — again as low-level communication between DARMS modules — be communicated to the executer Y, which is now able to execute p.

Note, that all necessary communication for handling the failure situation is performed by the DARMS modules. All communication the problem solvers have to do is with their own DARMS modules. The scheduler simply schedules jobs when they arrive, and informs the respective executer about them. Using DARMS, the executers get an explicit representation of the underlying assumptions the scheduler made, which are typically tied to states observable by the executer. Thus, they can check and verify or falsify relevant state in-

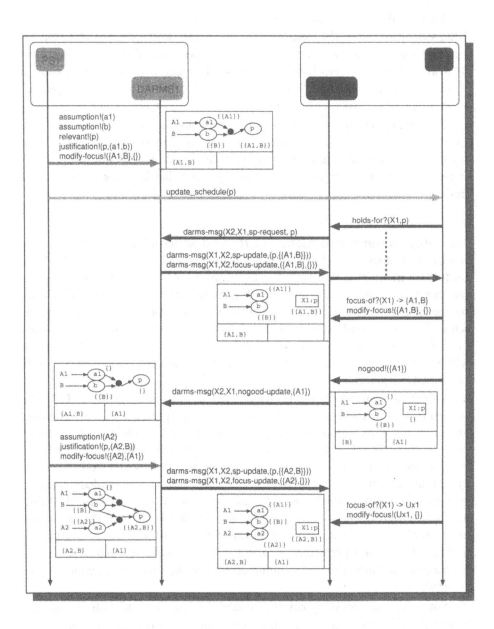

Figure 4.15: Handling failures using DARMS

formation in a very focused, goal-directed manner. The scheduler checks its
DARMS module for operations with empty labels on a regular basis and takes
measures to repair them. If repair can be done, it tells its DARMS module
about it, which automatically communicates and propagates changes to all
other affected DARMS.

Planning for Contingencies In the second scenario (Figure 4.16), we assume that tool $A1$ breaks very often, i.e. there is a significant likelihood that
it will break before executing operation p. In cases like this, contingency
planning must be considered. In other words, the scheduler anticipates the
situation that $A1$ breaks and provides alternative procedures to follow in this
situation.

In our example, the scheduler would consider both alternatives right away.
X's DARMS would have all the assumptions, nodes, and justifications as before
(with p now having the label $\{\{A1, B\}, \{A2, B\}\}$), plus the additional NOGOOD
$\{A1, A2\}$ representing that both tools cannot be used simultaneously. X would
indicate its preference of using $A1$ by including it into its focus. The executer
Y would try to adopt X's focus, as long as there is no conflicting information.
If $A1$ is declared NOGOOD before starting operation p, however, this alternative
cannot be carried out any more. However, there still is another environment in
$X{:}p$. As long as its assumptions can be included into the focus (i.e. the tool $A2$
can be configured and workpiece B is okay), the executer can still proceed, at
least with this particular operation. Again, low-level communication between
the DARMS modules will ensure that the scheduler X receives the information
about this change and can compute the appropiate consequences (e.g. a delay
of subsequent operations).

Note again, that no high level communication is necessary to handle the
failure situation here. Also, low-level communication is reduced, as the executer can directly react to the failure, without waiting for the scheduler to
come up with an alternative decision. However, the scheduler had to do the
extra work up front. In practical scenarios, the extra work may be limited
to provide one alternative operation only, without computing the effects of
actually using the contingency option (i.e. the alternative plan/schedule is developed only to depth one). However, since machine operations in practice
often take a aignificant amount of time (between several minutes up to several
hours), this kind of minimum reactivity in schedules may give the scheduler
just enough time to recompute the schedule, if such a failure situation arises.
This is certainly better than having the machine sit around doing nothing
while computing another schedule.

Advanced Use: A Perspective In this paragraph we want to give a rough
sketch of further types of useful applications of DARMS in planning, schedul-

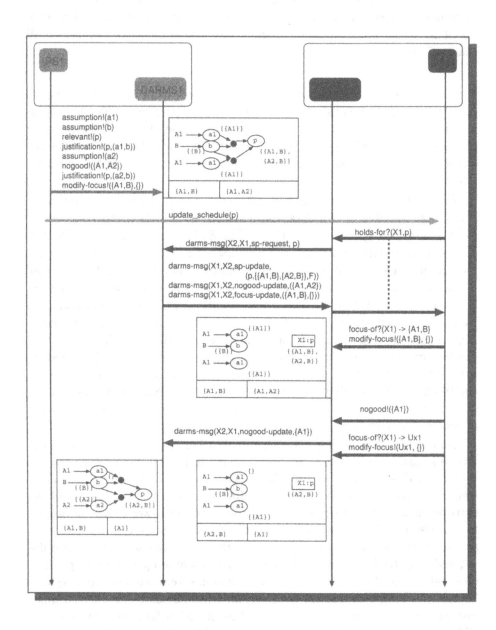

Figure 4.16: Planning contingencies using DARMS

ing, and control. The first application leads towards a solution of the following problem: If we cannot perform the (optimal) process plan given current constraints, when should we replan (use a less efficient process plan) and when should we reschedule (pre-empt other jobs, miss due dates)? We simply assume that a planner creates cost-optimal process plans assuming unlimited resources. The scheduler tries to use them and schedules its operations as good as it can. It then computes a cost penalty for this process plan with respect to its limited resources, by taking into account increased Work-In-Progress, job delays, etc. and informs the planner. The planner may now consider creating an alternative process plan that may be cheaper to schedule, but is by itself more expensive.

A different scenario could be the following: Process plans are not created in advance, but only on demand, i.e. when a job must be scheduled. Using abstractions, the scheduler informs the planner about its current resource situation. The planner then tries to come up with a process plan that is optimal given certain resource constraints. Possibly, a very close cooperation between planner and scheduler may yield best results: the planner has all the planning knowledge (what operations are available, etc.), but it asks the scheduler every time to evaluate alternative operations. The scheduler's evaluation of alternatives may depend on its current resource conditions and workload.

4.4.6.7 Discussion and Conclusions

Development of the DARMS system was a logical and important step into the right direction. An analysis of the desirable functionality opened up new insights and provided a much clearer view of the problem. The desire to provide a true distributed ATMS guided design and development.

However, a much more detailed analysis later on revealed the fact that there are a number of subtle issues about the design of DARMS which make it difficult to supply a precise formal characterization of DARMS behavior at best and render DARMS useless for many PEDE applications at worst.

Most of these problems are related to the problem of what agents in a multiagent setting consider relevant facts and assumptions. Or in other words, when, how, and to what extent does a DARMS module make previously unseen propositions and assumptions locally relevant, if they occur in queries? Under an ATMS-like reason maintenance scheme, adding a single assumption can at worst double the number of relevant environments. Adopting a rather liberal policy for dealing with unseen assumptions in queries thereby opens an avenue for unfair attacks by malevolent agents: Simply thrashing another agent's DARMS module with queries containing previously unseen assumptions can suffice in certain circumstances to blow the other agent's DARMS computationally.

Another problem of DARMS deals with NOGOODs. In the original DARMS specification, it was possible that an agent could get a positive response to a query regarding its belief into a communicated proposition, if it used an environment which was consistent locally, but not for the supplying agent. This oversight was later on repaired in [Dotzel, 1994], but as a consequence of this more stringent handling of NOGOODs almost all of them had to communicated and shared between almost al DARMS modules.

Aside of these pitfalls, there was still the open problem of efficiency: How can we efficiently maintain up to a million assumptions, a million dependencies, and a couple of hundred contexts in a multiagent system for PEDE applications? Thus, further work was necessary in order to obtain more suitable tools for PEDE applications.

4.5   Review of Multiagent Reason Maintenance

In section 4.1 we first investigated a multiagent meeting scheduling scenario, which exhibited many similarities, but also a few significant differences to the single agent scenario. One of the obvious and important differences was the need for communication between agents due to belief revision activities. Because belief revision activity crosses agent boundaries, we derived a need for distributed reason maintenance and showed that appropriate support systems could aid substantially in handling dependencies in multiagent domains.

Section 4.2 dealt with the formalization of the problem we analyzed previously. Various standard ways to formalize intentional notions, like modal logics of knowledge and belief, were reviewed, but altogether found to be more expressive and powerful than necessary. FHPL, a rather restricted, small logics was presented afterwards and discussed in some detail. The section concluded with a demonstration of how to apply FHPL to the multiagent meeting scheduling example used in the problem analysis.

With the problem analysis and formalization as background, Section 4.3 was devoted to the informal specification of a basic, generic set of functionalities for multiagent reason maintenance systems.

Section 4.4 reviewed previously available technology, which led to the conclusion that none of the existing systems is actually well-suited for multiagent planning and scheduling applications. Thus, new technology is required, and in the next chapter we try to make a first step towards this technology.

Chapter 5

MXFRMS:
A Multiagent Focus-Based
Reason Maintenance System

The chapter presents MXFRMS,[1] which provides a flexible and robust *base layer* for building advanced multiagent reason maintenance systems. In particular, MXFRMS allows for the construction of sophisticated, special-purpose multiagent context management and coordination facilities as needed e.g. in application systems that solve PEDE problems. Furthermore, it is designed to be extensible such that functionality for supporting temporal reasoning and for maintaining plans and schedules can be added.

5.1 Overview on MXFRMS

The main purpose of MXFRMS is to manage the beliefs and contexts of multiple agents in the presence of logical dependencies between their propositional data and the exchange of such data via inter-agent communication processes. MXFRMS is designed to be a flexible and extensible general-purpose distributed reason maintenance tool that is useful for a wide variety of applications utilizing multiagent systems technology.

The Generality/Specificity Dichotomy and MXFRMS Functionality Depending on one's viewpoint, the required functionality for belief and context management in multiagent systems may vary significantly. Including support for e.g. conflict resolution and coordination in a DRMS extends the

---

[1]MXFRMS is an acronym for Multiagent eXtended Focus-Based Reason Maintenance System

functionality of the system, but makes it also more specific and probably narrows its applicability. Regarding conflict resolution and multiagent coordination, there does not seem to exist a single, widely accepted scheme for either one of these problems. Usually, the approaches presented in the literature (e.g. [Sycara, 1993], [Petrie et al., 1994b]) have been designed for particular domains or applications. However, their use for other types of problems is at least questionable. Choosing any one of the approaches in the implementation of MXFRMS would significantly limit its possible uses. The fundamental question then arising is what functionality MXFRMS should provide in order to take a reasonable compromise between generality and specificity.

From an MXFRMS view, context management functionality can be divided into an application-specific (or domain-dependent) part and a general part. The application-specific part includes the *selection of interesting contexts* and *strategies for conflict resolution*, both of which tend to require specialized solutions tailored to the problem on hand. Because of their dependence on the domain or a particular application, it does not seem to make much sense to provide such functionality in a general-purpose tool such as MXFRMS. However, the general part of context management functionality, which is actually covered by MXFRMS, supports various approaches to solve these problems by providing functionality related to the *maintenance of contexts* and the *identification of conflicts*. Consequently, MXFRMS includes functionality for

- representing a (potentially large) number of relevant (propositional) problem solver data (from multiple problem solvers), including data communicated between agents,

- maintaining a (potentially large) number of logical dependencies among these propositional data,

- finding (with reasonable effort) logical consequences of assumptions with respect to the logical dependencies of a group of agents,

- determining the consistency of sets of assumptions within a group of agents, and

- representing and maintaining multiple contexts.

By providing these functionalities, MXFRMS supports the solution of

- the *distributed consequence determination problem*,

- the *distributed (local) context determination problem*,

- and the *distributed belief revision problem*

in multiagent systems which perform multiple-context, assumption-based reasoning.

Key Design Requirements The general goals in designing MXFRMS were *belief autonomy* and *local control*. By belief autonomy we mean that an agent's belief cannot be manipulated by other agents in uncontrollable and unforeseeable ways. Above all, this means that there is no way whatsoever that other agents somehow influence those beliefs of an agent which are purely local and do not dependent on communicated information. Also, other agents cannot force an agent to get interested in particular contexts. Belief autonomy will be described more specifically later on. Local control is an important aspect in *distributed* implementations of MXFRMS. It means that none of the MXFRMS algorithms may require some kind of global control scheme in order to perform reason maintenance functionality for an agent. In particular, a distributed implementation is worth the effort only if it provides some real concurrency and does not require a global serialization of the interactions with the problem solvers. Again, the concept and effect of local control will be explained in detail later on.

Key Design Ideas An essential, enabling element for achieving belief autonomy is the use of a suitable language for representing problem solver data; if the language is not expressive enough to model agents having different assumptions, dependencies, beliefs and contexts, then there is little hope for true belief autonomy. Thus, the underlying logic used by the agents to formulate their data and the dependencies between these data is assumed to be FHPL.

A design idea suggested by the underlying logic is that of structuring the MXFRMS data into facets, thereby yielding a natural unit for defining the grain size of distribution: different facets may be represented by different MXFRMS modules (which may be implemented as separate processes on different hosts), but a single facet is always represented in a non-distributed fashion. This structure is complemented by several other ideas that directly or indirectly affect representation of problem solver data: remote belief queries, local representation of communicated data (communicated beliefs), update contracts, and directed communication. Remote belief query means that an agent's problem solver addresses all requests related to other agents' beliefs to its own MXFRMS module, i.e. the MXFRMS module handling the agent's facet. The MXFRMS module takes care of all necessary communication with other agents' MXFRMS modules. Local representation of communicated data and update contracts mean that communicated beliefs are stored locally at the MXFRMS module of the requesting agent and that this modules receives update messages from the MXFRMS module of the agent providing the belief whenever changes to the belief occur. Directed communication means that agent need not perform mutual exchange of beliefs, i.e. if an agent requests a belief from another agent, the other agent does not automatically get the requestign agent's belief about the same proposition.

In contrast to HPL in the single agent case, where *environments* (sets of assumptions) uniquely determine contexts, FHPL contexts are determined by a *pair* (called a *focus structure* or simply focus) consisting of a *group* (a set of facets) and an *environment* (a set of assumptions). Two further key concepts related to focus structures are *context coherence* and *shared inconsistency*. Context coherence is simply group coherence as already introduced in the discussion of FHPL and means that in each context all agents referenced in the group of the underlying focus structure assume the same set of propositions. Shared inconsistency means that a context must be group consistent, i.e. in order to determine the consistency of a focus structure we must ensure that the proposition $\perp$ is not derivable in any facet referenced in the group.

MXFRMS extends the basic focus structure as follows:

- Each focus is assigned a set of facets called *owners*, for which the focus — and thus, the context — is relevant. Any focus owned by more than one facet is a *shared focus*, all others are *local focus structures*. A shared focus is created if a second facet *hooks* into an existing focus that has previously been created by another facet. While a local focus can only be used by its single owner in queries, a shared focus can be used in queries by any of its owners.

- Another attribute, the *public write permit*, determines whether foci are *public* or *private*. Private foci are always owned by only a single facet, while public foci can be owned by multiple facets (a group). Any shared focus must be public.

- A third focus attribute is the *modification token holder*. It identifies a single facet among the owners which is allowed to modify the focus structure. Possible modifications are to expand the group, to expand the environment, to extend the owners, to publish the focus, and to pass the modification token to another facet.

These extensions allow for flexible manipulation of focus structures and thereby provide a powerful basis for building customized coordination schemes.

As we cannot expect the computational requirements for managing multiple contexts in a multiagent setting to be any easier than in the single agent case, the main idea is to follow the approach taken by the XFRMS system: the MXFRMS *manages* multiple contexts, but it is up to the problem solvers to determine *which contexts* are of interest. The underlying assumption for this approach is that for most large applications, the number of contexts the problem solvers are interested in is orders of magnitudes smaller than the number of contexts an ATMS-like system would have to manage. Based on this assumption, the MXFRMS presented in this chapter shows that multiagent reason maintenance services for multiple-context assumption-based reasoning can be provided very efficiently.

For simplicity, but without restricting generality, we make two assumptions for the remainder of this chapter: The first assumption is that all agents know each other, i.e. each problem solver can freely reference all relevant facets. The second one is that each agent informs all other agents about all propositions and all assumptions it makes relevant (in the sense that these propositions can be used in queries, e.g. to form environments). Both assumptions deal with the congruence problem identified earlier and with issues related to data distribution. The assumptions taken here significantly simplify the specification and formal description of MXFRMS. Because facets, propositions, and assumptions are made known to everyone when they become relevant (a kind of *eager information exchange*), the functionality for checking the validity of data occurring in communication between agents becomes much less complex. The alternative would be to develop schemes for exchanging the relevant information *on demand*, but this often requires additional data structures with more complex schemes for updating the information represented by them. It certainly results in more complex procedures for the basic RMS functionality, which is in the focus of our discussion here. Note, however, that these decisions do not affect the design goal of *belief autonomy*, nor do they hurt *efficiency* very much: As will become obvious from the implementation description later on, the exchange of the above information is handled in a rather simple way; for instance, it usually does neither require to actually make the information locally relevant nor does it require label updates. Of course, one can easily conceive application scenarios where making these assumptions would be a bad idea. In such a situation, an actual implementation can easily provide additional functionality for dealing with these issues explicitly; the extension comes at the price of a little more complex data structures and algorithms, but does not require fundamental changes to the version of MXFRMS described here.

5.2 MXFRMS System Architecture

The design of the MXFRMS architecture is guided by the goals of flexibility and generality. Because the MXFRMS must coexist with a multiagent system, the architectures of both components should match or at least correlate in well-defined ways in order to yield good overall system behavior and performance. Thus, a look at typical characteristics of multiagent systems architectures is necessary first in order to determine possible consequences for the MXFRMS design and architecture. Then, we introduce three different perspectives of viewing the MXFRMS architecture and discuss each view in detail. The architecture discussion yields a negative and a positive result. The negative one is that it is not possible to provide a single fixed architecture for a general-purpose tool like MXFRMS. The positive one is that all functionality related to reason maintenance can be embodied in a so-called MXFRMS facet module which builds the basic building block for a particular MXFRMS implementation. As a consequence, we can provide the structure of an *open* MXFRMS architecture, which is presented at the end.

5.2.1   Multiagent System Architecture

We consider a typical multiagent system MAS, which consists of a set PS = $\{p_1, \ldots, p_k\}$ of k agents (problem solvers). It is assumed that any two agents may engage in communication of information. The set of agents may dynamically change, but due to our restriction to monotonic reason maintenance the set may only grow, i.e. agents may be added to but not removed from the multiagent system.[2] For simplicity, we assume in the following that all of the agents perform (monotonic) multiple-context, assumption-based reasoning and need to use the services of MXFRMS.

A major indicator for flexibility and generality of a system architecture is its independence of particular implementation decisions. Implementation independence is particularly difficult to achieve for software such as multiagent systems, because there exists a very wide spectrum of possible implementations. At one end of this spectrum the whole multiagent system is realized as a single process running on a single machine. An implementation where each agent is a separate process is somewhat in the middle of the implementation spectrum. In this case, several agents/processes may share the same host or run on different computers connected via local or wide area networks. At the far end of the spectrum we encounter designs where even single agents are implemented in a distributed manner (see Figure 5.1 for illustration).

Different implementation architectures require different means for implementing communication between agents. In scenario A in Figure 5.1, simple function calls can be used to implement agent communication. Scenario C requires more sophisticated functionality and could be realized with mechanisms like inter-process communication (IPC), remote procedure calls (RPC), and Internet communication facilities such as TCP/IP or electronic mail.

One of the most desirable features of an multiagent programming environment is to provide for adequate abstractions (through suitable language constructs) such that these implementation details are hidden from the implementor of an agent in the system. In particular, one would like to abstract from the way how agents are related to processes, how processes are mapped to hosts, and what the appropriate means are for communicating with another agent. The underlying implementation framework may choose to give the programmer explicit control over such allocation and other implementation is-

---

[2]See the Future Work section in the final chapter of this book for a discussion of possibilities to remove this restriction.

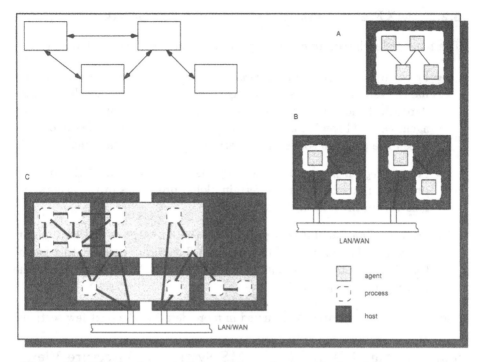

Figure 5.1: The implementation spectrum for a typical multiagent system.

The top left part of the figure shows the conceptual level of the multiagent system. The agents comprising the system are connected via links that indicate some form of interaction between the agents. The lower and right part shows three different implementation scenarios. In scenario A the complete multiagent system is implemented as a single process that – naturally – runs on a single processor. In scenario B each agent is realized as a separate process. The processes may run on the same host or on different hosts connected via some kind of communication network. Finally, in scenario C even single agents are realized in a distributed fashion as separate processes, which may be allocated on different hosts across the network.

sues. However, when programming an agent, all the programmer should need to know are the identity of other agents and an agent communication protocol such as KQML.[3]

A feature related to the previous one are mobile agents. If agents are allowed to travel from one host to another, one must solve a range of additional problems, e.g. how the delivery of messages send to an agent's previous location can be ensured. In the following, we will permit mobile agents but we simply assume that the implementation framework will provide functionality to solve such low-level problems.

---

[3]There actually exist implementations of KQML that, depending on what agent is addressed in a communication request, use various communication mechnisms such as function calls, TCP/IP, and electronic mail to actually transmit the information.

5.2.2   MXFRMS System Architecture Perspectives

The MXFRMS architecture can be viewed from three different perspectives:

- From an *agent-oriented perspective*, the (distributed) reason maintenance system should look to an agent's problem solver just like a standard RMS and permit a two-level agent architecture similar to the single
  agent case. This will have consequences for the way work is divided between the problem solver and its associated MXFRMS module.

- From a *logical perspective*, the MXFRMS is viewed as a single coherent
  program unit which ensures certain global properties of the agents' beliefs within the multiagent system.

- From an *implementational perspective*, the MXFRMS should have an architecture that promotes efficiency and flexibility. Usually, this means
  that the architecture should somewhat match the architecture of the
  multiagent system itself.

Each of these perspectives is discussed in more detail in the next few sections.

5.2.3   Agent-Oriented MXFRMS System Architecture View

The agent-oriented view may also be tagged *local view,* *agent view,* or *facet
view*, because it focuses on an agent's local perspective of reason maintenance.
From an agent-oriented view, each problem solver in the multiagent system is
assigned its own unique MXFRMS *facet module*.[4] The MXFRMS facet module can
be imagined as a kind of local logical representation and reasoning space. It
is the architectural equivalent of a facet in FHPL, which is used by an agent's
problem solver to formulate relevant propositions and logical dependencies.
Because an agent's reasoning is formally represented by a single facet and a
facet is realized as single MXFRMS facet module, an agent usually is not allowed
to use two MXFRMS facet modules at the same time.[5] A MXFRMS facet module
looks to its associated agent just like a local reason maintenance module which
provides at least the capabilities and services of a single-agent multiple-context
assumption-based reason maintenance system such as XFRMS, but provides
additional representational and inferential power (in comparison to a single-
agent reason maintenance system) by allowing the problem solvers to specify
base literal references in MXFRMS interface functions. Thus, a problem solver
can require from its MXFRMS facet module reason maintenance services that
involve other agents' beliefs, such as declaring other agents' belief status on

---

[4]Often simply referred to as MXFRMS module.

[5]In such a case, the result may be *schizophrenic* or some other kind of *brain-damaged*
agents. Logically, such an agent is represented by two facets, and it cannot be determined
which of the two "identities" is actually supposed to represent the agent.

certain propositions as relevant or determining whether some proposition is
group derivable for a particular group of agents.

The locality principle presented above forces the MXFRMS facet modules
to maintain local representations of communicated beliefs. All communication related to the acquisition and update of communicated beliefs must be
performed automatically without requiring any kind of additional reasoning
or control by the problem solver.

A central MXFRMS feature is that it promotes the use of an internal two-
level agent architecture and tries to hide most of the communication and information processing details related to reason maintenance. Taking the agent-
oriented perspective, communication between agents is structured into two
independent layers (see Figure 5.2):

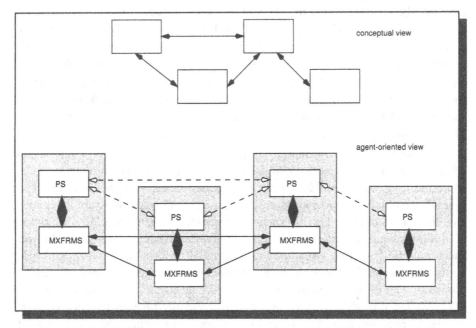

Figure 5.2: Agent-oriented view of the MXFRMS architecture.

As a consequence of the internal two-level agent architecture, communication between agents
can also be structured into two layers: Dashed lines between the agents' problem solvers
indicate application-specific communication. Thorough lines between the agents' MXFRMS
modules represent communication related to reason maintenance. An agent's problem solver
always interacts only with its own MXFRMS module (illustrated by black diamonds), but
never with other agent's MXFRMS modules.

- Communication between problem solvers is application- or domain-specific.
  For instance, it may include messages related to a conflict *resolution*
  protocol. As the agents' problem solvers must explicitly initiate such
  communication, they are also explicitly aware of it.

- Communication between the agent's MXFRMS modules is related to reason maintenance services. Such communication is automatically initiated by the MXFRMS modules and the problem solvers are *not* aware of
  it. Thereby, almost all communication related to reason maintenance
  (except for aforementioned messages related to conflict resolution) is
  hidden from the problem solvers.

The separation of communication in two layers, one of which is automatically
handled by an off-the-shelf general tool such as MXFRMS, reduces the overall
system complexity and significantly eases design, construction and maintenance of multiagent systems.

The agent-oriented view imposes a close relationship between problem
solver and its associated MXFRMS facet module, which can be exploited to
simplify the problem solver interface of MXFRMS: A particular implementation
can reduce the syntactic complexity of the PS interface by allowing the agents
to omit the outermost facet in all literals. Based on the assumption that an
MXFRMS facet module can distinguish messages from its problem solver from
messages sent by other MXFRMS modules, it can provide automatic facetification of formulas. Thus, many logical dependencies formulated by an agent
look just as HPL formulas and the MXFRMS automatically transposes them to
the equivalent FHPL formula.

Obviously, the agent-oriented view suggests a distributed implementation
of MXFRMS such that each agent is equipped with a MXFRMS facet module.
Whether an agent's problem solver and MXFRMS facet module are realized as
a single process or as two separate processes does not really matter; the resulting differences of these two alternative design choices are essentially restricted
to different communication mechanisms between problem solver and MXFRMS
facet module (function calls, vs. some form of process communication) and
should be hidden by the implementation environment as previously outlined.
However, the designer should be aware that an agent's problem solver and
MXFRMS facet module should, at least in principle, be able to work concurrently. Concurrent operation of problem solver and MXFRMS module is at least
advantageous, if not necessary, because an MXFRMS module may have to interact with other agents' MXFRMS modules while its associated problem solver
is engaged in possibly lengthy computations. Forcing other agents to wait for
an answer to a query until the MXFRMS under consideration will eventually
be given control by its problem solver would most likely lead to significant
performance bottlenecks.

5.2.4   Logical MXFRMS System Architecture View

From a logical view, the MXFRMS provides a mechanism for representing in and
reasoning with FHPL, very much like a relational database system provides the

functionality to represent tables and to perform certain operations on them. Similar to a database management system, the MXFRMS must enforce certain (global) logical properties, e.g. between base literals and base literal references. The global logical properties enforced by MXFRMS are discussed in detail in the formal specification of MXFRMS. Because of this emphasis of the global logical properties, the logical view may also be tagged *global view*.

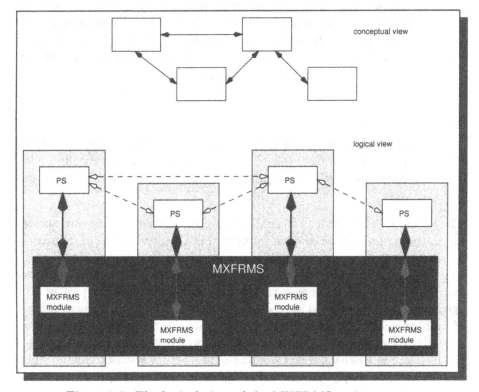

Figure 5.3: The logical view of the MXFRMS architecture.

Logically, the MXFRMS (large, dark box) can be viewed as a single monolithic system which implements the logic FHPL, i.e. it allows to respresent formulas of the logical language $\mathcal{L}_{\mathsf{FHPL}}$ and provides the reasoning capabilities of the logic's calculus $\mathcal{C}_{\mathsf{FHPL}}$. When using an appropriate internal structure for the MXFRMS (as shown above) the agent-oriented view is compatible with the logical view.

It should be noted that the logical view is compatible to the agent-oriented view; this is illustrated in Figure 5.3 by overlaying the logical view with the relevant agent-oriented structure. The difference between the two views can be further illustrated with the help of **FHPL**:

- In the agent-oriented view, each MXFRMS module box represents the relevant data and their dependencies of a *single* facet x as told by the MXFRMS module's associated problem solver, i.e. it captures a set Γ of

FHPL formulas with the property

$$\text{facetset}*(\Gamma) \quad = \quad \{x\}$$

The relationship between base literals and base literal references is only captured by the links between the MXFRMS module boxes.

- In the logical view, the MXFRMS encompasses a representation of the relevant data and dependencies from *all* agents. In addition, it includes all contract clauses which establish the necessary update relationships between base literals and base literal references. That means, just taking the formulas Γ_{x_i} of all MXFRMS facet modules x_i together yields still only a subset of the set Γ all MXFRMS formulas:

$$\bigcup_{x_i \in \Upsilon} \Gamma_{x_i} \quad \subseteq \quad \Gamma$$

The difference is just the set of contract clauses, which are never specified explicitly by a problem solver, but must be added automatically by the MXFRMS whenever a problem solver declares a base literal reference as relevant.

The logical view of MXFRMS suggests an implementation architecture according to the centralized server idea (presented in Chapter 1). In this approach, all reason maintenance functionality is concentrated in a single process, which avoids — for the reason maintenance level — most of the complexities of distributed systems development. Usually, the (problem solver part of the) agents will be implemented as separate processes. Design and implementation of problem solver interaction with the MXFRMS can be significantly eased by providing a *virtual* MXFRMS interface module, which provides a (local) function call interface to MXFRMS, thereby hiding all process or network communication details, and can simply be included in agents by their developers.

5.2.5   Implementational MXFRMS System Architecture View

The implementational perspective of the MXFRMS architecture focuses on the actual process and module structure of the MXFRMS implementation. The design of this structure may be both guided and constrained by various design goals and technological restrictions. Examples are the desire to minimize the occupation of bandwidth in the network connecting the computers or to reduce the amount of inter-process communication on a particular host. Running modules which intensively interact with each other and exchange a lot of information on the same host contributes to the former goal; implementing such modules as a single processes contributes to the latter. Designing particular multiagent systems according these lines leads to the spectrum of implementation architectures discussed previously (Section 4.4.2). By applying

the two-level architecture principle and separating each agent into a problem
solver and a reason maintenance module, the range of implementation archite-
cures becomes even wider. Determining a single implementation architecture
for MXFRMS therefore seems to be an ill-conceived idea and is not attempted
here. Rather, we look at the range of possibilities, determine certain commonalities and differences, and then try to draw some conclusions for MXFRMS
design. At the same time, we discuss how the agent-oriented and logical views
relate to a particular implementation architecture.

Figure 5.4 picks out — for the exemplary MAS architecture used in the
previous two sections — a few characteristic implementational architectures
from the wide range of possibilities.[6] The four selected scenarios exhibit an
increasing degree of distribution.

- Scenario A implements the complete multiagent system as a single process running on a single host. As shown, both the agent-oriented and
  the logical view relate well to this architecture; they can even be directly
  supported with an appropriate module structure, if the implementation
  environment provides adequate means for doing so. Communication between (problem solver or MXFRMS facet) modules can be performed via
  simple function calls. Because this architecture does not permit concurrency among the modules, it is easy to implement. However, this is an
  extreme case which is probably rarely encountered in practice.

- Scenario B shows a much more typical implementation architecture,
  where each agent is realized as a separate process. Processes may run on
  the same or different hosts. This architecture matches the agent-oriented
  view more or less directly, but requires a distributed implementation of
  the MXFRMS. As a consequence, the MXFRMS modules shown should
  incorporate the functionality to ensure the properties required by the
  logical view. PS/MXFRMS communication is simple while communication with other MXFRMS modules requires inter-process or network-based
  communication. However, an agent implementor should ensure that an
  agent's MXFRMS module can interact with other agents' MXFRMS modules when needed (i.e. it temporarily receives control in order to update
  labels or to respond to queries), even if the agent's problem solver is
  engaged in lengthy computations. This feature is also called the server
  capability of an MXFRMS facet module.

- Scenario C illustrates two things: an alternative way to structure the
  system into processes and a means to ensure the server capability. The
  former is illustrated by the two left-most agents in scenario C: instead of
  implementing agents as processes (which is close to the agent-oriented

---

[6]For simplicity and lack of space, we omitted the conceptual level and left out all links
representing some kind of communication, but focussed on structural issues instead.

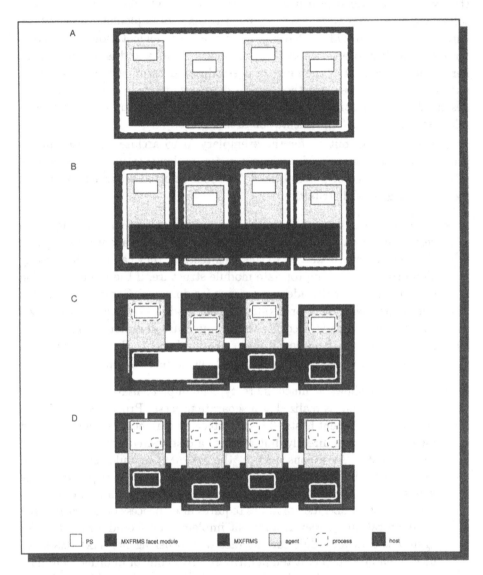

Figure 5.4: Implementational view of the MXFRMS architecture.

The figure picks out four characteristic cases from a wide range of possible implementation architectures. Structural hierarchy is illsutrated via containment of boxes. Boxes stretching several underlying boxes (problem solvers, agents, and MXFRMS) indicate a distributed implementation of the module or system the box stands for. Although not explicity illustrated in the figure, the implementational complexity of the communication facilities becomes clear when drawing a line between the two communicating modules: lines within a single process box can be implemented via simple function calls; every time the line leaves a process box inter-process communication must be used, and every time the line leaves a host box some kind of network communication facility must be available.

view), one can choose to combine several MXFRMS facet modules into a single process which serves the problem solvers of several agents.[7] An architecture with a single MXFRMS process incorporating all MXFRMS facet modules can be considered a direct implementation of the logical view. In general, an approach as depicted in scenario C corresponds to the idea of a hybrid implementation architecture of MXFRMS. Note, that similar to scenario B one must ensure the server capability of MXFRMS modules — although this time within an MXFRMS process. Both in this and the former case, the server capability can always be achieved simply by implementing both the problem solver and its associated MXFRMS facet module as separate processes.

- Finally, scenario D shows a case where even problem solver modules are implemented in a distributed fashion. The notable feature of this architecture is the structure of the MXFRMS part, where MXFRMS facet modules are always realized as single process. This expresses the design idea, motivated below, that distribution should not go beyond a single MXFRMS facet module

The following conclusions are drawn from the above spectrum of implementation architectures:

- A MXFRMS facet module is the smallest MXFRMS implementation unit. It provides reason maintenance services directly for exactly one problem solver and indirectly for all other MXFRMS facet modules. It should operate autonomously with respect to its associated problem solver and to other MXFRMS modules, regardless of its exact implementation details (process/host). The functionality of the MXFRMS facet module is occasionally referred to as the MXFRMS *facet level*.

- A MXFRMS module is (possibly together with other MXFRMS modules) wrapped by implementation framework-specific code which is referred to as the MXFRMS *system level*.

- Different implementational constellations of problem solvers and their associated MXFRMS facet modules mainly affects communication between these modules. As pointed out earlier, an appropriate implementation framework should provide means to take care of such low-level communication issues. Alternatively, the MXFRMS system level may have to provide this functionality. In any case, on the MXFRMS facet level we assume that generic communication primitives are available, which take care of all low-level details.

---

[7]As pointed out later on, there is even some potential for optimization buried in this approach, but exploiting it is expected to yield limited improvements while exhibiting other drawbacks, such as causing problems with mobile agents.

- For simplicity, we assume that each MXFRMS facet module explicitly knows about all other MXFRMS modules. Any special protocol to acquire and maintain this knowledge is considered part of the MXFRMS system level. In particular, whenever new agents are added, the new MXFRMS facet module is created and made known to all others automatically.

- Mobile agents need not add much complexity to the implementation architecture; if the implementation framework supports agent mobility, it should provide the necessary constructs such that agents can securely communicate with each other without knowing much about locations. It should also pose no significant problems to make MXFRMS facet modules mobile, if necessary. In any case, this issues are also considered a pure implementation problem, which should be solved on the MXFRMS system level, but not influence MXFRMS facet module functionality itself.

- As the MXFRMS will usually be implemented in a distributed fashion, all means for ensuring that global logical properties are met must be built into MXFRMS facet modules.[8]

- No distributed implementation of a single MXFRMS facet module is considered here.

Summarizing we can say that due to the range of possible multiagent system architectures it is not useful to fix a single architecture for the MXFRMS. Because functionality and architecture tend to influence each other more or less tightly, we encounter a dilemma. The best we can do in this case is to provide an *open* architecture, which is presented in the next section.

5.2.6   An Open MXFRMS Architecture

The *open* MXFRMS architecture presented here fixes only the structure and functionality related to reason maintenance while leaving sufficient freedom to allow for a variety of different implementations that take into account system-specific and/or application-specific requirements set forth by a particular implementation effort. Through this distinction, the MXFRMS functionality can be divided into a *facet level* and a *system level*.

The MXFRMS facet level provides all reason maintenance functionality. For a multiagent system with a set $\mathcal{PS} = \{\mathfrak{p}_1, \ldots, \mathfrak{p}_k\}$ of k problem solvers, the MXFRMS facet level consists of a matching set $\mathcal{FM} = \{\mathfrak{m}_1, \ldots, \mathfrak{m}_k\}$ of k

---

[8]Several MXFRMS facet modules can only jointly ensure these properties. Because they may have to rely on communication in order to interact with each other, it is not a priori obvious, *whether* these properties will actually hold, *when* they will hold, and *how* this can possibly be proved.

MXFRMS facet modules. Thus, each problem solver has exactly one MXFRMS module associated with it, i.e. there exist two total, bijective function

$$\text{associated-mxfrms} : \mathcal{PS} \longmapsto \mathcal{FM}$$
$$\text{associated-ps} : \mathcal{FM} \longmapsto \mathcal{PS}$$

that map problem solvers to their associated MXFRMS module and vice versa, respectively. For simplicity, we assume the mappings such that the indices coincide.

$$\text{associated-mxfrms}(\mathfrak{p}_a) =_{\text{def}} \mathfrak{m}_a$$
$$\text{associated-ps}(\mathfrak{m}_b) =_{\text{def}} \mathfrak{p}_b$$

Note, that the above-mentioned sets $\mathcal{PS}$ and $\mathcal{MXFRMS}$ refer to modules in a software architecture, not to the facet constants used in languages provided by facet logics such as FHPL. To simplify the formal framework we will assume total, bijective mappings

$$\text{mxfrms-to-facet} : \mathcal{FM} \longmapsto \Upsilon_X$$
$$\text{ps-to-facet} : \mathcal{PS} \longmapsto \Upsilon_X$$

between a set of PS modules $\mathcal{PS} = \{\mathfrak{p}_1, \ldots, \mathfrak{p}_k\}$, a set of MXFRMS facet modules $\mathcal{FM} = \{\mathfrak{m}_1, \ldots, \mathfrak{m}_k\}$, and a set of facet constants $\Upsilon_X = \{x_1, \ldots, x_k\}$ as follows:

$$\text{mxfrms-to-facet}(\mathfrak{m}_a) =_{\text{def}} x_i \qquad \text{mxfrms-to-facet}^{-1}(x_i) =_{\text{def}} \mathfrak{m}_a$$
$$\text{ps-to-facet}(\mathfrak{p}_a) =_{\text{def}} x_i \qquad \text{ps-to-facet}^{-1}(x_i) =_{\text{def}} \mathfrak{p}_a$$

Note further, that in multiagent systems consisting of a dynamically varying set of agents[9] the above mentioned sets and the mappings between them may have to be dynamically extended as well.

The MXFRMS system level contains all implementation-specific details, which happen to deal mostly with issues related to agent communication, agent mobility, and agent dynamics. These details can be easily and cleanly separated from the core reason maintenance functionality provided by the facet level.[10] Due to the implementation-specific nature of the MXFRMS system level, the specification of MXFRMS in the next section (Section 5.3) contains only an informal characterization of the MXFRMS system level functionality.

The facet level can be thought of as providing the core functionality as required by the agent-oriented and logical architecture views. The facet level is

---

[9]Due to our restriction to monotonic reason maintenance systems, the set of agents may only grow.

[10]This is similar to separating the application-specific functionality of conflict management from the application-independent part.

wrapped by the system level, which adds a particular implementation structure — for instance, integrated with all problem solvers in a centralized system (see Figure 5.4, part A), or each facet module individually integrated with its associated problem solver (part B of the same figure), or each facet module as its own process (part D of the same figure) — and additional implementation-dependent functionality such as the ability to dynamically create new facet modules or to make them mobile.

The next section specifies MXFRMS facet level functionality in a formal manner and the system level functionality in an informal manner. The internal architecture of a single MXFRMS facet module is discussed thereafter.

5.3   MXFRMS Specification

In Section 4.3 we presented a scheme for specifying DRMSs. This scheme was motivated from a reason maintenance perspective and is now applied to guide and structure the specification of the MXFRMS facet level. In order to account for logical and agent-oriented perspectives discussed in the architecture section, we provide two different but complementary definitions of the MXFRMS state (Sections 5.3.1 and 5.3.2). A few general remarks on the structure of interface function specifications are given before the various PS/MXFRMS interfaces are specified (Sections 5.3.3 to 5.3.5). At the end of this section, we include an informal specification of the MXFRMS system level functionality, which arises from implementation-specific needs (Section 5.3.6).

5.3.1   MXFRMS Global Logical State

The MXFRMS global logical state provides a *global* logical representation of the data and dependencies that have been declared relevant by *all* agents in the multiagent system (i.e. any agent) and is defined as follows:

DEFINITION 5.3.1 (MXFRMS GLOBAL LOGICAL STATE)
Let FHPL be a facetted Horn propositional logic with language $\mathcal{L}_{\mathsf{FHPL}}$ over an alphabet $\Lambda[\Upsilon, \Sigma]$ and calculus $\mathcal{C}_{\mathsf{FHPL}}$.

*The **global logical state** $\mathfrak{s}$ of MXFRMS is defined as a tuple*

$$\mathfrak{s} = \langle \mathcal{L}_{\mathsf{FHPL}}, \Upsilon_X, \Gamma_P, \Gamma_A, \Gamma_Q, \Gamma_J, \Gamma_K, \Pi_F, \Xi_f \rangle \tag{5.1}$$

where the following conditions hold:

1. *$\mathcal{L}_{\mathsf{FHPL}}$ fixes the logical language provided by the MXFRMS; this language must be used by the problem solvers of the multiagent system to represent relevant data and dependencies between them. Note, that $\mathcal{L}_{\mathsf{FHPL}}$ may be defined over an alphabet $\Lambda[\Upsilon, \Sigma]$ with infinite (but enumerable) sets of constants Υ and Σ.*

2. Υ_X is the set of **relevant facet constants** which must satisfy the following conditions:

$$\Upsilon_X \subseteq \Upsilon$$
$$\exists_{n \in \mathbb{N}} : [\, \|\Upsilon_X\| \leq n \,]$$

That is, Υ_X is a finite subset of the facet constants Υ of the alphabet Λ and represents the set of all problem solvers the MXFRMS knows of. Only these facet constants can be used in arguments for interface functions.

3. Γ_P is a finite set of **relevant base literals** each of which represents a relevant proposition in some facet. Γ_P must satisfy the following conditions:

$$\Gamma_P \subseteq \Gamma_{blit*}$$
$$facetset*(\Gamma_P) \subseteq \Upsilon_X$$
$$\forall_{x_i \in \Upsilon_X} : [\, \{x_i.\top, x_i.\bot\} \subseteq \Gamma_P \,]$$
$$\exists_{n \in \mathbb{N}} : [\, \|\Gamma_P\| \leq n \,]$$

The second condition ensures that for any relevant facet Γ_P contains at least the literals representing true and false.

4. Γ_A is the set of **assumptions**, which must satisfy the following condition:

$$\Gamma_A \subseteq \Gamma_P$$

The set Γ_A defines for each facet $x \in \Upsilon_X$ a finite subset of the propositional variables Σ of alphabet Λ which the problem solver represented by the facet intents to use as assumptions.

5. Γ_Q is a set of **relevant base literal references** each of which represent beliefs communicated between facets. Γ_Q must satisfy the conditions:

$$\Gamma_Q \subseteq \Gamma_{lref*}$$
$$\forall_{y:x.p \in \Gamma_Q} : [\, x.p \in \Gamma_P \text{ and } y \in \Upsilon_X \,]$$
$$\forall_{x \in \Upsilon_X} \forall_{y \in \Upsilon_X} : [\, \{y:x.\top, y:x.\bot\} \subseteq \Gamma_Q \,]$$

The latter two conditions ensure that for any communicated belief the original belief is relevant for the provider and that the literals representing true and false are communicated beliefs as well.

6. Γ_J is a set of **facet clauses** that represent how local beliefs logically depend on other local or communicated beliefs. Γ_J must satisfy the con-

ditions:

$$\Gamma_J \subseteq \Gamma_{fcl}$$
$$\text{antes}(\Gamma_J) \subseteq (\Gamma_P \cup \Gamma_Q)$$
$$\text{cons}(\Gamma_J) \subseteq \Gamma_P$$

7. Γ_K *is a set of* **contract clauses** *which represent update contracts between facets regarding a particular proposition.* Γ_K *must satisfy the conditions:*

$$\Gamma_K \subseteq \Gamma_{ccl}$$
$$\forall_{(x.p \rightsquigarrow y:x.p) \in \Gamma_K} : [\, x.p \in \Gamma_P \text{ and } y:x.p \in \Gamma_Q \,]$$
$$\forall_{y_i : x_i . p_i \in \Gamma_Q} \exists_{(x.p \rightsquigarrow y:x.p) \in \Gamma_K} : [\, y:x.p = y_i : x_i . p_i \,]$$

8. Π_F *is a set of* **relevant focus structures** *of the form* $f = \langle g, e, m, o, w \rangle$, *where g is the* **group** *of facets relative to which derivability is determined. e is the* **environment**, *i.e. the set of propositions which are assumed in all facets of the group. m is the* **modification token holder**, *i.e. the facet which can modify the group and the environment or delete the focus structure. o describes the* **owners** *of the focus structure (i.e. the set of facets to which the focus structure is relevant); any focus structure with more than one owner is a shared focus structure. w is the* **public write permit**, *which must be set to $\top$ at least for all shared focus structures and indicates whether the modificaton token may be passed between owners of the focus structure or not. Formally,* Π_F *is a relation*

$$\Pi_F \subseteq \mathfrak{P}(\Upsilon_X) \times \mathfrak{P}(\Gamma_A) \times \Upsilon_X \times \mathfrak{P}(\Upsilon_X) \times \{\top, F\}$$

and must satisfy the following conditions:

$$\forall_{f = \langle g, e, m, o, w \rangle \in \Pi_F} : [\, m \in o \subseteq g \subseteq \Upsilon_X \,]$$
$$\forall_{f = \langle g, e, m, o, w \rangle \in \Pi_F} \forall_{\phi \in e} : [\, \phi \in \Gamma_A \,]$$
$$\forall_{f = \langle g, e, m, o, w \rangle \in \Pi_F} : [\, m . \top \in e \,]$$

The last condition ensures that all premises are contained in the context of a focus structure. The set Π_F^* *of* **shared** *or* **publicly extensible focus structures** Π_F^* *is defined as follows:*

$$\Pi_F^* =_{\text{def}} \{\, f = \langle g, e, m, o, w \rangle \mid f \in \Pi_F \text{ and } w = \top \,\}$$

9. Ξ_f *defines exactly one* **current focus** f *for each facet x. It contains a set of pairs* $\langle x, \langle g, e, m, o, w \rangle \rangle$ *consisting of a single facet identifier x and a focus structure* $\langle g, e, m, o, w \rangle$. *The set of current foci* Ξ_f *is a relation*

$$\Xi_f \subseteq \Upsilon_X \times \Pi_F$$

which must satisfy the following conditions:

$$\forall_{x \in \Upsilon_X} \exists_{\langle x, f \rangle \in \Xi_f} : [\, f = \langle g, e, m, o, w \rangle \text{ and } x \in o \,]$$

$$\forall_{\langle x_i, f_i \rangle, \langle x_j, f_j \rangle \in \Xi_f} : [\, x_i = x_j \implies f_i = f_j \,]$$

The set of all possible focus structures is denoted by $\mathfrak{F}$. The set of all possible logical MXFRMS states is denoted by $\mathfrak{S}$.

The first three components of the global MXFRMS logical state describe a kind of least common denominator for the problem solvers of the multiagent system: the common language for representing relevant data and expressing logical dependencies, the set of actually relevant facets representing the problem solvers' reasoning spaces, and the set of actually relevant propositional variables. The latter two define a kind of upper bound for the groups and environments that can be used in focus structures. The next two components, Γ_P and Γ_Q, describe *all* data relevant to the problem solvers. Due to the syntactic structure of $\mathcal{L}_{\text{FHPL}}$, these data could all be put into a single set, but we chose to separate local and communicated data for easier reference later on. The two components Γ_J and Γ_K describe *all* logical dependencies between data. While Γ_J contains all facet clauses that express the agents' dependencies between their local data, Γ_K consist of all contract clauses that describe an update relationship between two agents for some communicated belief. The final two components of the global logical state, Π_F and Ξ_f, contain focus structures, i.e. logical descriptions sufficient to construct the relevant contexts. Π_F is the set of all relevant focus structures. Ξ_f is the set of current focus structures and contains for each facet exactly one focus structure refering that facet in its owner component.

Altogether, the logical state is a unified description of the problem solving knowledge (more specifically: of the relevant data plus data dependencies) of *all* agents of the multiagent system *plus* of their mutual information exchange relationships.

5.3.2 MXFRMS Facet Logical State

Given a global MXFRMS logical state, a characterization of the logical state of a particular facet x_i, which represents a particular agent's local reasoning space, is now given. The basic idea is to carry over the *structure* of the global logical state description $\mathfrak{s}$ to the definition of the MXFRMS facet logical state $\mathfrak{s}_i$, i.e. $\mathfrak{s}_i$ is similar to the following form:

$$\mathfrak{s}_i = \langle \mathcal{L}_{\text{FHPL}i}, \Upsilon_{Xi}, \Gamma_{Pi}, \Gamma_{Ai}, \Gamma_{Qi}, \Gamma_{Ji}, \Gamma_{Ki}, \Pi_{Fi}, \Xi_{f_i} \rangle$$

The definition of $\mathfrak{s}_i$ below will actually be a slight variation of this structure. What needs to be done first in order to fix a particular MXFRMS facet logical state s_i for a facet x_i, is to provide a precise definition of the facet-specific component sets in the structure given above. This will be done by specifying facet-specific subsets of the respective components of the global logical state. However, as there is considerable freedom in how one can define these components, it is quite illuminating to first illustrate what effects different definitions could have, before we actually provide these definitions. These effects become obvious when we take into consideration the facet logical state of all facets and look at the relationships holding between certain components of different facet logical states, and between facet-specific and global components. Let us look at an arbitrary global state component, e.g. a set Γ of formulas, and the set of Γ_i of facet-specific components. If the set of Γ_i is a partitioning of the set Γ, then Γ is represented in a fully distributed manner. At the other end of the spectrum, each Γ_i could simply be defined to equal Γ, i.e. the set Γ is fully replicated. In other words, the set Γ is globally shared by all agents. In all other cases, the Γ_i will be true subsets of Γ. Different sets Γ_i and Γ_j may have a non-empty intersection (we also say, they overlap), which just describes the set of data replicated in both agents or, in other terms, the data shared between the respective agents. Replicated data are readily available at the locations they occupy, thereby decreasing time and effort necessary to access them. On the other side, whenever replicated data exists, the facets must ensure appropriate updating of all replicas. For part of the MXFRMS functionality, this is exactly what is needed. However, the more update responsibilities a facet has, the more communication it has to perform, which decreases efficiency. Thus, one is interested in getting as much distribution as possible while allowing for sufficient overlap in order to ensure the desired local availability of data and the update functionality necessary to keep the replicated data updated.

After these general remarks, we can discuss these issues more specifically for each global state component in turn:[11]

- The first component of the global logical state, $\mathcal{L}_{\mathsf{FHPL}}$, *designates* the language to be used by the problem solvers for formulating data and logical dependencies.[12] We will generally define the language component of facet logical states to be the same as in the global logical state, i.e. all agents share a *common language* in which they express relevant data and dependencies. This simplifies a lot of technicalities and avoids a lot of syntactic and semantic problems arising when different languages are used, e.g. different names denoting the same data, communication

---

[11]The order of discussing them does not match their position within the structure for reasons that become obvious soon.

[12]Note, that any implementation of a global or a facet-specific state will be limited to the explicit representation of finite sets, and therefore can never actually encompass an extensional representation of an infinite language.

of data for which the receiver has no language terms available, etc. It is not, however, restricting the generality of the concepts presented here.

- The sets Γ_P, Γ_A, Γ_Q, and Γ_J can be naturally partitioned by using the function facet as follows

$$\Gamma_{Pi} =_{\text{def}} \Gamma_{P\lceil x_i \rceil} = \{ x.p \mid x.p \in \Gamma_P \text{ and } \text{facet}(x.p) = x_i \}$$
$$\Gamma_{Ai} =_{\text{def}} \Gamma_{A\lceil x_i \rceil} = \{ x.p \mid x.p \in \Gamma_A \text{ and } \text{facet}(x.p) = x_i \}$$
$$\Gamma_{Qi} =_{\text{def}} \Gamma_{Q\lceil x_i \rceil} = \{ y{:}x.p \mid y{:}x.p \in \Gamma_Q \text{ and } \text{facet}(y{:}x.p) = x_i \}$$
$$\Gamma_{Ji} =_{\text{def}} \Gamma_{J\lceil x_i \rceil} = \{ (\Phi{\to}\varphi) \mid (\Phi{\to}\varphi) \in \Gamma_J \text{ and } \text{facet}((\Phi{\to}\varphi)) = x_i \}$$

Thus, we reduce the respective global state component to the group consisting just of the facet on hand, which yields facet-specific subsets with empty mutual intersection, i.e.

$$\forall_{x_i,x_j \in \Upsilon_X} : [\, \Gamma_{Pi} \cap \Gamma_{Pj} = \varnothing \,]$$
$$\forall_{x_i,x_j \in \Upsilon_X} : [\, \Gamma_{Pi} \cap \Gamma_{Pj} = \varnothing \,]$$
$$\forall_{x_i,x_j \in \Upsilon_X} : [\, \Gamma_{Qi} \cap \Gamma_{Qj} = \varnothing \,]$$
$$\forall_{x_i,x_j \in \Upsilon_X} : [\, \Gamma_{Ji} \cap \Gamma_{Jj} = \varnothing \,]$$

The elements of these sets represent the respective sets of local and communicated data and the dependencies between them that are relevant for a particular facet.

- The set Γ_K contains the set of contract clauses each of which describes an update relationship between two facets for a particular proposition. Obviously, a facet needs to keep track of its own update committments, i.e. it needs at least a local representation of those contract clauses where the source is a proposition local to that facet, or, put differently, where the facet is contractor. This set of clauses, denoted by $\Gamma_{S_{x_i}}$, is defined by

$$\Gamma_{S_{x_i}} =_{\text{def}} \{\phi \mid \phi \in \Gamma_K \text{ and } \text{facet}(\text{source}(\phi)) = x_i\}$$

However, in order to increase flexibility, e.g. for implementations using different kind of communication protocols to implement the update functionalities, for mobile agent support, for retraction facilities, for explanation generation, for implementing nested beliefs, and for fine-grained status information reporting, it is useful for a facet to have explicitly available the set of contract clauses where the destination is a communicated proposition local to that facet, i.e. the facet is the subscriber in the contract clause. This set of contract clauses is denoted by $\Gamma_{R_{x_i}}$ and defined by

$$\Gamma_{R_{x_i}} =_{\text{def}} \{ \phi \mid \phi \in \Gamma_K \text{ and } \text{facet}(\text{dest}(\phi)) = x_i \}$$

As anything else does not make much sense to include we can define the facet-specific set of contract clauses as

$$\Gamma_{Ki} = \Gamma_{K_{x_i}} =_{\text{def}} \Gamma_{R_{x_i}} \cup \Gamma_{S_{x_i}}$$

which can alternatively be characterized by the following definition:

$$\Gamma_{K_{x_i}} =_{\text{def}} \{ \phi \mid \phi \in \Gamma_K \text{ and } x_i \in \text{facetset}(\phi) \}$$

- The set Π_F represents the set of relevant focus structures. An arbitrary focus structure $f = \langle g, e, m, o, w \rangle$ is relevant to a facet x_i, if one of the following conditions holds: i) the facet can contribute to the beliefs derivable in the context it represents ($x_i \in g$), ii) the facet has the right to modify it ($x_i = m$), or iii) the focus structure represents a relevant focus for the facet ($x_i \in o$), Because by definition $x \in o \subseteq g$, we define the set of focus structures relevant to a facet simply as follows:

$$\Pi_{Fi} = \Pi_{F_{x_i}} =_{\text{def}} \{ f \mid f = \langle g, e, m, o, w \rangle \in \Pi_F \text{ and } x_i \in g \}$$

- In contrast to Π_F, the set Ξ_f describes the agents current focus, of which we allow only one at any time. Because focus structures can be owned by several facets, the global logical state had to associate a focus structure with a particular facet that has chosen it as current focus in order to get a precise and unambiguous description of all current foci of all agents. For the facet logical state, it is sufficient to just pick out the single focus structure that represents the facet's current focus, i.e.

$$\Xi_{f_i} = \Xi_{f_{x_i}} =_{\text{def}} f_{x_i} = \langle g, e, m, o, w \rangle \quad \text{where} \quad \langle x_i, f_{x_i} \rangle \in \Xi_f$$

- The set Υ_X is the set of relevant facets. It is a nontrivial problem to determine a suitable and well-definable facet-local version Υ_{Xi}, because slightly different notions can be captured in such a definition. The basic intentions for having this component is to have an explicit representation for the facets that can be used to i) send out requests for information ii) to accept received requests for information, and iii) to construct groups for use in queries and in focus structures. Defining this component simply to equal Υ_X raises a problem with agent dynamics, because a new relevant facet must be made known to all existing ones whenever a new facet is added to the system. On the other hand, defining Υ_{Xi} to contain only the minimal set of relevant facets, which includes all those the facet has subscribed from or provided to information and all those which occur in the group component of an agent, raises the problem of how such a set is modified. For example, it could be automatically extended if a request for providing information is received by a previously unknown facet. However, any such scheme ultimately relies on a higher-level protocol between agents to acquaint themselves and an extension of the PS/MXFRMS interface to make new acquaintances known to their problem solvers. Of course, this is not really difficult to do in a particular implementation, but it unnecessarily complicates the specifications of the interfaces. Therefore, we will stick with the former option and define this component to be a global one.

An issue which is not relevant for the global logical state but arises in the definition of the facet logical state is the congruence problem: how can we describe query capabilities of an agent, or put differently, how does an agent know that it can use certain literals in queries or in focus structures? If we assume that we do not represent this information explicitly, then all the problems described in the context of the congruence problem can occur: either queries to other agents are often denied to be processed, or all literals in queries are automatically made relevant. The disadvantage of the former case is obvious. In the latter case the querying agent can force another agent to swamp its database with lots of utterly irrelevant information, simply by asking a lot of queries. To solve this problem, we take the following approach: Both the set of assumptions Γ_A as well as the set of base literals Γ_P are made globally known in each facet logical state as sets $\Sigma_{A_{x_i}}$ and $\Sigma_{P_{x_i}}$. This seems to be a very drastic step, but in fact it is not as bad as all. First of all, if an agent x knows what base literals are relevant to agent y, it makes only sense to use these in queries to y. Thus, x knows exactly what it can query y about. On the other side, it is perfectly alright now for y to deny any queries containing literals not relevant to y. The whole scheme is acceptable only if we find a way such that, for x, knowing which literals are relevant for y does not automatically mean that x must declare them relevant as well.[13] Such a scheme is presented for MXFRMS later on.

With the above preliminary definitions, the local logical state for a facet can be defined:

DEFINITION 5.3.2 (MXFRMS LOCAL LOGICAL STATE)
Let $\mathfrak{s} = \langle \mathcal{L}_{\mathsf{FHPL}}, \Upsilon_X, \Gamma_P, \Gamma_A, \Gamma_Q, \Gamma_J, \Gamma_K, \Pi_F, \Xi_f \rangle$ *be an* MXFRMS *global logical state. For each agent represented by a facet* $x_i \in \Upsilon$, *the* MXFRMS *local logical state is defined by a tuple*

$$\mathfrak{s}_i =_{\mathrm{def}} \langle \mathcal{L}_{\mathsf{FHPL}}, \Upsilon_X, \Sigma_{P_{x_i}}, \Sigma_{A_{x_i}}, \Gamma_{P\lceil x_i \rceil}, \Gamma_{A\lceil x_i \rceil}, \Gamma_{Q\lceil x_i \rceil}, \Gamma_{J\lceil x_i \rceil}, \Gamma_{K_{x_i}}, \Pi_{F_{x_i}}, f_{x_i} \rangle$$
$$(5.2)$$

where

- $\mathcal{L}_{\mathsf{FHPL}}$ *is equal to the respective component of the global logical state,*

---

[13] In such a case, one could fall back to a global database approach.

- $\Sigma_{P_{x_i}}, \Sigma_{A_{x_i}}$ are equal to the components Γ_P and Γ_A of the global logical state, respectively,

- $\Gamma_{P\lceil x_i \rceil}, \Gamma_{A\lceil x_i \rceil}, \Gamma_{Q\lceil x_i \rceil}, \Gamma_{J\lceil x_i \rceil}$ are the group reductions to group $g = \{x_i\}$ of the respective components of the global logical state,

- $\Gamma_{K_{x_i}}$ is the facet-related subset of clauses in Γ_K where x_i is either provider or subscriber,

- $\Pi_{F_{x_i}}$ is the facet-related subset of focus structures in Π_F, where x_i is referenced by the group component of the focus structure, and

- $\Xi_{f_{x_i}}$ is the uniquely determined focus structure f_{x_i} describing the facets current focus.

For later reference, we introduce abbreviations for the following sets of FHPL formulas for logical MXFRMS states $s = \langle \mathcal{L}_{\text{FHPL}}, \Upsilon_X, \Gamma_P, \Gamma_A, \Gamma_Q, \Gamma_J, \Gamma_K, \Pi_F, \Xi_f \rangle$ and for focus structures $f = \langle g, e, m, o, w \rangle$:

$$\forall_{g \subseteq \Upsilon_X} : \qquad \Gamma_{\top \lceil g \rceil} =_{\text{def}} \{x_i.\top \mid x_i \in g\}$$

$$\forall_{g \subseteq \Upsilon_X} : \qquad \Gamma_{\bot \lceil g \rceil} =_{\text{def}} \{x_i.\bot \mid x_i \in g\}$$

$$\forall_{f = \langle g, e, m, o, w \rangle \in \Pi_F} : \qquad \Gamma_A(f) =_{\text{def}} \{x_i.\phi_i \mid x_i \in g \text{ and } \phi_i \in e\}$$

$$\Gamma_{s,f} =_{\text{def}} (\Gamma_J \cup \Gamma_K)_{\lceil g \rceil} \cup \Gamma_{\top \lceil g \rceil} \cup \Gamma_A(f)$$

This concludes the necessary definitions of states and state-related sets.

Preliminary Notes on MXFRMS Interface Function Specifications
The MXFRMS interface function specifications presented below will refer to problem solvers, MXFRMS facet modules, and MXFRMS global logical states. Some preliminary comments on their role in the specifications are in order first.

As the definition of the MXFRMS logical state already suggests, logical state plays a vital role in the specification of MXFRMS behavior. In fact, the result of each interface function depends on the MXFRMS global logical state at the point of time when the function is called. Hence, the space of (global) logical states is specified as one of the inputs for the mappings defining interface functions. However, the logical state is assumed to be embodied in the MXFRMS system, most likely in a distributed manner as suggested by the facet logical states that we just defined. Hence, there is no need for the problem solver to provide the state as an explicit argument, and the function call notation of interface functions will omit the state as an argument. Likewise, if global logical states are specified as outputs, they describe the side effects of an interface function on the global logical state rather than an explicit return value. Note, that this way of specifying the interface functions does by no means imply that the MXFRMS as a whole or even a single facet module needs to have access to the complete global logical state in order to execute the interface functions; this becomes more obvious and is discussed in detail in the section on MXFRMS implementation later on. Specifications in terms of the global logical state rather than the facet logcal states allows to describe the global effects of PS/MXFRMS interactions in a much more concise manner.

Another two arguments occurring in the interface specifications are the identifier denoting the problem solver calling the interface function and the identifier denoting the MXFRMS facet module that is actually executing the function. These arguments serve two purposes:

- First, they allow to precisely formalize the underlying restrictions regarding the use of MXFRMS functionality by various problem solvers. In general, a MXFRMS module m_a will provide its services only to its associated problem solver $p_a = \text{associated-ps}(m_a)$, i.e. the following conditions must hold:

$$\text{ps-to-facet}(p_a) = x_i = \text{mxfrms-to-facet}(m_a)$$

- Second, they allow for a uniform specification of the core functionality of interface functions across all MXFRMS modules.

These two arguments should be supplied (filled in) automatically by an actual implementation.

All the reader should keep in mind for the next few sections is that these arguments are explicitly stated in the mapping notation of an interface function, but omitted in its function call notation.

5.3.3 MXFRMS Logical Query Interface

The logical query interface functions require access to the derivability relation in order to provide certain services of interest. The following set of functions, all of which leave the logical state unchanged, is defined for the MXFRMS:

DEFINITION 5.3.3 (MXFRMS LOGICAL QUERY INTERFACE)
The logical query interface of MXFRMS *consists of the following functions:*

$$
\begin{array}{lll}
\text{follows-from?}: & \mathfrak{G} \times \mathcal{PS} \times \mathcal{FM} \times \mathfrak{F} \times \Gamma_{lit*} & \longmapsto \{T, F\} \\
\text{holds-in?}: & \mathfrak{G} \times \mathcal{PS} \times \mathcal{FM} \times \mathfrak{F} \times \Gamma_{lit*} & \longmapsto \{T, F\} \\
\text{context-of?}: & \mathfrak{G} \times \mathcal{PS} \times \mathcal{FM} \times \mathfrak{F} & \longmapsto \mathfrak{P}(\Gamma_{lit})
\end{array}
$$

The first argument of each function is the global logical state, which is implicitly known by an MXFRMS *implementation and need not be provided as an explicit argument. The second and third arguments are the identifiers of the problem solver calling the function and the* MXFRMS *facet module executing the function. The fourth argument is a particular focus structure which designates the context relative to which the query is to be answered. Then, these functions are defined under the constraints*

$$\forall_{s=\langle \mathcal{L}_{\text{FHPL}}, \Upsilon_X, \Gamma_P, \Gamma_A, \Gamma_Q, \Gamma_J, \Gamma_K, \Pi_F, \Xi_f \rangle \in \mathfrak{S}}$$

$$\forall_{\mathfrak{p}_a \in \mathcal{PS}} : [\ \textit{ps-to-facet}(\mathfrak{p}_a) = z \ \text{and} \ z \in \Upsilon_X \ ]$$

$$\forall_{\mathfrak{m}_b \in \mathcal{FM}} : [\ \textit{mxfrms-to-facet}(\mathfrak{m}_b) = z' \ \text{and} \ z' \in \Upsilon_X \ \text{and} \ z' = z \ ]$$

$$\forall_{f=\langle g,e,m,o,w \rangle \in \mathfrak{F}} : [\ f \in \Pi_F \ \text{and} \ z \in o \ ]$$

as follows:

$$\forall_{\phi \in (\Gamma_P \cup \Gamma_Q),\ \textit{facet}(\phi)=z} \ :$$

$$\textit{follows-from?}(\mathfrak{p}_a, \mathfrak{m}_b, f, \phi) = \begin{cases} T & \text{if } \Gamma_{s,f} \vdash_{\text{FHPL}} \phi \\ F & \text{otherwise} \end{cases}$$

$$\forall_{\phi \in (\Gamma_P \cup \Gamma_Q),\ \textit{facet}(\phi)=z} \ :$$

$$\textit{holds-in?}(\mathfrak{p}_a, \mathfrak{m}_b, f, \phi) = \begin{cases} T & \text{if } \Gamma_{s,f} \vdash_{\text{FHPL}} \phi \\ & \quad \text{and } \forall_{\psi \in \Gamma_{\perp\lceil g \rceil}} : \Gamma_{s,f} \not\vdash_{\text{FHPL}} \psi \\ F & \text{otherwise} \end{cases}$$

$$\textit{context-of?}(\mathfrak{p}_a, \mathfrak{m}_b, f) = \{\ \phi \mid \phi \in (\Gamma_P \cup \Gamma_Q)$$
$$\text{and } \textit{facet}(\phi) = z$$
$$\text{and } \textit{holds-in?}(\mathfrak{p}_a, \mathfrak{m}_b, f, \phi) = T\ \}$$

Because the MXFRMS *maintains for each problem solver a current focus in its state, the following variants of the above functions are provided:*

follows-from-focus? :	$\mathfrak{S} \times \mathcal{PS} \times \mathcal{FM} \times \Gamma_{lit*}$	$\longmapsto \{T, F\}$
holds-in-focus? :	$\mathfrak{S} \times \mathcal{PS} \times \mathcal{FM} \times \Gamma_{lit*}$	$\longmapsto \{T, F\}$
context-of-focus? :	$\mathfrak{S} \times \mathcal{PS} \times \mathcal{FM}$	$\longmapsto \mathfrak{P}(\Gamma_{lit})$

The type and order of arguments is just as for the versions not referring to the current focus, with the exception that the focus structure argument is omitted. Then, these functions are defined under the constraints

$$\forall_{s=\langle \mathcal{L}_{\text{FHPL}}, \Upsilon_X, \Gamma_P, \Gamma_A, \Gamma_Q, \Gamma_J, \Gamma_K, \Pi_F, \Xi_f \rangle \in \mathfrak{S}}$$

$$\forall_{\mathfrak{p}_a \in \mathcal{PS}} : [\ \textit{ps-to-facet}(\mathfrak{p}_a) = z \ \text{and} \ z \in \Upsilon_X \ ]$$

$$\forall_{\mathfrak{m}_b \in \mathcal{FM}} : [\ \textit{mxfrms-to-facet}(\mathfrak{m}_b) = z' \ \text{and} \ z' \in \Upsilon_X \ \text{and} \ z' = z \ ]$$

$$[\ f_z \in \Pi_F \ \text{and} \ \langle z, f_z \rangle \in \Xi_f \ ]$$

in terms of their more general logical query interface function counterparts as follows:

$$\forall_{\phi \in (\Gamma_P \cup \Gamma_Q), facet(\phi)=z} : \quad \text{follows-from-focus?}(z, z', \phi) = \text{follows-from?}(z, z', f_z, \phi)$$

$$\forall_{\phi \in (\Gamma_P \cup \Gamma_Q), facet(\phi)=z} : \quad \text{holds-in-focus?}(z, z', \phi) = \text{holds-in?}(z, z', f_z, \phi)$$

$$\text{context-of-focus?}(z, z') = \text{context-of?}(z, z', f_z)$$

An error is returned by the above functions, if the arguments do not meet the conditions specified by the quantifications.

The logical query interface functions provide the means for solving the distributed consequence determination problem and the distributed context determination problem. Deciding the consistency of a context actually is a special case of the consequence determination problem. Also, some cases of the distributed belief revision problem (context switching by changing the set of assumptions) can be solved with these functions.

5.3.4 MXFRMS State Change Interface

The problem solvers of the multiagent system can modify the logical state of MXFRMS by using the state change interface functions specified in the next definition. All of these functions are called for effect only; the return value is not of interest and omitted from the specification. The state change interface can be roughly divided into five categories of functions:

- Functions for extending the relevant part of FHPL.

- Functions for adding and deleting focus structures.

- Functions for modifying group and environment of focus structures.

- Functions for handling shared focus structures.

- Functions for manipulating a facet's current focus.

Because the MXFRMS state change interface consists of more functions than the comparable XFRMS interface and because the formal specifications are somewhat more elaborate, we split the definition into three parts according to these categories in order to avoid overly long definitions. After each definition, an informal explanation explains the formal specification in plain words.

Due to the more complex overall structure of a multiagent system, which is already manifested by the more complex structure used to describe the logical state, an actual implementation will feature an even more elaborate state change interface and provide e.g. functions to add new facets for representing dynamically created agents. Section 5.3.6 contains a brief discussion of such possible extensions and additions.

DEFINITION 5.3.4 (MXFRMS STATE CHANGE INTERFACE, PART I)
The state change interface of MXFRMS *provides the following functions for extending the relevant part of* FHPL:

$$
\begin{array}{rll}
\text{add-proposition!} : & \mathfrak{S} \times \mathcal{PS} \times \mathcal{FM} \times \Gamma_{blit} & \longmapsto \mathfrak{S} \\
\text{add-assumption!} : & \mathfrak{S} \times \mathcal{PS} \times \mathcal{FM} \times \Gamma_{blit} & \longmapsto \mathfrak{S} \\
\text{add-reference!} : & \mathfrak{S} \times \mathcal{PS} \times \mathcal{FM} \times \Gamma_{lref} & \longmapsto \mathfrak{S} \\
\text{add-justification!} : & \mathfrak{S} \times \mathcal{PS} \times \mathcal{FM} \times \Gamma_{fcl} & \longmapsto \mathfrak{S}
\end{array}
$$

The first three arguments are identical to those of logical query interface functions. The fourth argument is the new FHPL *formula to be made relevant. Then, these functions are defined under the constraints*

$$
\forall_{s=\langle \mathcal{L}_{\mathsf{FHPL}}, \Upsilon_X, \Gamma_P, \Gamma_A, \Gamma_Q, \Gamma_J, \Gamma_K, \Pi_F, \Xi_f \rangle \in \mathfrak{S}}
$$
$$
\forall_{p_a \in \mathcal{PS}} : [\ \textit{ps-to-facet}(p_a) = z \text{ and } z \in \Upsilon_X\ ]
$$
$$
\forall_{m_b \in \mathcal{FM}} : [\ \textit{mxfrms-to-facet}(m_b) = z' \text{ and } z' \in \Upsilon_X \text{ and } z' = z\ ]
$$

as follows:

$$
\forall_{\phi \in (\Gamma_{blit} \smallsetminus \Gamma_P), \textit{facet}(\phi) = z} :
$$
$$
\text{add-proposition!}(p_a, m_b, \phi) = \langle \mathcal{L}_{\mathsf{FHPL}}, \Upsilon_X, \Gamma_P', \Gamma_A, \Gamma_Q, \Gamma_J, \Gamma_K, \Pi_F, \Xi_f \rangle
$$
$$
\textit{where } \Gamma_P' = \Gamma_P \cup \{\phi\}
$$

$$
\forall_{\phi \in \Gamma_P, \textit{facet}(\phi) = z} :
$$
$$
\text{add-assumption!}(p_a, m_b, \phi) = \langle \mathcal{L}_{\mathsf{FHPL}}, \Upsilon_X, \Gamma_P, \Gamma_A', \Gamma_Q, \Gamma_J, \Gamma_K, \Pi_F, \Xi_f \rangle
$$
$$
\textit{where } \Gamma_A' = \Gamma_A \cup \{\phi\}
$$

$$
\forall_{\phi \in (\Gamma_{lref} \smallsetminus \Gamma_Q), \textit{facet}(\phi) = z, \textit{source}(\phi) = \psi \in \Gamma_P} :
$$
$$
\text{add-reference!}(p_a, m_b, \phi) = \langle \mathcal{L}_{\mathsf{FHPL}}, \Upsilon_X, \Gamma_P, \Gamma_A, \Gamma_Q', \Gamma_J, \Gamma_K', \Pi_F, \Xi_f \rangle
$$
$$
\textit{where } \Gamma_Q' = \Gamma_Q \cup \{\phi\}
$$
$$
\textit{and } \Gamma_K' = \Gamma_K \cup \{(\psi \rightsquigarrow \phi)\}
$$

$$
\forall_{(\Phi \to \varphi) \in (\Gamma_{fcl} \smallsetminus \Gamma_J), \textit{lits}((\Phi \to \varphi)) \in (\Gamma_P \cup \Gamma_Q), \textit{facetset*}(\Phi) = \{z\}, \textit{facet}(\varphi) = z} :
$$
$$
\text{add-justification!}(p_a, m_b, (\Phi \to \varphi)) = \langle \mathcal{L}_{\mathsf{FHPL}}, \Upsilon_X, \Gamma_P, \Gamma_A, \Gamma_Q, \Gamma_J', \Gamma_K, \Pi_F, \Xi_f \rangle
$$
$$
\textit{where } \Gamma_J' = \Gamma_J \cup \{(\Phi \to \varphi)\}
$$

The easiest part of the update interface are the functions for declaring additional FHPL language elements relevant.

The add-proposition function can be used by a problem solver to declare a *local* proposition (w.r.t. the problem solver's facet) as relevant for its associated

MXFRMS facet, if the proposition was not already known.[14] The effect on the global logical state is that the proposition is added to the set of relevant propositions.

The **add-assumption!** function is used by the problem solver to declare that is intents to use the propositional variable as assumption. The propositional variable is added to the set of assumptions Γ_A. Note, that under the constraints set up for MXFRMS earlier (see Section 5.3.2) this function has a *global* effect: Any problem solver can now construct focus structures referring to that assumption.

The **add-reference!** function is used by a problem solver to make a communicated belief relevant. More precisely, the problem solver uses **add-reference!** to initiate communication of a certain belief of a particular problem solver. The effects of the function are again twofold:

- The communicated belief is added to the set of relevant base literal references.

- The contract clause representing the update contract between the original belief and the communicated belief is added to the set of relevant contract clauses.

The original belief must already be relevant. The problem solver can use state query interface functions (defined below) to find out whether a particular proposition is relevant for another problem solver. Constraining the set of possible communicated beliefs to the set of already existing original beliefs (base literals) is a safety measure. If the request to add a communicated belief could cause addition of an original belief, then a malevolent problem solver could swamp its own MXFRMS facet module with such requests, which would force other agent's MXFRMS facet modules to add a lot of irrelevant propositions.

The third function, **add-justification!**, adds a new logical dependency between *local* literals of a problem solver's facet. All literals involved must already have been declared relevant. The appropriate facet clause is added to the set of justifications and the belief state is updated accordingly.

The next three parts of the MXFRMS state change interface provide functions for manipulating the set of focus structures. The first part provides two functions for adding and removing focus structures.

DEFINITION 5.3.5 (MXFRMS STATE CHANGE INTERFACE, PART II)
MXFRMS *state change interface provides two basic functions for manipulating*

---

[14]For an actual implementation, it would probably be desirable to slightly refine the specification such that calling the function with an already known proposition argument results in an unchanged global logical state, but would not raise an error. This also holds for many other state change interface functions. For simplicity and brevity, we left this convenience out of the specifications.

the set of relevant focus structures:

$$\text{add-focus! :} \qquad \mathfrak{G} \times \mathcal{PS} \times \mathcal{FM} \times \mathfrak{F} \qquad \longmapsto \mathfrak{G}$$
$$\text{remove-focus! :} \qquad \mathfrak{G} \times \mathcal{PS} \times \mathcal{FM} \times \mathfrak{F} \qquad \longmapsto \mathfrak{G}$$

The first three arguments are identical to those of logical query interface functions. The fourth argument is in both cases the focus structure to be added or removed. These functions are then defined under the constraints

$$\forall_{s=\langle \mathcal{L}_{\text{FHPL}}, \Upsilon_X, \Gamma_P, \Gamma_A, \Gamma_Q, \Gamma_J, \Gamma_K, \Pi_F, \Xi_f \rangle \in \mathfrak{G}}$$
$$\forall_{\mathfrak{p}_a \in \mathcal{PS}} : [\ \textit{ps-to-facet}(\mathfrak{p}_a) = z \text{ and } z \in \Upsilon_X\ ]$$
$$\forall_{\mathfrak{m}_b \in \mathcal{FM}} : [\ \textit{mxfrms-to-facet}(\mathfrak{m}_b) = z' \text{ and } z' \in \Upsilon_X \text{ and } z' = z\ ]$$

as follows:

$$\forall_{f=\langle g,e,m,o,w \rangle \in (\mathfrak{F} \smallsetminus \Pi_F), e \subseteq \Gamma_A, m=z, o=\{z\}, w \in \{T, F\}} :$$
$$\text{add-focus!}(\mathfrak{p}_a, \mathfrak{m}_b, f) = \langle \mathcal{L}_{\text{FHPL}}, \Upsilon_X, \Gamma_P, \Gamma_A, \Gamma_Q, \Gamma_J, \Gamma_K, \Pi_F', \Xi_f \rangle$$
$$\text{where} \quad \Pi_F' = \Pi_F \cup \{f\}$$

$$\forall_{f \in \Pi_F, m=z, f \neq f_z} :$$
$$\text{remove-focus!}(\mathfrak{p}_a, \mathfrak{m}_b, f) = \langle \mathcal{L}_{\text{FHPL}}, \Upsilon_X, \Gamma_P, \Gamma_A, \Gamma_Q, \Gamma_J, \Gamma_K, \Pi_F', \Xi_f \rangle$$
$$\text{where} \quad \Pi_F' = \Pi_F \smallsetminus \{f\}$$

More informally described, the function **add-focus!** establishes a new focus structure. The problem solver provides the group and the environment as arguments and specifies whether it is supposed to be a shared focus or not. MXFRMS constructs the focus structure, with the facet representing the problem solver calling the function as initial modfication token holder and single owner of the focus structure. The focus structure is added only if it does not already exist.

Interface function **remove-focus!** removes an existing focus structure. Only the modification token holder can call this function.

MXFRMS focus structures are a little bit more complex than the XFRMS environments and require a more elaborate set of functions for manipulating them. Just for remembrance, a focus structure consists of the five components *group, environment, modification token holder, owners,* and *public write permit.* The first two components together determine a logical context. Often, the problem solver wants to change the context in one of the following two particular ways: include another facet into the scope of a context or making additional assumptions. This functionality is covered by the following part of the interface:

DEFINITION 5.3.6 (MXFRMS STATE CHANGE INTERFACE, PART III)
The MXFRMS *state change interface provides the following two functions for
modifying the group and environment components of focus structures:*

$$\text{extend-focus-group!} \; : \quad \mathfrak{G} \times \mathcal{PS} \times \mathcal{FM} \times \mathfrak{F} \times \mathfrak{P}(\Upsilon) \quad \longmapsto \mathfrak{G}$$

$$\text{extend-focus-environment!} \; : \quad \mathfrak{G} \times \mathcal{PS} \times \mathcal{FM} \times \mathfrak{F} \times \mathfrak{P}(\Sigma) \quad \longmapsto \mathfrak{G}$$

*Again, the first three arguments are identical to those of logical query interface
functions. The fourth argument is the focus structure to be manipulated, while
the fifth argument is a group in the first case and an environment in the second
case. These functions are then defined under the constraints*

$$\forall_{s=\langle \mathcal{L}_{\text{FHPL}}, \Upsilon_X, \Gamma_P, \Gamma_A, \Gamma_Q, \Gamma_J, \Gamma_K, \Pi_F, \Xi_f \rangle \in \mathfrak{G}}$$

$$\forall_{\mathsf{p}_a \in \mathcal{PS}} \; : \; [\; \textit{ps-to-facet}(\mathsf{p}_a) = z \; \text{and} \; z \in \Upsilon_X \;]$$

$$\forall_{\mathsf{m}_b \in \mathcal{FM}} \; : \; [\; \textit{mxfrms-to-facet}(\mathsf{m}_b) = z' \; \text{and} \; z' \in \Upsilon_X \; \text{and} \; z' = z \;]$$

as follows:

$$\forall_{f=\langle g,e,m,o,w \rangle \in \Pi_F, (m=z) \vee (w=T \wedge z \in o)} \forall_{g^+ \subseteq \Upsilon_X} \; :$$
$$\text{extend-focus-group!}(\mathsf{p}_a, \mathsf{m}_b, f, g^+) \; =$$
$$= \quad \langle \mathcal{L}_{\text{FHPL}}, \Upsilon_X, \Gamma_P, \Gamma_A, \Gamma_Q, \Gamma_J, \Gamma_K, \Pi_{F}', \Xi_f \rangle$$
$$\text{where} \quad \Pi_{F}' \; = \; (\Pi_F \smallsetminus \{f\}) \cup \{f'\}$$
$$\text{and} \quad f' = \langle (g \cup g^+), e, m, o, w \rangle$$

$$\forall_{f=\langle g,e,m,o,w \rangle \in \Pi_F, (m=z) \vee (w=T \wedge z \in o)} \forall_{e^+ \subseteq \Gamma_A} \; :$$
$$\text{extend-focus-environment!}(\mathsf{p}_a, \mathsf{m}_b, f, e^+) \; =$$
$$= \quad \langle \mathcal{L}_{\text{FHPL}}, \Upsilon_X, \Gamma_P, \Gamma_A, \Gamma_Q, \Gamma_J, \Gamma_K, \Pi_{F}', \Xi_f \rangle$$
$$\text{where} \quad \Pi_{F}' \; = \; (\Pi_F \smallsetminus \{f\}) \cup \{f'\}$$
$$\text{and} \quad f' = \langle g, (e \cup e^+), m, o, w \rangle$$

In less formal terms, the function extend-focus-group! allows to extend the
scope of a focus structure to include relevant propositions and logical dependencies of additional facets in the group underling the focus structure by
incrementally increasing group size. The function extend-focus-environment!
is the complemetary function to extend-focus-group! and allows to extend the
scope of a focus structure to incude additional assumptions by incrementally
increasing the environment size. Both functions may be called only be the
modification token holder, if the focus structure is private to facet z. The set
of potential callers of this function includes all owners from set o, if the focus
structure is a public focus.

The final one of the three parts dealing with manipulation of focus structures deals with shared focus structures:

DEFINITION 5.3.7 (MXFRMS STATE CHANGE INTERFACE, PART IV)
*For manipulaton of shared focus structures the following additional functions
are provided:*

$$\text{add-focus-owner!} \ : \qquad \mathfrak{G} \times \mathcal{PS} \times \mathcal{FM} \times \mathfrak{F} \times \Upsilon \qquad \longmapsto \mathfrak{G}$$
$$\text{remove-focus-owner!} \ : \qquad \mathfrak{G} \times \mathcal{PS} \times \mathcal{FM} \times \mathfrak{F} \times \Upsilon \qquad \longmapsto \mathfrak{G}$$

*The first three arguments are again identical to those of logical query interface
functions. The fourth argument is the focus structure to be manipulated, while
the fifth argument is a facet identifier. These functions are then defined under
the constraints*

$$\forall_{s=\langle \mathcal{L}_{\text{FHPL}}, \Upsilon_X, \Gamma_P, \Gamma_A, \Gamma_Q, \Gamma_J, \Gamma_K, \Pi_F, \Xi_f \rangle \in \mathfrak{G}}$$
$$\forall_{\mathfrak{p}_a \in \mathcal{PS}} \ : \ [\ \text{ps-to-facet}(\mathfrak{p}_a) = z \ \text{and} \ z \in \Upsilon_X \ ]$$
$$\forall_{\mathfrak{m}_b \in \mathcal{FM}} \ : \ [\ \text{mxfrms-to-facet}(\mathfrak{m}_b) = z' \ \text{and} \ z' \in \Upsilon_X \ \text{and} \ z' = z \ ]$$

as follows:

$$\forall_{f=\langle g,e,m,o,w \rangle \in \Pi_F} \forall_{x \in \Upsilon_X, x=z, x \in (g \smallsetminus o)} \ :$$
$$\text{add-focus-owner!}(\mathfrak{p}_a, \mathfrak{m}_b, f, x) = \langle \mathcal{L}_{\text{FHPL}}, \Upsilon_X, \Gamma_P, \Gamma_A, \Gamma_Q, \Gamma_J, \Gamma_K, \Pi_{F'}, \Xi_f \rangle$$
$$\text{where} \ \ \Pi_{F'} = (\Pi_F \smallsetminus \{f\}) \cup \{f'\}$$
$$\text{and} \ \ f' = \langle g, e, m, (o \cup \{x\}), w \rangle$$

$$\forall_{f=\langle g,e,m,o,w \rangle \in \Pi_F} \forall_{x \in \Upsilon_X, x \in o, x \neq m, f \neq f_x} \ :$$
$$\text{remove-focus-owner!}(\mathfrak{p}_a, \mathfrak{m}_b, f, x) = \langle \mathcal{L}_{\text{FHPL}}, \Upsilon_X, \Gamma_P, \Gamma_A, \Gamma_Q, \Gamma_J, \Gamma_K, \Pi_{F'}, \Xi_f \rangle$$
$$\text{where} \ \ \Pi_{F'} = (\Pi_F \smallsetminus \{f\}) \cup \{f'\}$$
$$\text{and} \ \ f' = \langle g, e, m, (o_i \smallsetminus \{x\}), w \rangle$$

Shared focus structure require the functionality defined in the last definition
because of the restrictive way the logical query interface is defined: Only
owners of a focus structure can pose queries referencing this focus structure.
On the other hand, if a focus structure is created, the facet representing the
problem solver creating the focus structure is the only owner. Thus, there
must be a way for other agents to become owner (and to undo becoming an
owner), which is exactly the purpose of the two functions in the last definition:

- The function add-focus-owner! can be called by an eligible problem solver
  if it wants to *hook* itself *onto* a shared focus. Only agents represented
  by facets in the group of the focus structure are eligible to perform this
  operation. Thus, the owners component of a focus structure cannot grow
  larger than the group component. Note, however, that the group component itself can be extended dynamically. The effect of add-focus-owner!
  on the focus structure, and on the state as a whole, is simple and obvious: The group component is adapted accordingly and as an effect of
  this the new owner can pose queries referencing this focus structure.

- remove-focus-owner! is used to undo the effect of add-focus-owner! and is needed, because an owner which is not the modification token holder cannot remove a focus structure. Furthermore, the specification requires that the owner requesting its removal from the owner set does not use this focus structure as its current focus. Otherwise, the MXFRMS could end up with facets having no current focus, which is an ill-defined state.

Note, that both of the above functions are the only state change functions that permit problem solvers to manipulate focus structure for which they are not modification token holder.

Last, but not least, the state change interface should allow problem solvers to shift their current focus. This functionality is specified in the following definition.

DEFINITION 5.3.8 (MXFRMS STATE CHANGE INTERFACE, PART V)
Finally, there exists a MXFRMS *state change interface functions for updating the current facet focus:*

$$\text{set-current-focus!} : \quad \mathbb{G} \times \mathcal{PS} \times \mathcal{FM} \times \mathfrak{F} \quad \longmapsto \mathbb{G}$$

The first three arguments are as usual. The fourth argument is the new current focus of for the facet. Then, the function set-current-focus! *is defined under the constraints*

$$\forall_{s=\langle \mathcal{L}_{\text{FHPL}}, \Upsilon_X, \Gamma_P, \Gamma_A, \Gamma_Q, \Gamma_J, \Gamma_K, \Pi_F, \Xi_f \rangle \in \mathbb{G}}$$
$$\forall_{\mathfrak{p}_a \in \mathcal{PS}} : [\ \textit{ps-to-facet}(\mathfrak{p}_a) = z \text{ and } z \in \Upsilon_X\ ]$$
$$\forall_{\mathfrak{m}_b \in \mathcal{FM}} : [\ \textit{mxfrms-to-facet}(\mathfrak{m}_b) = z' \text{ and } z' \in \Upsilon_X \text{ and } z' = z\ ]$$

as follows:

$$\forall_{f=\langle g, e, m, o, w \rangle \in \Pi_F, z \in o} :$$
$$\text{set-current-focus!}(\mathfrak{p}_a, \mathfrak{m}_b, f) = \langle \mathcal{L}_{\text{FHPL}}, \Upsilon_X, \Gamma_P, \Gamma_A, \Gamma_Q, \Gamma_J, \Gamma_K, \Pi_F, \Xi_f' \rangle$$
$$\text{where} \quad \Xi_f' = (\Pi_F \smallsetminus \{\langle z, f_z \rangle\}) \cup \{\langle z, f \rangle\}$$

The definition of set-current-focus! is very simple: it replaces the facet's current focus by a new one as specified by the problem solver.

Note that the state change interface described above provides only functionality for modifying the MXFRMS state based on a fixed set of facets. A rough sketch of some useful functionality to loosen this restriction is given in a section later on.

5.3.5   MXFRMS State Query Interface

Occasionally, a problem solver may have the need to query its MXFRMS facet module for the state components. An exemplary state query interface for MXFRMS is specified in this section.

DEFINITION 5.3.9 (MXFRMS STATE QUERY INTERFACE)
MXFRMS provides a function for retrieving the current focus of a facet as follows:

$$\text{current-focus?} \; : \quad \mathfrak{S} \times \mathcal{PS} \times \mathcal{FM} \longmapsto \mathfrak{F}$$

$$\forall_{s = \langle \mathcal{L}_{\text{FHPL}}, \Upsilon_X, \Gamma_P, \Gamma_A, \Gamma_Q, \Gamma_J, \Gamma_K, \Pi_F, \Xi_f \rangle \in \mathfrak{S}}$$

$$\forall_{\mathfrak{p}_a \in \mathcal{PS}, \, \text{ps-to-facet}(\mathfrak{p}_a) = z, \, z \in \Upsilon_X}$$

$$\forall_{\mathfrak{m}_b \in \mathcal{FM}, \, \text{mxfrms-to-facet}(\mathfrak{m}_b) = z', \, z' \in \Upsilon_X, \, z' = z}$$

$$\text{current-focus?}(\mathfrak{p}_a, \mathfrak{m}_b) \; = \; f_z \quad \text{iff} \quad \langle z, f_z \rangle \in \Xi_f$$

Additionally, MXFRMS *provides the following state query interface functions for querying the existence) of various items in* MXFRMS *logical state components (or relevance for the problem solvers):*

is-facet? :	$\mathfrak{S} \times \mathcal{PS} \times \mathcal{FM} \times \Upsilon$	$\longmapsto \{T, F\}$
is-local-proposition? :	$\mathfrak{S} \times \mathcal{PS} \times \mathcal{FM} \times \Gamma_{blit*}$	$\longmapsto \{T, F\}$
is-proposition-for? :	$\mathfrak{S} \times \mathcal{PS} \times \mathcal{FM} \times \Upsilon \times \Gamma_{blit*}$	$\longmapsto \{T, F\}$
is-local-assumption? :	$\mathfrak{S} \times \mathcal{PS} \times \mathcal{FM} \times \Gamma_{blit*}$	$\longmapsto \{T, F\}$
is-assumption-for? :	$\mathfrak{S} \times \mathcal{PS} \times \mathcal{FM} \times \Upsilon \times \Gamma_{blit*}$	$\longmapsto \{T, F\}$
is-reference? :	$\mathfrak{S} \times \mathcal{PS} \times \mathcal{FM} \times \Gamma_{lref*}$	$\longmapsto \{T, F\}$
is-justification? :	$\mathfrak{S} \times \mathcal{PS} \times \mathcal{FM} \times \Gamma_{fcl}$	$\longmapsto \{T, F\}$
is-local-focus? :	$\mathfrak{S} \times \mathcal{PS} \times \mathcal{FM} \times \mathfrak{F}$	$\longmapsto \{T, F\}$
is-focus-for? :	$\mathfrak{S} \times \mathcal{PS} \times \mathcal{FM} \times \Upsilon \times \mathfrak{F}$	$\longmapsto \{T, F\}$

Again, the first three arguments are identical to those of logical query interface functions. The fourth argument is the item whose presence in MXFRMS *state components is to be checked. These functions are then defined under the constraints*

$$\forall_{s = \langle \mathcal{L}_{\text{FHPL}}, \Upsilon_X, \Gamma_P, \Gamma_A, \Gamma_Q, \Gamma_J, \Gamma_K, \Pi_F, \Xi_f \rangle \in \mathfrak{S}}$$

$$\forall_{\mathfrak{p}_a \in \mathcal{PS}} \; : \; [\, \text{ps-to-facet}(\mathfrak{p}_a) = z \text{ and } z \in \Upsilon_X \,]$$

$$\forall_{\mathfrak{m}_b \in \mathcal{FM}} \; : \; [\, \text{mxfrms-to-facet}(\mathfrak{m}_b) = z' \text{ and } z' \in \Upsilon_X \text{ and } z' = z \,]$$

as follows:

$\forall_{x \in \Upsilon} :$

$$\text{is-facet?}(\mathfrak{p}_a, \mathfrak{m}_b, x) \quad = \quad \begin{cases} T & \text{if } x \in \Upsilon_X \\ F & \text{otherwise} \end{cases}$$

$\forall_{\phi \in \Gamma_{blit*}} :$

$$\text{is-local-proposition?}(\mathfrak{p}_a, \mathfrak{m}_b, \phi) \quad = \quad \begin{cases} T & \text{if } \phi \in \Gamma_P \text{ and } \textit{facet}(\phi) = z \\ F & \text{otherwise} \end{cases}$$

$\forall_{\phi \in \Gamma_{blit*}} :$

$$\text{is-proposition-for?}(\mathfrak{p}_a, \mathfrak{m}_b, x, \phi) \quad = \quad \begin{cases} T & \text{if } \phi \in \Gamma_P \text{ and } \textit{facet}(\phi) = x \\ F & \text{otherwise} \end{cases}$$

$\forall_{\phi \in \Gamma_{blit*}} :$

$$\text{is-local-assumption?}(\mathfrak{p}_a, \mathfrak{m}_b, \phi) \quad = \quad \begin{cases} T & \text{if } \phi \in \Gamma_A \text{ and } \textit{facet}(\phi) = z \\ F & \text{otherwise} \end{cases}$$

$\forall_{\phi \in \Gamma_{blit*}} :$

$$\text{is-assumption-for?}(\mathfrak{p}_a, \mathfrak{m}_b, x, \phi) \quad = \quad \begin{cases} T & \text{if } \phi \in \Gamma_A \text{ and } \textit{facet}(\phi) = x \\ F & \text{otherwise} \end{cases}$$

$\forall_{\phi \in \Gamma_{lref*}} :$

$$\text{is-reference?}(\mathfrak{p}_a, \mathfrak{m}_b, \phi) \quad = \quad \begin{cases} T & \text{if } \phi \in \Gamma_Q \text{ and } \textit{facet}(\phi) = z \\ F & \text{otherwise} \end{cases}$$

$\forall_{(\Phi \to \varphi) \in \Gamma_{fcl}} :$

$$\text{is-justification?}(\mathfrak{p}_a, \mathfrak{m}_b, (\Phi \to \varphi)) \quad = \quad \begin{cases} T & \text{if } (\Phi \to \varphi) \in \Gamma_J \text{ and } \textit{facet}((\Phi \to \varphi)) = z \\ F & \text{otherwise} \end{cases}$$

$\forall_{f = \langle g, e, m, o, w \rangle \in \mathfrak{F}} :$

$$\text{is-focus?}(\mathfrak{p}_a, \mathfrak{m}_b, f) \quad = \quad \begin{cases} T & \text{if } f \in \Pi_F \text{ and} \\ & \quad [\, m = z \text{ or } (w = T \text{ and } z \in o) \,] \\ F & \text{otherwise} \end{cases}$$

For a more complete assessment of currently relevant FHPL *structures,* MXFRMS *additionally provides the following state query interface functions:*

$$
\begin{array}{rll}
\text{all-facets? :} & \mathfrak{S} \times \mathcal{PS} \times \mathcal{FM} & \longmapsto \mathfrak{P}(\Upsilon) \\
\text{all-local-propositions? :} & \mathfrak{S} \times \mathcal{PS} \times \mathcal{FM} & \longmapsto \mathfrak{P}(\Gamma_{blit*}) \\
\text{all-propositions? :} & \mathfrak{S} \times \mathcal{PS} \times \mathcal{FM} & \longmapsto \mathfrak{P}(\Gamma_{blit*}) \\
\text{all-local-assumptions? :} & \mathfrak{S} \times \mathcal{PS} \times \mathcal{FM} & \longmapsto \mathfrak{P}(\Gamma_{blit*}) \\
\text{all-assumptions? :} & \mathfrak{S} \times \mathcal{PS} \times \mathcal{FM} & \longmapsto \mathfrak{P}(\Gamma_{blit*}) \\
\text{all-references? :} & \mathfrak{S} \times \mathcal{PS} \times \mathcal{FM} & \longmapsto \mathfrak{P}(\Gamma_{lref*}) \\
\text{all-justifications? :} & \mathfrak{S} \times \mathcal{PS} \times \mathcal{FM} & \longmapsto \mathfrak{P}(\Gamma_{fcl}) \\
\text{all-foci? :} & \mathfrak{S} \times \mathcal{PS} \times \mathcal{FM} & \longmapsto \mathfrak{P}(\mathfrak{F})
\end{array}
$$

All these functions take three arguments, which are the standard first three arguments as in all other interface functions. These functions are then defined under the constraints

$$
\begin{aligned}
&\forall_{s=\langle \mathcal{L}_{\text{FHPL}}, \Upsilon_X, \Gamma_P, \Gamma_A, \Gamma_Q, \Gamma_J, \Gamma_K, \Pi_F, \Xi_f \rangle \in \mathfrak{S}} \\
&\forall_{p_a \in \mathcal{PS}} : [\ \textit{ps-to-facet}(p_a) = z \text{ and } z \in \Upsilon_X\ ] \\
&\forall_{m_b \in \mathcal{FM}} : [\ \textit{mxfrms-to-facet}(m_b) = z' \text{ and } z' \in \Upsilon_X \text{ and } z' = z\ ]
\end{aligned}
$$

as follows:

$$
\begin{aligned}
\text{all-facets?}(p_a, m_b) &= \Upsilon_X \\
\text{all-local-propositions?}(p_a, m_b) &= \Gamma_{P\lceil z \rceil} \\
\text{all-propositions?}(p_a, m_b) &= \Gamma_P \\
\text{all-local-assumptions?}(p_a, m_b) &= \Gamma_{A\lceil z \rceil} \\
\text{all-assumptions?}(p_a, m_b) &= \Gamma_A \\
\text{all-references?}(p_a, m_b) &= \Gamma_{Q\lceil z \rceil} \\
\text{all-justifications?}(p_a, m_b) &= \Gamma_{J\lceil z \rceil} \\
\text{all-foci?}(p_a, m_b) &= \{\, f \mid f \in \Pi_F \text{ and is-focus?}(f) = T \,\}
\end{aligned}
$$

The state query interface could be extended to include the possibility to query the system about other agents' relevant data etc., but — as becomes clear later on — this would require the implementation to include an extension of the belief query and manipulation protocol between MXFRMS facets. Such an extension also raises a number of unresolved questions regarding semantical issues, like what data communicated from other agents to the local MXFRMS facet are supposed to mean, if these data are supposed to be not even relevant for the local facet. Therefore, we leave the state query interface as defined above.

5.3.6   MXFRMS System Level Functionality

In the section on MXFRMS system architecture, we motivated a division of overall system functionality into facet-level interface and system-level interface in order to separate general-purpose functionality from more implementation-specific functionality. The former kind of functionality has been specified in detail in the previous sections. In this section, we give a rough sketch of the kind of system-level functionality that can be built into a particular implementation of MXFRMS.

Agent Dynamics and Agent Mobility   The facet-level functionality specified above assumes a fixed set of facets, because the dynamic creation of new facet modules requires the determination of a substantial amount of implementation-specific information, like where and how the facet module is allocated, setting up communication connections, etc. Dynamic changes to the set of relevant facets must be handled by a facet dynamics interface (described below), which should provide among others at least the function:

$$\text{new-facet! :} \qquad \mathbb{G} \times \mathcal{PS} \times \mathcal{FM} \times \mathcal{PS} \times \mathcal{FM} \times \Upsilon \longmapsto \mathbb{G}$$

which can under the constraints

$$\forall_{s=\langle \mathcal{L}_{\mathsf{FHPL}}, \Upsilon_X, \Gamma_P, \Gamma_A, \Gamma_Q, \Gamma_J, \Gamma_K, \Pi_F, \Xi_f \rangle \in \mathbb{G}}$$
$$\forall_{p_a \in \mathcal{PS}} : [\; \mathsf{ps\text{-}to\text{-}facet}(p_a) = z \text{ and } z \in \Upsilon_X \;]$$
$$\forall_{m_b \in \mathcal{FM}} : [\; \mathsf{mxfrms\text{-}to\text{-}facet}(m_b) = z' \text{ and } z' \in \Upsilon_X \text{ and } z' = z \;]$$

be defined as follows:

$$\text{new-facet!}(p_a, m_b, x) = \langle \mathcal{L}_{\mathsf{FHPL}}, \Upsilon_X', \Gamma_P', \Gamma_A', \Gamma_Q', \Gamma_J, \Gamma_K', \Pi_F', \Xi_f' \rangle$$
$$\text{where } \Upsilon_X' = \Upsilon_X \cup \{x\}$$
$$\text{and } \Gamma_P' = \Gamma_P \cup \{x.\bot, x.\top\}$$
$$\text{and } \Gamma_A' = \Gamma_P \cup \{x.\top\}$$
$$\text{and } \Gamma_Q' = \Gamma_Q \cup \{y{:}x.\phi \mid y \in (\Upsilon_X \smallsetminus \{x\}) \text{ and } \phi \in \{\top, \bot\}\}$$
$$\text{and } \Gamma_K' = \Gamma_K \cup \{(x.\phi {\rightsquigarrow} y{:}x.\phi) \mid y \in (\Upsilon_X \smallsetminus \{x\}) \text{ and } \phi \in \{\top, \bot\}\}$$
$$\text{and } \Pi_F' = \Pi_F \cup \{\langle \{x\}, \{x.\top\}, x, \{x\}, \mathsf{F} \rangle\}$$
$$\text{and } \Xi_f' = \Xi_f \cup \{\langle x, \langle \{x\}, \{x.\top\}, x, \{x\}, \mathsf{F} \rangle \rangle\}$$

Note that with the above specification any exiting problem solver can instruct its associated MXFRMS facet module to establish a new MXFRMS facet module, which upon creation becomes available for service to its associated problem solver and becomes known as an additional facet to all available MXFRMS facet modules

The allocation of a facet module to an MXFRMS process or a particular host need not necessarily stay fixed. In the presence of mobile agents, it can make sense for a facet module to move along network connections together with its associated problem solver. Implementation-specific functionality is needed for maintaining communication with those MXFRMS facet modules where belief contracts exist.

Communication and Distribution   Another strongly implementation-dependent feature is the association of problem solver modules and MXFRMS facet modules to processes. Unless transparent agent communication protocols, which hide the actual transportation mechanisms and low-level features like port number, TCP/IP addresses, or INTERNET URLS, the way problem solvers and MXFRMS facet modules can communicate with each other and among themselves depends on process-related features of the underlying implementation architecture. The system-level interface of MXFRMS should abstract from such implementation details and supply functionality for agent-based or facet module-based communication based on symbolic addresses.

Furthermore, it may make sense to dynamically change the allocation of facet modules to processes. For example, on multiprocessor machines the efficiency of a big MXFRMS process with a large number of facet modules could be dynamically replaced by two MXFRMS processes with just half of the MXFRMS facet modules each. Or a large agent process with a problem solver module and a MXFRMS modules could be split up into two processes, such that the process with the MXFRMS facet module can work in the background while the problem solving process is thinking about its next steps or communicating with other agents.

Access Rights and PS Callback Interfaces   Finally, the above specification permits a MXFRMS module to communicate any local belief to another facet module. Security and privacy precautions could necessitate the inclusion of elaborate functionality for maintaining access rights, on a per agent and a per literal basis. One possibility to include such functionality would be via a problem solver callback interface: the MXFRMS facet module can call problem solver functions in order to determine whether communicating a belief is permitted or not. Such a PS call back interface could also be useful in those cases, where ensuring global knowledge of relevant facets and assumptions is not possible: the MXFRMS module could request its problem solver for permission to make it relevant, if a previously non-relevant proposition occurs in a query posed by some other agent.

The above items give just a rough idea of the nature of system-level functionality, which must be analyzed and determined separately when some more details about the overall multiagent system architecture are known.

5.4 MXFRMS Facet Module Architecture

Section 5.2 discussed the overall system architecture of an MXFRMS that is embedded in a multiagent system. The main problem was that the wide spectrum of possible implementation architectures for multiagent systems makes it virtually impossible to come up with a single, fixed architecture for MXFRMS. The solution to this problem was provided by an abstraction process, which created a separation of the overall MXFRMS system functionality into facet-level and system-level functionality. The *facet module* was the central concept in this separation process. Like the implementation architecture itself, ystem-level functionality is application-specific and must be left to a particular implementation effort. Facet-level functionality is generic and was specified in the previous section. This section dicusses *architectural issues* for the implementation of a facet module and leads the way towards the general discussion of how MXFRMS can be implemented.

The architecture of an MXFRMS facet module is similar to the architecture of the XFRMS system and graphically illustrated in Figure 5.5. Thus, the MXFRMS facet module consists of the three submodules dependency net unit (DNU), context management unit (CMU), and communication and control unit (CCU).

- The **dependency net unit** (DNU) is the backbone of an MXFRMS facet module. It maintains the local dependencies dependencies between local and communicated beliefs (base literals and base literal references). The dependency net consists of three types of nodes and links which together make up a directed, bipartite graph, possibly with cycles (for details, see below). Among other information, the nodes representing beliefs carry labels which allow to determine the logical consequence relation in avery efficient manner.

- The **context management unit** (CMU) manages focus structures, which are the principal component of labels, and their associated contexts. Furthermore, the CMU is responsible for maintaining the current focus of a facet, which represents the context the problem solver is currently reasoning in.

- The **communication and control unit** (CCU) controls the interaction between DNU and CMU and handles all necessary communication with the associated problem solver *and* all other MXFRMS facet modules. As part of the communication protocol, the CCU translates problem solver data into some normal form such that it can be easily communicated

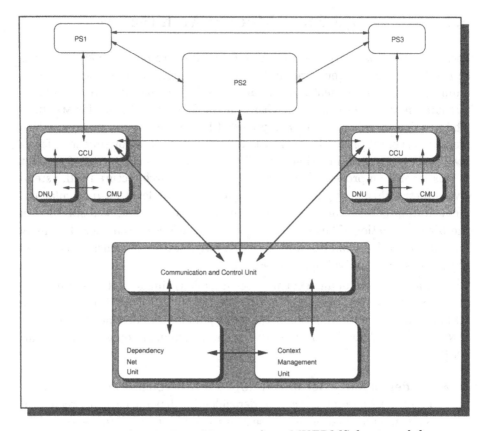

Figure 5.5: A generic architecture for a MXFRMS facet module.

between facet modules. The CCU also handles the mapping of problem solver data to internal data structures and vice versa.

The generality and the advantages of the generic reason maintenance architecture proposed in Chapter 3 becomes now obvious: we have structured the overall functionality into reasonably self-contained submodules with well-defined interactions among them such that the extension to the multiagent case now requires only comparatively limited changes in each of the units. This is discussed in more detail in the next section.

5.5   MXFRMS Implementation

In this section, we investigate the implementation of MXFRMS facet modules a little bit more closely. Like a distributed database system, MXFRMS can be viewed as a collection of modules, where each module has internal state for persistent storage of relevant information and provides a set of operations to query and change the internal state. The internal state of a MXFRMS facet module is called simply MXFRMS facet module state; the state of the overall system is called MXFRMS global system state or simply MXFRMS state. Section 5.3.2 showed how the global MXFRMS logical state can be divided up into a set of facet-local logical states. Using this natural division of the global state, it remains to be shown how a facet-local logical state is represented by a MXFRMS facet module state. A set of integrity constraints is defined on the set of module states, which ensure that all properties of the global logical states are met.

The update operations in the MXFRMS state change interface modify MXFRMS state and must ensure that the integrity constraints are violated only temporarily during the execution of the operation, but will hold again after the operation has been completed. In other words, the MXFRMS problem solver interface functions are similar to database transactions [Gray and Reuter, 1993]. Because the integrity constraints span multiple, sometimes even all MXFRMS facet modules communication between facet modules may be necessary. A MXFRMS inter-facet communication protocol is specified to handle such communication. Note, that this communication interface depends strongly on the design of the implementation; therefore, it did not make sense to provide its specification earlier, e.g. in Section 5.3.

The following sections discuss all these issues in some more detail. Because the implementation of a MXFRMS module has significant commonalities with the XFRMS implementation, we will omit details that have already been explained in Section 3.4 and concentrate on the differences instead.

5.5.1   Representation: Mapping Logical State to MXFRMS State

The basic implementation ideas are to use a modified variant of the XFRMS implementation to implement a MXFRMS facet module, and to let such a MXFRMS facet module represent exactly one facet-local logical state as defined in Section 5.3.2. Thus, the global state of an MXFRMS serving k problem solvers is described as a k-ary vector of k MXFRMS facet module states. Furthermore, each MXFRMS facet module state is structured according to the module architecture described above (Section 5.4) and consists of the states of the three units DNU, CMU, and CCU   (see also 5.6).

The state components of the three units of an MXFRMS facet module are either sets of *nodes* or *tables*. The nodes are structured data objects (C structs or CLOS object) which represent particular problem solver data, i.e. items of various logical state components, e.g. base literals, base literal references, justifications, or focus structures. The tables represent binary relations which implement mappings between problem solver data and MXFRMS internal node data structures.

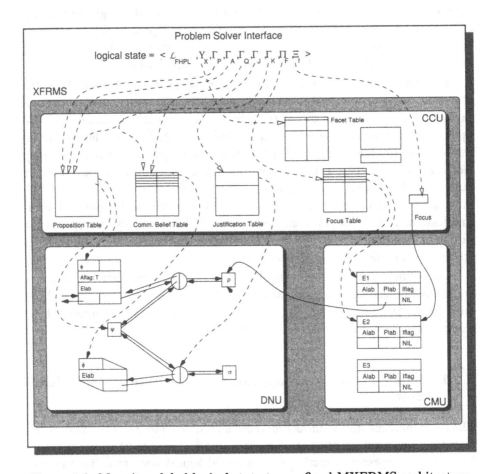

Figure 5.6: Mapping global logical state to a refined MXFRMS architecture.

In the DNU, local propositions (base literals) are drawn as rectangular nodes, communicated beliefs (base literal references) as trapezoid nodes, and local justifications as circular nodes. Arrows illustrate reference to other structures and are stored as pointers in attribute fields. Focus structures in the CMU are also drawn as rectangles. Some of the nodes have been zoomed out to display some important aspects of their internal structure. Bidirectional hash tables are used by the CCU to represent the mappings between problem solver data and MXFRMS internal data.

The DNU uses *proposition nodes*, *communicated nodes*, and *justification nodes* to represent the logical state components Γ_P, Γ_Q, and Γ_J, respectively. Justifications nodes have the same structure as in the XFRMS. Proposition nodes are a slightly extended variant of those in XFRMS: the extra attributes are a flag Cflag for fast indication that the node represents the falsum and a field Qset which represents the set of facets to which the base literal represented by the proposition node has been communicated and which need to be informed about changes. Communicated nodes are new in MXFRMS, but have a structure that weakly resembles a proposition node: The proposition node attributes for storing pointers to justifications justifying the node, the flag indicating the node representing an assumption, and the attribute for storing the set of facets to which the node has been communicated are not needed for communicated nodes, because they can neither be justified, nor be assumptions, nor be communicated to other agents (at least not in our implementation). Proposition nodes and communicated nodes have additional attributes (*labels*) which represent contextual information in a concise manner and aids in query processing. All three kinds of nodes are appropriately linked together such that they form a dependency network, the topological structure of which is exploited to efficiently ensure consistency after updates of the information stored in the DNU.

The CMU uses the fourth kind of node — *focus nodes* — to represent the set of relevant focus structures (in the same sense as defined for facet-local logical state) in an MXFRMS facet module. The focus nodes carry attributes which represent their associated contexts. The focus nodes of the CMU and the proposition nodes and communicated nodes of the DNU are appropriately interlinked for speeding up query processing and updates. The CMU also has a variable which points to the focus node representing the facet's current focus.

Finally, the CCU uses *facet nodes* to represent the set of all known facets, including their relevant propositions, assumptions, and focus structures. In addition, focus nodes may store implementation-dependent information related to facets, e.g. addresses or message queues necessary for communication, which is not further discussed here. The other components of the CCU are bidirectional hash tables which implement mappings between problem solver data expressed in FHPL and MXFRMS internal data structures.

5.5.2 Labels

A key role in achieving sufficient efficiency in query processing play *labels*, which are special attributes that proposition nodes, communicated nodes, and focus structures carry.

The label of a proposition node representing some base literal $\phi = x.p$ or a communicated node $\phi = y{:}x.p$ is called *focus label* and denoted by $\mathsf{Flab}(x.p)$

and Flab(y:x.p), respectively. It describes the set of all relevant focus structures f, for which the following holds:

$$\Gamma_{s,f} \vdash_{\mathsf{FHPL}} \phi$$

Thus, in order to provide an answer for a query like follows-from?($\mathfrak{p}_a, \mathfrak{m}_b, f, \phi$), for appropriate $\mathfrak{p}_a, \mathfrak{m}_b$, it will suffice to check whether the focus node representing f is referenced in the focus label Flab(ϕ) of the node representing ϕ. Conceptually, each focus structure $f = \langle g, e, m, o, w \rangle$ introduces a unique marker, which is by definition inserted into all focus labels of the nodes representing elements of g.e. The label propagation procedures discussed below ensure that the unique marker is passed on to all other nodes for which the above relationship holds. In addition to other necessary restrictions, the integrity constraints discussed in the next section, will ensure that the above relationship is enforced.

The labels of focus nodes are called *belief labels* and are denoted by Blab(f). A belief label contains references to all proposition nodes and communicated nodes that are (locally in the curret facet) believed in the context determined by the focus under consideration. Belief labels can be imagined as a kind of inverted list of focus labels.

Both kind of labels implement an *explicit, distributed representation* of the derivability relation $\vdash_{\mathsf{FHPL}}$. Distribution of the derivability relation is actually in two stages:

- **Distribution across the set of facets:** A particular facet stores only derivability information local to the facet.

- **Distribution across sets of nodes:** Within a facet the distribution is, in the case of focus labels, across the (local) set of proposition nodes and communicated belief nodes representing relevant problem solver data, and in the case of belief labels, across the set of focus structures relevant for the local facet.[15]

5.5.3   Integrity Constraints

A substantial number of integrity constraints must be ensured by the MXFRMS in order to keep the information represented by the MXFRMS consistent. Obviously, any constraint that has been defined for logical states (see Section 5.3.1) must have an equivalent constraint on MXFRMS facet module states. However,

---

[15]Note, that a focus structure relevant for a MXFRMS facet module $\mathfrak{m}_b$ does not necessarily have to be relevant for its associated problem solver $\mathfrak{p}_a$: The former is the case for any focus structure $f = \langle g, e, m, o, w \rangle$ with mxfrms-to-facet($\mathfrak{m}_b$) $\in g$, while the latter is the case only if ps-to-facet($\mathfrak{p}_a$) $\in o$.

because of the additional information represented by the various nodes, additional constraints must be defined, e.g. ones that ensure correct linking of proposition and justification nodes or a unique and complete representation of the logical state. Again, a complete set of these constraints is formally given in a separate technical report; here, we only present the constraints pertaining to labels.

DEFINITION 5.5.1 (MXFRMS STATE CONSTRAINTS)
Let $\mathfrak{s} = \langle \mathcal{L}_{\mathsf{FHPL}}, \Upsilon_X, \Gamma_P, \Gamma_A, \Gamma_Q, \Gamma_J, \Gamma_K, \Pi_F, \Xi_f \rangle \in \mathfrak{S}$ be a logical RMS state, $\phi \in \mathsf{FHPL}$ be a base literal x.p or a base literal reference y:x.p, $f = \langle g, e, m, o, w \rangle$ be a relevant focus structure, and $\Gamma_{\mathfrak{s},f}$ be the set $\Gamma_{\lceil g \rceil} \cup g.\top \cup g.e$.

The following constraints must be met by proposition node labels, communicated node labels, and environment node labels in any MXFRMS state:[16]

C1 $\quad \forall_{\phi \in (\Gamma_P \cup \Gamma_Q)} \forall_{f \in \Pi_F} :$ $\qquad [\, f \in \mathit{Flab}(\phi) \implies \Gamma_{\mathfrak{s},f} \vdash_{\mathsf{FHPL}} \phi \,]$ $\qquad$ (5.3)

C2 $\quad \forall_{\phi \in (\Gamma_P \cup \Gamma_Q)} \forall_{f \in \Pi_F} :$ $\qquad [\, \Gamma_{\mathfrak{s},f} \vdash_{\mathsf{FHPL}} \phi \implies f \in \mathit{Flab}(\phi) \,]$ $\qquad$ (5.4)

C3 $\quad \forall_{\phi \in (\Gamma_P \cup \Gamma_Q)} \forall_{f \in \Pi_F} :$ $\qquad [\, \phi \in \mathit{Blab}(f) \implies \Gamma_{\mathfrak{s},f} \vdash_{\mathsf{FHPL}} \phi \,]$ $\qquad$ (5.5)

C4 $\quad \forall_{\phi \in (\Gamma_P \cup \Gamma_Q)} \forall_{f \in \Pi_F} :$ $\qquad [\, \Gamma_{\mathfrak{s},f} \vdash_{\mathsf{FHPL}} \phi \implies \phi \in \mathit{Blab}(f) \,]$ $\qquad$ (5.6)

Constraints C1 and C2 ensure soundness and completeness of proposition node and communication node labels, while C3 and C4 ensure soundness and completeness of focus node labels.

5.5.4 Process Structure of Facet Modules

A MXFRMS facet module remains inactive unless it must process requests from its associated problem solver or other MXFRMS facet modules. Requests arrive via some communication channel and are queued in an inbox. Whenever the inbox is non-empty, the MXFRMS facet module process is activated and processes all pending requests one-by-one, in the order they arrived. The processing of a single request works roughly as follows:

1. First of all, the CCU tests the eligibility of the request. For instance, only the problem solver associated with the MXFRMS facet module may pose a follows-from? request, while the functionality to update the label of base literal reference can be invoked only by the MXFRMS module that originally supplied the communicated belief.

2. Next, the CCU tries to map the problem solver data supplied as arguments into internal data structures of the MXFRMS. If the CCU cannot

---

[16]Because the MXFRMS data objects are not yet formally defined, the specification of these constraints refers to entities of the logical state, although they actually constrain the nodes representing these entities.

perform this mapping, an error is reported and the problem solver request is discarded.

3. Otherwise, the CCU calls the appropriate internal functions of the CMU or DNU to process the query or update request.

4. The CCU takes the results provided by the internal functions of the DNU and CMU, maps them into problem solver data, and sends the answer back to the unit that posed the request.

This cycle is further illustrated in the next section, which shows how labels are exploited in query processing.

5.5.5   Exploitation of Labels in Query Processing

Maintaining labels as a distributed representation (across the set of nodes representing relevant data) of the derivability relation pays off when a MXFRMS facet module m_b receives requests from a problem solver p_a to answer queries using functions of the logical query interface, e.g. follows-from?, holds-in?, and context-of?. These queries can be locally processed without any communication with other entities.

Both follows-from? and holds-in? are defined only for the problem solver directly associated with the MXFRMS facet module on hand, i.e. in the first step of the cycle the CCU checks the condition ps-to-facet(p_a) $= z = z' =$ mxfrms-to-facet(m_b), which must be satisfied if the request is to be further processed. In the second step, the problem solver data supplied as arguments in the request are mapped into MXFRMS data. Then, the main work is done by the DNU, which executes the appropriate internal function in order to provide the answer to the query. The results are mapped back to problem solver data and returned to the problem solver.

The functions used by the DNU to provide the above functionality are sketched in the following two function definitions:[17]

FUNCTION 5.5.1 (FOLLOWS-FROM?)

```
1  function follows-from?(p_a, m_b, f, φ)  ≡
2         if [ f ∈ Flab(φ) ]
3            then return(T)
4            else return(NIL)
```

---

[17]The functions and procedures are specified in *mathematical pseudocode*. The pseudocode is tagged mathematical, because we sometimes use mathematical notation for parts that are obviously easy to implement, e.g. set union, element tests, or subset tests. Pseudocode keywords are underlined. Words set in sans serif font are function, procedure, or data structure attribute names.

```
5        fi
6 end
```

Function follows-from? performs a simple element test: it checks whether the environment is contained in the proposition node's label. Depending on the number of environments actually used, an implementation of labels based on bit vectors may be advisable in order to make the element test fast.

FUNCTION 5.5.2 (HOLDS-IN?)

```
1 function holds-in?($p_a, m_b, f, \phi$) $\equiv$
2        if [[ lflag($f$) == NIL ] $\wedge$ [ $f \in$ Flab($\phi$) ]]
3            then return(T)
4            else return(NIL)
5        fi
6 end
```

Query function holds-in? first tests the lflag flag of the environment node in order to find out whether the environment is consistent. The remainder is equivalent to follows-from?.

The logical query functions follows-from? and holds-in? can actually be processed both by the DNU and the CMU; usually the DNU will provide the response faster, unless the average number of environments in a proposition node label exceeds the average number of proposition nodes in an environment node label.

The answer to the logical query function context-of? is always provided by the context management unit:

FUNCTION 5.5.3 (CONTEXT-OF?)

```
1 function context-of?($p_a, m_b, f$) $\equiv$
2        if [ lflag($f$) == T ]
3            then return($\varnothing$)
4            else return(Blab($f$))
5        fi
6    end
```

Function context-of? simply returns the (proposition) label of the respective environment node, if the environment is consistent. Otherwise, it returns the empty set.

The three focus-related variants of the above query functions do not take an explicit environment argument, but use the known problem solver focus instead. As an example, the function follows-from-focus? is given:

FUNCTION 5.5.4 (FOLLOWS-FROM-FOCUS?)

```
1  function follows-from-focus?(p_a, m_b, φ)  ≡
2          if [ f_z ∈ Flab(φ) ]
3              then return(T)
4                else return(NIL)
5          fi
6  end
```

The functions specified in state query interface are obviously trivial to implement: they require only a lookup in the appropriate CCU tables. Thus, they
are not further discussed here; however, they are included in the appendix.

5.5.6   Label Propagation

Achieving total locality of query processing as described in the previous section
while delivering correct and complete answers to queries is possible only if the
various labels attached to the nodes are always kept up-to-date. That this
is always the case is ensured by the integrity constraints specified earlier.
Integrity constraints are endangered by requests pertaining to the functions
specified in the MXFRMS state change interface, which a problem solver in
the multiagent system must use in order to update its relevant beliefs and
dependencies. Like in the XFRMS, an incremental label propagation mechanism
is used to ensure that the integrity constraints hold after a state change invoked
by a problem solver. If an update request is received by an MXFRMS facet
module, it must check whether the logical consequence relation is affected. If
this is indeed the case, then the MXFRMS facet module must initiate

- a local, incremental label propagation which updates the labels of the
  local nodes affected by the change caused by the problem solver,

  and,

- for every base literal that i) has been communicated to other MXFRMS
  facet modules and ii) has been updated during the local label propagation step, communication of an appropriate message to each MXFRMS
  facet module that the base literal has been communicated to.

In this section, we discuss this incremental label propagation mechanism. The
next section then explains in detail, how and when the mechanism is invoked
for each state change interface function. Contrary to the XFRMS, which is a
system oriented towards a single agent, and hence, single-facetted, the extent
of label propagation in the MXFRMS can cover several facet modules. The
functions for handling communication between MXFRMS facet modules are
described in the section thereafter. The last section of the chapter on MXFRMS
implementation considers correctness of label propagation.

In order to understand the MXFRMS label propagation mechanism it is useful to outline its similarities and differences to the XFRMS label propagation mechanism. MXFRMS focus structures play a similar role as XFRMS environments: they fix the group of problem solvers to be considered and the assumptions this group of problem solvers wants to make in the focus on hand. Given a database of logical dependencies (facet clauses and contract clauses in MXFRMS), the context associated with a focus structure is uniquely determined. The context information is represented in the MXFRMS, in a distributed fashion, in the labels of various nodes introduced earlier. The construction and maintenance of these labels is done by the label propagation mechanism and is very similar to the way XFRMS handles environments, except for two things which are both related to contract clauses:

- Every node representing a base literal has an attribute which stores a list of facets (agents) which have contracted the base literal. These agents must be informed if derivability of a base literal represented by the node changes.

- Base literal references are represented by a new type of nodes: communicated nodes. Their label is never updated due to a local label propagation; rather, the facet module must receive an update message from the facet module which maintains the source object, i.e. the base literal.

The basic task of the label propagation mechanism is to pass the focus markers along the (global) dependency net, which is constructed from the database of logical dependencies (facet clauses and contract clauses), to other nodes which represent base literals and base literal references in the focus structure's context (see also Figure 5.7). In order to be included in the context, a datum must be derivable from the set of assumptions and in the group of facets determined by the focus structure. A derivation is constructed by applying the LMP or CMP inference rules defined in C_{FHPL}, which require the presence of appropriate facet clauses or contract clauses, respectively, in the database of logical dependencies. This database can be separated into the subset of facet clauses and the subset of contract clauses, which are represented and handled differently in the MXFRMS.

The set of facet clauses (justifications) is naturally divided into subsets belonging to a single facet and is represented in a distributed fashion: each such subset of facet clauses builds a local dependency net represented in a facet module's DNU. Label propagation across justifications has been treated extensively in XFRMS; their treatment in MXFRMS is almost equivalent to that of XFRMS: a single justification behaves like a multiple input logical AND gate, which passes the focus marker to the consequent node label iff it is present at all antecedent node labels, while multiple justifications for a single propo-

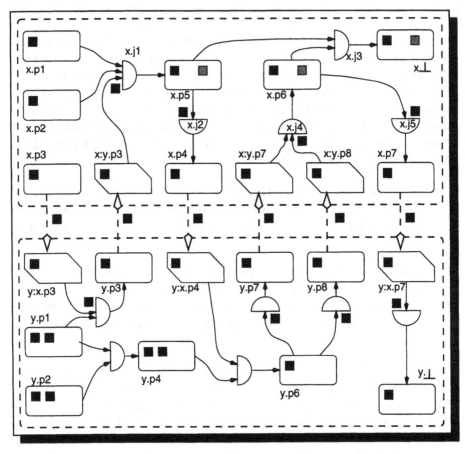

Figure 5.7: The MXFRMS label propagation mechanism.

The dependency nets of two facets are shown and the propagation of a extend-focus-environment! operation is shown. The black box represents a focus structure $f = \langle g, e, m, o, w \rangle$ with $g = \{x, y\}$ and $m = y$. The initial environment e was $\{y.p_1, y.p_2\}$, and y just extended it such that it includes $y.p_3$. Note, that this has no direct effect on facet y at first, but the message being sent to x regarding the update of the focus structure f causes x to label $x.p_3$ with focus f (illustrated by the black box). Then the label update ripples through the network, hopping back and forth several times between x and y, until finally — in our case — all nodes are updated. Note, however, that the overall update is broken down into several small local update transactions: whenever no further local updating is possible, such a local transaction is finished. The MXFRMS module can resume to serve requests from its associated problem solver. When another message is received, it is handled like an independent request, which has no obvious relationship to previous updates.

sition (i.e. all justifications have the same antecedents) behave like a multiple input logical OR gate, which adds the focus marker to the node label iff at least one justification passes the label to it. Considering all focus structures simultaneously, this means that the label passed by a justification node to its consequent node must be the intersection of the labels of its antecedents, and the label of a proposition node must be the union of the labels passed by all justifications with the proposition as consequent.

Contract clauses (or belief update contracts) connect a base literal to a base literal reference in another facet. The node representing a base literal reference should include a focus node in its Flab label iff the focus structure occurs in the base literals label and the facet containing the base literal reference occurs in the focus structure's group. Facet clauses are not explicitly represented by nodes. Instead, each proposition node stores a list of facet identifiers for which it has committed to an update contract regarding the proposition node.

In the next few paragraphs, we now look at the actual procedures that perform the incremental label propagation. The label propagation is called inremental, because whenever an update of labels is necessary, it tries to compute and propagate only *label differences* instead of computing full labels from scratch.

Propagation of labels across justifications (facet clauses) is performed by the function mxrms-propagate, which is specified as follows:

PROCEDURE 5.5.5 (MXFRMS-PROPAGATE)

```
1  procedure mxfrms-propagate(φ, Φ, Δ_{F+})  ≡
2         if [ Δ_{F+} = ∅ ]
3            then Δ_{F+}' ← ∩_{φ∈Φ} Flab(φ)
4            else Δ_{F+}' ← Δ_{F+} ∩ ∩_{φ∈Φ} Flab(φ)
5         fi
6         if [ Δ_{F+}' ≠ ∅ ]
7            then mxfrms-update-prop-label(φ, Δ_{F+}')
8         fi
9  end
```

The procedure mxfrms-propagate can be used both for full label computation as well as incremental propagation of label changes. Let us consider a justification $(\Phi \rightarrow \varphi)$:

- Computation of a full label for the consequent of the justification is achieved by the following function call:

$$\text{mxfrms-propagate}(\varphi, \Phi, \varnothing)$$

For example, mxfrms-add-justification! invokes mxfrms-propagate like this.

- If incremental label propagation is asked for, e.g. because the label of some antecedent node ϕ_i of a justification has just been updated with some incremental label Δ_{F+}, the antecedent node causing the update is removed from the antecedent list (for the procedure call, only), and the resulting procedure call looks then like this:

$$\text{mxfrms-propagate}(\varphi, (\Phi \smallsetminus \{\phi_i\}), \Delta_{F+})$$

During label propagation, most calls to mxfrms-propsgate are of this type.

Most of the label propagation work is actually done by mxfrms-update-prop-label, which updates the label of proposition nodes. In the following, we assume that the facet represented by the facet module executing the procedure on hand is z.

PROCEDURE 5.5.6 (MXFRMS-UPDATE-PROP-LABEL)

```
 1  procedure mxfrms-update-prop-label(φ, Δ_F+) ≡
 2          Δ_F' ← Δ_F+ ∖ Flab(φ)
 3          if [ Δ_F' ≠ ∅ ]
 4              then Flab(φ) ← Flab(φ) ∪ Δ_F'
 5                  foreach [ f ∈ Δ_F' ] do
 6                      Blab(f) ← Blab(f) ∪ {φ}
 7                  od
 8                  if [ prop(φ) = ⊥ ]
 9                      then foreach [ f ∈ Δ_F' ] do
10                          Iflag(f) ← T od
11                  fi
12                  if [ Qset(n_φ) ≠ ∅ ]
13                      then foreach [ x ∈ Qset(φ) ] do
14                          Δ_F+" ← ∅
15                          foreach [ f ∈ Δ_F+' ] do
16                              if [ x ∈ g ]
17                                  then Δ_F+" ← {f}
18                              fi
19                          od
20                          mxfrms-send(x, update-belief, x:φ, Flab, Δ_F+")
21                      od
22                  fi
23                  foreach [ (Φ→φ) ∈ Γ_J where φ ∈ Φ ] do
24                      Φ' ← Φ ∖ {φ}
25                      mxfrms-propagate(φ, Φ', Δ_F+')
26                  od
27          fi
28  end
```

The mxfrms-update-prop-label procedure first checks whether an update of the node's label is necessary at all. If all focus structures referenced in the incremental label are already in the node's Flab label, then it immediately exits.[18] Otherwise, the label difference computed in the first step is added to the Flab label of the node. Then, the proposition node is added to the Blab labels of all focus nodes just added to the proposition node label. The next step checks whether the proposition node on hand is the falsum. If this is the case, all focus structures represented by focus nodes which have been added to the proposition node label become inconsistent and the appropriate flag is set on each focus node. After that, communication with other facet modules is dealt with. If the proposition node has never been communicated to another facet, nothing has to be done. Otherwise, for each facet x in the Qset attribute, the subset of the incremental label relevant to x is computed by checking whether x occurs in the focus structure's group, and the resulting subset Δ_{F+}'' is communicated to x using the appropriate facet communication message (see Section 5.5.8). Finally, mxfrms-update-prop-label invokes the mxfrms-propagate procedure for every justification which references the proposition node in its antecedents.

Communicated nodes permit a slightly simplified update procedure, because base literal references can neither be justified localy (i.e. they cannot occur as consequent in facet clauses) nor be used as assumptions, nor passed on to other facets. Thus, communicated node have a simplified structure. The procedure used to udate their Flab labels is as follows:

PROCEDURE 5.5.7 (MXFRMS-UPDATE-COMM-LABEL)

```
 1  procedure mxfrms-update-comm-label(φ, Δ_F+) ≡
 2        Δ_F' ← Δ_F+ \ Flab(φ)
 3        if [ Δ_F' ≠ ∅ ]
 4        then Flab(φ) ← Flab(φ) ∪ Δ_F'
 5             foreach [ f ∈ Δ_F' ] do
 6                Blab(f) ← Blab(f) ∪ {φ}
 7             od
 8             if [ prop(φ) = ⊥ ]
 9             then foreach [ f ∈ Δ_F' ] do
10                     lflag(f) ← T
11                  od
12             fi
13             foreach [ (Φ→φ) ∈ Γ_J where φ ∈ Φ ] do
14                Φ' ← Φ \ {φ}
```

---

[18]Such a situation occurs for instance, if a new justification is added which produces just an alternative way of deriving a datum in an existing context, in which the datum was already derivable.

15   mxfrms-propagate$(\varphi, \Phi', \Delta_{F+}')$

16   <u>od</u>

17   <u>fi</u>

18 <u>end</u>

Except for the part handling the propagation of label updates to other facet modules, the mxfrms-update-comm-label procedure is equivalent to procedure mxrms-update-prop-label. Note, however, the purpose of line 2 in this procedure: Because it is possible that, for an arbitrary focus structure f in the incremental label argument Δ_{F+}, i) the owner of f removes the focus structure while an incremental label update process involving f is still in progress, and ii) the message initiating the removal of f may have already been processed at some facet y when a message for updating some communicated node with an incremental label Δ_{F+} with $f \in \Delta_{F+}$ arrives, mxfrms-update-comm-label throws out all focus structures in Δ_{F+} that do not exist any more. This is achieved by intersecting it with the set of all currently known focus structures.

5.5.7   Updating MXFRMS States

In this section, we describe for each state change interface function in detail which label propagation function it invokes in order to ensure that all integrity constraints are met. Also, we include all necessary communication between MXFRMS facet modules in this description as well. Note, that communication between MXFRMS facet modules does not necessarily lead to label updates; in particular, some simplifying assumptions made earlier, e.g. that facets, propositions, and assumptions are supposed to be known to all MXFRMS facet modules, require such communication.[19] In the following, we continue to consider a particular agent consisting of some problem solver $\mathfrak{p}_a$ and MXFRMS facet module $\mathfrak{m}_b$ with ps-to-facet$(\mathfrak{p}_a) = z = z' = $ mxfrms-to-facet$(\mathfrak{m}_b)$. For each state change interface function, we first discuss its effect on the derivability relation, then the necessary updates in the MXFRMS facet modules are outlined.

- Making a new base literal $z.p$ relevant does not affect derivability much: the base literal cannot be locally derivable unless it is justified with facet clauses (that have the base literal as consequent) or becomes an

---

[19]The discussion also shows that these assumptions do in fact have an effect that is far less constraining than one would assume. Nevertheless, an actual implementation of MXFRMS could, of course, be designed such that these assumptions do not have to hold. However, as already outlined earlier, a finer-grained protocol for making facets, propositions, assumptions, and focus structures known to other agents would be necessary. Such an approach raises a number of issues which belong more to the areas of communication, distributed systems in general, agent-oriented programming, and mobile computing, all of which are not within the focus of this work.

assumption and is included into a focus structure of the local probelem solver. However, other facet modules could have focus structures with the following two properties: i) the facet z is in the focus structure's group, and ii) the propositional constant p of the base literal is used in the focus structure's environment. The group coherence property of MXFRMS focus structures requires the new base literal to be an assumption for such a focus, and hence, the new base literal must be derivable in it.

The problem solver makes a new base literal relevant with a call to add-proposition!, which creates a new proposition node in the DNU of m_b (with an empty label). Then the following two steps are performed for each other known facet x_i:

1. The new proposition is made known to x_i via a message

$$\text{mxfrms-send}(x_i, \text{update-facet}, \text{Propositions}, z.p).$$

   Upon receival of this message, x_i updates its facet node for z appropriately, but no further updates or label propagation happen.

2. If x_i has already declared the literal $x_i.p$ an assumption, then for each of the known focus structures structures f_i of x_i, the facet modules m_b checks whether $x_i.p$ is in the focus structures environment (by looking into the group and environment components of the data structure representing the focus structure). If so, then the focus structure f_i is inserted into the label of the node $z.p$ via a call to

$$\text{mxfrms-update-prop-label}(z.p, \{f_i\})$$

Note, that the second step cannot lead to any further label updates, because a newly added proposition node can neither occur in any justifications nor could it have been communicated to other agents; thus, label propagation stops already at $z.p$.

- Turning a base literal $z.p$ into an assumption does not change derivability at all; the only effect is that the base literal may be used to form environments for new or extended local focus structures.

When a MXFRMS facet module receives a problem solver request for executing add-assumption!, it sets the assumption flag of the local proposition node $z.p$ and sends a message

$$\text{mxfrms-send}(x_i, \text{update-facet}, \text{Assumptions}, z.p)$$

to each known facet x_i. Again, facet x_i updates its facet node for z, but no further updates or label propagation occur.

- Making a base literal reference $z{:}x.p$ relevant has an effect similar to adding a new base literal: the base literal reference will be locally derivable in facet z for all existing focus structures f_i, for which the two conditions i) $\Gamma_{s,f} \vdash_{\mathsf{FHPL}} x.p$ and ii) $z \in g$ hold.

For the implementation the above means that a call to add-reference! causes the initialization of a new communicated node to a non-empty label. The correct initial label of the communicated node will always be a subset, for which the above two conditions hold, of the label of the original proposition. However, this label is actually computed by the MXFRMS facet module representing facet x and is requested from x by sending a message

$$\mathsf{mxfrms\text{-}send}(x, \mathsf{request\text{-}belief}, x.p).$$

Because communication between MXFRMS facet modules is assumed to be asynchronous — z does not wait for the answer from x —, the communicated node is initialized with an empty label and proceeds to respond to requests from its problem solver or other facet modules.

When receiving this message, the facet x computes the appropriate subset Δ_F of the label of base literal $x.p$, i.e. it selects all focus structures in the label where $z \in g$ holds, and sends the answer back to z via a message

$$\mathsf{mxfrms\text{-}send}(z, \mathsf{update\text{-}belief}, x.p, \Delta_F).$$

When z receives this message from x, it simply calls

$$\mathsf{mxfrms\text{-}update\text{-}comm\text{-}label}(z{:}x.p, \Delta_F),$$

which will install the correct initial label in the communicated node. As the communicated node cannot yet occur in any local justifications — by definition of FHPL, it can neither occur as consequent in justifications nor as assumption in focus structures anyway — the necessary label modifications are limited to the new communicated node.

- In contrast to the state change functions just discussed, adding a justification $(\Phi \rightarrow \varphi)$ via a call to add-justification! can have dramatic effect of the derivability relation. In the worst though highly unlikely case, almost all relevant data (both base literals and base literal references could be affected. The direct effect is that derivability of the justification's consequent φ could change. The justification produces candidate focus structures for updating the consequent: any focus structure which allows to derive each antecedent of the justification also allows to derive the consequent. Derivability of φ actually changes, if there exists at least one candidate focus structure for which φ was not already derivable. For any focus structure for which φ was already derivable, the new justification produced just a new means for deriving φ, i.e. it produced one or more new proofs. If this is the case for all candidate focus structures, then derivability is not affected any further. Otherwise, if φ becomes derivable in additional focus structures, then the derivability of all consequences of and references to φ may also change, i.e. the change must be propagated across all facet clauses where φ is antecedent and all contract clauses where φ is source object.

In the implementation, almost all of the work described above is performed by the label propagation procedures described previously. After creating and properly initializing a new justification node, the procedure add-justification! simply performs the call

$$\text{mxfrms-propagate}(\varphi, \Phi, \varnothing).$$

This way of calling mxfrms-propagate invokes the incremental label propagation mechanism such that a full label is produced for the consequent; actually, it computes a set of candidate focus structures and leaves it up to mxfrms-update-prop-label to do the rest of the work (see also Section 5.5.6): selecting the focus structures which are not already in the consequent node's label, communicating the label update to all base literal references of φ, and (recursively) invoking the incremental label propagation mechanism for all facet clauses where φ is antecedent.

- Defining a new focus structure $f = \langle g, e, m, o, w \rangle$ via a call to add-focus! introduces a single new context. The effect on the derivability relation of this new context can be described in three parts:

  1. All assumptions $z.p_i \in e$ in the focus structure's environment e are derivable by definition. Note, that all assumptions must actually exist, i.e. every base literal in e must have been declared as a relevant proposition and as assumption by m.

  2. For all facets $x_i \in (g \setminus \{m\})$, all literals $x_i.p_i$ are derivable, if they exist, i.e. if they have already been declared relevant by facet x_i. Although group coherence requires the derivability of all these literals, it is not necessary to enforce their creation if their occurrence as an assumption in a focus structure is the only reason: As the problem solver associated with facet x_i does not consider it relevant, it cannot use such a literal in a query. Also, there can neither exist any facet clause in x_i with a reference to such a literal, nor a base literal reference to it in any other facet. Thus, explicitly creating such a literal for a focus structure does not really contribute anything to the context, except for itself. Note, however, that care

must be taken to ensure integrity, if such a literal is made relevant later on; this problem is dealt with in the add-proposition! state change interface function.

3. Finally, the deductive closure must be computed with respect to the group g.

The implementation of the add-focus! interface function first creates a new focus node in facet z. Then, for reasons that become more obvious later on, the first and second item above are performed in reversed order: In the second step, the new focus structure is made known to all facets $x_i \in g$ by sending each x_i a message

$$\text{mxfrms-send}(x_i, \text{update-facet}, \text{Foci}, +f)$$

The reception of such a message by a facet x_i will lead to an update of x_i's facet node representing z and, as a side effect of this, the function call

$$\text{mxfrms-update-prop-label}(x_i.p_i, f)$$

is executed for every base literal $x_i.p_i$ which is relevant in x_i and for which $z.p_i \in e$ holds. Thus, the second step ensures that the second part of computing the context is achieved. The first part is taken care of in the third step of add-focus!. The function call

$$\text{mxfrms-update-prop-label}(z.p_i, f)$$

is performed for each $z.p_i \in e$. Computation of the deductive closure of the context is actually taken care of automatically by the incremental label propagation mechanism.

- Removing an existing focus structure $f = \langle g, e, m, o, w \rangle$ with remove-focus! deletes a single context. The system must ensure that the focus f is removed in all facets of the group g.

In the implementation, removing a focus structure is extremely simple and consists of two steps:

1. Instruct each group member $x_i \in (g \setminus \{m\})$ to remove the focus structure by sending a message

$$\text{mxfrms-send}(x_i, \text{update-facet}, \text{Foci}, -f)$$

to each $x_i \in g$.

2. Each group member — those in $g \setminus \{m\}$ upon receival of the above message, m directly — removes the focus structure from the labels of all in f locally derivable nodes. This local set of nodes is easily determined by looking up the set of local proposition and communicated nodes in the focus node representing f.

- Extending the group g of a focus structure $f = \langle g, e, m, o, w \rangle$ with a set g^+ of additional facets via extend-focus-group! can be seen as a stripped-down variant of add-focus!. The effects on derivability can be separated into direct and indirect effects. The direct effects are that the focus structure's set of assumptions, which are derivable by definition, is extended. The set of additional assumptions is determined by the extended set of group members g^+ and the environment e in a way similar to add-focus!. The indirect effects are that the deductive closure will have to be extended as a consequence of extending the focus structure's set of assumptions. First, the local consequences of the assumptions in the facets added to the focus structure's group have to be computed, and second, — as a consequence of the first — base literal references with source objects that have become derivable in the first step have to be updated.

The interface function extend-focus-group! can be initiated either by the modification token holder, or by an arbitrary owner of a shared focus structure. A problem we have to solve in the implementation of extend-focus-group! (and the other interface functions modifying focus structures) is how to ensure that multiple, independently invoked updates of shared focus structure are correctly dealt with and how we can ensure that multiple updates do not harmfully interfere with each other. The solution taken is to assign the reponsibility for focus structure updates always to the facet module representing the modification token holder. Thus, the extend-focus-group! interface function just sends the following message

$$\text{mxfrms-send}(m, \text{update-focus}, f, \text{Group}, g^+)$$

The message queue of the facet module representing the focus structure's modification token holder then serves as a natural serialization mechanism. When receiving such a message the facet m has to do the following two steps:

1. It must inform all facets $x_i \in g$ of the change, such that they can update their local information on the focus structure. This is done via the same kind of messages as shown above, i.e. the messages have the form

$$\text{mxfrms-send}(x_i, \text{update-focus}, f, \text{Group}, g^+)$$

2. It must instruct all facets $x_j \in g^+$ to add the focus structure $f' = \langle (g \cup g^+), e, m, o, w \rangle$. Sending a message of the form

$$\text{mxfrms-send}(x_j, \text{update-facet}, \text{Foci}, +f')$$

will achieve the appropriate changes in each of the facets added to the focus structure's group.

The second step automatically invokes the appropriate label updates in all facet added to the group, and the incremental label update mechanisms ensures that the effects are propagated through the local dependency networks and — if labels of base literals communicated to other facets of the extended group are updated — also to base literal references in other facets of the extended group.

- Extending the environment of a focus structure $f = \langle g, e, m, o, w \rangle$ by a set of extra assumptions e^+ via a call to extend-focus-environment! is somewhat similar to extending a focus structure's group. Again, the effects on derivability can be classified into direct and indirect effects. The direct effects are concerned with the additional assumptions that have to be made: all literals $x_i.p_j$ become derivable by definition of the focus structure, if $x_i \in g$ and $p_j \in e^+$. The indirect effect is that the deductive closure must be updated as well.

Like the interface function extend-focus-group!, extend-focus-environment! can be invoked either by the modification token holder or an arbitrary owner, if f is a shared focus. For the reasons outlined above, and analogous to extend-focus-group!, that the extend-focus-environment! interface function sends the following message

$$\mathsf{mxfrms\text{-}send}(m, \mathsf{update\text{-}focus}, f, \mathsf{Env}, e^+)$$

to the facet module representing the modification token holder. When receiving this message, the modification token holder m performs the following two steps:

1. It sends a message of the form

$$\mathsf{mxfrms\text{-}send}(x_i, \mathsf{update\text{-}focus}, f, \mathsf{Env}, e^+)$$

   to all facets $x_i \in (g \setminus m)$.

2. It executes the function call

$$\mathsf{mxfrms\text{-}update\text{-}prop\text{-}label}(m.p_i, \{f\})$$

   for each assumption $m.p_i$ with $p_i \in e^+$.

Every facet module x_i receiving a message of the kind specified in the first step performs the second step for each assumption $x_i.p_i$ with $p_i \in e^+$, if the respective base literal has aleady been declared relevant in x_i. The label propagation mechanism ensures that the deductive closure of the focus structure is appropriately updated.

- Hooking onto a shared focus structure $f = \langle g, e, m, o, w \rangle$ does not affect derivability at all, because derivability depends solely on the focus structure components g and e, which are not modified by this function. The only effect of this function is that a facet can adopt a sharable focus structure created by another facet module as one of its own relevant focus structures and use it in queries.[20] Thus, a facet can only hook itself onto a sharable focus.

  As add-focus-owner! can be called by any member $x_i \in g$ of the group of a shared focus structure, the problem of potentially interfering focus structure updates must be dealt with. The implementation used the same approach already applied in the previous two functions and assigns the sole responsibility to actually initiate updates to the facet module of the modification token holder. Thus, a call to add-focus-owner! results in a message

  $$\text{mxfrms-send}(m, \text{update-focus}, f, \text{Oset}, +x_i)$$

  being sent to the modification token holder m. When m receives this message, it performs the following two steps:

  1. It sends analogous copies of the above message to all members x_j of the group g.

  2. It updates the owners attribute its local focus node for f.

  Each facet module x_j receiving a message as sent by the modification token holder in the first step just updates the onwers attribute of its local focus node representing f.

- Unhooking from a shared focus structure is performed via a function call to remove-focus-owner!, which just reverses the effect of add-focus-owner!. Derivability is not affected for the same reasons as for add-focus-owner!.

  The implementation of remove-focus-owner! uses the same basic scheme as add-focus-owner!, except that the messages being sent have the format

  $$\text{mxfrms-send}(x_j, \text{update-focus}, f, \text{Oset}, -x_i),$$

  and that the facet supplied as argument is not added, but removed from the owners atribute of the focus nodes representing focus structure f.

---

[20]Note, that owners and the modification token holder have slightly different rights regarding the modification of focus structures: only the modification token holder can delete a focus structure. However, for an arbitrary owner, unhooking from a shared focus can be considered the operation equivalent to deleting a relevant focus structure for the modification token holder.

- Setting the current focus of a facet via set-current-focus! does affect derivability at all, because the new current focus must have been delared relevant before calling this function. Thus, set-current-focus! does not necessitate any label updates.

  In the implementation, the only effect of set-current-focus! is that the current focus pointer maintained by the CMU of the MXFRMS facet module is changed such that it oints to the focus node representng the new current focus.

The above state change interface function allow the problem solvers in the multiagent system to modify the sets of relevant data and logical dependencies as well as manipulate the set of relevant focus structures. The only logical state component that remains stable for all calls of the above functions (except for the logical language used in the multiagent system, of course) is the set of facets. If a new agent is added to the system, this set needs to be updated. Adding a new facet x with the system-level interface function new-facet! causes the following updates in the MXFRMS:

1. A new MXFRMS facet module m_b for x is created. This is implementation specific.

2. A facet node for x is created.

3. The propositions $x.\top$ and $x.\bot$ are made relevant.

4. The propositions $x.\top$ is turned into an assumption

5. The focus structure $\langle\{x\}, \{x.\top\}, x, \{x\}, F\rangle$ is added.

6. The above focus structure is made the current focus of the facet.

7. Facet nodes for all facets are generated.

8. A message is generated for all facets to inform them of the new facet.

Upon reception of the last kind of message, each facet y of the previously existing facets performs the following steps:

1. Create a facet node for the new facet.

2. Make the base literal references $y{:}x.\top$ and $y{:}x.\bot$ relevant.

This describes, of course, only the part of new-facet! relevant to the logical state and the facet-level interfaces of MXFRMS.

5.5.8 MXFRMS Facet Communication Interface

Throughout this chapter, we sporadically referred to the communication interface of a MXFRMS facet and already introduced a number of messages as examples for the use of this interface. In this section, we give a brief overview on the communication interface, summarize the set of messages exchanged between MXFRMS facet modules, and, if not already discussed in the previous section, outline how messages relate to functions executed by the MXFRMS facet module receiving the messages.

The function used above to specify that a message is being sent to a facet module was mxfrms-send. Although we do not want to discuss the — typically implementation-specific — communication mechanism in detail, it is important to point out the following underlying assumption: If a facet module z executes a call to mxfrms-send, e.g.

$$\text{mxfrms-send}(x, MsgType, Arg_1, \ldots, Arg_n),$$

then a message of the form

$$\langle z, x, MsgType, Arg_1, \ldots, Arg_n \rangle$$

is transmitted to facet module x and enqueued into its inbox.[21] Problem solver requests can be handled in a similar way. The process associated with facet module x (see Section 5.5.4) dequeues messages from the inbox and invokes message dispatching, which is based on the message content. After some a priori error checking, e.g. to prevent the processing of messages which have erroneously been delivered to the wrong facet module, the message dispatcher interprets the $MsgType$ and, if necessary, further arguments of the message and invokes the apropriate function for processing the request. For the problem solver interfaces, message dispatching is rather trivial, because of the way communication between a problem solver and its associated MXFRMS facet module is designed:

1. The problem solver executes a function call as specified in the interface definitions.

2. In the problem solver process, the function call is encoded into a message which is sent to the facet module.

3. The message is decoded into the equivalent function call on the facet module side.

---

[21] For brevity and clarity, we simply used the facet identifiers for specifying sender and receiver of a message throughout the chapter on MXFRMS implementation. A communication mechanism will usually require addresses it can send message to. For instance, problem solver and MXFRMS facet module names like p_a or m_b could serve this role. If this is the case, the implementation can automatically map facet identifiers to such addresses; however, this is implementation-specific, of course.

4. The function call is executed.

5. If the function call returns a result, the result is sent back to the problem solver.[22]

Thus, if we i) assume a unique, bijective encoding of problem solver function calls into messages and ii) ensure the availability of the same set of functions both on the problem solver side and the MXFRMS facet module side, then disptaching of problem solver messages is indeed trivial.

The only issue that remains to be solved is communication between MXFRMS facet modules. Messages exchanged between facet modules can be classified into the following three categories:

- Messages for updating information related to facets.

- Messages for requesting and updating communicated beliefs.

- Messages for updating information related to focus structures.

In the remainder of this section, we discuss the messages in these three categories and ouline the effect on label propagation within the receiver of the message.

Updating information related to facets   Each facet module z has a facet node for each known facet x where it maintains certain information about that facet. The information that needs to be updated encompasses the propositions, assumptions, and (a subset of) focus structures relevant to x. While in the current version of MXFRMS the sets of propositions and assumptions can only monotonically grow, focus structures can be added *and* deleted. Together, this requires the following four kinds of messages related to updating facet information:

$$\langle z, x, \text{update-facet}, \text{Propositions}, z.p \rangle$$
$$\langle z, x, \text{update-facet}, \text{Assumptions}, z.p \rangle$$
$$\langle z, x, \text{update-facet}, \text{Foci}, +f \rangle$$
$$\langle z, x, \text{update-facet}, \text{Foci}, -f \rangle$$

Note the positive or negative sign in front of the last argument in the latter two kinds of messages, which indicates whether a focus structure is to be added or removed.

---

[22] In order to allow the problem solver to easily associate results received from the facet module, the interface can be easily extended such that the problem solver, for each of its requests, supplies a unique token which the facet module sends back with the appropriate answer.

The first two functions have no side effect related to label propagation and just update the appropriate attributes in the facet node representing the sender. Messages related to focus structures are received only if $x \in g$, i.e. if the receiver is in the focus structure's group. This also means that label propagation must be initiated. If a request to add a focus structure $f = \langle g, e, m, o, w \rangle$ is received from z, then x creates a new focus node and executes the function call

$$\text{mxfrms-update-prop-label}(x.p, f)$$

for each p if $z.p \in e$ and $x.p$ is a relevant base literal. Handling a request from z to remove a focus structure is even easier: x simply removes the focus node representing f from the Flab labels of all DNU nodes referenced in the Blab label of f.

At least one additional message is necessary for assisting the system-level functionality of adding a new facet. This is not further discussed here, though.

Requesting and updating communicated beliefs An essential functionality in a multiagent reason maintenance system is the ability to build and maintain update contracts for communicated beliefs, i.e. to implement the role contract clauses play in FHPL. Naturally, two facet modules z, x must communicate in order to set up and maintain such a contract. The following two kinds of messages are used for that:

$$\langle z, x, \text{request-belief}, x.p \rangle$$
$$\langle x, z, \text{update-belief}, z{:}\phi, \text{Flab}, \Delta_{F+} \rangle$$

The first message is the one that sets up a contract. It does not itself lead to any label propagation. However, it leads to the exchange of an initial message of the second kind, whith the relevant subset of focus structures in the Flab label of $x.p$ as argument Δ_{F+}. This subset is installed in the Flab label of $z{:}x.p$ by executing a function call

$$\text{mxfrms-update-comm-label}(z{:}x.p, \Delta_{F+})$$

Any subsequent update of the Flab labe of $x.p$ leads to another message of the second kind, and an appropriate update of the Flab label of $z{:}x.p$ via the same mechanism.

Updating information related to focus structures The information related to a particular focus structure $f = \langle g, e, m, o, w \rangle$ is maintained — in a distributed fashion — in a set of focus nodes: one focus node in each facet $x \in g$. Whenever focus structures are modified, the changes must be communicated to all members of the group. The operations available to modify focus structures are to monotonically extend the group g or the environment e and to add or remove owners to shared focus structures. The following four types of messages are used to exchange information related to these operations between facet modules:

$$\langle z, x, \text{update-focus}, f, \text{Group}, g^+ \rangle$$
$$\langle z, x, \text{update-focus}, f, \text{Env}, e^+ \rangle$$
$$\langle z, x, \text{update-focus}, f, \text{Oset}, +y \rangle$$
$$\langle z, x, \text{update-focus}, f, \text{Oset}, -y \rangle$$

As outlined earlier, the first, third and fourth kind of message do not affect derivability. Thus, no label propagation must be initiated, and only attributes of the focus node are updated. The second kind of message does change derivability, and label propagation must be invoked. Extending a focus structure's environment is actually quite similar to adding a new focus, except that the focus node already exists and need not be created. Invocation of label propagation is achieved by executing the function call

$$\text{mxfrms-update-prop-label}(x.p, f)$$

for each p if $z.p \in e$ and $x.p$ is a relevant base literal.

5.5.9   Correctness of Label Propagation

In the last few sections, we described i) the incremental label propagation mechanism, ii) whether and how problem solver interface functions invoke label propagation, iii) whether and how problem solver interface function invoke communication between MXFRMS facet modules, and iv) whether and how facet module communication invokes label propagation. Our claim is that, taken together, these measures ensure the integrity constraints specified in Section 5.5.3, i.e. that the incremental label propagation mechanism is correct. In this section, we will substantiate this claim a bit more precisely by showing

- correctness of an incremental mxfrms-propagate step,
- correctness of mxfrms-propagate after adding justifications,
- correctness of an mxfrms-update-prop-label step,
- correctness of an mxfrms-update-comm-label step, and
- termination of label propagation.

Furthermore, we will discuss the following issues related to the fact that MXFRMS is a distributed system:

- asynchronous communication and integrity constraints,

- interaction and interference of concurrent updates, and

- the systems dynamics of distributed marker propagation mechanisms.

Complexity consideration are deferred to the next section.

Correctness of an incremental mxfrms-propagate **step**   We look at a particular facet z and assume that the Flab label of some node ϕ (a proposition node $x.p$ or a communicated node $y{:}x.p$) has just been extended by a set of focus structures, i.e. an incremental label Δ_{F+}. The incremental label is now propagated across a justification $(\Phi \rightarrow \varphi)$ with $\phi \in \Phi$ via the call

$$\text{mxfrms-propagate}(\varphi, (\Phi \smallsetminus \{\phi\}), \Delta_{F+}).$$

The task of mxfrms-propagate is to compute an incremental label $\Delta_{F+}{}'$ for φ,which is contributed by the justification $(\Phi \rightarrow \varphi)$ and contains all additional focus structures that now allow to derive φ by using the justification. Obviously, the incremental label $\Delta_{F+}{}'$ for φ must be a subset of the incremental label Δ_{F+} which just arrived at ϕ. $\Delta_{F+}{}'$ contains only focus structures f from Δ_{F+}, which also allow to derive all remaining antecedents of the justification, i.e. if f is an element of $\bigcap_{\phi_i \in (\Phi \smallsetminus \{\phi\})} \text{Flab}(\phi_i)$. Thus, the incremental label is

$$\Delta_{F+}{}' = \Delta_{F+} \cap \bigcap_{\phi_i \in (\Phi \smallsetminus \{\phi\})} \text{Flab}(\phi_i).$$

This is exactly what is computed by line 4 of procedure mxfrms-propagate, if it is invoked with arguments as described above. If this incremental label (produced by justification $(\Phi \rightarrow \varphi)$) is empty (none of the focus structures added to the label of the recently updated antecedent node occurs in all other antecedent node labels as well), then no new derivations involving this justification are possible, and propagation stops. Otherwise, the incremental label must be merged into the consequent node's Flab label, which is achieved by calling mxfrms-update-prop-label in line 7 of procedure mxfrms-propagate.

Correctness of mxfrms-propagate **after adding justifications**   The previous paragraph showed that mxfrms-propagate works correctly for existing justifications, if an incremental label produced by updating one of the justification's antecedents needs to be propagated across a justification. This situation is, however, different from adding a new justification $(\Phi \rightarrow \varphi)$, where all members of the set of antecedents Φ already have a well-formed Flab label. The candidate label for the consequent computed by mxfrms-propagate must be the intersection of the labels of all antecedents, because only focus structures that allow to derive all antecedents also allow to derive the consequent via the added justification. When discussing the problem solver interface function add-justification! above, we claimed that calling

$$\text{mxfrms-propagate}(\varphi, \Phi, \varnothing)$$

correctly produces the label increment for updating φ. In the definition of mxfrms-propagate, we used the same technique as in the XFRMS version: The second argument Φ now contains *all* antecedents and the incremental label argument Δ_{F+} is empty, while in the incremental mxfrms-propagate step discussed above the second argument contains all antecedents *except* the one just updated with the incremental label supplied as third argument. mxfrms-propagate computes in both cases the intersection of the labels of all nodes in the second argument. In the case of adding a justification, this does the job, i.e. a full candidate label for the conseuqent is computed. We only have to prevent mxfrms-propagate to intersect the result with the empty set supplied as third argument. The conditional in lines 2-5 of mxfrms-propagate take care of the two cases.

Correctness of an mxfrms-update-prop-label step   The update procedure mxfrms-update-prop-label must merge (incremental) labels, produced either by propagating label updates across justifications (mxfrms-propagate) or directly by state update procedures (e.g. extend-focus-environment!, add-focus!) into the Flab labels of proposition nodes representing base literals $\phi = x.p$. Only those focus structures not already contained in an focus label Flab(ϕ) must actually be included and propagated further through the dependency net. The appropriate subset Δ_{F+}' of the label increment Δ_{F+} is obtained by computing

$$\Delta_{F+}' = \Delta_{F+} \setminus \text{Flab}(\phi),$$

which is what mxfrms-update-prop-label computes in line 2. If the resulting set Δ_{F+}' is empty, all focus structures in the incremental label were already present and nothing further needs to be done (conditional in line 3). Otherwise, the new, reduced label increment Δ_{F+}' is merged into the proposition node's focus label (line 4) and the proposition node is added to the belief label Blab of all focus nodes referred in Δ_{F+}' (lines 5 to 7). If the currently updated node represents the local facet's *falsum*, all focus structures in the incremental label allow to derive a contradiction in the local facet and therefore become inconsistent (lines 8 to 11). Adding a focus structure to a proposition node's focus label Flab represents that the node has become derivable in the context determined by that focus strcuture. This has the following consequences:

- Any contract clause which refers to the updated proposition node as its source object (the base literal $\phi = x.p$) may now allow to derive the destination object (the base literal reference $y{:}x.p$). This is indeed the case for every base literal reference $y{:}x.p$ and every focus structure $f = \langle g, e, m, o, w \rangle$ for which $y \in g$ holds.

- Any justification $(\Phi \rightarrow \varphi)$ which refers the updated proposition node in its antecedents may now allow to derive further base literals (proposition nodes) of the local facet in the context based on the focus structure added to the label.

The first issue is dealt with by mxfrms-update-prop-label in lines 12 to 22 as follows: If there exist no base literal references to the base literal $x.p$, nothing has to be done (conditional in line 12). Otherwise, for every facet y that the base literal has been communicated to (for loop in line 13) we determine a subset $\Delta_{F+}{}''$ of focus structures of the incremental label $\Delta_{F+}{}'$ (lines 14 to 19). This subset contains only the focus structures relevant to y which is determined by checking whether $y \in g$ holds. Thereby, we have determined the incremental label $\Delta_{F+}{}''$ for the base literal reference and communicate it to the subscriber y (line 20).

The second issue is dealt with by propagating the label increment $\Delta_{F+}{}'$ (containing the focus structure with which the label has actually been extended by mxfrms-update-prop-label) across all justifications which refer the updated node in its antecedents, with the set of antecedents except the updated node as second argument and the incremental label as third argument. This ensures that the deductive closure of all focus structures in the incremental label will be updated appropriately.

Correctness of an mxfrms-update-comm-label **step**   The update procedure mxfrms-update-comm-label is just a simplified variant of mxfrms-update-prop-label: Because base literal references cannot be communicated to other facets (at least not in the current version of MXFRMS), the part dealing with propagating label updates across contract clauses is not needed. The remainder is equivalent to mxfrms-update-prop-label and need not repeated explicitly.

Termination of label propagation   So far, we only considered isolated propagation steps involving mxfrms-propagate, mxfrms-update-prop-label and mxfrms-update-comm-label. However, these steps are tightly linked and mutually call each other. We must ensure, that the incremental label propagation process always finishes after a finite number of steps; in particular, if cycles are present in the dependency net of a local facet, or — even worse — cycles exist in the combined dependency structure of several facets. Figure 5.8 illustrates an example of the update work a single problem solver state change request can cause and how it is distributed across space (facets) and time. The problem solver $\mathfrak{p}_a$ of some agent represented by facet z calls a state change interface function of its associated MXFRMS facet module m_a. When executing the interface function, this facet module computes all local effects and updates its local data structures. While doing so, the update process can generate messages that are sent to other MXFRMS facet modules, e.g. to some facet x. Such an (asynchronously sent) message may arrive at x, be processed by x and lead to further messages, e.g. back to z *before* the initial update at z is finished. However, as already outlined before, a facet module never works on two update requests at the same time. Thus, the message coming back from x is enqueued until the initial (local) update work is completed. Then, the secondary effects of an update are processed, which may again lead to messages being sent to other facet modules. Under certain circumstances, this process can happen many times. However, termination is guaranteed because of the following facts:

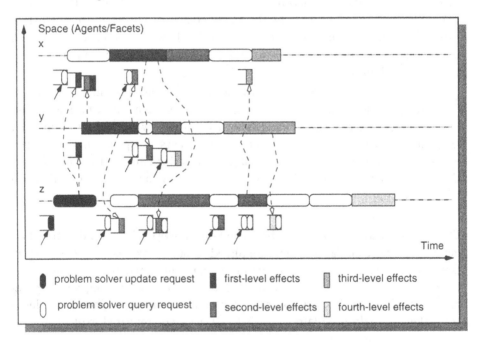

Figure 5.8: Example of the distribution of label update work across space and time.

The effects of a single problem solver update are illustrated in the figure. The content of the message queues of the three facets is shown at various points of time. Short solid lines represent the arrival of problem solver requests at the facet modules. Dashed lines represent communication between facet modules.

1. The overall size of focus labels is bounded by the number of relevant focus structures in the MXFRMS.

2. The size of an individual focus label is monotonically ascending, because

focus structures are not removed from focus labels during the incremental label propagation mechanism. The only exception is the complete removal of a focus structure, which is not handled by the label propagation mechanism.

3. The incremental label propagation mechanism itself does not create any new focus structures.

4. The size of the incremental label is bounded by the number of relevant focus structures in the MXFRMS.

5. Once label propagation is invoked, the size of the incremental label is monotonically descending.

6. Label propagation stops whenever the label increment becomes empty.

Further details about termination are provided by the next few paragraphs and the discussion of complexity considerations in the next section.

Interaction and interference of concurrent updates Because we assume that both problem solvers and MXFRMS facet modules work concurrently and use asynchronous communication, it is possible that two or more label updates are initiated at roughly the same time at different places (facet modules) in the system. The questions arising here are

1. how concurrent updates do interact, and

2. whether any kind of interference between such updates is possible.

Unique ownership of access rights to data structures, the MXFRMS facet process structure (see Section 5.5.4), and the precautions we have taken in the mxfrms-update-comm-label procedure together guarantee that no harmful interference between concurrent updates can occur. This conclusion is justified by the following line of reasoning:

- From a gobal view, concurrent updates overlap (see also Figure 5.9). However, from a local, facet-oriented view updates consist of a bunch of small, atomic transactions which do not overlap.

- Each facet performs a single atomic transaction at any one point of time. Execution of a transaction encompasses the computation of all local updates and the creation and transmission of all necessary messages to other agents. Thus, there is no direct interaction between concurrent updates or atomic transactions, and interference is possible only, if concurrent updates access the same data.

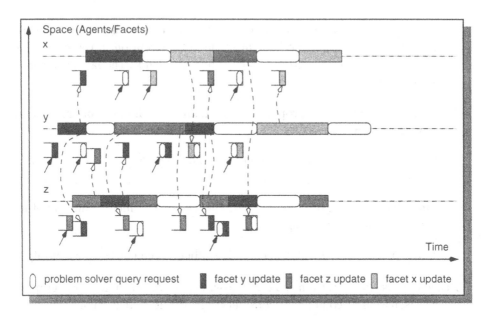

Figure 5.9: Concurrent execution and temporal overlap of multiple update requests.

- Data, in particular the various kinds of nodes, are updated by the facet that maintains the data. As all requests arriving at some facet z are locally serialized and processed one at a time, there cannot occur any interference in the access of data. Moreover, for each datum there is also a single facet who has the capability to *initiate* a modification of that datum. For example, only facet z can cause updates to facet nodes representing z. Thus, all facet node update requests arriving at some facet x which pertain to facet z must have been initiated by facet z. The same holds for focus nodes: the modification token holder is the one ultimately responsible for initiating any changes to a focus structure, in particular, its Blab belief label and the set of owners.

- Because we assumed that the communication mechanism preserves message order, we can also exclude any problems that could arise from permutating messages.

- Thus, the only possibility remaining open are the Flab focus labels of proposition nodes and communicated nodes. However, the kind of labels we use and the way the label propagation mechanism is structured also guarantee that no harmful interference occurs. Basically, labels montonically grow. If the incremental labels Δ_{F+} of two label update requests both contain some particular focus structure f, it does not really mattter, which one is processed first: The focus structure is added only once, and this change is propagated only once. The second try to add f will simply have no effect.

The only case where harmful interference may occur is the following case: We assume some focus $f = \langle g, e, m, o, w \rangle$ with $g = \{x, y, z\}$ and $m = z$. Furthermore, y has a communicated node from x with currently empty Flab label. z decides to delete its focus f and informs x and y about that. y receives the message and updates its information about z accordingly. However, just before x receives the message about f, it has added a justification, which results in f being in the incremental label that x sends to y. Facet y receives a message which tells it to update its communicated node from x with an incremental label that contains a non-existing focus! However, the problem can easily be dealt with by the label update procedure mxfrms/update-comm-label, which simply filters out all non-existing focus structures from any incremental labels it receives.

Asynchronous communication and integrity constraints   Another question raised by the fact that MXFRMS facet modules work concurrently is related to the integrity constraints that we required to hold. When do our integrity constraints hold? The easy answer is that they hold if all problem solver requests including facet communication messages have been processed and no further messages are pending in the message queues of any MXFRMS facet module. However, a look at Figure 5.9 reminds us that this condition can be quite difficult to determine. An easy case is if an update request (e.g. in facet z) does not lead to communication with other facet modules. Then the integrity constraints will hold already after the initial local update transaction has been performed. This is, e.g. the case for requests that manipulate private and completely local focus structures $f = \langle g, e, m, o, w \rangle$ with $g = \{z\}$. A few other update requests are not very problematic either, because their effects on other facet modules can be predicted quite well. For example, adding a proposition or an assumption in z results in messages to other facets allowing them to update their information on z. At some arbitrary facet x, such messages can neither lead to label updates nor to facet communication with other facet modules. Function add-proposition! can, however, lead to local label updates and consequently to label update messages being sent to other facet modules. Of course, this propagation will also occur for interface procedures like add-justification!, add-focus!, extend-focus-environment!, and so on. The problem is that z has no means to determine, whether its messages to other facets will in turn result in further update messages being sent to itself. Thus, z cannot tell when an incremental label propagation process that it invoked has stopped.

There are two ways to deal with this situation:

- We can consider the behavior we described above as a feature of situatedness and simply live with it: *all* problem solver requests will always be answered relative to the information the associated facet module has received up to the point in time the query was posed. A single problem solver update of the logical state could invalidate all answers to prior queries.[23] In a multiagent scenario, situatedness is even stronger: while in a single agent scenario, the problem solver knows when it changes its database, and thus, when prior queries may have been invalidated, this is virtually impossible to know in a multiagent scenario. However, it is a phenomenon that is quite natural, at least in many daily areas. Consider e.g. markets, where a supplier sends out offers or price lists, but does not know whether and when any response will come, or if any responses are still being prepared.

- We can look into mechanisms for deciding distributed termination. Such mechanisms do exist and could be integrated into MXFRMS. However, the question is what we win by doing this: If a problem solver always want to wait until all the global effects of updating its logical state have been computed, then this policy will usually turn into a serious performance bottleneck; besides that, the use of some other technology, like a central database, might be more advisable in such a case. If the problem solver does not want to wait, then it is not really important to know whether all global effects have been computed or not.

In our opinion, the former option is more promising for the kind of domains and applications we have in mind.

The systems dynamics of distributed marker propagation mechanisms   The previous chapter seems to seriously question the role of the integrity constraints defined earlier on. If a problem solver cannot determine when these constraints hold, are they worth anything? The answer is, of course, yes. In order to understand the role of the integrity constraints, we lend some terminology from dynamical systems theory in order to explain the dynamic behavior of MXFRMS. Naturally, we can give only an informal overview of how the systems dynamics of MXFRMS look like and a more detailed account must be deferred to future work.

A dynamical system is a system whose future state depends on its current state and inputs in a principled way. Dynamical systems theory is a body of mathematics that provides a language for characterizing a system's behavior over time and the way this behavior depends on parameters. For a brief overview, see [Beer, 1995] In the following, we briefly outline how dynamical

---

[23]The update/query behavior of databases is similar: in principle, a single database update could make the result of any previous query obselete.

system theory could be applied to formally prove various computational issues of MXFRMS, like termination, stability, and deterministic behavior:

The state space of a particular MXFRMS implementation consists of the Cartesian product of domains of all system variables. The constraints defined for permissable logical states and the integrity constraints together define equilibrium points in this state space. A particular logical state specified by two problem solvers has exactly one equivalent equilibrium point in the MXFRMS state space. If the actual state of the MXFRMS at some point of time is equal to the equilibrium point associated with the current logical state, then nothing happens, and the MXFRMS remains in this state (and the integrity constraints are met, of course). If the MXFRMS is not at the equilibrium point associated with the logical state, then the incremental label update mechanism will move the system towards this equilibrium point. Problem solver requests to update the MXFRMS logical state can be viewed as pertubators, which move the system out of the equilibrium point in the direction of the equilibrium point associated with the new logical state. The incremental label mechanism then ensures that the system will eventually get to this equilibrium point.

An important point to verify using dynamical systems theory would be to ensure that the asymptotic behavior of MXFRMS converges to equilibrium *points* only, and that no other, higher-dimensional limit sets exist. If one could show that the state space has e.g. a limit cycle, this means that MXFRMS can exhibit periodic or oscillatory behavior, and that some form of endless loop would be possible.

5.6   MXFRMS Complexity Considerations

MXFRMS is claimed to provide its reason maintenance services efficiently. In this final section before the summary of MXFRMS, we want to make our claims more precise by looking into the space and runtime complexity of MXFRMS and provide some informal arguments for these claims. A detailed formal investigation requires much more space and effort than we can spend here. Furthermore, we refer to the complexity considerations made for the XFRMS, which are obviously directly relevant for the MXFRMS as well.

In the following, let $\|S\|$ denote the cardinality of a set S. For brevity, we introduce the following notational conventions: Let c_x, c_p, c_q, c_j, and c_f denote the number of all relevant facets, base literals (proposition nodes), base literal references (communicated nodes), facet clauses (justification nodes), and focus structures, respectively. Furthermore, we denote with m_a the maximum number of antecedents any particular facet clause may have, and with m_j the maximum number of facet clauses for any particular base literal:

$$c_x \quad =_{\text{def}} \quad \|\Gamma_P\|$$

$$c_p \quad =_{\text{def}} \quad \|\Gamma_P\|$$

$$c_q \quad =_{\text{def}} \quad \|\Gamma_Q\|$$

$$c_j \quad =_{\text{def}} \quad \|\Gamma_J\|$$

$$c_f \quad =_{\text{def}} \quad \|\Pi_F\|$$

$$m_a \quad =_{\text{def}} \quad \max_{(\Phi \to \varphi) \in \Gamma_J} \|\text{ANset}((\Phi \to \varphi))\|$$

$$m_j \quad =_{\text{def}} \quad \max_{\phi \in \Gamma_P} \|\{(\Phi \to \varphi) \mid (\Phi \to \varphi) \in \Gamma_J \text{ and } \varphi = \phi\}\|$$

5.6.1   Space Complexity

At any point of time, MXFRMS represents a particular logical state. The space required by MXFRMS for this consists of the space required for the internal data structures used by the MXFRMS to represent the logical state plus the space required for the mappings between problem solver data and internal data structures. For each element of the logical state components Υ_X, Γ_P, Γ_Q, Γ_J, and Π_F the MXFRMS allocates exactly one internal node data structure. Thus, the number of nodes grows linearly with the number of relevant data. Furthermore, the size of all node attributes (which usually contain sets of pointers to other nodes), is bounded by the number of relevant data they can refer. For instance, the Flab label of proposition nodes and communicated nodes cannot grow any larger than the overall number of relevant focus structures. Thus, the logical state can be efficiently represented by MXFRMS.

5.6.2   Runtime Complexity

Like in the XFRMS, all query interface functions of the MXFRMS are very efficient: Aside of the time necessary to perform the mapping to and from problem solver data to internal data structures (see Section 3.5.2), only simple membership tests, flag tests, or simple value assignments are performed.

Due to the incremental label propagation mechanism and the type of labels used, the state update functions also have very reasonable performance characteristics.

If label propagation is not invoked, only simple updates of local data structures, like adding an entry to a hash table and creating and initializing a new node, and the communication of messages are performed. These operations are not critical, especially because they cannot lead to secondary effects, like the update of labels does.

Estimating the runtime requirements for incremental label propagation is more difficult. However, just like in XFRMS we take a global view and look at how many invocations of a particular label propagation procedure could have happened in the history of a certain logical state. The line of reasoning is then almost equivalent to the XFRMS case: We look at the Flab label of a particular proposition node and ask how many times mxfrms-update-prop-label could have been called. As the label is initially empty, its size is bounded by c_f, and label propagation in MXFRMS is monotonic, — everything just like in the XFRMS—, it follows that c_p, c_f, and m_j together impose an upper bound of $O(c_p \times c_f \times (_s f \times m_j)$ on the number of possible calls to mxfrms-update-prop-label. It is equally easy to see that the number of calls to mxfrms-update-comm-label is bounded by $O(c_q \times c_f)$. Analogously, we can derive an upper bound for the number of calls to procedure mxfrms-propagate of at most $c_j \times c_f \times m_a$.

These boundaries limit the sum of all procedure calls to mxfrms-propagate, mxfrms-update-prop-label, and mxfrms-update-comm-label that can have occurred in the history of producing a particular logical state. Single state update operations usually have far smaller complexity.

Chapter 6

Conclusions

6.1 History and Review of Work Done

The work described in this book has its roots in the PEDE project. Its goal is to develop a general framework and specific methods and tools for computer-aided planning and scheduling in distributed environments. Within the PEDE scenario it is assumed multiple agents jointly plan and execute tasks in order to solve their goals. The use of multiagent technology was and still is considered most promising in our case, because it allows — in principle, at least — to combine sufficient autonomy (by making agents reasonably autonomous) with sufficient coordination and cooperation (by applying multiagent coordination techniques). However, it was very soon clear, that the multiagent technology available at that time did not provide adequate support for planning and scheduling applications. In particular, task analysis for typical planning and scheduling domains indicated the value of explicitly maintaining the dependencies hidden in plans and schedules, especially if fast response to unexpected changes or replanning/rescheduling are required, but the techniques available were not suited to build large planning applications upon them. Thus, we started to investigate this problem and to gradually develop the necessary technology to solve the problem in applications.

Within AI, the logical starting point to look for potential candidate technology was the area of truth or reason maintenance. As described in Section 4.4, none of the available distributed RMSs provided the required characteristics. In a first effort, we tried to re-implement the DATMS and to fix some of its problems. The resulting system was named DARMS and is described in [Fuhge, 1993], [Beckstein et al., 1993], [Beckstein et al., 1994], and [Beckstein, 1994]. A detailed analysis and formalization of DARMS exhibited several problems (some of which were described in Section 4.4.6). The attempt to solve these problems led to the general approach, taken also in this text, of starting out by defining a sufficiently small and restricted logic, then

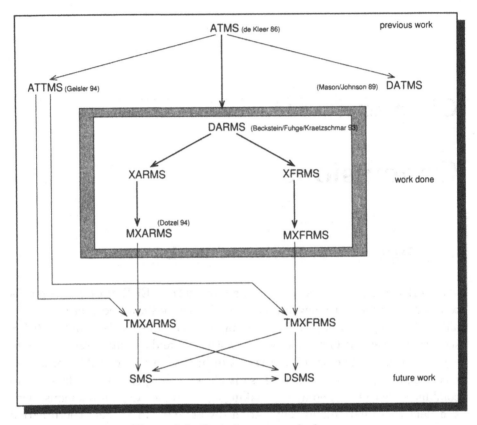

Figure 6.1: Overview on work done.

specifiying the desired functionality, and finally implementing it.[1] The actual development work performed after the initial DARMS can be structured into two families of RMSs:

- ARMS family

- FRMS family

A graphical overview on the relationships between the various topics covered in this book and its relationships to other related work is given in Figure 6.1.

---

[1]This approach is very similar to the VPP method described in [Stoyan, 1988] and [Stoyan, 1991].

6.2 Major Results and Contributions

The main results and contributions of this work — classified into the four categories problem analysis, problem formalization, RMS architectures, and RMS systems — can be summarized as follows:

Problem Analysis

- By giving two elaborate examples, we showed that maintenance of dependencies is a fundamental problem for the PEDE domain, and multiagent systems in general. We identified the distributed consequence determination problem, the distributed context determination, and the distributed belief revision problems, as the *core problems* to be solved in order to provide computational support for maintaining plans and schedules. Also, we identified the *congruence problem* that arises in multiagent reason maintenance systems.

- We summarized the strengths and weaknesses of existing single agent and multiagent RMS technology. The overall conclusion of this anaylsis was that previously developed systems are not well-suited for the PEDE domain. For single context systems, the main reason for this was that the capability to maintain a single context only is not suffcient for the PEDE domain. For multiple context systems we discovered that the ability to maintain multiple contexts must be bought at prohibitive costs.

Problem Formalization

- For the single agent case, we introduced HPL, a very small propositional Horn logic sufficient to formalize single agent multiple context, assumption-based reason maintenance problems.
- For multiagent scenarios, we presented the concept of Facetted Horn Propositional Logics (FHPL), which allow to easily formalize multiagent reason maintenance problems, especially from the PEDE domain. FHPL logics have syntax similar to modal propositional logics, but far simpler and more intuitive semantics.
- In FHPL, we presented formal definitions for several concepts of interest in multiagent systems, like group consequence, group derivability, group consistency, and group coherence.

RMS Architecture

- We presented a generic architecture for a single agent reason maintenance module. The architecture, consisting of three sub-units

DNU, CMU, and CCU,   improves the software structure of reason maintenance modules and eases design, maintenance, and extension of RMSs.

- We showed that a slightly extended variant of the generic architecture can serve as a flexible, generic component in the construction of multiagent reason maintenance systems.

RMS Systems

- We presented XFRMS, a single agent, multiple context, assumption-based, and focus-based reason maintenance system, which allows to efficiently maintain large sets of data, assumptions, and dependencies while considering multiple, but a comparatively small number of contexts; in particular, XFRMS solves — for the PEDE domain — the computational problems of ATMS-style systems.
- For multiagent scenarios, we presented MXFRMS, the multiagent variant of XFRMS. MXFRMS allows a group of agents to use reason maintenance services, like the ones provided by XFRMS. Additionally, MXFRMS supports the exchange of beliefs between agents, to establish update contracts for maintaining such beliefs over time, and to perform a variety of joint (group-based) reasoning functions, like determining consequences and contexts of coherent assumption sets in a group and determining the consistency of focus structures

Of course, a disclaimer is in order as well. This text does not treat reason maintenance techniques relevant for domains that equire sophisticated *non-monotonic* reasoning capabilities. Also, it is not an attempt to provide the full functionality of de Kleer's ATMS for multiagent scenarios. In particular, we have omitted explanation facilities and all capabilities that allow to construct interpretations. Sometimes ATMS-based systems (mis)use the ATMS as a kind of search engine that is expected to deliver (i.e construct) a set of solutions to a problem on hand. Neither the XFRMS nor the MXFRMS are claimed to provide a solution for the problems such an approach incurs. However, as we have motivated on several occasions throughout this book, we consider XFRMS and MXFRMS to provide a solid basic functionality that we believe is essential for the PEDE domain.

6.3   The Work in Perspective

At this point, it is time to roam about a few intented and potential uses of the work described in this book. Knowing about where we are heading to will also prepare the ground for describing the things that remain to be done in the section on future work.

The main feature of the XFRMS and MXFRMS technology is that it allows to efficiently maintain multiple contexts for large sets of assumptions and logical dependencies. Thus, good opportunities for using XFRMS and MXFRMS technologies are applications where this capability is needed. Such applications often occur in the following areas:

- planning, scheduling, and control

- configuration and design

- network services

- systems management

- programming

- authoring

The multiagent version MXFRMS is, of course, required whenever the application is implemented as a multiagent system, or in some other distributed fashion.

The next few paragraph give a short illustration and example for potential applications in some of these areas.

Logistics as a PEDE Domain Transportation of goods is prototypical example for a PEDE problem. In work described elsewhere (see for example [Riederer, 1993], [Reinema, 1993], and [Reinema and Kraetzschmar, 1993]), we have performed an in-depth analysis of several just-in-time (JIT) supply processes at the car manufacturing unit of Mercedes-Benz in Sindelfingen. These processes involve several (semi-)autonomous decision makers, involve a large number of additional agents executing plans and schedules made by the decision makers, and are distributed across space, time and functionality. [Riederer, 1993] provides a range of eye-opening examples for things routinely going wrong. These failures typically cause significant costs. For example, in the JIT supply process for indoor covers of cars, it happens several times a day that the required parts are not available when they are needed. As a consequence, the doors of a car often cannot be assembled on time and require the whole car to be shifted out of the line. Naturally, all assembly processes after door assembly (here referred to as post-door assemblies) are disturbed by such a measure, because it is usually not possible for the people and systems controlling these post-door assemblies to react fast enough to such a unforeseen change. Riederer also presents an analysis of these processes which shows that the problem often is caused by the fact, that the agents (people and systems) where a failure of some kind occurs (e.g. in door assembly, that the required door is not available) do not inform other agents, which depend on the results produced by the former agents, about these failures. As we have shown, formalizing and explicitly maintaining such dependencies, and integrating this service into the information processing infrastructure used by Mercedes-Benz could lead to dramatically reduced failure rates and allows for large savings of costs. However, this domain requires the maintenance of a very large number of propositions, assumptions, and logical dependencies, and previously existing technology like the ATMS does not scale up to problems of this size. Systems based on XFRMS and MXFRMS seem to be much more promising in this area, although some simplifying assumptions taken here, like the eager communication of relevant propositions and assumptions, might have to be removed. That this is possible with reasonable effort was argued before.

Electronic Markets in Logistics A very promising technology to apply in the logistics domain is market-oriented programming [Wellman, 1993]. The basic principle is to apply ideas from markets and economics in order to design flexible and robust distributed resource allocation schemes. A simple example involves the application of the contract net protocol [Davis and Smith, 1983]: Customers wishing to have some goods transported from place A to place B announce this task as a job to be performed. Agents capable of doing the job (e.g. logistics companies) react to this announcement by submitting offers which specify the conditions for performing the job. The customer then selects the offer that suits his needs best and assigns a contract. However, there are still a large number of unresolved problems with this new approach. A central one is the stability of the system as a whole, and of particular system properties. For example, if contractors do not fulfill their committments and cancel already assigned contracts, difficulties begin to arise. These difficulties become real problems, and may cause the system to become unstable and exhibit chaotic behavior,[2] if the contracting process is a multistage process: for some particular task, z gives contracts for subtasks to $y_1, y_2, \ldots, y_1$ subcontracts $x_{11}, x_{12}, \ldots$, and so on. Equipping all participating agents with multiagent reason maintenance technology can open a pathway leading to solutions for this problem.

Design Decision Support Another are loaden with the ubiquituous presence of dependencies is design. At the Center for Design Research at Stanford University, Charles Petrie investigates methods for recording design rationales and exploiting the explicit maintenance of such rationales to improve design processes [Petrie et al., 1994a]. So far, Petrie

---

[2]For the analysis of the dynamical behavior of large distributed systems, see work done by Huberman, Hogg, Clearwater et al. at XEROX PARC.

has only used single context reason maintenance technology, mainly because of the computational complexity of multiple context technology like the ATMS. However, the need for multiple contexts in design is obvious. Besides the fact, that multiple contexts are necessary in order to allow for concurrent engineering (design different components concurrently by several design groups), they allow to maintain customer-specific design requirements, multiple design alternatives, and country-specific information.

Software Installation Assistance A much smaller, but nevertheless equally interesting area is system management and installation. Typically, system administrators have to administer a network of computers,[3] and a large range of software,[4] while suffering a very large overall workload. As anyone with software installation experience knows, even the initial installation and configuration of a machine in such a complex environment is a complex process that is loaden with dependencies. The most prominent ones of a single software package can be recovered from the set of `Makefiles`. In a typical scenario, the system administrator does neither have the time nor the need to touch a particular machine after its initial installation and configuration for several weeks or even months. When the need to perform system maintenance tasks on this machine arises again, then all the knowledge about how the system was installed, what problems occurred and how they were solved, has vanished a long time ago, and must be recovered in a tedious and time-consuming process. We believe that better support for maintaining heterogeneous hardware and software environments is urgently needed, and that the technology developed here can be a valable contribution to such support systems.

Software Installation Assistance A much smaller, but nevertheless equally The development of large software systems is a cooperative process that usually involves a group of software designers and programmers. Furthermore, the presence of dependencies between various software components is obvious. The number of dependencies increases fast as multiple versions and configurations of a software system must be maintained. Thus, software development and version and configuration management are worthwhile areas for the application of multiagent reason maintenance technology.

---

[3]Say, 20-30 UNIX workstations connected via an Ethernet local area network, several printers, modems, scanners, and other devices such as tapes and disks, plus special hardware like a parallel processor

[4]At our department in Ulm, this ranges from UNIX operating systems, programming language development environments, large editors and compilers, networking software, and typesetting environments like TEXand LATEX, all the way to neural network and robotic simulators.

Joint Authoring and Document Configuration Management An area
that exhibits a lot of similarities to the software development area is
joint authoring of large documents, especially if these documents must
be maintained in multiple versions and variants. Good examples can be
found in technical documentation, where several product variants also
require several variants of technical documentation, often in several languages. A group of people, consisting e.g. of writers, graphics designers,
layouters, and technical specialists, is usually involved in the creation
and maintenance of complex documents. Thus, joint authoring and document configuration management tools can profit from the application
of multiagent reason maintenance technology.

It is clear that the problem discussed in this text is almost ubiquituous in many
domains and that there is quite a number of potential applications. However,
for many of these areas additional functionality is needed in computational
support systems. The work described here is only a first step towards the right
direction. XFRMS and MXFRMS provide well-founded base layer substrates for
implementing more application-specific, higher-level functionality. The next
section outlines a few potential lines of future work.

6.4   Future Work

Although XFRMS and MXFRMS already provide the basic functionality required
for many multiagent applications where multiple context assumption-based
reasoning is needed, more elaborate and specialized support services are desirable for several of the domains mentioned above. The development of such
higher-level functionality remains a rich field for future work.

Desirable extensions can roughly be decomposed into two subproblems:

- integrating some special capability, such as temporal reasoning, with
  reason maintenance services, and

- developing the appropriate multiagent functionality for the added capabilities.

Based on the work described here, one could pursue an extension effort in the
following four steps:

1. Select a candidate capability required in a single agent, higher-level support system and develop an approach for providing the additonal functionality.

2. Integrate this functionality with XFRMS.

3. Extend the additional functionality to the multiagent domain, by carefully analyzing the problem in the multiagent scenario, formalizing it appropriately, and developing an approach for providing the functionality in multiagent systems.

4. Integrate this functionality with MXFRMS.

The underlying assumption in this approach is that one is researching an application domain where basic multiagent RMS functionality like the one provided by XFRMS and MXFRMS is useful.

What are such candidate functionalities one could think about to add? Two such areas, where the application of XFRMS and MXFRMS technology seems very promising, are temporal reasoning and plan or schedule management:

Temporal Reasoning The capability to explicitly reason with and manipulate temporal data is definitely a must for scheduling applications and also for many planning applications. There have aleady been several attempts to combine reason maintenance and temporal reasoning for single agent scenarios.[5] An ATTMS, developed in our research group by Tim Geisler [Geisler, 1994], combines temporal reasoning techniques based on constraint propagation with an ATMS. However, the use of the system is severely limited due to computational limitations imposed by the ATMS approach. A reimplementation of the ATTMS using the XFRMS instead of the ATMS seems very promising and is very likely to avoid these problems.

Plan and Schedule Management Systems A step further towards off-the-shelf components for planning and scheduling applications requires the availability of support systems for plan and schedule management. Using RMS technology, in particular the ATMS, in this area has some tradition (see e.g. [Morris and Nado, 1986], [Beetz and Lefkowitz, 1989b], [Beetz and Lefkowitz, 1989a], and [Lindner, 1992]), although success was somewhat limited so far. At least up to now, these approaches have not found widespread use in standard planning and scheduling architectures. The commonly cited reasons for this fact are again the computational limitations of the underlying ATMS. Using XFRMS and MXFRMS technology seems very promising in this area.

Two further areas, where the potential benefits of applying XFRMS and MXFRMS technology are much more vague, are the following:

Support for Spatial Reasoning Spatial reasoning has some intriguing analogies to temporal reasoning; some approaches simply view certain spatial

---

[5]For a review, see [Geisler, 1994].

reasoning problems as multi-dimensional temporal reasoning problems. For example, Geisler has used this approach in his diploma thesis to develop a system that performs semi-automatic layouting of graphical user interfaces. It is unclear, but seems an intellectually challenging task, whether the technology developed in this thesis could also be beneficial for spatial reasoning applications. Candidate domains include all areas which require assignment of space (e.g. in trucks, ships, or planes) or robotics (e.g. multirobot scenarios).

Reasoning with Uncertainty All the way through this book, we only considered problem solvers with very limited capabilities for dealing with uncertainty. All logical dependencies are certain information, for example. If all antecedents hold, then the consequent also holds. In many domains, however, formalizing problems without using a mechanism for explicitly expressing uncertainty is very difficult. Examples can be found in robotics or medical reasoning. Dubois and Prade have extensively researched the problem of combining reason maintenance services with e.g. probabilistic or possibilistic reasoning mechanisms [Dubois et al., 1991].

It would be very interesting to find out whether their work could be improved by integrating ideas found in XFRMS and MXFRMS.

Of course, this list is incomplete and many more lines of future work, like adding nonmonotonic capabilites or investigating parallel implementations of MXFRMS, can be pursued.

6.5 Summary

We have identified the problem of maintaining logical dependencies as a problem that is typical in the PEDE domain. We have analyzed dependency maintenance both in the single agent and the multiagent case in reasonable depth and provided the two logics HPL and FHPL, which allow to formalize and reason about these problems. Furthermore, the logics open the way for providing computational support for handling these problems. We have provided formal specifications for the functionality desirable for such support systems and provided an architecture for implementing such systems. Finally, we designed and implemented the two systems XFRMS (for the single agent scenario) and MXFRMS (for the multiagent scenario), which provide the desired kind of functionality. With these two systems, we could demonstrate that it is possible to maintain multiple contexts with great efficiency.

A lot of work remains to be done in order to yield systems that are suitable components for building flexible, distributed PEDE applications, but we have provided a solid stepping stone and a technological key component for getting in this direction.

Bibliography

[AAAI, 1991] AAAI (1991). *Proceedings of the Ninth National Conference on Artificial Intelligence*, Anaheim, CA, USA. American Association for Artificial Intelligence, AAAI Press.

[AAAI, 1992] AAAI (1992). *Proceedings of the Tenth National Conference on Artificial Intelligence*, San Jose, CA, USA. American Association for Artificial Intelligence, AAAI Press.

[AAAI, 1993] AAAI (1993). *Proceedings of the Eleventh National Conference on Artificial Intelligence*, Washington, D.C., USA. American Association for Artificial Intelligence, AAAI Press.

[AAAI, 1994] AAAI (1994). *Proceedings of the Twelfth National Conference on Artificial Intelligence*, Seattle, WA, USA. American Association for Artificial Intelligence, AAAI Press.

[Abramsky et al., 1992] Abramsky, S., Gabbay, D. M., and Maibaum, T. S. E., editors (1992). *Background: Mathematical Structures*, volume 1 of *Handbook of Logic in Computer Science*. Clarendon Press, Oxford, UK.

[Allen et al., 1990] Allen, J., Hendler, J., and Tate, A., editors (1990). *Readings in Planning*. Morgan Kaufmann, San Mateo, CA, USA.

[Allen et al., 1991] Allen, J. F., Kautz, H. A., Pelavin, R. N., and Tenenberg, J. D. (1991). *Reasoning About Plans*. Morgan Kaufmann Publishers, San Mateo, CA, USA.

[Appelt and Konolige, 1988] Appelt, D. and Konolige, K. (1988). A nonmonotonic logic for reasoning about speech acts and belief revision. In Reinfrank, M., de Kleer, J., Ginsberg, M. L., and Sandewall, E., editors, *Non-Monotonic Reasoning — Proceedings of the Second International Workshop*, pages 164–175. Springer-Verlag, Heidelberg, Germany. LNAI Volume 346.

[Barwise and Perry, 1983] Barwise, J. and Perry, J. (1983). *Situations and Attitudes*. The MIT Press, Cambridge, MA, USA.

[Beckstein, 1992] Beckstein, C. (1992). Reason Maintenance Systeme. Vorlesung im Hauptstudium, Universität Erlangen.

[Beckstein, 1994] Beckstein, C. (1994). *Architektur und logische Grundlagen monotoner Systeme zur Begründungsverwaltung.* Habilitation thesis, Universität Erlangen-Nürnberg, Erlangen.

[Beckstein et al., 1993] Beckstein, C., Fuhge, R., and Kraetzschmar, G. K. (1993). Supporting Assumption-Based Reasoning in a Distributed Environment. In Sycara, K. P., editor, *Proceedings of the 12th Workshop on Distributed Artificial Intelligence*, Hidden Valley Ressort, Pennsylvania, USA.

[Beckstein et al., 1994] Beckstein, C., Kraetzschmar, G. K., and Schneeberger, J. (1994). Distributed Plan Maintenance for Scheduling and Execution. In Bäckström, C. and Sandewall, E., editors, *Current Trends in AI Planning*, pages 74–86, Amsterdam, The Netherlands. IOS Press.

[Beer, 1995] Beer, R. D. (1995). Introduction to dynamics. in: Practice and Future of Autonomous Agents, Volume II. Notes from a Tutorial given at AA-95, Monte Verita, Switzerland.

[Beetz and Lefkowitz, 1989a] Beetz, M. and Lefkowitz, L. S. (1989a). PNMS: A belief revision system for planning. Technical report, University of Massachussetts.

[Beetz and Lefkowitz, 1989b] Beetz, M. and Lefkowitz, L. S. (1989b). Reasoning about justified events: a unified treatment of temporal projection, planning rationale and domain constraints. Technical report, University of Massachussetts.

[Beetz et al., 1992] Beetz, M., Lindner, M., and Schneeberger, J. (1992). Temporal Projection for Hierarchical, Partial-Order Planning. In *Tenth National Conference on Artificial Intelligence, Workshop on Implementing Temporal Reasoning*.

[Bell and Grimson, 1992] Bell, D. A. and Grimson, J. (1992). *Distributed Database Systems.* International Computer Science Series. Addison-Wesley, Wokingham.

[Bench-Capon, 1990] Bench-Capon, T. J. M. (1990). *Knowledge Representation: An Approach to Artificial Intelligence*, volume 32 of *The A.P.I.C. Series*. Academic Press, London, UK.

[Bond and Gasser, 1988a] Bond, A. H. and Gasser, L. (1988a). An analysis of problems and research in distributed artificial intelligence. In Bond, A. H. and Gasser, L., editors, *Readings in Distributed Artificial Intelligence*. Morgan Kaufmann, San Mateo, CA, USA.

[Bond and Gasser, 1988b] Bond, A. H. and Gasser, L. (1988b). *Readings in Distributed Artificial Intelligence*. Morgan Kaufmann Publishers, San Mateo, Calif.

[Brachman and Schmolze, 1985] Brachman, R. J. and Schmolze, J. G. (1985). An overview of the KL-ONE knowledge representation system. *Cognitive Science*, 9:171–216.

[Bridgeland and Huhns, 1990] Bridgeland, D. and Huhns, M. (1990). Distributed truth maintenance. In *Proceedings of AAAI-90*, pages 72–77. AAAI.

[Brownston et al., 1985] Brownston, L., Farrell, R., Kant, E., and Martin, N. (1985). *Programming Expert Systems in OPS5: An Introduction to Rule-Based Programming*. Addison-Wesley, Reading, MA, USA.

[Chellas, 1980] Chellas, B. F. (1980). *Modal Logic: An Introduction*. Cambridge University Press, Cambridge, UK.

[Cohen and Levesque, 1990a] Cohen, P. and Levesque, H. (1990a). Intention is choice with commitment. *Artificial Intelligence*, 42:213–261.

[Cohen and Levesque, 1990b] Cohen, P. and Levesque, H. (1990b). Rational interaction as the basis for communication. In Cohen, P., Morgan, J., and Pollack, M., editors, *Intentions in Communication*, pages 221–256. The MIT Press, Cambridge, MA, USA.

[Cohen and Perrault, 1979] Cohen, P. and Perrault, C. (1979). Elements of a plan-based theory of speech acts. *Cognitive Science*, 3(177–212).

[Collins and DeCoste, 1991] Collins, J. W. and DeCoste, D. (1991). CATMS: An ATMS Which Avoids Label Explosions. In *Proceedings of AAAI-91*. AAAI.

[Cormen et al., 1990] Cormen, T. H., Leiserson, C. E., and Rivest, R. L. (1990). *Introduction to Algorithms*. The MIT Press, Cambridge, MA, USA.

[Davies, 1992] Davies, N. J. (1992). A First Order Theory of Knowledge, Belief and Action. In Neumann, B., editor, *Proceedings of ECAI 92*, pages 408–412. John Wiley and Sons.

[Davis, 1990] Davis, E. (1990). *Representations of Commonsense Knowledge*. Morgan Kaufmann Publishers, San Mateo, CA, USA.

[Davis and Smith, 1983] Davis, R. and Smith, R. (1983). Negotiation as a metaphor for distributed problem solving. *Artificial Intelligence*, 20:63–109.

[de Kleer, 1986a] de Kleer, J. (1986a). An Assumption-based TMS. *AI-Journal*, 28:127–224.

[de Kleer, 1986b] de Kleer, J. (1986b). Extending the ATMS. *AI-Journal*, 28:127–224.

[de Kleer, 1986c] de Kleer, J. (1986c). Problem-Solving with the ATMS. *AI-Journal*, 28:127–224.

[DeCoste and Collins, 1991] DeCoste, D. and Collins, J. W. (1991). CATMS: An ATMS Which Avoids Label Explosions. Technical report, Institute for the Learning Sciences, Northwestern University.

[Dotzel, 1994] Dotzel, C. (1994). Design und Implementierung verteilter Reason Maintenance Systeme. Diplomarbeit, University of Erlangen.

[Doyle, 1979] Doyle, J. (1979). A Truth Maintenance System. *AI-Journal*, 12:231–272.

[Dressler and Farquhar, 1991] Dressler, O. and Farquhar, A. (1991). Putting the Problem Solver Back in the Driver's Seat. In Martins, J. P. and Reinfrank, M., editors, *Proc. ECAI-90 Workshop on Truth Maintenance Systems*, Heidelberg, Germany. Springer-Verlag.

[Dubois et al., 1991] Dubois, D., Lang, J., and Prade, H. (1991). A possibilistic assumption-based truth maintenance system with uncertain justifications, and its application to belief revision. In Martins, J. P. and Reinfrank, M., editors, *Truth Maintenance Systems*. Springer-Verlag, Berlin.

[ECAI, 1992] ECAI (1992). *Proceedings of the 1992 European Conference on Artificial Intelligence*, Vienna, Austria. ECCAI.

[ECAI, 1994] ECAI (1994). *Proceedings of the 1994 European Conference on ARtificial Intelligence*, Amsterdam, The Netherlands. ECCAI.

[Enderton, 1972] Enderton, H. B. (1972). *A Mathematical Introduction to Logic*. Academic Press, New York, NY, USA.

[Farwer et al., 1993] Farwer, B., Kasten, P., Köster, A., and Kopka, M. (1993). Nichtklassische logiken. Diplomarbeit, University of Hamburg, Fachbereich Informatik, Theoretische Grundlagen der Informatik, Hamburg, Germany.

[Fikes et al., 1987] Fikes, R., Morris, P., and Nado, B. (1987). Use of Truth Maintenance in Automatic Planning. In *DARPA Knowledge-Based Planning Workshop*, Austin, TX.

[Findler, 1979] Findler, N. V., editor (1979). *Associative Networks - The Representation and Use of Knowledge in Computers*. Academic Press, New York, NY, USA.

[Finin et al., 1993a] Finin, T., Weber, J., Wiederhold, G., Genesereth, M., Fritzson, R., McKay, D., McGuire, J., Pelavin, R., Shapiro, S., and Beck, C. (1993a). Specification of the KQML Agent-Communication Language. Unpublished draft manuscript, Enterprise Integration Technologies Corp., Palo Alto, CA, USA.

[Finin et al., 1993b] Finin, T., Weber, J., Wiederhold, G., Genesereth, M., Fritzson, R., McKay, D., McGuire, J., Pelavin, R., Shapiro, S., and Beck, C. (1993b). Specification of the kqml agent-communication language. Unpublished draft manuscript, Enterprise Integration Technologies Corp., Palo Alto, CA, USA.

[Fitting, 1993] Fitting, M. (1993). Basic modal logic. In Gabbay, D. M., Hogger, C. J., and Robinson, J., editors, *Handbook of Logic in Artificial Intelligence and Logic Programming, Volume I: Logical Foundations*, pages 365–448. Clarendon Press, Oxford, UK.

[Foner, 1993] Foner, L. N. (1993). What's An Agent, Anyway? A Sociological Case Study. Agents Memo 93-01, Agents Group, MIT Media Lab, Cambridge, MA, USA.

[Forbus and de Kleer, 1993] Forbus, K. D. and de Kleer, J. (1993). *Building Problem Solvers*. The MIT Press, Cambridge, MA, USA.

[Forgy, 1981] Forgy, C. L. (1981). The OPS5 users manual. Technical Report CMU-CS-79-132, Carnegie-Mellon University, Computer Science Department, Pittsburgh, PA, USA.

[Fuhge, 1993] Fuhge, R. (1993). Verteilte Begründungsverwaltung. Studienarbeit, Universität Erlangen-Nürnberg.

[Geisler, 1994] Geisler, T. (1994). Ein anwendungsunabhängiges Unterstützungssystem zum integrierten annahmenbasierten und temporalen Schlie"sen. Diplomarbeit, University of Erlangen.

[Genesereth et al., 1993a] Genesereth, M. R., Fikes, R. E., Bobrow, D., Brachman, R., Gruber, T., Hayes, P., Letsinger, R., Lifschitz, V., MacGregor, R., McCarthy, J., Norvig, P., Patil, R., and Schubert, L. (1993a). Knowledge Interchange Format Version 3.0 Reference Manual. Report Logic-92-1, Logic Group, Computer Science Department, Stanford University, Stanford, CA, USA.

[Genesereth et al., 1993b] Genesereth, M. R., Fikes, R. E., Bobrow, D., Brachman, R., Gruber, T., Hayes, P., Letsinger, R., Lifschitz, V., MacGregor, R., McCarthy, J., Norvig, P., Patil, R., and Schubert, L. (1993b). Knowledge Interchange Format Version 3.0 Reference Manual. Report Logic-92-1, Logic Group, Computer Science Department, Stanford University, Stanford, CA, USA.

[Genesereth and Nilsson, 1987] Genesereth, M. R. and Nilsson, N. J. (1987). *Logical Foundations of Artificial Intelligence*. Morgan Kaufmann Publishers, Los Altos, CA, USA.

[Ginsberg, 1993] Ginsberg, M. (1993). *Essentials of Artificial Intelligence*. Morgan Kaufmann Publishers, Inc., San Mateo, California, USA.

[Giunchiglia and Serafini, 1994] Giunchiglia, F. and Serafini, L. (1994). Multilanguage hierarchical logics, or: how we can do without modal logics. *Artificial Intelligence*, 65(1):29–70.

[Gray and Reuter, 1993] Gray, J. and Reuter, A. (1993). *Transaction Processing*. Morgan Kaufmann, San Mateo, CA, USA.

[Haddadi and Bussmann, 1994] Haddadi, A. and Bussmann, S. (1994). Scheduling Meetings by Multi-Agent Negotiation. In [Petrie et al., 1994b].

[Halpern, 1986] Halpern, J. Y. (1986). Reasoning about knowledge: An overview. In Halpern, J. Y., editor, *Proceedings of the 1986 Conference on Theoretical Aspects of Reasoning About Knowledge*, pages 1–18, San Mateo, CA, USA. Morgan Kaufmann Publishers.

[Halpern, 1987] Halpern, J. Y. (1987). Using reasoning about knowledge to analyze distributed systems. *Annual Review of Computer Science*, 2:37–68.

[Halpern, 1990] Halpern, J. Y. (1990). Knowledge and common knowledge in a distributed environment. *Journal of the ACM*, 37(3).

[Halpern and Moses, 1985] Halpern, J. Y. and Moses, Y. (1985). A guide to the modal logics of knowledge and belief. In *Proceedings of IJCAI-85*, pages 480–490. IJCAI.

[Halpern and Moses, 1992] Halpern, J. Y. and Moses, Y. (1992). A guide to completeness and complexity for modal logics of knowledge and belief. *Artificial Intelligence*, 54:319–379.

[Hammond, 1994] Hammond, K., editor (1994). *Second International Conference on Artificial Intelligence Planning Systems*, Chicago, IL, USA. AAAI.

[Hendler and McDermott, 1992] Hendler, J. and McDermott, D., editors (1992). *First International Conference on Artificial Intelligence Planning Systems*, College Park, MD, USA. AAAI.

[Hintikka, 1962] Hintikka, J. (1962). *Knowledge and Belief.* Cornell University Press, Ithaca, NY, USA.

[Horstmann, 1991] Horstmann, T. C. (1991). Distributed Truth Maintenance. Technical Report D-91-11, Deutsches Forschungszentrum für Künstliche Intelligenz GmbH, Kaiserslautern.

[Hughes and Cresswell, 1968] Hughes, G. E. and Cresswell, M. J. (1968). *An Introduction to Modal Logic.* Methuen and Co., London, United Kingdom.

[IJCAI, 1991] IJCAI (1991). *International Joint Conference on Artificial Intelligence*, Sydney, Australia. IJCAI.

[IJCAI, 1993] IJCAI (1993). *International Joint Conference on Artificial Intelligence*, Chambery, France. IJCAI.

[IJCAI, 1995] IJCAI (1995). *International Joint Conference on Artificial Intelligence*, Montreal, Canada. IJCAI.

[Kean and Tsiknis, 1992] Kean, A. and Tsiknis, G. (1992). Assumption-based reasoning and clause management systems. *Computational Intelligence*, 8(1).

[Kean and Tsiknis, 1993] Kean, A. and Tsiknis, G. (1993). Claus management systems (CMS). *Computational Intelligence*, 9(1):11–40.

[Kelleher and van der Gaag, 1993] Kelleher, G. and van der Gaag, L. (1993). The LazyRMS: Avoiding Work in the ATMS. *Computational Intelligence*, 9(3):239–253.

[Konolige, 1982] Konolige, K. (1982). A first-order formalization of knowledge and action for a multi-agent planning system. In Hayes, J., Michie, D., and Pao, Y., editors, *Machine Intelligence 10*, pages 41–72. Ellis Horwood, Chichester, UK.

[Konolige, 1986] Konolige, K. (1986). *A Deduction Model of Belief.* Pitman Publishing, London, UK.

[KR, 1992] KR (1992). *International Conference on Knowledge Representation.* AAAI.

[KR, 1994] KR (1994). *International Conference on Knowledge Representation.* AAAI.

[Kraetzschmar, 1996a] Kraetzschmar, G. K. (1996a). Mxfrms. Technical report, FORWISS.

[Kraetzschmar, 1996b] Kraetzschmar, G. K. (1996b). Xfrms. Technical report, FORWISS.

[Kripke, 1963a] Kripke, S. (1963a). Semantical analysis of modal logic. *Zeitschrift für Mathematische Logik und Grundlagen der Mathematik*, 9:67–96.

[Kripke, 1963b] Kripke, S. (1963b). Semantical considerations on modal logic. *Acta Philosophica Fennica*.

[Lakemeyer and Nebel, 1994] Lakemeyer, G. and Nebel, B., editors (1994). *Foundations of Knowledge Representation*, volume 810 of *Lecture Notes in Artificial Intelligence*. Springer-Verlag, Berlin, Germany.

[Lesser, 1995] Lesser, V., editor (1995). *Proceedings of the First International Conference on Multiagent Systems*, San Francisco, CA, USA. WWW Page http://dis.cs.umass.edu/icmas.html.

[Levesque, 1984] Levesque, H. J. (1984). A logic of explicit and implicit belief. In *Proceedings of AAAI-84*, pages 198–202. AAAI.

[Lindner, 1992] Lindner, M. (1992). ATMS-basierte Plangenerierung. Diplomarbeit, Intellektik/Informatik, Technische Hochschule Darmstadt.

[Liu and Sycara, 1994] Liu, J. and Sycara, K. P. (1994). Distributed constraint-directed meeting scheduling. In [Petrie et al., 1994b].

[Lux and Schupeta, 1994] Lux, A. and Schupeta, A. (1994). PASHA - Personal Assistant for Scheduling Appointments. In [Petrie et al., 1994b].

[Maier, 1983] Maier, D. (1983). *The Theory of Relational Databases*. Computer Science Press, Potomac, MD, USA.

[Maier and Warren, 1988] Maier, D. and Warren, D. S. (1988). *Computing with Logic: Logic Programming with Prolog*. Benjamin Cummings, Menlo Park, CA, USA.

[Malheiro et al., 1994] Malheiro, B., Jennings, N. R., and Oliveira, E. (1994). Belief revision in multi-agent systems. In Cohn, A., editor, *ECAI 94. Proceedings of the 11th European Conference on Artificial Intelligence*. John Wiley & Sons.

[Martins, 1991] Martins, J. P. (1991). The Truth, the Whole Truth, and Nothing But the Truth: An Indexed Bibliography to the Literature of Truth Maintenance Systems. *AI-Magazine*, II(5):7–25.

[Mason and Johnson, 1989] Mason, C. L. and Johnson, R. R. (1989). DATMS: A Framework for Distributed Assumption Based Reasoning. In Huhns, M. N. and Gasser, L., editors, *Distributed AI Volume II*, pages 293–317. Pitman Publishers London.

[McAllester, 1990] McAllester, D. (1990). Truth maintenance. In *Proceedings of the Eighth National Conference on Artificial Intelligence (AAAI-90)*, pages 1109–1116, Menlo Park, CA, USA. AAAI, AAAI Press.

[McCarthy and Hayes, 1969] McCarthy, J. and Hayes, P. J. (1969). Some philosophical problems from the standpoint of artificial intelligence. In Meltzer, B. and Michie, D., editors, *Machine Intelligence 4*, pages 463–502. American Elsevier, New York, NY, USA.

[McDermott, 1991] McDermott, D. V. (1991). A general framework for reason maintenance. *Artificial Intelligence*, 50(3):289–329.

[McDermott, 1982] McDermott, J. (1982). R1: A rule-based configurer of computer systems. *Artificial Intelligence*, 19(1):39–88.

[McDermott, 1984] McDermott, J. (1984). R1 revisited: Four years in the trenches. *AI magazine*, 5(Fall):21–32.

[Minsky, 1975] Minsky, M. (1975). A framework for representing knowledge. In Winston, P., editor, *The Psychology of Computer Vision*, pages 211–277. McGraw-Hill, New York, NY, USA.

[ML, 1993] ML (1993). *International Conference on Machine Learning*.

[Moore, 1977] Moore, R. (1977). Reasoning about knowledge and action. In *Proceedings of the Fifth International Joint Conference on Artificial Intelligence (IJCAI-77)*, Cambridge, MA, USA. IJCAI.

[Moore, 1980] Moore, R. (1980). Reasoning about knowledge and action. Technical Note 191, SRI International, Menlo Park, CA, USA.

[Moore, 1990] Moore, R. (1990). A formal theory of knowledge and action. In Allen, J. F., Hendler, J., and Tate, A., editors, *Readings in Planning*, pages 480–519. Morgan Kaufmann Publishers, San Mateo, CA, USA.

[Morris and Nado, 1986] Morris, P. B. and Nado, R. A. (1986). Representing Actions with an Assumption-Based Truth Maintenance System. In *Fifth National Conference on Artificial Intelligence*.

[Moses and Shoham, 1993] Moses, Y. and Shoham, Y. (1993). Belief as defeasible knowledge. *Artificial Intelligence*, 64(2):299–321. also directly relevant.

[Müller, 1993] Müller, J., editor (1993). *Verteilte Künstliche Intelligenz*. B.I. Wissenschaftsverlag, Mannheim.

[Nebel and Köhler, 1995] Nebel, B. and Köhler, J. (1995). Plan reuse versus plan generation: A theoretical and emprical analysis. *Artificial Intelligence*.

[Neches et al., 1991a] Neches, R., Fikes, R., Finin, T., Gruber, T., Patil, R., Senator, T., and Swartout, W. R. (1991a). Enabling Technology for Knowledge Sharing. *AI magazine*, 12(3):36–56.

[Neches et al., 1991b] Neches, R., Fikes, R., Finin, T., Gruber, T., Patil, R., Senator, T., and Swartout, W. R. (1991b). Enabling technology for knowledge sharing. *AI magazine*, 12(3):36–56.

[Nilsson, 1991] Nilsson, N. J. (1991). Logic and artificial intelligence. *Artificial Intelligence*, 47:31–56.

[Oezsu and Valduriez, 1991] Oezsu, M. and Valduriez, P. (1991). *Principles of Distributed Database Systems*. Prentice-Hall, Englewood Cliffs, NJ. USA.

[Park and Birmingham, 1994] Park, S. and Birmingham, W. P. (1994). Meeting Scheduling using Negotiation. In [Petrie et al., 1994b].

[Perlis, 1985] Perlis, D. (1985). Languages with self reference I: Foundations. *Artificial Intelligence*, 25:301–322.

[Perlis, 1988a] Perlis, D. (1988a). Languages with self reference II: Knowledge, belief, and modality. *Artificial Intelligence*, 34:179–212.

[Perlis, 1988b] Perlis, D. (1988b). Meta in logic. In Maes, P. and Nardi, D., editors, *Meta-Level Architectures and Reflection*, pages 37–49. Elsevier Science Publishers, Amsterdam, The Netherlands.

[Petrie et al., 1994a] Petrie, C., Cutkosky, M., and Park, M. (1994a). Design space navigation as a collaborative aid. In *3rd Intl. Conference on AI in Design*, Lausanne, Switzerland.

[Petrie et al., 1993] Petrie, C., Tenenbaum, J. M., and Huhns, M. (1993). CAIA-94 Workshop on Coordinated Design and Planning: Call for participation. Available via WWW from http://cdr.stanford.edu/pub/caia-wrkshp.

[Petrie et al., 1994b] Petrie, C., Tenenbaum, J. M., and Huhns, M., editors (1994b). *Proceedings of the CAIA-94 Workshop on Coordinated Design and Planning*. Also available via WWW from http://cdr.stanford.edu/pub/caia-wrkshp.

[Petrie, 1991] Petrie, C. J. (1991). *Planning and Replanning with Truth Maintenance*. PhD thesis, The University of Texas at Austin, Austin, TX, USA.

[Reinema, 1993] Reinema, R. (1993). PEDE-Lab — Aufbau und Entwicklung einer Experimentierumgebung für Multi–Agenten–Systeme. Diplomarbeit, Universität Erlangen-Nürnberg.

[Reinema and Kraetzschmar, 1993] Reinema, R. and Kraetzschmar, G. K. (1993). PEDE-Lab — Eine Experimentierumgebung für die Verteilte Künstliche Intelligenz. In Müller, J., editor, *Beiträge zum Gründungsworkshop der Fachgruppe Verteilte Künstliche Intelligenz*, pages 102–113, Saarbrücken. Deutsches Forschungszentrum für Künstliche Intelligenz, Document D-93-06.

[Riederer, 1993] Riederer, M. (1993). Just-In-Time Beschaffungsprozesse in der Automobilproduktion als PEDE-Problem. Diplomarbeit, IMMD VIII, Universität Erlangen.

[Schneider, 1982] Schneider, H.-J., editor (1982). *Distributed Database Systems*.

[Searle, 1969] Searle, J. (1969). *Speech Acts: An Essay in the Philosophy of Language*. Cambridge University Press, Cambridge, UK.

[Seel, 1989] Seel, N. (1989). *Agent Theories and Architectures*. Ph.d. thesis, Surrey University, Guildford, UK.

[Sen, 1994] Sen, S. (1994). Contract-based distributed meeting scheduling. In [Petrie et al., 1994b].

[Singh, 1991] Singh, M. P. (1991). Towards a formal theory of communication for multi-agent systems. In *Proceedings of the Twelfth International Joint Conference on Artificial Intelligence (IJCAI-91)*, pages 69–74, Sydney, Australia. IJCAI, Morgan Kaufmann Publishers.

[Stoyan, 1988] Stoyan, H. (1988). *Programmiermethoden der Künstlichen Intelligenz*, volume 1 of *Studienreihe Informatik*. Springer Verlag, Berlin, Germany.

[Stoyan, 1991] Stoyan, H. (1991). *Programmiermethoden der Künstlichen Intelligenz*, volume 2 of *Studienreihe Informatik*. Springer Verlag, Berlin, Germany.

[Stoyan et al., 1992] Stoyan, H., Beckstein, C., Kraetzschmar, G. K., and Lutz, E. (1992). Erstellung und Ausführung von Plänen in verteilten Systemen. In *Antrag an die Deutsche Forschungsgemeinschaft auf Fortsetzung des Sonderforschungsbereichs 182 - Multiprozessor- und Netzwerkkonfigurationen*. Universität Erlangen-Nürnberg.

[Sycara, 1993] Sycara, K. P., editor (1993). *Proceedings of the 12th Workshop on Distributed Artificial Intelligence (to appear)*, Hidden Valley Ressort, Pennsylvania, USA.

[Sycara, 1990] Sycara, K. S., editor (1990). *Innovative Approaches to Planning, Scheduling and Control*, San Mateo, CA, USA. Morgan Kaufman.

[Tatar, 1994] Tatar, M. M. (1994). Combining the lazy label evaluation with focusing techniques in an atms. In Cohn, A., editor, *ECAI 94. Proceedings of the 11th European Conference on Artificial Intelligence*. John Wiley & Sons.

[Thayse, 1989] Thayse, A., editor (1989). *From Modal Logic to Deductive Databases*. John Wiley & Sons, Chichester, UK.

[Thayse and Gochet, 1988] Thayse, A. and Gochet, P. (1988). *From standard logic to logic programming*. Wiley, Chichester, UK.

[Waltz, 1975] Waltz, D. (1975). Understanding line drawings of scenes with shadows. In Winston, P., editor, *The Psychology of Computer Vision*, pages 19–91. McGraw-Hill, New York, NY, USA.

[Wedekind, 1988] Wedekind, H., editor (1988). *Datenverteilung in Rechnernetzen*. Universität Erlangen, Erlangen, Germany.

[Wedekind, 1992] Wedekind, H. (1992). Multiprozessor- und netzwerkkonfigurationen. Sonderforschungsbereich 182, Antrag an die DFG auf Förderung in den Jahren 1993-1995.

[Wedekind, 1994] Wedekind, H., editor (1994). *Verteilte Systeme: Grundlagen und zukünftige Entwicklung aus der Sicht des Sonderforschungsbereichs 182 "Multiprozessor- und Netzwerkkonfigurationen"*. B.I. Wissenschaftsverlag, Mannheim, Germany.

[Wellman, 1993] Wellman, M. P. (1993). A Market-Oriented Programming Environment: Preliminary Explorations. In Sycara, K. P., editor, *Proceedings of the 12th Workshop on Distributed Artificial Intelligence (to appear)*, Hidden Valley Ressort, Pennsylvania, USA.

[Werner, 1988] Werner, E. (1988). Toward a theory of communication and cooperation for multiagent planning. In Vardi, M. Y., editor, *Proceedings of the Second Conference on Theoretical Aspects of Reasoning About Knowledge (TARK-II)*, pages 129–144, San Mateo, CA, USA. Morgan Kaufmann Publishers.

[Wooldridge and Jennings, 1995] Wooldridge, M. and Jennings, N. R. (1995). Intelligent Agents: Theory and Practice. *Knowledge Engineering Review (to appear)*.

[Wooldridge, 1992] Wooldridge, M. J. (1992). *The Logical Modelling of Computational Multi-Agent Systems*. PhD thesis, Department of Computation, University of Manchester.

[Zweben and Fox, 1994] Zweben, M. and Fox, M. S., editors (1994). *Intelligent Scheduling*. Morgan Kaufmann Publishers, San Francisco, CA, USA.

List of Figures

1.1 Assumptions and dependencies in dynamic planning and scheduling domains. 6

1.2 Assumptions and dependencies in distributed planning and scheduling. 8

1.3 The two-level software architecture. 14

1.4 Multiagent system using standard RMS technology. 16

1.5 Multiagent system using centralized RMS technology. 18

1.6 Multiagent system using multiagent RMS technology. 19

2.1 The layered architecture approach. 31

2.2 Graphical illustration of some dependencies in Patricia's initial schedule. 40

2.3 Families of reason maintenance systems. 51

3.1 A generic reason maintenance system architecture. 65

3.2 Mapping a logical state to a (refined) XFRMS architecture. . . 67

3.3 Illustration of XFRMS Label Propagation. 72

4.1 A typical multiagent meeting scheduling situation. 85

4.2 Initial information given to the secreatries by their managers. . 86

4.3 Generation of two initial schedule alternatives. 87

4.4 Reactions to rescheduling requests and changes in availability. . 89

4.5 Graphical illustration of the congruence problem. 94

4.6 The possible metalogical states of a proposition. 96

4.7 The layered architecture approach for multiagent systems. . . . 97

4.8 Graphical illustration of initial schedule dependencies. 129

4.9 The basic two-level software architecture of each agent. 144

4.10 Multiagent system using centralized RMS technology. 145

4.11 Multiagent system using multiagent RMS technology. 146

4.12 Multiagent system using hybrid multiagent RMS technology. . 147

4.13 Families of multiagent reason maintenance systems. 148

4.14 The architecture of DARMS modules 156

4.15 Handling failures using DARMS 166

4.16 Planning contingencies using DARMS 168

5.1 The implementation spectrum for a typical multiagent system. 177

5.2 Agent-oriented view of the MXFRMS architecture. 179

5.3 The logical view of the MXFRMS architecture. 181

5.4 Implementational view of the MXFRMS architecture. 184

5.5 A generic architecture for a MXFRMS facet module. 212

5.6 Mapping global logical state to a refined MXFRMS architecture. 214

5.7 The MXFRMS label propagation mechanism. 222

5.8 Example of the distribution of label update work across space
     and time. 242

5.9 Concurrent execution and temporal overlap of multiple update
     requests. 244

6.1 Overview on work done. 252

List of Tables

2.1   Patricia's first schedule.   28
2.2   Patricia's second schedule.   29

4.1   Overview on initial availability knowledge.   87
4.2   Local knowledge after the initial solution generation stage. . . .   88
4.3   Local scheduling alternatives after the initial solution genera-
      tion stage.   89
4.4   Local knowledge after the final solution generation stage. . . .   90
4.5   Local scheduling alternatives after the final solution generation
      stage.   90
4.6   Summary of possible constellations in the congruence problem.   93

List of Acronyms

Several names and notions occurring several times in the text have unwieldy and long names. The same holds for a number of well-known or newly developed systems, which are sometimes given names consisting of up to eight words in order to distinguish them from other systems. For abbreviation, the acronyms listed in the following table are used in most occurrences. Acronyms in small capitals are names of implemented or drafted systems.

AAAI	American Association for Artificial Intelligence. Also the official name for their national conference, sometimes called NCAI.
AI	Artificial Intelligence.
AIPS	Conference on AI Planning and Scheduling.
ARPA	Advanced Research Program Agency. U.S. funding agency; formerly known as DARPA (Defense ARPA).
ARMS	Assumption-Based Reason Maintenance System. See [Dotzel, 1994].
ATMS	Assumption-Based Truth Maintenance System. See [de Kleer, 1986a].
ATTMS	Assumption-Based Temporal Truth Maintenance System. See [Geisler, 1994].
BRTMS	Backward Reasoning Truth Maintenance System. See [Horstmann, 1991].
CAIA	Conference on Artificial Intelligence Applications.
CCU	Communication and Control Unit. A module in the generic RMS architecture.

CLOS   Common Lisp Object System.
The object-oriented extension of COMMONLISP.

CMS   Clause Management System.
See [Kean and Tsiknis, 1992] and [Kean and Tsiknis, 1993].

CMU   Context Management Unit.
A module in the generic RMS architecture.

CMXFRMS   Centralized Multiagent Extended Focus-Based Reason Maintenance System.

CRMS   Centralized (Multiagent) Reason Maintenance System.

DAI   Distributed Artificial Intelligence.

DARMS   Distributed Assumption-Based Reason Maintenance System.
See [Beckstein et al., 1993].

DATMS   Distributed Assumption-Based Truth Maintenance System.
See [Mason and Johnson, 1989].

DBMS   Data Base Management System.

DMXFRMS   Distributed Multiagent Extended Focus-Based Reason Maintenance System.

DNU   Dependency Network Unit.
A module in the generic RMS architecture.

DRMS   Distributed Reason Maintenance System.

DTMS   Distributed Truth Maintenance System.
See [Bridgeland and Huhns, 1990].

ECAI   European Conference on Artificial Intelligence.

FHPL   Facetted Horn Propositional Logic.

HPL   Horn Propositional Logic.

ICMAS   International Conference on Multiagent Systems.

IJCAI   International Joint Conference on Artificial Intelligence.

IMSA   Intelligent Meeting Scheduling Assistant.
An imaginary piece of smart code that aids in meeting scheduling.

IPC	Inter-Process Communication. Socket-based process communication on UNIX machines.
JTMS	Justification-Based Truth Maintenance System. See [Doyle, 1979].
KIF	Knowledge Interchange Format. See [Genesereth et al., 1993b].
KQML	Knowledge Query and Manipulation Language. See [Finin et al., 1993b].
KR	Knowledge Representation. Also the acronym for the conferences of the KR community.
KSE	Knowledge Sharing Effort. A large ARPA-sponsored project [Neches et al., 1991b].
LTMS	Logical Truth Maintenance System. See [McAllester, 1990].
MAAMAW	Modelling Autonomous Agents in Multi-Agent Worlds. European DAI workshop.
MAS	Multiagent System.
ML	Machine Learning. Also the acronym for the conference of the ML community.
MRMS	Multiagent Reason Maintenance System.
MXFRMS	Multiagent Extended Focus-Based Reason Maintenance System.
MXARMS	Multiagent Assumption-Based Reason Maintenance System.
NCAI	National Conference on Artificial Intelligence.
NMJTMS	Nonmonotonic JTMS. For example, Doyle's original TMS [Doyle, 1979].
PEDE	Planning and Execution in Distributed Environments. A joint FORWISS/IMMD-8 project [Stoyan et al., 1992].
PNMS	Plan Network Maintenance System. A system for maintaining nonlinear plans. Developed by Beetz, Lindner, and Schneeberger [Lindner, 1992], [Beetz et al., 1992].
PNSMS	Plan Network and Schedule Maintenance System.

PS   Problem Solver.

RMS,RMS   Reason Maintenance System.
                      Also the name of McDermott's system described in [McDermott, 1991].

RPC   Remote Procedure Call.
                      A mechanism for executing code on remote machines.

TMS,TMS   Truth Maintenance System.
                      Also the name of Doyle's original system described in [Doyle, 1979],
                      which is here referred to as JTMS.

TCP/IP   Transmission Control Protocol/Internet Protocol.

TRMS   Temporal Reason Maintenance System.

URL   Uniform Resource Locator.
                      The INTERNET names for network-accessible information.

URA   Uniform Resource Agent.
                      An approach to provide a uniformly structured agent archi-
                      tecture.

XCON   The name of a large expert system developed at DEC for
                      the configuration of VAX computer systems.

XFRMS   Extended Focus-Based Reason Maintenance System.

Index

2vATMS, 54

AAAI, 1
accessibility relation, 102
acquaintances, 136
action theory, 9
add-assumption!, 47, 138
    MXFRMS, 200, 227
    XFRMS, 62
add-environment!, 47
    XFRMS, 62
add-facet!, 138
add-focus!, 138
    MXFRMS, 202, 229
add-focus-owner!
    MXFRMS, 204, 233
add-justification!, 47, 138
    MXFRMS, 200, 228
    XFRMS, 62
add-proposition!, 47, 138
    MXFRMS, 200, 227
    XFRMS, 62
add-reference!, 138
    MXFRMS, 200, 228
agent, i
    acquaintances, 136
    architecture, 13
    autonomous, 17
    autonomy, ii, 96, 142, 251
    deliberative, 5
    dynamics, 209
    identifier, 100
    infrastructure, 16
    knowledge-based, 3
    malevolent, 142, 169

    mobility, 209
    planning, 10
    rational, 5
    scheduling, 10
    trusted, 96
AI systems, i
all-assumptions?
    MXFRMS, 208
    XFRMS, 64
all-environments?
    XFRMS, 64
all-facets?
    MXFRMS, 208
all-foci?
    MXFRMS, 208
all-justifications?
    MXFRMS, 208
    XFRMS, 64
all-local-assumptions?
    MXFRMS, 208
all-local-propositions?
    MXFRMS, 208
all-propositions?
    MXFRMS, 208
    XFRMS, 64
all-references?
    MXFRMS, 208
appointment scheduling, 26, 83
    multiagent, 84
architecture
    layered, 30, 31, 97
    two-level, 7, 13
ARMS family, 252
artificial intelligence, 1, 251
    distributed, 1

assimilation of information approach, 95

assumption, 6, 7, 31, 33, 46, 255
  about future world states, 6
  communicated, 91

assumption-based reasoning, 25
  multiagent, 11, 83
  multiple-context, 11

asymptotic behavior, 247

ATMS, i, 7, 13, 52
  complexity, 54
  complexity problems, 57
  deficiencies, 13
  dependency network, 52
  focussing techniques, 54
  label, 52
    completeness, 53
    consistency, 53
    minimality, 53
    soundness, 53
    update, 53
  nogoods, 53

ATTMS, 259

automatic facetification, 180

axiom 4, 100

axiom 5, 100

axiom K, 100

axiom T, 100

base layer substrates, 258

base literal references, 178

belief, 10
  communicated, 11, 92
  local, 92

belief autonomy, 17, 132, 142

belief consistency, 11

belief merge, 123

belief revision problem, 2, 11, 57, 61
  distributed, 3, 12, 153, 199, 253

belief update, 91
  communication of, 91

brain-damaged agents, 178

BRTMS, 149, 150

bulk updates, 55

c-subsumption, 54

CAIA-94, 84

CATMS, 54

CCU, 20, 65, 211, 213, 254

centralized server approach, 17, 144, 182

clause database, 10, 63
  update, 11

clause retraction, 63

clauses, 10

client-server architecture, 2

CMU, 20, 65, 211, 213, 254

communicated belief, 189

communicated nodes, 155

communication, 4, 99
  of beliefs, 11

communication and control, 65

communication and control unit, 15, - 65, 211

complex task, 5

complexity, 20, 33, 57

computational complexity, ii

computational cost, ii

computational support, 4, 253

conceptualization, 38

configuration management, 257

conflict resolution, 171

conflict resolution protocol, 179

conflicting goals, 27

conflicts, 11

congruence problem, 93, 132, 142, 175, 195, 253

consequence, 32
  logical, 46

consequence determination problem, 57
  distributed, 12, 199, 253

consequence finding, i, 10

consequential closure, 100

consistency, 32

global, 92
local, 11
of an environment, 46
plan, 10
schedule, 10
shared, 115
consistency checking, i, 68
constraint, 33
constraints, 27
logical, 10
context, 10, 32, 46, 98
deletion, 15
inconsistent, 10
information, 13
maintenance, 57
management, 13
of an environment, 46
revision, 32
context coherence, 174
context determination, i
context determination problem, 2, 10, 57
distributed, 3, 12, 199, 253
context management, ii, 65, 155
application-specific, 172
explicit, 58
general, 172
multiagent, 171
context management unit, 15, 65, 211
context-of?, 46, 138
MXFRMS, 197, 219
XFRMS, 60
contingency planning, 164
contract net protocol, 256
contradiction, 10, 11
cooperation problem, 4
coordination
multiagent, 171
coordination problem, 5
correctness, 20
correspondence theory, 102
CPL, 35

current environment, 14
current-focus?
MXFRMS, 206

DAI, 1
DARMS, 150, 152, 251
ATMS expressiveness, 163
belief merge, 164
communication and control, 158
context management, 157
cyclic communication, 164
dependency net management, 156
derivability, 160
formal specification, 160
functional interface, 158
handling failure situations, 165
integrity constraints, 162
module architecture, 155
NOGOODs, 159
planning for contingencies, 167
remote belief query, 158
data
communicated, 11
consistency, 2
integrity, 2
relevant, 31
DATALOG, 34
DATMS, 149, 151, 251
decision
planning, 6
scheduling, 6
deduction
concurrent, 105
simultaneous, 105
deductive closure, 71
denial of service approach, 93
dependencies, i
between data, 39
causal, 9
data, iii
logical, i, 7, 255
maintenance of, 253
temporal, 8, 9

dependency
  between data, 31
  communicated, 91
  local, 91
dependency net, ii, 13, 65
dependency net unit, 15, 65, 211
dependency network, 52
derivability, 71
derivability relation
  partial representation, 44
design decision support, 256
design rationale maintenance, 256
diagnosis, i
directed communication, 155
distributed, i
  belief revision problem, 199
  consequence determination problem, 199
  context determination problem, 199
  control, i
  databases, 2
  environment, i
  planning, i, 4
  proofs, 122
  reason maintenance, i
  reason maintenance system, 12, 91, 97, 251
  resource allocation, 256
  scheduling, i, 4
  systems, iii
distributed system approach, 18, 145
distribution
  functional, 4, 255
  spatial, 4, 255
  temporal, 4, 255
DNU, 20, 65, 211, 213, 254
document configuration management, 258
domain theory, 9, 39
DRMS, 97, 131
DTMS, 149, 150
dynamical systems, 246

theory, 246
eager information exchange, 175
ECAI, 1
electronic markets, 256
environment, 10, 46, 174
  consistent, 46
  context, 46
equilibrium point, 247
explanation, i
explanation generation, 57
extend-environment!
  XFRMS, 62
extend-focus-environment!
  MXFRMS, 203, 232
extend-focus-group!
  MXFRMS, 203, 231

facet, 105
Facetted Horn Propositional Logic, 17, 105
falsum, 67, 74
FHPL, ii, 17, 34, 99, 104, 105, 253
  α-model, 114
  α-satisfiable, 114
  α-unsatisfiable, 114
  α-interpretation, 113
  α-semantics, 111
  ω-interpretation, 111
  ω-semantics, 111
  alphabet, 106
  base literal references, 107
  base literals, 107
  belief autonomy, 122
  calculus, 118
    base belief completeness, 106
    completeness, 106
    contract modus ponens, 118
    incompleteness, 119
    literal completeness, 106, 119
    local modus ponens, 118
    soundness, 106, 119
    common consistency, 115
    common environment, 117

connectives
  precedence order, 107
contexts, 122
contract clauses, 109
contract delivery object, 109
contract source object, 109
contractor, 109
deduction theorem, 106, 121
derivability, 118
  global, 106
  group, 106
  local, 106
derivability relation
  distributed representation, 216
facet, 108
facet clauses, 108
facet connectives, 106
facet constants, 106
facet group, 110
facet theorem, 106, 121
facetset, 109
facetset*, 110
g-coherent, 117
g-consequence, 115
g-consistency, 115
g-consistent, 115
g-derivable, 119
g-inferable, 119
g-provable, 119
group, 110
group coherence, 106, 117, 253
group consequence, 115, 253
  monotonicity of, 116
group consistency, 106, 115, 253
group consistency lemma, 116
group derivability, 118, 253
group reduction, 110
Horn clauses, 108
inter-facet clauses, 109
inter-facet communication, 106
intra-facet clauses, 108
joint consequence, 115
literals, 107

local consequence, 117
local consistency, 117
logical connectives, 106
logical consequence
  global, 106
  group, 106
  local, 106
nogood clauses, 108
premise clauses, 108
prop, 108, 109
propositional variables, 106
propset, 109, 110
propset*, 110
receiver, 109
remote literals, 107
road map to, 105
semantics, 111
sender, 109
shared consistency, 115
shared environment, 117
special symbols, 106
subscriber, 109
syntax, 106
well-formed formulas, 110
focus, 14, 54
focus?
  XFRMS, 64
focus structure, 174
  environment, 174
  group, 174
follows-from?, 46, 137
  MXFRMS, 197, 219
  XFRMS, 60
formalization, 11
frame, 33
FRMS family, 252
function call notation, 197

generality/specificity dichotomy, 171
global coherence, 142
global consistency, 149
goal, 5, 99
goal conflict, 27

group, 98, 174
group coherence, 174, 253
group consequence, 253
group consistency, 253
group derivability, 253

holds-in?, 46, 137
   MXFRMS, 197, 219
   XFRMS, 60
Horn Propositional Logic, 20, 34
HPL, 20, 32, 34, 72, 253
   alphabet
      logical connectives, 34
      parentheses, 34
      propositional variables, 34
      special symbols, 34
   axiom
      verum, 35
   calculus, 35
      derivability relation, 72
      incompleteness, 36
      literal completeness, 37
      soundness, 36
   complex formulas, 34
   definite clauses, 34
      antecedent, 34
      consequent, 34
      Horn, 34
      nogood, 34
      premise, 34
   derivability, 36
   inference rule
      modus ponens, 35
   language, 34
      alphabet, 34
   literals, 34
      extended set of, 34
      set of, 34
   logical consequence, 35
      monotonicity of, 35
   well-formed clauses, 35
   well-formed formulas, 34
hybrid systems approach, 146

IJCAI, 1
IMSA, 38
inconsistency, 92
   condition for, 32
   material, 10
   of environments, 74
inconsistent
   context, 10
   situation, 9
information hiding, 15, 58
intentional notions, 99
intentions, 99
interpretation, ii
   construction, 57
is-assumption?
   XFRMS, 64
is-assumption-for?
   MXFRMS, 206
is-environment?
   XFRMS, 64
is-facet?
   MXFRMS, 206
is-focus-for?
   MXFRMS, 206
is-justification?
   MXFRMS, 206
   XFRMS, 64
is-local-assumption?
   MXFRMS, 206
is-local-focus?
   MXFRMS, 206
is-local-proposition?
   MXFRMS, 206
is-proposition?
   XFRMS, 64
is-proposition-for?
   MXFRMS, 206
is-reference?
   MXFRMS, 206

JIT, 255
joint authoring, 258
just-in-time supply processes, 255

justification, 7, 33
    structure, 63
justified-by?, 46
justifies?, 46

Künstliche Intelligenz, 1
    Verteilte, 1
KL-ONE, 34
knowledge
    incomplete, 27
    representation, 30
        constraints, 33
        frames, 33
        production rules, 33
        semantic nets, 33
knowledge axiom, 100
Kripke structure, 102

label, 52
    propagation, 13
    structure, 15
labelling scheme, ii
labels, 13
language
    logical, 34
lazy evaluation, 54
LazyRMS, 54
local consistency, 149
local focus, 174
logic, 34
    calculus, 33, 34
      axioms, 34
      completeness, 33
      deduction rules, 34
      literal completeness, 36
      soundness, 33
    classical, 34
    consequence relation, 35
    deductive consequence relation,
      36
    derivability, 36
    derivability relation, 45
    first-order, 33
    Horn clause, 10

    definite, 10
    HPL, 32
    language, 34
      semantics, 34
      syntax, 34
    modal, 17
    monotonic, 35
    predicate, 33
    propositional, 33
      classical, 34
    semantics, 33
    sentential, 34
    syntax, 33
logical consequence, 10, 12
logical omniscience problem, 100
logical query function, 46
logics, i, 32, 33
    FHPL, 105, 253
    HPL, 253
    intentional, 104
    language
      hierarchical, 104
      self-referential, 104
    metalanguage, 103
    modal, 99
      axioms, 100
      logical omniscience, 100
      material axioms, 101
      necessitation, 101
      of knowledge and belief, 99
      possible world semantics, 100
    multiagent, 99
    of belief, 99
    of knowledge, 99
    proof theory, 101
    self-referential, 103
    syntactic theories, 103
logistics, 4, 255

MAAMAW, 1
maintenance
    design rationale, 256
maintenance system, i

plan, i
schedule, i
management system
    plan, 259
    schedule, 259
mapping notation, 197
market-oriented programming, 256
MAS, 1
material axioms, 101
mathematical pseudocode, 69
meeting scheduling
    multiagent, 84
Mercedes-Benz, 255
metalanguage logics, 99
metalogical state, 95
mixed approach, 18
mobile agents, 177
modal logics, 99
modus ponens, 35, 71
MRMS
    architectures, 143
    centralized server approach, 144
    classification
        expressive power, 148
        level of consistency, 148
        number of contexts, 148
    current focus, 136
    design tradeoffs, 142
    distributed systems approach,
        145
    distribution of control, 146
    families, 147
    focus structures, 136
    global consistency, 149
    hybrid systems approach, 146
    local consistency, 149
    shared consistency, 149
    specification, 134
        callback interface, 135
        components, 134
        context, 137
        extended facet interface, 135
        focus, 137

global logical state, 134
local logical state, 134
logical query interface, 134,
    136
logical state, 135
multiagent logical state, 134
state change interface, 134,
    138
state query interface, 134, 139
    synchronization, 146
multiagent, i
    communication, 97
    context, 98
        environment, 98
        group, 98
    context management, 171
    cooperation, 251
    coordination, 171, 251
    logics, 99
    planning, 6, 8
    planning systems, 97
    reason maintenance, i, 83
    scheduling, 6, 8
    scheduling systems, 97
    systems, i
    technology, 251
multiagent reason maintenance
    generic functionality, 131
    system
        specification, 134
multiagent RMS, ii, 253
    design requirements, 173
multiagent system, 1
    architecture, 176
multiagent systems, 8
multiagent temporal reasoning, 258
multiple context, 8, 255
MXFRMS, i, 171, 254, 256
    access rights, 210
    add-assumption!, 200, 227
    add-focus!, 202, 229
    add-focus-owner!, 204, 233
    add-justification!, 200, 228

add-proposition!, 200, 227
add-reference!, 200, 228
agent dynamics, 209
agent mobility, 209
all-assumptions?, 208
all-facets?, 208
all-foci?, 208
all-justifications?, 208
all-local-assumptions?, 208
all-local-propositions?, 208
all-propositions?, 208
all-references?, 208
assumptions, 189
asynchronous communication, 245
belief labels, 216
CCU, 211
    facet nodes, 215
CMU, 211
    focus nodes, 215
communication and control unit,
    211
communication and distribution,
    210
complexity, 247
    runtime, 248
    space, 248
concurrent updates, 243
context management unit, 211
context-of?, 197, 219
contract clauses, 190
current focus, 190
current-focus?, 206
dependency net unit, 211
design ideas, 173
    communicated beliefs, 173
    directed communication, 173
    facets, 173
    remote belief queries, 173
    update contracts, 173
design requirements, 173
    belief autonomy, 173
    local control, 173
DNU, 211

communicated nodes, 215
justification nodes, 215
proposition nodes, 215
extend-focus-environment!, 203,
    232
extend-focus-group!, 203, 231
facet clauses, 190
facet communication interface,
    235
facet level, 185, 186
facet module, 178, 185, 217
    CCU, 213, 215
    CMU, 213, 215
    DNU, 213, 215
    internal state, 213
    state update, 226
facet module architecture, 211
focus label, 215
focus structure, 174
    environment, 174, 190
    group, 174, 190
    modification token holder, 174,
        190
    owners, 174, 190
    public write permit, 174, 190
follows-from?, 197, 219
holds-in?, 197, 219
implementation, 212
    representation of state, 213
integrity constraints, 213, 216,
    245
is-assumption-for?, 206
is-facet?, 206
is-focus-for?, 206
is-justification?, 206
is-local-assumption?, 206
is-local-focus?, 206
is-local-proposition?, 206
is-proposition-for?, 206
is-reference?, 206
label propagation, 220
    correctness, 238
    incremental mechanism, 220

systems dynamics, 246
  termination, 241
labels, 215
local focus (structure), 174
mxfrms-propagate, 223
mxfrms-send, 235
mxfrms-update-comm-label, 226
mxfrms-update-prop-label, 225
new-facet!, 209, 234
open system architecture, 186
private focus (structure), 174
PS callback interface, 210
public focus (structure), 174
query processing, 218
relevant base literal references,
    189
relevant base literals, 189
relevant facet constants, 189
relevant focus structures, 190
remove-focus!, 202, 230
remove-focus-owner!, 204, 233
set-current-focus!, 205, 234
shared focus (structure), 174,
    190
specification, 188
  facet logical state, 191
  global logical state, 188
  logical query interface, 197
  state change interface, 199
  state query interface, 206
  system level functionality, 209
system architecture, 175
  agent-oriented perspective, 178
  implementational perspective,
    178
  locality principle, 179
  logical perspective, 178
  perspectives, 178
system level, 185, 186
systems dynamics, 246
virtual interface module, 182
mxfrms-propagate
  MXFRMS, 223

mxfrms-send
  MXFRMS, 235
mxfrms-update-comm-label
  MXFRMS, 226
mxfrms-update-prop-label
  MXFRMS, 225

necessitation, 101
negative introspection, 100
new-facet!
  MXFRMS, 209, 234
node
  label, 52

on demand information exchange,
    175

PEDE, iii, 3, 251
  problem, 3, 4
  project, 3, 251
  research approach, 3
perfect knowledge, 101
plan, 5
  adaptation, 7
  alternative, 9
  consistency, 10
  coordination, 97
  inconsistency
    mutual, 11
  maintenance, 253
  partial, 6
  representation, 9
planner, 6
planning, i, 251
  agent, 10
  data, 30
  decision, 6, 9
  distributed, 4
  knowledge, 30
  multiagent, 6, 8
planning, scheduling, and control
  integration of, 164
PNMS, 9
PNSMS, 97

positive introspection, 100
possible world semantics, 100, 102
premise, 10, 32
private focus, 174
problem analysis, 19
problem formalization, 19
problem solver, i, 7, 43
problem solver interface
    language-based, 58
problem solver modules, 132
problem solver queries, 13
production rule, 33
proof procedure, 34
proof theories, 101
proposition, 6
    communicated, 91
    local, 91
    relevant, 7
protocol assumptions, 47, 139
    reduction of syntactic complex-
        ity, 141
    relaxation of, 47, 139
public focus, 174

reason maintenance, i, 2, 251
    assumption-based, i
    distributed, i
        systems, 4
    monotonic, 63
    multiagent, i, 83
    multiple context, i
    single agent, 25
        generic functionality, 43
    system, i, 43
        architecture, i, 50
        specification, 44
    systems
        classification of, 13
        distributed, 12
        XFRMS, 57
    technology, i
reasoning, i, 30
    assumption-based, i, 25

formal analysis of, 33
logics for, 33
multiple context, i
nonmonotonic, 254
possibilistic, 260
probablitistic, 260
spatial, 259
temporal, 258
    multiagent, 258
with uncertainty, 260
reasoning space, 105
reducing failure rates, 256
relevance autonomy, 132, 142
remote belief query, 155
remote procedure call, 2
remove-environment!
    XFRMS, 62
remove-focus!
    MXFRMS, 202, 230
remove-focus-owner!
    MXFRMS, 204, 233
replanning, 164
representation
    distributed, 105
results
    problem analysis, 253
    problem formalization, 253
    RMS architecture, 253
    RMS systems, 253, 254
retraction, 63
RMS, 7, 43
    all context, 52
    architecture, 19, 50, 58
        three-unit, 64
    classes, 50
    complexity, 57
    design tradeoffs, 48
    distributed, 91
    families, 50
    generic architecture
        CCU, 254
        CMU, 254
        DNU, 254

implementation
  pure database approach, 49
  theorem proving approach, 48
logical query interface
  generic, 45
  MXFRMS, 197
  XFRMS, 60
logical state, 47
  generic, 45
  MXFRMS, 188
  XFRMS, 58
module, 50, 254
monotonic, 63
multiagent, 253
multiple context, 51
MXFRMS, 254
problem solver interface, 65
single context, 51
specification, 44
  components, 44
  logical query interface, 44
  logical state, 44
  state change interface, 44
  state query interface, 45
state change interface
  generic, 47
  MXFRMS, 199
  XFRMS, 61
state query interface
  generic, 47
  MXFRMS, 206
  XFRMS, 63
system, 19
systems
  distributed, 251
technology
  multiagent, 253
  single agent, 253
  XFRMS, 254

safe-add-assumption!, 48
safe-add-justification!, 140
schedule, 5

alternative, 9, 28, 87, 91
conflict-free, 91
consistency, 10, 91
maintenance, 253
revision, 91
scheduler, 6
scheduling, 251
  agent, 10
  conflicts, 85
  constraints, 84
  data, 30
  decision, 6, 9
  distributed, 4
  knowledge, 30
  multiagent, 6, 8
  of appointments, 26, 83
  tasks, 84
schema variable, 35
schizophrenic agents, 178
semantic net, 33
semantics, 33, 34
set-current-focus!
  MXFRMS, 205, 234
set-focus!
  XFRMS, 62
shared beliefs, 123
shared consistency, 149
shared focus, 174
shared inconsistency, 155, 174
software components, 12
software development, 257
software installation assistance, 257
software technology, 12
spatial reasoning, 259
speech act theories, 99
state space, 247
support systems, 12
syntactic theories, 99
  expressive power, 103
syntax, 34
system installation, 257
system management, 257

temporal reasoning, 258, 259
   multiagent, 258
theorem prover, 33
TRMS, 97
trust, 96
truth maintenance, 251
truth maintenance systems, 12
two-level architecture, 154, 179

uncertainty, 27
update
   incremental, 32
update contract, 155

veridicality, 100
version management, 257
verum, 35, 67
virtual RMS, 18
VPP method, 252

world
   dynamic, 6
   static, 6

XFRMS, i, 15, 57, 254, 256
   add-assumption!, 62
   add-environment!, 62
   add-justification!, 62
   add-proposition!, 62
   all-assumptions?, 64
   all-environments?, 64
   all-justifications?, 64
   all-propositions?, 64
   architecture, 64, 66
   CCU, 65, 69
   CMU, 65, 66, 69
   complexity, 78
      runtime, 79
      space, 79
   context label, 68
   context-of?, 60, 70
   dependency net, 67
   DNU, 65, 66, 69, 74
   environment label, 68

environment node label, 68
   completeness, 69
   soundness, 69
environment nodes, 68
extend-environment!, 62
focus?, 64
follows-from?, 60, 70
follows-from-focus?, 71
holds-in?, 60, 70
implementation, 66
   logical state, 66
integrity constraints, 68
is-assumption?, 64
is-environment?, 64
is-justification?, 64
is-proposition?, 64
justification nodes, 67
label constraints, 69
label propagation, 67, 71
   correctness, 74
   termination, 78
   xfrms-propagate, 72, 73
   xfrms-update-label, 72, 73
labels, 68
logical query interface, 60
logical state, 58
   assumptions, 59
   clauses, 59
   current context, 59
   current environment, 59
   environments, 59
   focus, 59
   relevant propositions, 59
node, 66
   flags, 66
   labels, 66
problem solver focus, 68
problem solver interface, 65
proposition label, 68
proposition node label, 68
   completeness, 69
   soundness, 69
proposition nodes, 67

query processing, 69
remove-environment!, 62
representation
   logical state, 66
set-focus!, 62
specification, 58
state, 67
state change interface, 61
state query interface, 63
state updates, 74

Lecture Notes in Artificial Intelligence (LNAI)

Vol. 1171: A. Franz, Automatic Ambiguity Resolution in Natural Language Processing. XIX, 155 pages. 1996.

Vol. 1177: J.P. Müller, The Design of Intelligent Agents. XV, 227 pages. 1996.

Vol. 1187: K. Schlechta, Nonmonotonic Logics. IX, 243 pages. 1997.

Vol. 1188: T.P. Martin, A.L. Ralescu (Eds.), Fuzzy Logic in Artificial Intelligence. Proceedings, 1995. VIII, 272 pages. 1997.

Vol. 1193: J.P. Müller, M.J. Wooldridge, N.R. Jennings (Eds.), Intelligent Agents III. XV, 401 pages. 1997.

Vol. 1195: R. Trappl, P. Petta (Eds.), Creating Personalities for Synthetic Actors. VII, 251 pages. 1997.

Vol. 1198: H. S. Nwana, N. Azarmi (Eds.), Software Agents and Soft Computing: Towards Enhancing Machine Intelligents. XIV, 298 pages. 1997.

Vol. 1202: P. Kandzia, M. Klusch (Eds.), Cooperative Information Agents. Proceedings, 1997. IX, 287 pages. 1997.

Vol. 1208: S. Ben-David (Ed.), Computational Learning Theory. Proceedings, 1997. VIII, 331 pages. 1997.

Vol. 1209: L. Cavedon, A. Rao, W. Wobcke (Eds.), Intelligent Agent Systems. Proceedings, 1996. IX, 188 pages. 1997.

Vol. 1211: E. Keravnou, C. Garbay, R. Baud, J. Wyatt (Eds.), Artificial Intelligence in Medicine. Proceedings, 1997. XIII, 526 pages. 1997.

Vol. 1216: J. Dix, L. Moniz Pereira, T.C. Przymusinski (Eds.), Non-Monotonic Extensions of Logic Programming. Proceedings, 1996. XI, 224 pages. 1997.

Vol. 1221: G. Weiß (Ed.), Distributed Artificial Intelligence Meets Machine Learning. Proceedings, 1996. X, 294 pages. 1997.

Vol. 1224: M. van Someren, G. Widmer (Eds.), Machine Learning: ECML-97. Proceedings, 1997. XI, 361 pages. 1997.

Vol. 1227: D. Galmiche (Ed.), Automated Reasoning with Analytic Tableaux and Related Methods. Proceedings, 1997. XI, 373 pages. 1997.

Vol. 1228: S.-H. Nienhuys-Cheng, R. de Wolf, Foundations of Inductive Logic Programming. XVII, 404 pages. 1997.

Vol. 1229: G. Kraetzschmar, Distributed Reason Maintenance for Multiagent Systems. XIV, 296 pages. 1997.

Vol. 1236: E. Maier, M. Mast, S. LuperFoy (Eds.), Dialogue Processing in Spoken Language Systems. Proceedings, 1996. VIII, 220 pages. 1997.

Vol. 1237: M. Boman, W. Van de Velde (Eds.), Multi-Agent Rationality. Proceedings, 1997. XII, 254 pages. 1997.

Vol. 1244: D. M. Gabbay, R. Kruse, A. Nonnengart, H.J. Ohlbach (Eds.), Qualitative and Quantitative Practical Reasoning. Proceedings, 1997. X, 621 pages. 1997.

Vol. 1249: W. McCune (Ed.), Automated Deduction – CADE-14. Proceedings, 1997. XIV, 462 pages. 1997.

Vol. 1257: D. Lukose, H. Delugach, M. Keeler, L. Searle, J. Sowa (Eds.), Conceptual Structures: Fulfilling Peirce's Dream. Proceedings, 1997. XII, 621 pages. 1997.

Vol. 1263: J. Komorowski, J. Zytkow (Eds.), Principles of Data Mining and Knowledge Discovery. Proceedings, 1997. IX, 397 pages. 1997.

Vol. 1266: D.B. Leake, E. Plaza (Eds.), Case-Based Reasoning Research and Development. Proceedings, 1997. XIII, 648 pages. 1997.

Vol. 1265: J. Dix, U. Furbach, A. Nerode (Eds.), Logic Programming and Nonmonotonic Reasoning. Proceedings, 1997. X, 453 pages. 1997.

Vol. 1285: X. Jao, J.-H. Kim, T. Furuhashi (Eds.), Simulated Evolution and Learning. Proceedings, 1996. VIII, 231 pages. 1997.

Vol. 1286: C. Zhang, D. Lukose (Eds.), Multi-Agent Systems. Proceedings, 1996. VII, 195 pages. 1997.

Vol. 1297: N. Lavrač, S. Džeroski (Eds.), Inductive Logic Programming. Proceedings, 1997. VIII, 309 pages. 1997.

Vol. 1299: M.T. Pazienza (Ed.), Information Extraction. Proceedings, 1997. IX, 213 pages. 1997.

Vol. 1303: G. Brewka, C. Habel, B. Nebel (Eds.), KI-97: Advances in Artificial Intelligence. Proceedings, 1997. XI, 413 pages. 1997.

Vol. 1307: R. Kompe, Prosody in Speech Understanding Systems. XIX, 357 pages. 1997.

Vol. 1314: S. Muggleton (Ed.), Inductive Logic Programming. Proceedings, 1996. VIII, 397 pages. 1997.

Vol. 1316: M.Li, A. Maruoka (Eds.), Algorithmic Learning Theory. Proceedings, 1997. XI, 461 pages. 1997.

Vol. 1317: M. Leman (Ed.), Music, Gestalt, and Computing. IX, 524 pages. 1997.

Vol. 1319: E. Plaza, R. Benjamins (Eds.), Knowledge Acquisition, Modelling and Management. Proceedings, 1997. XI, 389 pages. 1997.

Vol. 1321: M. Lenzerini (Ed.), AI*IA 97: Advances in Artificial Intelligence. Proceedings, 1997. XII, 459 pages. 1997.

Vol. 1323: E. Costa, A. Cardoso (Eds.), Progress in Artificial Intelligence. Proceedings, 1997. XIV, 393 pages. 1997.

Vol. 1325: Z.W. Ras, A. Skowron (Eds.), Foundations of Intelligent Systems. Proceedings, 1997. XI, 630 pages. 1997.

Lecture Notes in Computer Science

Vol. 1292: H. Glaser, P. Hartel, H. Kuchen (Eds.), Programming Languages: Implementations, Logics, and Programs. Proceedings, 1997. XI, 425 pages. 1997.

Vol. 1293: C. Nicholas, D. Wood (Eds.), Principles of Document Processing. Proceedings, 1996. XI, 195 pages. 1997.

Vol. 1294: B.S. Kaliski Jr. (Ed.), Advances in Cryptology — CRYPTO '97. Proceedings, 1997. XII, 539 pages. 1997.

Vol. 1295: I. Prívara, P. Ružička (Eds.), Mathematical Foundations of Computer Science 1997. Proceedings, 1997. X, 519 pages. 1997.

Vol. 1296: G. Sommer, K. Daniilidis, J. Pauli (Eds.), Computer Analysis of Images and Patterns. Proceedings, 1997. XIII, 737 pages. 1997.

Vol. 1297: N. Lavrač, S. Džeroski (Eds.), Inductive Logic Programming. Proceedings, 1997. VIII, 309 pages. 1997. (Subseries LNAI).

Vol. 1298: M. Hanus, J. Heering, K. Meinke (Eds.), Algebraic and Logic Programming. Proceedings, 1997. X, 286 pages. 1997.

Vol. 1299: M.T. Pazienza (Ed.), Information Extraction. Proceedings, 1997. IX, 213 pages. 1997. (Subseries LNAI).

Vol. 1300: C. Lengauer, M. Griebl, S. Gorlatch (Eds.), Euro-Par'97 Parallel Processing. Proceedings, 1997. XXX, 1379 pages. 1997.

Vol. 1301: M. Jazayeri, H. Schauer (Eds.), Software Engineering - ESEC/FSE'97. Proceedings, 1997. XIII, 532 pages. 1997.

Vol. 1302: P. Van Hentenryck (Ed.), Static Analysis. Proceedings, 1997. X, 413 pages. 1997.

Vol. 1303: G. Brewka, C. Habel, B. Nebel (Eds.), KI-97: Advances in Artificial Intelligence. Proceedings, 1997. XI, 413 pages. 1997. (Subseries LNAI).

Vol. 1304: W. Luk, P.Y.K. Cheung, M. Glesner (Eds.), Field-Programmable Logic and Applications. Proceedings, 1997. XI, 503 pages. 1997.

Vol. 1305: D. Corne, J.L. Shapiro (Eds.), Evolutionary Computing. Proceedings, 1997. X, 313 pages. 1997.

Vol. 1307: R. Kompe, Prosody in Speech Understanding Systems. XIX, 357 pages. 1997. (Subseries LNAI).

Vol. 1308: A. Hameurlain, A M. Tjoa (Eds.), Database and Expert Systems Applications. Proceedings, 1997. XVII, 688 pages. 1997.

Vol. 1309: R. Steinmetz, L.C. Wolf (Eds.), Interactive Distributed Multimedia Systems and Telecommunication Services. Proceedings, 1997. XIII, 466 pages. 1997.

Vol. 1310: A. Del Bimbo (Ed.), Image Analysis and Processing. Proceedings, 1997. Volume I. XXII, 722 pages. 1997.

Vol. 1311: A. Del Bimbo (Ed.), Image Analysis and Processing. Proceedings, 1997. Volume II. XXII, 794 pages. 1997.

Vol. 1312: A. Geppert, M. Berndtsson (Eds.), Rules in Database Systems. Proceedings, 1997. VII, 214 pages. 1997.

Vol. 1313: J. Fitzgerald, C.B. Jones, P. Lucas (Eds.), FME '97: Industrial Applications and Strengthened Foundations of Formal Methods. Proceedings, 1997. XIII, 685 pages. 1997.

Vol. 1314: S. Muggleton (Ed.), Inductive Logic Programming. Proceedings, 1996. VIII, 397 pages. 1997. (Subseries LNAI).

Vol. 1315: G. Sommer, J.J. Koenderink (Eds.), Algebraic Frames for the Perception-Action Cycle. Proceedings, 1997. VIII, 395 pages. 1997.

Vol. 1316: M. Li, A. Maruoka (Eds.), Algorithmic Learning Theory. Proceedings, 1997. XI, 461 pages. 1997. (Subseries LNAI).

Vol. 1317: M. Leman (Ed.), Music, Gestalt, and Computing. IX, 524 pages. 1997. (Subseries LNAI).

Vol. 1318: R. Hirschfeld (Ed.), Financial Cryptography. Proceedings, 1997. XI, 409 pages. 1997.

Vol. 1319: E. Plaza, R. Benjamins (Eds.), Knowledge Acquisition, Modeling and Management. Proceedings, 1997. XI, 389 pages. 1997. (Subseries LNAI).

Vol. 1320: M. Mavronicolas, P. Tsigas (Eds.), Distributed Algorithms. Proceedings, 1997. X, 333 pages. 1997.

Vol. 1321: M. Lenzerini (Ed.), AI*IA 97: Advances in Artificial Intelligence. Proceedings, 1997. XII, 459 pages. 1997. (Subseries LNAI).

Vol. 1323: E. Costa, A. Cardoso (Eds.), Progress in Artificial Intelligence. Proceedings, 1997. XIV, 393 pages. 1997. (Subseries LNAI).

Vol. 1324: C. Peters, C. Thanos (Ed.), Research and Advanced Technology for Digital Libraries. Proceedings, 1997. X, 423 pages. 1997.

Vol. 1325: Z.W. Ras, A. Skowron (Eds.), Foundations of Intelligent Systems. Proceedings, 1997. XI, 630 pages. 1997. (Subseries LNAI).

Vol. 1327: W. Gerstner, A. Germond, M. Hasler, J.-D. Nicoud (Eds.), Artificial Neural Networks — ICANN '97. Proceedings, 1997. XIX, 1274 pages. 1997.

Vol. 1329: S.C. Hirtle, A.U. Frank (Eds.), Spatial Information Theory. Proceedings, 1997. XIV, 511 pages. 1997.